NEW WORKS IN ACCOUNTING HISTORY

Richard P. Brief, *Series Editor*

Leonard N. Stern School of Business
New York University

STUDIES IN EARLY PROFESSIONALISM

Scottish Chartered Accountants
1853-1918

Edited by
Stephen P. Walker
and
Thomas A. Lee

Routledge
Taylor & Francis Group

LONDON AND NEW YORK

First published 1999 by Garland Publishing Inc.

Published 2017 by Routledge
2 Park Square, Milton Park, Abingdon, Oxon OX14 4RN
711 Third Avenue, New York, NY 10017, USA

Routledge is an imprint of the Taylor & Francis Group, an informa business

Library of Congress Cataloging-in-Publication Data
Studies in early professionalism : Scottish chartered accountants, 1853–1918 /
    edited by Stephen P. Walker and Thomas A. Lee.
        p. cm. — (New works in accounting history)
    Includes bibliographical references.
    ISBN 0-8153-3231-9
        1. Accounting—Scotland—History. 2. Accountants—Scotland—History.
    I. Walker, Stephen P. II. Lee, Thomas A. (Thomas Alexander) III. Series.
    HF5616.S36S78 1999
    657'.09411—dc21   99-34345

ISBN 13: 978-0-8153-3231-2 (hbk)

CONTENTS

Acknowledgments

The editors are grateful to Routledge, Elsevier Science Ltd, MCB University Press, and the editors of *The Accounting Historians Journal* and *Accounting History* for permission to reproduce the papers contained in this volume.

The appearance of this collection of papers also provides an opportunity to acknowledge the role of The Institute of Chartered Accountants of Scotland (ICAS) in encouraging and facilitating research on the history of the accounting profession. ICAS has permitted access to the source material which is the basis of much of the work reprinted in this book and its staff have consistently welcomed and accommodated academic researchers. This book is published under the auspices of the Scottish Committee on Accounting History of The Institute of Chartered Accountants of Scotland.

Grateful thanks are also due to Marsha Caplan, Department of Accounting and Business Method, Edinburgh University, and Kathy Rice, School of Accountancy, The University of Alabama, for their painstaking work in formatting the text.

Introduction: Early Scottish Professionalism in Accountancy

Thomas A Lee and Stephen P Walker

In 1971, The Institute of Chartered Accountants of Scotland (ICAS) formed the Scottish Committee on Accounting History (SCAH). The purpose of SCAH is to promote the study of accounting history as it relates to professionalised accountancy activity. Since its formation, SCAH has discharged this responsibility by funding and supervising a considerable number of projects world-wide. These projects have resulted in the publication of numerous books and articles on historical topics which not only advance academic scholarship but also inform professional accountants of past issues which have a contemporary relevance. Many of these contributions to the historical literature deal with the early professionalisation of accountancy in Scotland which is one of SCAH's current research themes. This collection of writings is dedicated to this theme.

Structure of the text

The text is intended to provide its reader with a sampler of relatively recent research on the early development of professional accountancy in Scotland. Limiting the literature selection to Scotland has no particular nationalistic intent. It reflects the volume of historical research on the profession in Scotland, the significance of events in Scotland to subsequent developments elsewhere, and the implications of the Scottish case for advancing our understanding of accounting professionalism. The selection reflects the availability of primary sources relating to professionalisation in Scotland and the willingness of a small number of researchers to scour the archives. We hope that the results of using the Scottish archives will encourage researchers in other countries to make use of similar local sources. Indeed, there is evidence that this is happening in Australia (Edwards, Carnegie and Cauberg, 1997).

The text is divided into two main sections containing fourteen selected items. For ease of identification in this introduction, we refer to the selections by the author's name and the chapter number used in the contents list. The first section deals mainly with formation events pertaining to The Society of Accountants in Edinburgh (SAE) founded in 1853, and The Institute of Accountants and Actuaries in Glasgow (IAAG) founded also in 1853 (i.e. Macdonald [1]; Briston and Kedslie [2]; Macdonald [3]; Kedslie [4]; Lee [5]; Walker [6]; and Lee [7]). The foundation of a third Scottish body, The Society of Accountants in Aberdeen (SAA) took place much later in 1866, and is covered only briefly in these writings. However, the involvement of the SAA in post-formation developments features more fully in several of the papers contained in the second part of the book.

The second section of the text deals with several of the post-foundation issues faced by the new professional bodies. These problems included the need to persistently and strategically defend the professional monopoly which had been nurtured by the organisations founded in 1853 and 1866 (Walker [8]); the sometimes friendly and sometimes argumentative political relations which existed between the Edinburgh, Glasgow and Aberdeen societies during the late nineteenth and early twentieth centuries (Shackleton [9]); the key role played by individuals in the institutionalisation process and its subsequent problems (Lee [10]); the nature of early professional accountancy practice in Scotland, revealing its original association with the law and the move into servicing the corporate sector (Walker [11]); the oversupply of Scottish accountants and a resultant emigration which had much to do with founding professional accountancy overseas (Lee [12]); the need to formally deal with ethical issues other than by uncodified expectations of gentlemanly conduct (Walker [13]; and the emerging issue of female challenges to an all-male world of professional accounting (Shackleton [14]).

Each of the fourteen contributions is introduced briefly below following an overview of the social and economic climate in which the formations of SAE, IAAG and SAA took place during the mid-nineteenth century.

Scotland prior to the formation events

It is clear from an examination of published research on the formations of the SAE and IAAG in 1853 that the founding of professional organisations in Edinburgh and Glasgow was the culmination of a much longer process of occupational development. With relatively few exceptions, the founding fathers were experienced accountants who had developed their practices over a number of years during a period of considerable economic and social change in Scotland. Professional organisation occurred during Hobsbawm's (1975) 'Age of Capital'. The demand for accounting services had grown in parallel with the emergence of an industrial-urban economy and a maturing agricultural sector (Stewart, 1977; and Kedslie, 1990). Edinburgh was the location for a considerable development in legal and financial services (particularly banking and insurance) (Cockerell and Green, 1994; and Saville, 1996), and was a major British centre of the old professions such as law and medicine (Walker, 1988; Kedslie, 1990; and Corfield, 1995). Glasgow was a major industrial and merchanting city on the navigable River Clyde (Marwick, 1909; and Shackleton, 1995).

Professional accountancy in Scotland was relatively well developed when the formations of the SAE, IAAG and SAA were considered and put into effect. Indeed, according to data researched by Brown (1905) and Kedslie (1990), there were well-established communities of professional accountants in both Edinburgh and Glasgow by the mid-nineteenth century. Brown (1905) identified 17 accountants working in Edinburgh in 1805, and 10 in Glasgow two years later. In contrast, Kedslie (1990) reports 132 publicly-listed Edinburgh accountants in 1850-1, and 135 in Glasgow in the same period. In other words, a compelling conclusion about the formation events discussed in the papers contained in Part 1 of this text is that they were engineered by experienced accountants who were particularly motivated at that time to place their profession on an institutional basis. In this regard, there is clear evidence that, particularly in Edinburgh, the professionalism of the founders was held in high esteem by members of other organised professions such as lawyers (Walker, 1995). Equally, there is no confounding evidence from Glasgow to suggest that accountants practicing in that city were not highly regarded within the local commercial community.

The initial focus on the formation events by accounting historians appears to have been to determine reasons why Scottish professional accountants in the mid-nineteenth century felt a pressing need to organise. As such, the contributions to the accounting history literature reproduced in this text describe a component of the emergence of the 'new' professions during the nineteenth century and what has been labelled as 'the rise of professional society', in which professionals not only became a dominant social group but where their values permeated wider society (Perkin, 1969, 1989).

Foundation events

Seven of the fourteen papers reproduced in this text cover the formation events, particularly around 1853 and 1854 as they affected the SAE and IAAG. The first paper by Macdonald (1) was published in 1984 in the *British Journal of Sociology*, and was therefore addressed primarily to students of the sociology of professional behaviour. Based on secondary data from biographies produced by Brown (1905) and Stewart (1977), and utilising the work of Larson (1977), Macdonald provides an analysis of the data to conclude that the formation of the SAE, IAAG and SAA provide evidence of market control and a quest for upward social mobility by the founding members. Briston and Kedslie (2) provide a response to this conclusion, basing their criticisms largely on the inaccuracy and unsuitability of the secondary data used by Macdonald, and arguing the purely economic nature of the foundations in relation to a perceived legislative threat to a monopoly held by Scottish accountants in the area of bankruptcy. Macdonald (3) provides a counter-response to Briston and Kedslie, and reinforces his earlier argument and conclusions. What these three contributions effectively provide for the reader is a start to a complex story about professional formation which contains intertwining socio-economic elements, and whose credibility depends on the depth of the archival trawl made by individual researchers, and their consequential ability to make reasonable interpretations from the data they find. Macdonald, for example, believes that his data are credible enough to make his interpretation. Briston and Kedslie, on the other hand, demand a deeper and more contextualised use of available data.

Kedslie (4) is an abbreviated version of her book (Kedslie, 1990), and reveals the basis for her earlier criticism with Briston of Macdonald. In the paper reproduced here, she explains the formation events within an economic context of nineteenth century expansion and technology which, in turn, created the need for professional accountancy services in cities such as Edinburgh, Glasgow and Aberdeen. Kedslie's main focus is the identification of the mainstream work of the early accountants generally, and its bias in Edinburgh toward court-related services such as bankruptcies, and in Glasgow to both bankruptcies and stock exchange services. Her thesis is that a legislative threat to the Scottish monopoly of bankruptcy work provided the stimulus to organise in the institutional form of the SAE. In making these connections, Kedslie briefly outlines the extremely speedy process to the grant of a royal charter by the organisations in Edinburgh and Glasgow, and the differences in social origins between the founding accountants in the two cities. The strong professional (especially legal) backgrounds of Edinburgh accountants are contrasted with the mercantile origins of a majority of the Glasgow founders. Kedslie's conclusions of differences in social origins but similarity in the economic reason for formation are consistent with the earlier conclusions of Macdonald.

As previously mentioned, Kedslie's research has been reported more fully in book form (Kedslie, 1990). This was reviewed by Lee (5) in 1991, and contrasted more specifically with the socio-demographic study of self-recruitment conducted by Walker (1988) in his history of the SAE to 1914. Lee's review concentrates on the need for theoretical rather than speculated reasons for the organization of accountants in Scotland. Without such prior theories he argues, collected data are difficult to interpret. In this sense, his arguments more closely match the approach of Macdonald (1) rather than that of Kedslie (4).

Walker's (6) paper constructs an explanation of the 1853 events based on critical-conflict theory and previously undiscovered evidence. Within his scenario, the SAE and IAAG formations are explained as collective community responses to external threats to the economic and social status of accountants. A proposed bill on bankruptcy *and* insolvency, and different from a narrower bill on bankruptcy identified by Kedslie (4), was observed by Walker as at the root of the problem. This proposed legislation on the mundane subject of insolvency excited considerable attention in Scotland, especially among the accountants of Edinburgh and Glasgow. Below the surface, within the socio-economic environment of the mid-nineteenth century, lay such matters as the effects in Scotland of mercantilism and free trade ideologies transported from England, and a nationalist counter-response which emphasised the perceived need to retain the separate identity and structure of the Scottish legal system. This argument is consistent with the importance to the SAE of its founders' legal relationships and origins, more fully described in Lee (7).

Lee (7) is the first in a series of research studies of the Scottish professional accountancy foundations which examine the social networking that was necessary to the success of the institutionalisation process. In this study, Lee identifies for the first time all 75 accountants who participated in the events leading to the granting of the SAE royal charter in 1854. This study also reconstructs the leadership group by means of identifying attendances at the formation events and meetings. Lee is able to conclude that the SAE formation was as much the institutionalisation of a social elite in Edinburgh as it was the protection by that elite against a threat to its economic monopoly of court-related services. In particular, he identifies an inner 'cabinet' within the SAE whose members did not necessarily join the initial SAE councils or committees. This conclusion is consistent with Macdonald's (1995) assertion that the Scottish formations were akin to the creation of elite clubs.

Post foundation events

Part 2 of the text deals with specific issues faced by the Scottish chartered accountancy bodies from the mid-nineteenth century onwards. First, Walker (8) presents an explanatory review of a persistent series of legal challenges to the credential-based monopoly of Scottish chartered accountants over the supply of accounting services. The challenges came from two other bodies of accountants in the form of court cases and Privy Council petitions for royal charters. These challenges covered a period from 1884 to 1905, and were typically grounded in the argument that Scottish chartered accountants had created a near monopoly of accounting work as a result of their chartered status. At great cost in terms of time and human resources, the three chartered bodies successfully rebutted each challenge by employing functionalist arguments to protect their professional status - i.e. by explicit appeals to the superiority of chartered accountancy quality standards of entry, training, examination, and practice, and the reputation of the holders of the professional designation 'CA.' The chartered bodies also made considerable use of their legal and political connections, revealing once again what had been an important ingredient in the success of the earlier formation events.

The Walker paper suggests a great deal of co-operation was necessary for the Scottish chartered bodies to succeed during the post-formation conflicts with rival bodies, and this was certainly the case in practice. Although not agreeing on all things, the SAE, IAAG and SAA pooled their efforts and resources to protect their right to own the title of chartered accountant. But all was not well within the Scottish family of chartered accountants. As observed by Shackleton (9), the evidence is clear that, from its inception, the SAE assumed a leadership role in Scottish professional accountancy. Its leaders and membership had unwavering views on institutional matters such as entry, training, and examination requirements, and these differed significantly from the equivalent views of the IAAG and the SAA. These matters became issues whenever there was a suggestion for the creation of one national body of chartered accountants in Scotland. Both the IAAG and SAA suggested such a body at various times, especially during the various challenges against Scottish chartered accountancy as documented by Walker (8). The major differences between the bodies which prevented merger were indenture fees and practice requirements. However, despite these differences, co-operation between the bodies did take place (regarding the formation of a unified examining system and a joint committee of governing councils). Shackleton's conclusion on these matters is an interesting one - that collaboration tended to follow external pressure to do so rather than internally-driven motivations. Thus, even within a small country such as Scotland, socially-driven differences leading to what now appear like petty rivalries could only be set aside when political expediency dictated. In this sense, early Scottish professional accountancy was little different from a dysfunctional family.

The tensions and strains which prevailed over the three Scottish chartered bodies following the formations in 1853 and 1854 are captured in Lee's (10) analysis of a period in the secretaryship of the SAE. A key player in the events which formed the various challenges to the chartered accountancy monopoly appears to have been the SAE's chief executive, Richard Brown. Lee's analysis is consistent with the conclusion of Shackleton (9) that the SAE assumed a leadership role in these and other events affecting Scottish chartered accountancy. Indeed, Lee's argument reveals that the SAE leadership generally, and

Brown in particular, often ignored the IAAG and SAA despite the existence of the Joint Committee of Councils. However, Brown's legacy to chartered accountancy appears to be his ability to bring the SAE, IAAG and SAA together when it mattered and despite their internal differences. As such, the history of Scottish chartered accountancy is as much about the role of individuals as it is about collective actions.

Walker's (11) paper brings the reader back to the heart of any profession - that is, its practice. In this case, his analysis covers a century of professional activity in one of Edinburgh's leading accountancy practices. The period covers the pre and post-formation events affecting the SAE, and the major actors in Lindsay, Jamieson & Haldane include some of the founding fathers. What is of importance in this study is the careful analysis of archival data of an unusually rich nature, and the findings about client service which run counter to the conventional wisdoms of earlier writers relying on secondary sources. In particular, the case of Lindsay, Jamieson & Haldane reveals the mix of early professional activity, the importance of insolvency work generally, the long-standing nature of audit work and a strong client link to landowners (and, thus, to the legal profession).

The 'demand side' development of professional accountancy practices in Edinburgh, Glasgow, and elsewhere in Scotland appears to have been outstripped in the second half of the nineteenth century by the 'supply side' production of qualified chartered accountants. This oversupply problem is mentioned by a contemporary observer (Brown, 1905) and is analysed by Walker (1988). Its affect on the initial and early formation of an accountancy profession in the United States is examined by Lee (12). Restricting his analysis to members of the SAE, Lee demonstrates the impact that SAE emigrants had on the foundation of professional firms and institutions in America. Indeed, one of the sons (John Niven) of one of the SAE founders (Alexander Niven) not only founded a firm which is now part of the so-called Big 5, but also became president of the leading body of professional accountants in the United States (The American Institute of Accountants). Thus, as this paper demonstrates, examination of the influence of Scots professional accountants should not be restricted to the relatively narrow confines of either Scotland or the United Kingdom.

One of the functional characteristics of a profession as described by traditional analysts such as Carr-Saunders and Wilson (1933) is the respectability of the professional in terms of his or her attitude and behaviour at work and in play. This was particularly pertinent to the founding members of the SAE, IAAG and SAA. In the case of the SAE, research reveals that, as a group, they occupied a high social position within Edinburgh society (Stewart, 1977; Macdonald, 1984; Walker, 1988; Kedslie, 1990; and Lee [7]). For that reason, it is surprising to learn from Walker (13) that two of the founding members of the SAE participated in criminal activity which resulted in their expulsion from the SAE, and influenced the speedy introduction of ethical provisions by that body to allow its council and members to deal with future inappropriate behaviour by individual members. No such provisions were felt necessary prior to the second discovery of crime in 1883, perhaps suggesting an unjustified feeling of complacency in the self-selections of the SAE founders.

The final professional issue in this text deals with the exclusion of women from the all-male profession of early Scottish accountancy. Shackleton (14) outlines events generally, and more specifically with respect to the Scottish accountancy profession, prior to the 1919 Sex Discrimination (Removal) Act. The subsequent reaction of the councils of the three Scottish bodies is outlined, and the conservative nature of the discussions and proposals is clear to see - especially the idea of creating a separate body for lady accountants. Eventually, the 1919 legislation opened the door of chartered accountancy to women, but Shackleton's empirical data reveals a muted response in terms of apprenticeships and qualifications.

Conclusions

Several conclusions may be permitted from a reading of the various research contributions to this text. The first relates to the founding of the SAE, IAAG and SAA in mid-nineteenth century Scotland. The foundations were the result of the efforts of men whose social backgrounds and practice experience suggested that institutionalisation was a needed solution to a serious problem facing developed professional communities. That organisation took place so speedily, and apparently without complication or challenge, further suggests that the founders were well-connected. Although there may have been measurable differences in origins, etc. between accountants in the three cities, the overwhelming conclusion is that the founding bodies were exclusive clubs designed to maintain if not enhance their members' socio-economic status.

The second conclusion from the analysis is that there appears to be a fundamental compulsion for institutionalised professionals to observe for intrusions into their socio-economic space, and to react accordingly by mobilising alliances cultivated with other key groups (in the case of Scottish accountants, with lawyers, civil servants and politicians). In order to achieve market control and upward social mobility, the early Scottish professionals spent several decades engineering social closure in their profession - first by royal charter, professional designation, and professional self-regulations, and then by repelling any competition. In a sense, this is a classic case of the 'survival of the fittest,' with fitness determined by the acquisition of social capital, the construction of occupational alliances, amassing economic resources and adherence to ideologies which optimise the achievement of desired results.

Our third conclusion from the previous review is the need for organised professional accountants not only to self-regulate, but also to demonstrate that self-regulation. Thus, as in the case of the early Scottish chartered accountants, there was a requirement to desist from the previous practice of assuming that all members were persons of integrity, and to recognise that black sheep might be present in the professional community from time to time and needed to be dealt with in a way which would maintain public confidence in the profession.

Fourth, it is clear from several papers in this collection that balancing the demand and supply of professional accountants in a constantly changing world is a less than precise science. Inevitably, client needs change and new services require to be offered. The leads and lags in this process, particularly in terms of ensuring a sufficient supply of suitably qualified accountants, are matters requiring constant attention. Also, societal changes are inevitable, and the accountancy profession has to respond accordingly, as in the case of admitting women to its ranks.

What is remarkable about these conclusions is that each derives from the results of research into a situation or issue which is many decades old. Yet each could equally be dealing with an item which is paralleled on a modern-day agenda for a council meeting of a body such as ICAS. It, and similar organisations are continuously concerned with the recruitment of the 'right kind' of professional. Each body has to take decisions which balance the obligation to be seen to serve the public interest with the need to maintain the economic position of its members. No professional body can exist today without good working relations with other bodies or with the state. Professional bodies have not only to be aware of socio-economic change, but also to anticipate it in terms of syllabus, examination, and training structures. Relations with clients, the maintenance of ethical standards, the challenge of information technology, removing barriers to the advancement of women in the profession, are all matters facing the current leaders of professional accountancy bodies. From that conclusion, it is an easy leap to suggest that reading about similar problems in a historical context is a rational way of understanding the persistence of issues and their resistance to solution. The studies in this text of the early Scottish accountancy profession are a reasonable first step in such a study.

Bibliography

Brown, R. (1905), *A History of Accounting and Accountants* (T.C. & E.C. Jack: Edinburgh).
Carr-Saunders, A. M. and Wilson, P.A. (1933), *The Professions* (Clarendon Press: Oxford).
Cockerell, H. A. L. & Green, E. (1994), *The British Insurance Business: A Guide to its History and Records* (Sheffield University Press: Sheffield).
Corfield, P. (1995), *Power and the Professions in Britain 1700-1850* (Routledge: London).
Edwards, J. R., Carnegie, G. D. and Cauberg, J. H. (1997), "The Incorporated Institute of Accountants, Victoria (1886): A Study of Founders' Backgrounds," in Cooke, T. E. and Nobes C. W. (eds.), *The Development of Accounting in an International Context: A Feschrift in Honour of R. H. Parker* (Routledge: London), pp.49-67.
Hobsbawm, E. (1975), *The Age of Capital 1848-1875* (Weidenfeld & Nicholson: London).
Kedslie, M. J. M. (1990), *Firm Foundations: The Development of Professional Accounting in Scotland 1850-1900* (Hull University Press: Hull).
Larson, M. S. (1977), *The Rise of Professionalism: A Sociological Analysis* (University of California Press: Berkeley, CA).
Lee, T. A. (1996), *Shaping the Accountancy Profession: The Story of Three Scottish Pioneers* (Garland Publishing: New York, NY).
Macdonald, K. M. (1995), *The Sociology of Professions* (Sage Publications: London).
Marwick, J. D. (1909), *The River Clyde and the Clyde Burghs* (J Maclehose & Sons: Glasgow).
Perkin, H. (1969), *The Origins of Modern English Society, 1780-1880* (Routledge: London).
Perkin, H. (1989), *The Rise of Professional Society: England Since 1880* (Routledge: London).
Saville, R. (1996), *Bank of Scotland: A History, 1695-1995* (Edinburgh University Press: Edinburgh).

Shackleton, K. (1995), "Scottish Chartered Accountants: Internal and External Political Relationships, 1853-1916," *Accounting, Auditing & Accountability Journal* (Vol.8, No.2), pp.18-46.

Stewart, J. C. (1977, 1986), *Pioneers of a Profession: Chartered Accountants to 1879* (Garland Publishing: New York, NY).

Walker, S. P. (1988), *The Society of Accountants in Edinburgh 1854-1914: A Study of Recruitment to a New Profession* (Garland Publishing: New York, NY).

PART 1

FORMATION EVENTS

CHAPTER 1

Professional Formation: The Case of Scottish Accountants

Keith M Macdonald

Introduction

The study of the rise of an occupational group is important to the continuing debate on the nature and bases of social stratification in industrial society.

The battle-lines in this debate have been drawn between the neo-Marxists who are concerned with working out how to draw class boundaries that make sense of contemporary stratification while still adhering to the structural principles of class laid down by Marx over 100 years ago,[1] and the Weberians who argue that the reality of social stratification requires the analysis of 'social closure' based not only on property in the means of production but on other criteria as well.[2] The most important of these criteria is 'credentialism', which is seen as being of the essence of the 'collective social mobility',[3] of 'professions' (although Parkin regards it rather differently, as part of bourgeois individualism).

Actual empirical studies of stratification, however, are usually interested in individual social mobility, where class is represented entirely by occupation (for instance, Goldthorp[4]), although the study of professions does provide a counter-balance with its concern with collective social mobility (e.g. Parry and Parry,[5] and Larson.[6])

Historical studies of the present kind are important because they give us an opportunity to see how *an occupational group deploys its resources in its struggle for collective social mobility.*

Reproduced from *British Journal of Sociology*, Volume 35, Number 2, June 84, pp 174-89, with kind permission from Routledge.

Collective social mobility

Larson's work has provided an important stimulus in recent years and the present study makes use of her two central concepts of 'collective social status' and 'market control'. However, there is little attempt either by Larson (or by other writers on this topic) to locate the aspiring occupations at all clearly in the stratification system of the nineteenth century. This tends to be regarded on a common sense basis as being a class society because it is the archetypal capitalist industrial society. The present study on the other hand is set in the context of recent historical work on nineteenth-century stratification, particularly Neale's[7] attempt to adapt modern theories of social class (especially Dahrendorf[8]) to the study of social mobility in the mid-nineteenth century.

A general outline of Larson's work may be presented by quoting and summarizing certain passages:

> Professionalism is . . . an attempt to translate one order of scarce resources - specialist knowledge and skills - into another - social and economic rewards. To maintain scarcity implies a tendency to monopoly: monopoly of expertise in the market, monopoly of status in a system of stratification.
>
> Professionalisation (is) the process by which producers of special services (seek) to constitute *and control* a market for their expertise. Because marketable expertise is a crucial element in the structure of modern inequality, professionalisation appears also as a collective assertion of special social status and as a process of collective upward social mobility.[9]

The nineteenth century development of professionalism constituted a new form of structured inequality that differed both from the model of aristocratic patrons and gentlemanly clients[10] and from the model of capitalist entrepreneurs and property in the means of production. Its central principle of legitimacy rested on education and credentialing, leading to socially recognized expertise. Important elements in the development of professions are however the conflicts between this new principle and those of aristocracy and entrepreneurship.

This outline contains two analytical elements: market control and collective social status. These two aspects are *analytically* distinct although on the whole they refer to much the same empirical material (the actions and the pronouncements of norms and values by individuals, firms and associations, for example). The other element is collective social status and mobility. 'The market', said Max Weber,[11] 'knows nothing of honour'. But as he goes on to discuss, those who are successful in the rational, non-affective market normally wish to be well-regarded and looked up to by their fellow citizens and therefore attempt to convert economic success into high social status.

For Larson, however, the connection is of a different order, because looking at *collective* social mobility it is apparent that many (if not all) of the means of market control are also the means to the other aspect of the professional 'project', namely status.

When an occupation successfully defines and delimits its area of expertise, its market and its membership it establishes a collective social status, and the efforts of the occupational association tend directly and indirectly to emphasize the socially valued and rewarded characteristics. In doing so they probably achieve for the members upward social mobility and operate the mechanism that Parry and Parry,[12] Parkin,[13] and others see as the most important by which middle class groups define and maintain their position, namely 'closure'.

Nineteenth century stratification

Any discussion of collective social mobility must be set against a background of the social stratification of the period in question, otherwise the analysis is going to rely on some kind of 'common sense' history. The examination of the emergence of any profession is therefore immediately presented with the problem that in most cases the structure of society was in a state of change during the period of that emergence and that any such process was itself part of the change. The development of the accountancy profession is a case in point because between 1800 (when there seem to have been about a dozen men in London calling themselves accountants) and 1880 (when a Royal Charter created the Institute of Chartered Accountants in England and Wales and 1200 were admitted) major changes in the structure of society had occurred.

In 1800 many aspects of the old order prevailed and many historians (e.g. Perkin[14]) emphasize that two-thirds of the population still lived in the countryside and that many of the pre-steam factories 'were self-conscious models of paternal benevolence and discipline, ideal examples of the old society in miniature'.[15]

> The old society, then was a finely graded hierarchy of great subtlety and discrimination, in which men were acutely aware of their exact relation to those immediately above and below them, but only vaguely conscious except at the very top of their connections with those of their own level.[16]

This continuum was held together by patronage in a great variety of forms.

> 'Vertical friendship', a durable two-way relationship between patrons and clients permeating the whole society, was a social nexus peculiar to the old society. Less formal and inescapable than feudal homage, more personal and comprehensive than the contractual employment relationships of capitalist 'Cash Payment'.[17]

Within thirty or forty years the dramatic social changes of rapidly advancing industrialism had made themselves felt. The working class had taken on its characteristic form[18] and contemporary sociological models of class can be usefully applied.[19,20] However two important observations must be noted before assuming that the social stratification system in which Accountancy emerged was essentially modern. The first point is made by Neale who claims that as compared with contemporary British class structure the following five-class model should be adopted.

FIGURE I *Five-class model*

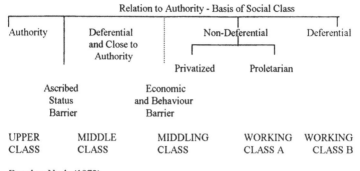

Relation to Authority - Basis of Social Class

Authority	Deferential and Close to Authority	Non-Deferential		Deferential
		Privatized	Proletarian	
	Ascribed Status Barrier	Economic and Behaviour Barrier		
UPPER CLASS	MIDDLE CLASS	MIDDLING CLASS	WORKING CLASS A	WORKING CLASS B

Based on Neale (1972)

The five classes are made up as follows:

(1) *Upper class*: aristocrat, landholding, authoritarian, exclusive.

(2) *Middle class*: industrial and commercial property-owners, senior military and professional men, aspiring to acceptance by the upper class.

(3) *Middling class*: petit bourgeois, aspiring professional men, other literates and artisans; individuated or privatized like the middle class but collectively less deferential.

(4) *Working class A*: industrial proletariat in factory areas, workers in domestic industries, collectivist and non-deferential.

(5) *Working class B*: agricultural labourers, other low-paid non-factory urban labourers, domestic servants, urban poor, deferential and dependent.

One should note in this model the distinction between a traditional deferential middle class and an aspiring privatized 'middling class'. If one reads this scheme in conjunction with the findings of Foster[21] it seems likely that these aspirants as they moved up either allied themselves with the 'county' or saw themselves as part of the urban (and ultimately national) bourgeoisie and stayed closer to their radical origins.

The second major point is that during the past decade research into nineteenth century stratification especially of elites has led historians to modify the usual history book view that Victorian society became dominated by the newly wealthy capitalist manufacturer, with the Reform Act of 1832 as the turning point. The work of Arnstein[22] and Rubinstein[23] show that the really wealthy were not in manufacturing, but in commerce and that they tended to be associated with the landed aristocracy, who continued to dominate the political arena: in the 60 years following the Reform Act only two cabinets had less than 50 per cent aristocrats (1868, Gladstone, 47 per cent and 1892, Gladstone, 41 per cent). The social world of the first half of the nineteenth century was therefore one in which the landed aristocracy still comprised the elite. However, the middle class can be seen to have more than one strand in it, distinguishing those who claim a 'gentlemanly' basis to their occupation plus those who manage to obscure the unfortunate origins of their wealth by allying themselves with 'the county' and becoming officers in the Yeomanry. Then there was Neale's 'middling' class of aspirants whose radical class consciousness he sees as an important element in nineteenth century social change. They were antagonistic to the patronage that lingered on from the old society, and instead emphasized ability, thereby contributing to the breakdown of the finely graded status system.

It should perhaps be emphasized that his middling class was provided with the opportunity for achieving its aspirations by the increasing division of labour occasioned by capitalist industrialization. In Marxist terminology (cf. Johnson[24]) 'global capital' required more 'control agents' as the industrialization developed and accountants in England and Scotland managed to establish themselves as legitimate occupants of that role in a manner which has had consequences for the development of accountancy throughout the capitalist world.[25] It should also be noted, with reference to the distinctions within the wealthy bourgeoisie just mentioned, that it was particularly the interest of 'finance capitalists'[26] that was served by the passing of the Companies Act of 1856 and 1862, legislation which was crucial in the development of the accountancy profession.

The 'middling class' and the 'unresolved dialectic'

Neale's five-class model of early to mid-nineteenth century social stratification gives prominence to the 'middling' class, which contains upwardly mobile working class 'literates', downwardly mobile people from the established middle class and the gentry, as well as the offspring of the previous generation of the middling class. This view of class seems reasonable, and it is in accord with both Marxian and Weberian theories of social class to divide the middle class into the established and propertied on the one hand, and the aspiring and propertyless on the other. The latter have to make the best use of their talents and training in order to succeed, and one would expect to find in this category not only the Philosophical Radicals (whose social position is Neale's *explicandum*), but the members of such occupations as accountancy who were attempting collective social mobility.

In the context of Neale's model it is also possible to test the concept of the 'unresolved dialectic' which plays an important part in a recent attempt to put the emergence of professional occupations in their historical context.[27] This thesis proposes that an ideal-typical classification of professions should be based on three 'variables', wealth, status, and power. These occupations have achieved their privileges in these three areas by social and political strategies which have combined mechanisms from both industrial and pre-industrial stages of society, mechanisms of both achievement and ascription: this combination of 'historical conjuncture'[28] constitutes the 'unresolved dialectic'.

Against the background of these two hypotheses we may observe the emergence of accountants on to the historical stage.

Table I shows the numbers of persons listed as 'accountant' only, in various city directories and omits those who combined accountancy with other occupations such as writing-master, teacher, agent or broker. At this point it will be useful to focus attention on Scottish Accountants for a number of reasons:

(a) The formation of Scottish accountancy bodies occurred some decades before that in England, or indeed anywhere else.
(b) The data are readily available to permit a sociological analysis of at least some aspects of the professionalisation process, which for England they are not.
(c) Perhaps the most important reason for studying Scottish Accountants is that in the annals of professionalization they are probably unique in that legal recognition was obtained by three *local* groups of practitioners within two years of formally setting up their Societies (Edinburgh 21 months, Glasgow 16 months, Aberdeen 11 months).

The second and third of these points make the Scottish case very different from the English one: some tentative explanation for this difference will be offered in the conclusions section of this paper.

TABLE I *Numbers of accountants in various British cities -*
1780 to 1870

Decade	London	Liverpool	Mancheste	Bristol	Edinburgh	Glasgow
1780					7	6
1790	5	5		1		
1800	25		4			
1810	47		14			
1820	99		24	20		
1830		37	32	28		
1840	107	69	52			14
1850	264		66		54	49
1860	310	91	84	74		
1870	467	139	159			

The occupation of 'accomptant' appears to have emerged much earlier in Scotland than in England. I say 'appears' because it must be borne in mind that in relying on secondary sources as this investigation does, the researcher is looking at material which has an ideological function. In looking into the past the accountant-historian is not only more likely to find material on the notable and successful practitioners, but will tend to emphasize such figures because they suit his (perhaps unconscious) interest in showing the long-standing respectability of his profession.

Having entered that *caveat* it is a matter of fact that accountancy in Scotland achieved recognition and 'professional' status earlier than its English counterpart and it is difficult to avoid the conclusion that this should be attributed in a general way to certain aspects of the culture, social structure and stratification system of Scotland in the eighteenth and early nineteenth centuries, and to particular characteristics of the operation of the Scottish courts in relation to bankruptcy.

Scottish culture and Scottish accountants

A number of authors have recently criticized the 'myth' of Scottish egalitarianism, which many historians have taken as established fact.[29,30] They do, however, conclude that various aspects of the pre-modern Scottish life did contribute to a genuine (if incomplete) *gemeinschaft* which formed the basis for the modern myth. In terms of social stratification this means that the continuity of status ranking which Perkin[31] discerns in England was also true of Scotland and may well have remained firmly in existence in the earlier stages of industrialization.

A significant aspect of this phenomenon for the present purpose is the closeness of the landed gentry and the legal profession which is documented by Smout[32] and Stewart.[33] Upper and middle status groups may have been even closer than they were in England, and it might be surmised that this was enhanced by three more character-istics of Scottish society

(a) its relatively small size as compared with England;
(b) the partial truncation of the status system because of the incorporation of the top echelon of the elite into an English system;
(c) as industrialization proceeded, the development of the dual metropoles of Edinburgh and Glasgow.

Support for the notion that the proto-accountants of the early industrial period came from a stratum of society closely linked to the gentry comes from the list of worthies paraded by Brown.[34] While the selection of such personages may well have an ideological function as suggested above, it is clear from the early City Directories that there were very few people calling themselves 'accomptants'. In the first Edinburgh Directory of 1773 there were seven, and six in Glasgow of 1783. So if Brown tells us of six individuals of that era in Edinburgh the picture cannot be greatly distorted.

Brown records eight Edinburgh accountants who died between 1760 and 1782, and it is clear that they were associated with the top strata of business and social life in the city. Six of them are known to have been on friendly terms with members of the nobility and gentry, three of them held important public or commercial positions, three of them belonged to prestigious clubs, one was also a solicitor and one had his portrait painted by Raeburn. The nature of their business activities betokens knowledge of, and perhaps training in, the law.

Of Glasgow accountants there seems to be less trace, largely because they were less involved in legal work, and more frequently described themselves as 'merchant and accountant'. Indeed Brown reports that some of them became accountants because they were merchants who had gone bankrupt and that this was the best way to employ their commercial skills when they had no financial resources. However, the details survive of the practice in 1824 of one Glasgow accountant: of ten activities specifically mentioned, seven had a definite legal component.

It has already been noted that the legal profession enhanced its status by close connection with the gentry; it also appears that Scottish accountants were able to establish their social status partly by the same kind of association and partly because they undertook specialist work that put them in the same position in relation to the Courts as lawyers. This point was actually made by the Edinburgh society in their petition for incorporation by Royal Charter, and refers to the fact that certain activities performed by accountants in Scotland are performed in England by lawyers called Masters in Chancery. The closeness of the association of accountancy with law is perhaps most graphically illustrated by a phrase from a much - quoted letter written by Sir Walter Scott in 1820 in which he says apropos accountancy '- in this, as in other branches of our legal practice.'[35]

But law was only one of three main strands in early accountancy in Scotland. In Edinburgh especially there was a strong connection with banking and insurance. Many accountants were directors, managers and agents for these institutions, and not a few also described themselves as actuaries because until well into the nineteenth century actuarial science was little developed and accountants had more expertise than most. The third strand was stock-broking. This was particularly important in Glasgow, where over 40 per cent of the profession were engaged in it to a greater or lesser extent (see Table III).

Thus it is possible to depict Scottish accountancy as an outgrowth of three areas of activity that provided its members with status and opportunities for high income.

Table II supports this view especially for Edinburgh, for it shows that 12 per cent came from the ranks of the gentry and that 48 per cent had fathers in the professions. Admittedly the situation in Glasgow was rather different where only 20 per cent in total came from these two backgrounds. Aberdeen while broadly similar had the distinction of having a peer among its members!

TABLE IIA *Father's occupation of Scottish chartered accountants 1853 to 1879*

	Edinburgh %	Glasgow %	Aberdeen %
Gentry and military	12	1	5
Professional	48	19	9
Lower professional	2	0	5
Merchants, manufacturers	2	6	5
Tradesmen, small businessmen	1	3	5
Farmers	3	3	5
No information	32	68	66
	100	100	100
(N)	180	144	22

TABLE IIB *Education of Scottish chartered accountants - 1853 to 1879 (per cent)*

Public school	30	0	0
Other named school	35	9	5
University	18	6	9

TABLE III *Activities of Scottish chartered accountants - 1853 to 1879 (per cent)*

	Edinburgh	Glasgow	Aberdeen
Church elder	11	16	27
J.P.	7	12	5
Volunteer officer	6	10	5
Charity, education work	16	17	9
Arts, learned society	14	12	9
Politics (local and national)	5	9	0
Stockbroker	2	42	18
Company director	23	12	55
Prestigious memberships	4	2	5
(N)	180	144	22

Table III likewise shows the prestigious educational background of Edinburgh accountants with a third of them attending the Royal High School or Edinburgh Academy, and nearly a fifth attending (but not necessarily graduating from) University. This table also shows that sizeable proportions of the membership of the Edinburgh and Glasgow Institutes had other roles which enhanced their status - such as J.P., Officer in a Volunteer Regiment or an Elder of the Kirk, and that in a number of ways the Glasgow membership makes good by these means the deficiencies in family and educational background.

Collective social mobility

How, then, do these data fit with Neale's hypothesis of the aspirant 'middling' class, whom he sees as providing an important dynamic to nineteenth century social mobility? In some respects it appears that Scottish accountants constituted a well-established and respected occupation, which had grown out of a number of prestigious activities, but against this must be set a number of important points.

(i) The data must be considered in the light of the caveat entered above. They come from works written by accountants with the very objective of emphasizing the standing and achievements of the occupation.[36, 37] This is not to say that they are inaccurate, but just they are themselves part of the process by which an occupation establishes and maintains its collective status and if there is bias, it will be in the occupation's favour.

(ii) Although the Scottish accountants of 1850 were on average respectable, well-educated and well-trained in comparison with most occupations of that time, they lagged behind the law, medicine and the clergy. This was particularly true of the education of Glasgow accountants of whom only 6 per cent had been to University. So it must be noted that in contrast to the luminaries of the profession, the majority had only a modest education and that most Glasgow accountants and a sizeable minority of those in Edinburgh probably came from lower-middle or even working-class homes.

(iii) The incorporation of the societies seems to have been the outcome of a debate that had been going on for some time, but the secondary sources give no clue to the nature of the disagreements which appeared to have delayed matters in Edinburgh and Glasgow. However, leaving this question to one side, an analysis of the content of the petitions for Charters from the Edinburgh, Glasgow and Aberdeen societies (see Table V) shows that the two chief points of emphasis were (a) involvement in legal matters and work for the courts, and (b) the 'respectability' of the profession - the Glasgow petition mentions that word three times. Accountancy skills receive scant attention and specific training in them is confined to the phrase 'tend to secure the qualifications which are essential for the proper performance of their duties'.

TABLE IV *Characteristics of members of original council (Edinburgh) and those involved in foundation of Glasgow society*

	Edinburgh	Glasgow Senior	Junior
Father's occupation = gentry or professional	8	4	2
Education = named school.	4	4	3
university	2	2	2
Directorships, etc.	7	14	5
Stock Exchange member	0	9	15
J.P.	1	7	2
Volunteer officer	0	2	1
Legal training	2	1	3
Associations with Edinburgh	-	0	3
(N)	10	14	27

TABLE V *Factors mentioned in the petitions for charters of the Privy Council*

		No. of times mentioned		
	Total	Edinburgh	Glasgow	Aberdeen
Connections with courts and law	32	13	10	9
Standing, respectability of profession	13	4	6	3
Accounting skills	7	2	4	1
Importance of work content	7	4	0	3
Importance of liberal education	3	1	1	1
Incorporation would achieve:				
Unity	3	1	1	1
Qualifications	3	1	1	1
Public benefit	2	1		1

(iv) The study of professionalization as a process does not provide clear-cut hypotheses on factors leading to the incorporation of members of an occupation. It might be surmised, however, that it occurs when members feel that their position is threatened or made ambiguous by lower status or fringe practitioners or alternatively by lack of clear distinction from another occupation; further, that the initiative would be taken by the high status members, who would subsequently assume the leading roles in the newly formed professional body.

In Edinburgh it would appear that it was indeed the leading lights of the profession who took the initiative. From the terms of the petition it could be deduced that an important impetus came from the need to establish both equality with and distinctiveness from the legal profession. While a sizeable minority of Edinburgh accountants had some legal training, and some were in fact lawyers, they were only a minority and it seems probable that some distinctiveness was required to counterbalance this deficiency. The other important claims put forward are the long-standing and respectability of the profession and the intrinsic importance of the work content; once again these are attempts to rectify the deficiency in standardized training.

The way in which the Glasgow Society was formed shows certain important differences from Edinburgh and it may be supposed that somewhat different forces were at work. It appears that smaller numbers - in fact committees - were involved in the formation process, but this was just part of an interesting sequence of events. The initiative in Glasgow came not from the senior members but from the younger ones. A group of 27 accountants who had started in practice after 1 January 1841 addressed a letter to fifteen accountants who commenced practice before that date. The letter stated that the formation of a Society was in every way desirable, to advance their common professional interests, and referred in particular to impending changes in the Bankruptcy Law which would render some form of organization more necessary. After the favourable response to this letter, matters were handled either by the senior accountants or by committees from the two groups.

The 'old hands' responded promptly to the suggestions of the younger members, but it is noticeable that the Glasgow petition made less reference to law, none to the work content, and used the word 'respectable' or 'respectability' six times in a petition of only 350 words. So it was perhaps the younger members who felt under pressure, both in their own town and by comparison with Edinburgh accountants and that there was a tendency to compensate for their relative lack of legal training and lower level of formal education by an emphasis on 'respectability'.

The data seem to suggest therefore that those setting up as professional accountants in Glasgow between 1841 and 1853 (the junior group) were men of fewer social and business resources than their seniors and with two or three notable exceptions, achieved less success in these respects during their careers. Probably therefore this competent but less well endowed generation put pressure on their seniors to form an association which would enable the juniors to acquire some of the ascribed and inherited characteristics of their seniors. By this means they could achieve a 'closure'[38] and create a distinction between themselves and those of even lower attainment and background.

Conclusion

This study presents a picture of an occupation forming itself into a profession and at the same time into a constituent part of the emerging middle class. In some respects the personnel can be regarded as belonging to Neale's aspirant 'middling class' and the junior practitioners in Glasgow seem to fit into that category. But their success was clearly dependent upon the actions of the better placed senior accountants, and the Glasgow events must be seen in the light of the initiative taken by the Edinburgh accountants a few months earlier. In the Edinburgh case the senior members took the initiative, and these men of good education and middle-class background do not seem to correspond to the concept of aspirant middling class. This lack of fit with Neale's formulation suggests that his model of class needs amplification in two respects:

(a) It needs to take account of collective social mobility and the actions of collectivities, primarily occupations, to achieve closure. It is clear from the data on Scottish accountants that these processes were not merely the result of lower status aspirants' actions but were to a large extent handled by the senior members who in terms of background, education and successful practice were neither aspirant nor upwardly mobile. What the senior members did was to use their acquired and achieved characteristics to establish and give status to an occupational collectivity, which was advantageous to all members.

(b) This leads to the second point, the need for 'market control'. The advantages of social status and 'market control' are closely linked. Accountants wanted to control their 'market' by establishing their distinctive claims to specialist competence, especially in the eyes of the Courts. This recognition was obtained by the successful claim that all designated members were 'respectable', were trained in their specialism, and that their specialism included such esoteric and high status skills and knowledge as law, actuarial practice and accounting. This claim would be more likely to be accepted by the public in general and by the legal profession in particular, if it were made by men of acceptable middle class characteristics, who could vouch for the other members admitted to the professional body. Thus the technique of closure was employed by accountants to gain the acceptability required to achieve market control. In so doing they not only controlled entry (and thereby to a large extent the job market) but went a long way towards achieving a monopoly in accounting services.

In addition to these modifications, whose theoretical origins are to be found in Larson,[39] the 'unresolved dialectic'[40] can be seen to be one of the most important elements in the establishment of the Scottish accountancy profession. In so far as 'respectability' seemed to have taken precedence over all other virtues, it may be said that the ascriptive side of the dialectic was a *sine qua non*. The twin advantages of collective social mobility and market control were, in the present case, initially achieved by using the characteristics of the old status order to establish a distinctive and high position in the new class system. Members of the aspirant middling class certainly provided some of the impetus, but an alliance with those of the established middle class was necessary in order to give the occupation a firm and elevated position in the structure of the emergent industrial society.

Finally, a hypothesis, if not an explanation, can now be offered for the differences between professional formation in Scotland and in England. There are two main points to consider:

(a) In Scotland, between January 1853 and January 1855 two local Societies of Accountants (Edinburgh and Glasgow) were formed and obtained the grant of Royal Charters; Aberdeen followed a similar pattern twelve years later. The speed with which the Charters were obtained and the fact that they were granted to local bodies are both exceptional. In England local societies were formed (Liverpool and London in 1870, Manchester in 1873, Sheffield in 1877) but it was not until 1880 that a Royal Charter was granted - to a national body.

(b) The process of professional formation may be analysed in the Scottish case because the data are readily available in extremely detailed secondary sources. The material for England is sketchy and the standard history of accountancy in England by Stacey, glosses over the question of professional formation in the following way. After an account for the economic background to the demand for accountancy services in the 1850s, Stacey writes

> No wonder that some three associations of accountants were formed in Scotland, quickly in succession at the commencement of the second half of the nineteenth century. In England an accountancy body was not to see the light of day until 1870.[41]

What these points suggest is that on the one hand the Scottish accountants carried far more weight with the Privy Council than their English counterparts and on the other that there is little recorded about the personal details of the English founder members because they were much less worthy of note. One might therefore hypothesize that English accountants contained within their ranks far fewer of the established middle class than in Scotland and that they lacked the connection with the legal profession so important to their Scottish counterparts. The comparable functions in England had been performed by lawyers (Masters in Chancery) and in so far as accountants had encroached on lawyers' work, as a result of the Bankruptcy Act of 1831, they were regarded with disfavour if the words of Justice Quain (1875) are any guide.

> The whole affairs in bankruptcy have been handed over to an ignorant set of men called accountants, which is one of the greatest abuses introduced into law.[42]

The test of such an hypothesis must await detailed biographical study of nineteenth century English Accountants.

Notes and Bibliography

1.   G. MacKenzie, 'Class Boundaries and the Labour Process', in A. Giddens   and G. MacKenzie, *Social Class and the Division of Labour,* Cambridge, Cambridge University Press, 1982.
2.   F. Parkin, *The Marxist Theory of Class: a Bourgeois Critique,* London, Tavistock, 1979.

3. E. Hughes, *The Sociological Eye: Selected Papers*, Chicago/New York, Atherton, 1971.
4. J. H. Goldthorpe, *Social Mobility and Class Structure in Modern Britain*, Oxford, Clarendon Press, 1980.
5. N. C. A. Parry and J. Parry, *The Rise of the Medical Profession: a Study of Collective Social Mobility*, London, Croom Helm, 1976.
6. M. S. Larson, *The Rise of Professionalism*, London, University of California Press, 1977.
7. R. S. Neale, *Class and Ideology in the Nineteenth Century*, London, Routledge & Kegan Paul, 1972.
8. R. Dahrendorf, *Class and Class Conflict in Industrial Society*, London, Routledge & Kegan Paul, 1959.
9. Larson, op. cit., pp. xvi-xvii.
10. It should be noted that the modern usage of the word 'client' by lawyers, accountants, architects, etc. inverts the original usage, which is still employed in sociology and anthropology in which (say) the 'aristocrat' commissioning the building of a house is the patron and the architect the client.
11. M. Weber, *Economy and Society* (2 vols), New York, Bedminster Press, 1968.
12. N. C. A. Parry and J. Parry, op. cit.
13. F. Parkin, op. cit. and F. Parkin, 'Strategies of Social Closure in Class Formation', in Parkin, F. *The Social Analysis of Class Structure*, London, Tavistock, 1974.
14. H. Perkin, *The Origins of Modern English Society 1780-1880*, London, Routledge & Kegan Paul, 1969.
15. Ibid., p. 178.
16. Ibid., p. 24.
17. Ibid., p. 49.
18. E. P. Thompson, *The Making of the English Working Class*, Harmondsworth, Penguin, 1963.
19. J. Foster, *Class Struggle and the Industrial Revolution*, London, Weidenfeld & Nicolson, 1974.
20. R. S. Neale, op. cit.
21. J. Foster, op. cit.
22. W. L. Arnstein, 'The Survival of the Victorian Aristocracy', in F. C. Jaher, *The Rich, the Well-Born and the Powerful*, Chicago, University of Illinois Press, 1973.
23. W. D. Rubenstein, 'The Victorian Middle Classes: Wealth, Occupation and Geography', *Economic History Review*, 30, 1977, pp. 602-23 and W. D. Rubenstein, 'Wealth, Elites and the Class Structure of Modern Britain', *Past and Present*. 76. 1977, pp. 99-126.

24. T. J. Johnson, 'Professions in the Class Structure', in R. Scase (ed.), *Industrial Society: Class, Cleavage and Control*, London, Allen & Unwin, 1977, pp. 93-110.
25. T. J. Johnson and M. Caygill, 'The Development of Accountancy Links in the Commonwealth', in R. H. Parker (ed.), *Readings in Accounting and Business Research*, London, 1978.
26. J. Burnham, *The Managerial Revolution*, Harmondsworth, Penguin, 1941, 1962.
27. D. Portwood and A. Fielding, 'Privilege and the Professions', *Sociological Review*, *29*, 1981, pp. 749-73.
28. T. J. Johnson, 'Work and Power', in G. Esland and G. Salaman, *The Politics of Work and Occupations*, Milton Keynes, Open University Press, 1980.
29. D. McCrone, F. Bechhofer and S. Kendrick, 'Egalitarianism and Social Inequality in Scotland' in D. Robbins (ed.), *Rethinking Social Inequality*, London, Gower Press, 1982, pp. 127-47.
30. A. A. MacLaren, *Social Class in Scotland*, Edinburgh, John Donald, 1976.
31. H. Perkin, op. cit.
32. T. C. Smout, *A History of the Scottish People 1560-1830*, Fontana, 1972.
33. J. C. Stewart, *Pioneers of a Profession - Chartered Accountants to 1879*, Edinburgh, The Institute of Chartered Accountants of Scotland, 1977. J. C. Stewart, 'Early C.A. Apprentices: 1854-1863', *Accounting History*, vol. 2, no. 1, May 1977, pp. 23-33.
34. R. Brown, op. cit.
35. Ibid.
36. Ibid.
37. J. C. Stewart, op. cit.
38. N. C. A. Parry and J. Parry, 1976, op. cit.
39. M. C. Larson, op. cit.
40. D. Portwood and A. Fielding, op. cit.
41. N. A. H. Stacey, *English Accountancy 1800-1954*, London, Gee, 1954, p.20.

CHAPTER 2

Professional Formation: The Case of Scottish Accountants - Some Corrections and Some Further Thoughts

Richard J Briston and Moyra J M Kedslie

Introduction

In his analysis of the rise of the Scottish accounting profession recently published in this journal,[1] Keith Macdonald (KM) makes many unjustified inferences, which are caused partly by the defective nature of his source material and partly by the incorrect analysis of that data. The objective of this paper is to present additional data and facts, to correct some of the analysis in the earlier paper and to demonstrate that KM's conclusions are unwarranted.

Source material

KM does admit that his source material is entirely secondary, based as it is upon the work of Brown[2] and Stewart.[3] However, at the time that he wrote his paper the highly relevant work of Jones[4] was available and from that book he would also have found reference to a study by Kedslie[5] which gives still further information concerning the social characteristics of early Scottish accountants. Neither Brown nor Stewart intended their work to be treated as research and Stewart categorically states:

> I have tried to bring together such biographical notes about the first chartered accountants as could fairly easily be assembled

Reproduced from *British Journal of Sociology*, Volume 37, Number 1, March 1986, pp 122-30, with kind permission from Routledge.

without undertaking research on a scale for which I have neither the skill nor the temperament.

Given a disclaimer of this sort it is surely wrong of KM to use such data to attempt to draw conclusions about the evolution of the Scottish accounting profession; and this error is compounded by accusing the source authors of being biased in presenting an unduly favourable picture of the accounting profession and then using this unwarranted assumption as a basis for implying that any accountant whose social class was not stated would tend to be of a lower class than those who were identified.

Definition of accountant

KM does not explain precisely what he means by an accountant. In his Table I, which is in any case incomplete and inaccurate as explained below, he confines himself to persons listed in the trade directories as an accountant only. In view of the fact that it was common, particularly in Glasgow, for accountants to combine other occupations with their primary one, this significantly reduces the number of accountants included in his survey. Also he excludes the large number of financial accountants in industry and in the public service.[6] In fact, the census of 1841[7] shows 4,974 persons in England and Wales who were described as accountants. At the same date KM's Table I shows only 107 in London, 69 in Liverpool, 52 in Manchester and 14 in Glasgow.

KM is therefore only concerned with a very small part of the population of accountants, namely those who were self-employed. Admittedly, it was these who were the first to professionalize but they were quickly followed by accountants employed in the public and private sectors.

He shows a further lack of understanding by referring to accountants as legitimate occupants of the role of control agents as industrialization developed. However, at the time of the professionalization of Scottish accountants, using from henceforth the term to refer only to practising accountants, they were much more concerned with liquidation and bankruptcy work than with auditing, which did not appear to contribute more than about ten per cent of their fee income until 1880. Furthermore, although it is correct to argue that the Companies Acts of 1856 and 1862 were crucial to the development of the accounting profession, their influence was only gradual and was only felt as audit work passed from shareholder auditors to professional auditors towards the end of the century. Certainly those Acts had no effect upon the emerging accounting profession in Scotland and they were not even referred to in the minute books of the Edinburgh and Glasgow societies. Bankruptcy legislation was, however, referred to frequently and it was proposed changes in that legislation which was the catalyst for the formation of the two societies.

Number of accountants

The data in Table I must be challenged. In the first place KM gives three far from convincing reasons for concentrating upon Scottish accountants and then presents a table with three-quarters of the figures for Scotland missing. Furthermore, most of those which he provides are wildly incorrect. The 1840 directory for Glasgow[8] shows 48 accountants, not KM's 14, and that for 1850[9] shows 146 against his 49. Similarly the directory for Edinburgh for 1850[10] shows 132 and not 54. The figures for other years are readily available and reveal a fairly static number of accountants in both cities between 1845 and 1860, the period with which KM's research is concerned.

Differences between England and Scotland

In the paragraph below Table I KM quite unfairly criticizes his source authors for having an ideological bias in writing their books. Given that neither author is able to defend himself it seems rather unprofessional gratuitously to criticize their work in this way when the real fault lies in using it for a purpose for which it was never intended.

He then states that accountancy in Scotland achieved recognition and professional status earlier than its English counterpart and argues that this was due partly to characteristics of the culture, social structure and stratification system in Scotland and partly to the Scottish system of dealing with bankruptcy.

Of these two systems, as our research, which was admittedly not available to KM, has shown, bankruptcy was by far the most important and it was the threat to that work from an impending change in bankruptcy legislation which prompted the formation, first of the Edinburgh society, and then of the Glasgow society. Social factors were far less important and, if anything, the differences in culture, etc. between Glasgow and Edinburgh were much more significant than those between England and Scotland.

Furthermore, it is by no means clear that accountancy emerged much earlier in Scotland than in England. There were, after all, as many accountants in London in 1850 as there were in Glasgow and Edinburgh combined, using the corrected figures given above. Jones,[11] in fact suggests that 'in the latter part of the eighteenth century accountants appear to have been no more numerous in Scotland than they were in England.'

One main difference appears to have been that in Scotland, the accountant, particularly in Edinburgh, was seen as an adjunct to the legal profession and shared in the respect which that profession carried. Thus in the statement by Sir Walter Scott, of which KM only quotes part, an accountant is described as 'highly respectable' and as belonging to a branch of legal practice.

Glasgow, however, was a more important commercial centre than Edinburgh and its accountants performed a wider range of activities, though bankruptcy work was still of prime importance. Probably the Glasgow accountant was more comparable to his English counterpart, for whom bankruptcy work was also a major source of fees. Although neither of them would be as socially respectable as an Edinburgh accountant in the Edinburgh environment, there is no reason to suppose that their status in their own environment was significantly lower.

In fact, then, as far as social characteristics are concerned the real distinction lies between Glasgow and Edinburgh accountants (though it is a distinction of environment rather than of status) rather than between those of England and Scotland.

The other main difference, and by far the most important one, is that Scottish accountants, both in Edinburgh and Glasgow, were faced with a threat to the lucrative bankruptcy work which constituted such a large proportion of their fee income.

Social characteristics

KM virtually ignores the effect of bankruptcy legislation and concentrates upon the social characteristics of early Scottish accountants using the inappropriate sources referred to above. He first suggests that Scottish accountancy was an outgrowth of law, actuarial science and stockbroking and argues that his Table IIA supports this assertion.

However, in the first place his table is far from complete in that he has no information regarding the father's occupation of 32 per cent of the Edinburgh accountants, 68 per cent of the Glasgow accountants and 66 per cent of those from Aberdeen. Furthermore, he does not give details of the separate occupations included under 'professional'. Fortunately, we are able to provide additional evidence from our own research and Table I gives data in the same format as KM's Table IIA.

TABLE I *Father's occupation of Scottish chartered accountants, 1853-79*

	Edinburgh %	Glasgow %	Aberdeen %
Gentry and military	11	2	5
Professional	45	27	5
Lower professional	6	9	18
Merchant, manufacturers	5	25	32
Tradesmen, small businessmen	10	10	18
Farmers	4	11	13
No information	19	16	9
	100	100	100
(N)	180	144	22

This table demonstrates that the main difference between Glasgow and Edinburgh was that fewer of the Glasgow parents were 'professional' or 'gentry and military', while far more were 'merchants or manufacturers'. This does not mean, however, that they were from a lower class, for in Glasgow the position of merchant or manufacturer would have carried a much higher status than it did in Edinburgh.

When the 'professional' category is further analysed, KM's argument regarding the outgrowth of accounting from law, actuarial science and stockbroking is disproved:

TABLE II *Analysis of professional category in Table I*

	Edinburgh %	Glasgow %
Lawyers	45	24
Ministers	23	32
Accountants	18	42
Others	14	2
	100	100
(N)	80	38

Even allowing for difficulties in classification between professional and lower professional, the table confirms the emphasis upon law in Edinburgh and commerce in Glasgow. It also suggests that stockbroking, insurance and banking were not significant parental occupations, thus contradicting the outgrowth theory, and it also highlights the existing respectability of accountancy during these formative years in that both lawyers and ministers regarded it as a suitable career for their children.

KM's Table IIB is also open to criticism, for he does not make it clear that it includes only those accountants for whom Stewart provides information. Our own research suggests that the figures for Edinburgh are broadly correct, but that the 'other named school' category should increase to 17 per cent for Glasgow and to 14 per cent for Aberdeen. However, research has been hampered by the fact that the major named schools in Glasgow have not published registers of former pupils, whereas such registers are available for the Edinburgh named schools. As a result it is not surprising that fewer Glasgow accountants have been *identified* as attending a named school.

KM's Table III seems inconclusive and certainly nothing in this or in any of the other tables warrants the final conclusion that 'in a number of ways the Glasgow membership makes good by these means the deficiencies in family and educational background.' In fact, KM presents no valid evidence to suggest that the Glasgow membership, given the social and commercial environment in Glasgow, suffered any such deficiency.

Collective social mobility

On the basis of his data in his tables IIA, IIB and III KM concluded that Scottish accountants constituted a well-established and respected occupation, but against this he offered four caveats:

1. His data comes 'from works written by accountants with the very objective of emphasizing the standing and achievements of the profession'. This seems a very unfair accusation to make against two authors who were writing almost as a hobby. Stewart, for example, very humbly describes his book 'as the product of an amateur author working outside his normal field' and states that it 'suffers from obvious defects and that there are substantial gaps in the biographical information'. If any bias exists, it is in the unwarranted use of this material for drawing academic inferences given the author's own warning of its defects and incompleteness.

2. Although Scottish accountants of 1850 were generally well-respected, the majority had only a modest education and most Glasgow accountants and a sizeable minority of those in Edinburgh probably came from lower middle or even middle class families. These assertions are amazing given that he had no information as to the parental occupation of 68 per cent of the Glasgow accountants! Our own data presented in Table I show that KM's argument is wrong as far as parental occupation is concerned, and we have already explained how defective are the data regarding the education of Glasgow accountants.

3. It is suggested that the main aim of incorporation was to secure respectability for Scottish accountants. However, our own research suggests that accountants were already respectable; that, although there had been discussions about incorporation, it had not been felt that this would present any positive advantages, and that it was the threat to their earnings from bankruptcy work by a proposed change in law that was the main stimulus for incorporation. The wording of the actual petition for the Charter is surely unimportant, for this would have been prepared by a lawyer in a fairly standard format which would probably tell us more about the legal profession than about the accounting profession.

4. Great play is made of the fact that it was a junior group in Glasgow which provided the pressure for incorporation and it is argued that this was 'to compensate for their relative lack of legal training and lower level of formal education by an emphasis on

"respectablity". We have already criticized this argument, but would further point out that the older members were probably less interested in incorporation because they performed a wider range of commercial activities than did Edinburgh accountants and would have been less affected by the proposed change in the bankruptcy legislation. The most telling statistic is that only nine of the fifteen senior members were involved in bankruptcy work while twenty of the twenty-seven junior instigators were involved in such work.

Conclusions

Given the defective data on which KM's conclusions are based it is hardly surprising that they should be open to criticism. His argument that the method by which the younger Glasgow accountants invited the senior ones to form a society represents collective social mobility is unjustified by the facts. The senior accountants had attempted to form a society in the past and had concluded that there was not sufficient enthusiasm for this. It was only when the younger ones, who would have suffered more from a reduction in their bankruptcy work, were faced with such a reduction that the pressure towards incorporation increased. It was a purely economic stimulus which had nothing to do with respectability or collective social mobility.

The arguments about market control are also unsupported. KM argues that 'the technique of closure was employed by accountants to gain the acceptability required to achieve market control. In so doing they not only controlled entry (and thereby to a large extent the job market) but went a long way towards achieving a monopoly in accounting services.' However the stimulus to incorporation was the threat of the loss of a market and not the wish to gain acceptability. Reference to a monopoly in accounting services is unjustified because those services are not defined by KM. Audit work was unimportant in 1850 and the profession did not get a monopoly of it until 1948, and even then the monopoly was incomplete. Bankruptcy and liquidation work *was* all-important in 1850, yet accountants have never had a monopoly of it. Admittedly, the chartered accountants have often attempted to stifle the growth of other accounting bodies but they have been unsuccessful in this throughout their history. Thus there has been no clearly defined market for accounting services, no effective market closure and certainly no need to incorporate to gain a respectability which already existed.

Given these criticisms we would therefore deny that the 'unresolved dialectic' was one of the most important elements in the establishment of the Scottish accounting profession. The references to respectability, collective social mobility and market control are unsupported by the facts, facts which suggest that it was a purely economic motive which encouraged the incorporation of the profession.

Finally KM suggests a hypothesis to explain the fact that professional formation in Scotland was earlier than in England. This is that 'on the one hand the Scottish accountants carried far more weight with the Privy Council than their English counterparts and on the other that there is little recorded about the personal details of the English founder members because they were much less worthy of note.' As far as the first part of this hypothesis is concerned we would reiterate that Scottish accountants were faced with a loss of bankruptcy work due to a change in law which was to apply only in Scotland. There was, therefore, not the same incentive for English accountants to incorporate. The second part of the hypothesis is patently absurd. One might just as well argue that the lack of information on early English accountants proves that English accountants earn so much more than their Scottish counterparts that none of them can afford the time to become amateur authors to write pen pictures of early English accountants!

All in all, then, we strongly dispute the conclusions which KM draws from his data. In the first place, those data were never intended for academic analysis and are far more incomplete than KM implies. Our additional data fill in many of the gaps and facilitate a sounder analysis. In the second place, KM makes wrong assumptions regarding differences between English and Scottish accountants and this too leads him to incorrect conclusions.

Notes and Bibliography

1. K. M. Macdonald, 'Professional Formation: the Case of Scottish Accountants', *British Journal of Sociology*, vol. xxv, no. 2, March 1984, pp. 174-89.
2. R. Brown, *A History of Accounting and Accountants*, T. C. and E. C. Jack, Edinburgh, 1905.

3. J. C. Stewart, *Pioneers of a Profession - Chartered Accountants to 1897*, The Institute of Chartered Accountants of Scotland, Edinburgh, 1977.

4. E. Jones, *Accountancy and the British Economy 1840-1980 - The Evolution of Ernst & Whinney*, B. T. Batsford Ltd., London, 1981.

5. M. J. M. Kedslie, 'Social Origins of Scottish Chartered Accountants 1854-1904', Paper presented at the Third International Congress of Accounting Historians, London, 1980.

6. E. Jones, op. cit.

7. E. Jones, op. cit.

8. *Post Office Glasgow Directory* 1840-41, p. 255.

9. Op. cit., pp. 421-2.

10. *Edinburgh and Leith Post Office Directory,* 1850-1, p. 298.

11. E. Jones, op. cit. p. 80.

CHAPTER 3

Professional Formation: A Reply to Briston and Kedslie

Keith M Macdonald

The thoughts of Briston and Kedslie[1] on my paper *Professional Formation*[2] are welcome especially as they are accompanied by some research findings of their own. Their paper contains seven main headings, some of which contain sub-sections and this response is structured accordingly. Following their example I shall refer to my paper as KM and theirs as B and K.

I. Source material

B and K point out that KM has used incomplete data from secondary sources. It is only 'wrong to use such data' (B and K p. 123) if it is demonstrably biased or inaccurate. B and K data for Edinburgh confirms KM's, as indeed does Stewart 1977,[3] which has no omissions from the population studied. B and K's Glasgow data supplies much of the missing information and shows that with the exception of merchants and manufacturers the data is proportionately distributed over categories as shown in Table I (where 'Gentry' has been collapsed with 'professionals' because the former contains only two cases.)

KM's expectation that the missing data would be largely in working class occupations is not borne out. On the other hand the notion of the 'aspirant middle class' (KM p. 178) is strengthened. The other point that these new data raise is why, if merchants had as high a status as lawyers (B and K p. 125), were their sons so reticent about their background?

Reproduced from *British Journal of Sociology*, Volume 38, Number 1, March 1987, pp 106-111, with kind permission from Routledge.

TABLE I: *KM and B & K data compared: percentage increase in cell numbers*

	%
Gentry and professional	19
Lower professional	17
Merchants and manufacturers	36
Tradesmen, etc.	13
Farmers	15

2. Definition of accountant

While KM does not include a specific definition, there is nothing in the paper to suggest that it deals with anyone other than accountants in public practice to the virtual exclusion of other activities (KM p. 179). Scottish accountants certainly engaged in other activities (e.g. stockbroking) but the newly-formed societies eliminated these over time. Why the definition of accountants as 'control agents' (a reference to Johnson, 1977[4]) shows a 'lack of understanding' (B and K p. 123) is not clear; dealing with bankruptcy is just as regulative of capitalism as auditing.

3. The number of accountants

This is clearly tied up with the matter of definition, which probably explains the discrepancies between KM's Table I and B and K's figures. Their point is largely vitiated when they argue that the combined number of accountants in Edinburgh and Glasgow 'corrected' figure - was equal to the number in London 'uncorrected' figure (p. 125). This seems unlikely in view of the fact that the population of London was about five times that of Edinburgh and Glasgow combined.

4. Differences between England and Scotland

(a) *History as Ideology* It is hard to believe that many sociologists would take issue with KM p. 184 first paragraph. B and K's notion that this constitutes unfair criticism is rather strange (de mortuis nil nisi bonum it seems!) and their charge that 'it is unprofessional' is (unconsciously) ironic. It is not clear why they take issue so strongly with the suggestion (no more) that the works of accountants writing as amateur historians should have an ideological function - unless it is because Mr. Briston is himself a practising accountant.

(b) *England and Scotland, Glasgow and Edinburgh* KM is very cautious about such differences and much that is said was put in to suit an editor who wanted comparison. B and K, however, are quite categorical in their statements about the differences between England and Scotland and between Edinburgh and Glasgow; for example

> ... as far as social characteristics are concerned the real distinction lies between Glasgow and Edinburgh accountants (though it is a distinction of environment rather than of status) rather than those of England and Scotland.

The problems with this statement are:
(a) what terms like 'social characteristics' and 'environment' refer to
(b) the logical difficulty of showing small differences between England and Scotland when there are large differences between Edinburgh and Glasgow;
(c) the absence of either data or references.

5. Social characteristics

This section starts with the statement 'KM virtually ignores the effect of bankruptcy legislation'. KM refers to the matter quite explicitly four times (pp. 180, 182, 185 and 188). In addition, the source of the threat to accountants' bankruptcy work (to which B and K refer, rather mysteriously, on p. 125), is given (KM, p. 185).

B and K appear to have noticed, quite correctly, an elision in the argument on pp. 182-3 where it is stated that Table II supports the view that Scottish accountancy was an outgrowth of law, actuarial practice and stockbroking. In fact, Table II supports the claim earlier on (p. 182) about accountants' links with gentry and professionals. B and K's data amplifies KM's and their Table II does no more to disprove the claim than KM's to prove it, because it deals with fathers' occupations, not the accountants!

6. Collective social mobility

(a) The first of B and K's four points (secondary sources) has already been dealt with.

(b) The second, while correct, is far less substantial than they make out because the proportions with known social origin in military/gentry/ professional remains much the same (see Table II).

TABLE II

	Edinburgh %	Glasgow %
KM	60	20
B&K	56	29

(c) The third point brings to the fore the major problem with B and K's paper which is the failure to read the KM data in relation to its theoretical concern and to make their points in that context. If they had done this they would not read KM as saying 'the main aim of incorporation was *to secure respectability* for Scottish accountants' [my italics]. The point is that Scottish accountants put great emphasis on their respectability, which some of their members certainly possessed, in order to establish their market position (KM p. 187); and that Glasgow accountants, with fewer 'respectable' members, put more emphasis on it. It cannot be claimed in relation to the repeated used of 'respectable' in petitions to the Privy Council, that 'the actual wording is surely unimportant', unless it can be shown that in the context the word meant something else. KM's actual words, which were central to the paper were

> The advantages of social status and 'market control' are closely linked. Accountants wanted to control their 'market' by establishing their distinctive claims to specialist competence, especially in the eyes of the Courts. This recognition was obtained by the successful claim that all designated members were 'respectable', were trained in their specialism, and that their specialism included such esoteric and high

status skills and knowledge as law, actuarial practice and accounting. This claim would be more likely to be accepted by the public in general and by the legal profession in particular, if it were made by men of acceptable middle class characteristics, who could vouch for the other members admitted to the professional body. Thus the technique of closure was employed by accountants to gain the acceptability required *to achieve market control* [my italics].

7. Conclusions

1. The 'defective data' is similar to B and K's and their improvements do nothing to alter KM's cautious conclusions.

2. Their mistake about the direction of KM's argument relating respectability and market control is repeated on pp. 128 and 129. The argument about closure has been elaborated in a further paper.[5] Given this failure to understand the argument presented and the concepts derived from Larson,[6] Johnson[7] and Portwood and Fielding,[8] B and K's assertion that theory is 'unsupported by the facts' (p. 129) collapses. Once KM's argument is stated in its original form, it is clear that it does not lead to 'incorrect conclusions' (p. 129).

3. Scottish accountants had a strong specific motivation in 1852-5 to obtain incorporation. However, it must be emphasized that (a) Edinburgh and Glasgow accountants had been considering it for some time; (b) Aberdeen did not obtain it until 1867; (c) so far as can be judged from Millerson,[9] these were the only charters granted to *local* professional bodies in modern times. These events are not explicable by some mechanistic force exerted by the Bankruptcy Act.

The tentative hypothesis (p. 129) cannot be dismissed as 'absurd' when there are no data. It is in line with the paper's theoretical reasoning which remains intact.

To conclude by reviewing the points B and K make in their abstract, and the responses to them:

(i) KM's assumptions regarding the social characteristics of early Scottish accountants are wrong;

KM's findings (not assumptions) are the same as B and K's, with the exception of a greater proportion of merchants among the fathers of Glasgow accountants.

(ii) KM's inferences about the motivation of Scottish accountants to professionalize are mistaken;

B and K are themselves mistaken about what KM wrote.

(iii) KM's assertion of the importance of the difference between Scottish and English accountants is misguided;

KM asserts nothing but puts forward a tentative hypothesis for testing.

(iv) The distinction between the social environment of Glasgow and Edinburgh carried much more influence;

it is not clear from this what it was that was influenced.

It is useful when critical interest is shown in a paper, especially when accompanied by new data. It would have been more useful still if the critics had appreciated the theoretical framework and the line of reasoning employed.

Bibliography

1.   R. J. Briston and M. J. M. Kedslie. 'Professional Formation: The Case of Scottish Accountants - Some Corrections and Some Further Thoughts', *British Journal of Sociology*, vol. XXXVII, 1, pp. 122-30.

2.   K. M. Macdonald. 'Professional Formation: The Case of Scottish Accountants', *British Journal of Sociology*, vol. XXXV, 2, pp. 174-89.

3.   J. C. Stewart. 'Early C. A. Apprentices 1854-1863'. *Journal of Accounting History*, vol. 2, 1, May 1977, pp. 23-33.

4.   T. J. Johnson. 'Professions in the Class Structure' in R. Scase (ed.) *Industrial Society. Class, Cleavage and Control*, London: Allen & Unwin 1977, pp. 93-110.

5.   K. M. Macdonald. 'Social Closure and Occupational Registration: the Case of Accountancy in Britain'. *Sociology*, vol. 19, 4, November 1985, pp. 541-56.

6.   M. S. Larson. *The Rise of Professionalism*. London: University of California Press, 1977.

7.   T. J. Johnson *op cit.* and 'Work and Power' in G. Esland and G. Salaman *The Politics of Work and Occupations*, Milton Keynes: Open University Press, 1980.

8.   D. Portwood and A. Fielding. 'Privilege and the Professions'. *Sociological Review*, 29, 1981, pp. 749-73.

9.   G. Millerson. *The Qualifying Associations*, London: Routledge & Kegan Paul, 1964.

CHAPTER 4

Mutual Self Interest - A Unifying Force; The Dominance of Societal Closure Over Social Background in the Early Professional Accounting Bodies

Moyra J M Kedslie

Introduction

By the mid-1850s, Post Office Directories show that Scotland had at least four hundred men calling themselves accountants. The initial membership of the professional accounting bodies in Edinburgh and Glasgow at that time, however, was just one-third of that number. Indeed, it was not until the 1880s that their joint membership reached four hundred. Only a small part of the discrepancy can be explained by the geographical location of these accountants, for Glasgow and Edinburgh were by far the most dominant commercial centers in Scotland. The main explanatory factor was the exclusivity adopted by the new bodies immediately upon formation and maintained for at least a century thereafter.

The purpose of this paper is to examine the range of activities which were regarded as accounting in the mid-1850s and to explain the factors which brought about the narrowing of that definition in respect of the new professional bodies. These factors were largely social, yet, given that the Edinburgh and Glasgow societies were the forerunners of similar societies in England and Wales and in many countries around the world which were subject, either directly or indirectly, to British influence, they have assumed an importance which far transcends their initial Scottish confines.

Reproduced from *The Accounting Historians Journal,* Volume 17, Number 2, December 1990, pp 1-19, with kind permission of the Editor.

Finally, the paper highlights the continuing concern of the two bodies with professional closure, a further preoccupation which has characterized the activities of the numerous accounting bodies which can trace their existence back to the Scottish societal formation of the 1850s.

Early nineteenth century economic developments

Several industries played a role in the development of accountants in early Scotland. The most prominent are listed below:

Canals and railways

The development and construction of canals provided a great deal of work for men called accountants who might have been more appropriately called cashiers or book-keepers [Hadfield, 1971]. Apart from bringing together enormous volumes of employees and capital, canal companies also had large numbers of shareholders from diverse backgrounds. This necessitated the monitoring of construction costs often using elaborate systems [Gibb, 1935, pp. 186-7] and the preparation of either printed annual reports or more basic reports to be read to shareholders of smaller companies [Hadfield, 1955, p. 84]. While the role of the bookkeeper/cashier/accountant was important to the company, neither as a group nor individually do they appear to have had any impact on the professionalization of accountancy. Only sixteen canals were completed in Scotland and only eight were still operating when the first accounting society was formed [Lindsay, 1968, pp. 210-13]. In addition, no canal accountants appear to have been of sufficient status to be listed in any of the professional or trade directories of that period.

From the 1840s onwards, the essential role of canals as a means of more efficient transportation of goods and passengers was rapidly overtaken by railway companies. Again, the complexities of work, capital and shareholders necessitated the employment of cashiers and accountants during the construction phase as well as the efficient running of railway companies, and parliamentary records show that there was steady employment of approximately thirty cashiers/accountants on Scottish railway lines opened and under construction [BPP 1847-55]. Their employment had undoubtedly been encouraged by the Railway Clauses Consolidation Act of 1845 which required the preparation of annual accounts of receipts and expenditures and a statement of the balance of the account. The Act also produced another area of work for accountants in that it required these accounts to be audited. All of the Scottish railway lines which listed auditors consistently appointed at least one described as an accountant [Bradshaw's 1848 etc.].

Before 1854, the employment opportunities open to accountants in railway concerns were limited because of the small number of companies. One interesting difference, however, can he observed in those employed as accountants. None of the men who was employed in the internal management accounting of the companies were considered to he of sufficient importance to be listed in any of the city directories - an indication of their relatively low status. On the other hand, many of the accountant-auditors became founder members of the Scottish professional societies - an indication of their higher social status. Perhaps this difference arose from several factors. It was generally the case that auditors were required to hold shares in the company they were auditing. The availability of capital, therefore, was an essential prerequisite for the position. Second, the majority of the shares in such companies were often held by the directors, who would automatically appoint an auditor from their own class.

Banking, stockbroking and insurance

From the time of their foundation, all Scottish banks employed people designated as accountants, although it is difficult to establish exactly what was meant by the term. The lack of reference to them in directories of the day and in the first history of Scottish accounting [Brown, 1905] suggests that, although this specialist group was probably quite important in its own area, it was considered insignificant in the development of the accounting profession in Scotland. Banks differed from railways in their attitude toward auditing and generally did not have a system of independent audit since there was a strongly held view that this would interfere with the privacy demanded by the bank's customers [Tyson, 1974, p. 126].

Stock exchanges did not appear in Scotland until the 1840s, although the first recognized stockbrokers began trading in the mid-1820s. The attitude of early accountants toward this work was divided geographically. In Edinburgh, few accountants became involved in this work, which was viewed as being high risk and of low status [Michie, 1981, p. 17]. In Glasgow, which had a mercantile character and consequently closer links between accountants and industry, almost forty percent of the original members of the Glasgow stock exchange became professional accountants [*Records of Glasgow Stock Exchange*, 1927].

In the middle of the nineteenth century, much of the great expansion in Scotland in various kinds of insurance business was attributed to accountants [Brown, 1905, p. 195; Stewart, 1977, p. 18]. By 1854, eighty-one insurance companies were listed in Edinburgh and one hundred and fourteen in Glasgow. The involvement of chartered accountants was much stronger in Glasgow, where at least fifty-two percent of those involved in insurance work became chartered accountants. Even more significant is the fact that sixty-seven percent of the signatories of the application for the Royal Charter for the Glasgow Institute were involved in this type of work. Such employment, however, generally formed only a small part of the work load for any professional accountant of that period. He was more likely to be involved in the audit of insurance companies, which were quicker than banking companies to realize the importance of audit by professional accountants.

Bankruptcy

Men styling themselves as "accountants" had been involved in the settlement of bankrupt estates in Scotland from the latter part of the eighteenth century[1] and by the mid-nineteenth century had grown to be the most important occupational group so involved, being appointed trustees in 55 percent of the total number of cases and earning 78 percent of the total fee income. Sixty-nine percent of the cases dealt with by accountants were undertaken by men who later became members of one of the bodies of Scottish chartered accountants, and it is of note that they administered the most remunerative estates, taking 81 percent of the fees earned by accountants (Table I).

Not only were there differences between the number of trusteeships awarded to the two different groups of accountants, there were also significant differences between the awards in Edinburgh and Glasgow accountants. Although there was no significant difference between the numbers of the two groups of accountants who were involved in such work in the two cities, it is immediately apparent that Glasgow accountants, in both groups, dealt with a much larger proportion of cases than did their counterparts in Edinburgh (Table II). This fact is not really surprising since the Bankruptcy (Scotland) Act of 1839 gave extensive bankruptcy jurisdiction to the Sheriff Courts which resulted, in most cases, in the trusteeship being awarded in the county where the bankrupt traded. Glasgow was considerably larger as a center of population and trade and therefore gave rise to more bankruptcies.

TABLE I *Analysis of cases awarded and fee income earned on pre-1851 sequestrated estates per occupational group*

Occupational Group	Total Cases %	Fee Income %
Accountants - later chartered	38	63
Other accountants	17	15
Total accountants	55	78
Legal profession	13	8
Banking	5	3
Miscellaneous (non-professional)	27	11
	100	100

Total cases = 1,155; Total fee income = £89,000

Source: *The Alphabetical Compendium of Scotch Mercantile Sequestrations,* 1851.

A comparison of the cases dealt with by the group who later became CAs shows quite clearly that the more lucrative cases were dealt with by the Edinburgh CAs. This might be explained by the fact that complicated cases were often referred to the Court of Session in Edinburgh and such cases were almost always awarded to Edinburgh accountants. There can, however, be no doubt as to the importance of bankruptcy work to the first chartered accountants with 70 and 83 percent of founder members in Edinburgh and Glasgow being so involved.

This analysis of the areas of work undertaken by accountants in the mid-1850s suggests that, with the exception of the bankruptcy work in both cities and insurance and stockbroking in Glasgow, there was a clear distinction between the work undertaken by accountants who became members of the chartered societies and those who were excluded, perhaps reflecting the mid-Victorian view expressed by Trollope's Mrs. Marrable " . . . that when a man touched trade or commerce in any way he was doing that which was not the work of a gentleman" [Lewis & Maude, 1952, p. 48] and the chartered societies certainly saw themselves as being open only to gentlemen.

TABLE II *Comparison of pre-1851 sequestration work undertaken by two groups of accountants per location*

	Later CAs			Non CAs		
	No. of Accountants	*% Cases*	*% Fees*	*No. of Accountants*	*% Cases*	*% Fees*
Location						
Edinburgh	32	27	59	21	16	7
Glasgow	36	70	39	25	63	75
Aberdeen	1	<1	2	0	0	0
Dundee	3	3	*	4	8	7
Others	0	0	0	16	13	11
		——	——		——	——
		100	100		100	100
		——	——		——	——
Total	72	448	£56,811	66	196	£13,070
*Not disclosed						

Source: *The Alphabetical Compendium of Scotch Mercantile Sequestrations*, 1851.

Factors significant in societal formation

Edinburgh

Societal formation began successfully in Edinburgh on January 17, 1853 when A. W. Robertson sent a letter to fourteen accountants in practice in the city inviting them to a meeting in his office. The wording of his letter suggests that he was acting as spokesman for a few accountants who had been discussing the possibility of a society for some time. Those approached had an average age of forty-four, but only three of them were over the age of fifty. They had two common areas of professional interest, in that 67 percent were actively involved in insurance work of some description and 87 percent had an involvement in bankruptcy work [*Edinburgh and Leith Post Office Directory* 1853-54, pp. ixlii].

Six of the men approached, plus one who was presumably approached verbally, attended the meeting in Robertson's office on January 20, 1853 and determined that, although previous attempts to form a society had failed, the time was now ripe for incorporation. Robertson and his unknown group had prepared well since they produced a draft constitution and rules and regulations at this meeting and arranged to discuss these at a further meeting two days later. The meeting on January 22 was attended by eight recipients of the original invitation along with Robertson and three others who had been approached personally. Again the group had a strong interest in insurance, in which 58 percent were involved but, more significantly, 92 percent were active in bankruptcy work [*Edinburgh and Leith Post Office Directory*, 1853-54, pp. i-xlii].

TABLE III *Analysis of professional interests of early Edinburgh chartered accountants*

Significant Events	No.	Bankruptcy %	Insurance %	Stock Exchange %
January 17, 1853 Recipients of letter and sender	15	87	67	0
January 20, 1853 First meeting	8	88	63	0
January 22, 1853 Discussion of rules and regulations	12	92	58	0
February 4, 1853 Council and office bearers	11	64	82	0
October 23, 1854 Charter signatories	61	62	66	0

Source: *The Alphabetical Compendium of Scotch Mercantile Sequestrations,*1851; *Edinburgh and Leith Post Office Directory*, 1853-54, pp, i-xlii.

This small group was charged with the task of targeting practising accountants considered suitable for membership of what was envisaged as a prestigious new society. They were apparently successful in this since 47 men attended the next meeting on January 31. However, since the Edinburgh and Leith Directory for 1853-54 listed 132 accountants, the nucleus formed by Robertson was very selective in extending its invitations. This larger group was unanimous in appointing James Brown to the chair, although he had not previously been involved in the formation activities, and agreed that the society be called the Institute of Accountants in Edinburgh [Institute of Accountants, *Sederunt Book, Council Minutes*, No. 1, p. 5].

At the next meeting on February 4, office bearers and members of Council were appointed. This group of eleven accountants differed from the previous groups in several ways. First, five of them had not been on the list of those originally approached by Robertson and six of them had attended neither of the two formation meetings. In addition, the group's 82 percent involvement in insurance was stronger than any previous group while its involvement in bankruptcy was, at 64 percent, significantly lower. Clearly, the five members of this group who had not been involved in the initial stages of the society had been identified as being important to it. They were, with an average age of 58, a little older than the other founding members, four of them had an involvement in insurance work, but only one had an interest in bankruptcy. It would appear that their selection for office was based on the long experience that they had in accountancy practice in the city. At the date of societal formation, Brown had been in practice for 40 years and appears to have been the doyen of Edinburgh accountants of that period. Three of the others had been in practice for 30 years and the fifth for almost 20. As a group, they brought to the new society long experience and their no doubt well-established respectability in their professional field would reflect on the image of the group they had been invited to join [Brown, 1905, p. 205].

Having settled the most immediate matter of determining entry procedures, qualifications and cost, the Institute of Accountants in Edinburgh moved rapidly, on April 8, 1853, to a discussion on the matter of most concern to them - the proposed changes in bankruptcy law, which would have abolished the office of Interim Factor (which was often undertaken by an accountant) and passed its duties to the Sheriff Clerk, a legal officer. By May 11, a report had been prepared, and the extent of the society's interest evidenced by the claim that five-sixths of all Scottish bankrupt estates were dealt with by accountants - at that time averaging about 250 cases per year. The report was subsequently submitted to the Lord Advocate and clearly had the desired effect, for, when the Bankruptcy (Scotland) Act was passed on August 4, 1853, the offending clause had been removed and the Act did no damage whatsoever to the work previously undertaken by accountants [Scottish Records Office CS 322/1 etc. *Annual Report of The Accountant of Bankruptcy in Scotland*].

Once the threat of one of their main sources of fee income had been removed, the Council of the Edinburgh Institute met on May 29, 1854, to discuss applying for a Charter. The Charter was dated October 23 and registered December 11, 1854, under the name of the Society of Accountants in Edinburgh. Sixty-one members signed the Charter, 66 percent of whom were involved with insurance work and 62 percent in bankruptcy [*Edinburgh and Leith Post Office Directory*, 1853-54, pp. i-xlii].

Glasgow

The professionalization of Glasgow accountants began from an initiative in September 1853 by 27 accountants already established in practice in the city contacting a further 14 accountants of similar experience. From this group, a steering committee met and discussed and agreed to the proposal that a society of accountants be formed in Glasgow. A President was appointed and a small committee entitled the "Committee of Elder Members" was formed to ensure the rapid transformation of the idea into actuality. Within six weeks, office bearers had been elected and a Constitution agreed upon, and within two months of its formation the members of the society had appointed a committee to examine the proposed changes in Scottish bankruptcy law [Institute of Accountants in Glasgow, *Minute Book*, No. 1, p. 14].

No record survives to indicate which one of the 27 accountants who signed the requisition was responsible for bringing the group together, but the members did share several professional areas of interest. Seven of them were members of the Glasgow stock exchange and, presumably, met from time to time at the exchange. Seventeen of them were actively involved in insurance activities within the city, generally as managers and agents. Most significantly, 23 (85 percent) of them were active in bankruptcy work, which they were no doubt anxious to protect for themselves [*The Alphabetical Compendium of Scotch Mercantile Sequestrations*, 1851].

Although no minutes survive, this group or its representatives must have had at least one meeting to determine a strategy that would result in the successful formation of a society, at which they prepared a list of accountants who would be targeted for support. The average age of the members of the first group was 36, with several being in their late twenties or early thirties. The group approached for support, and presumably considered essential to the success of any accounting society in the city, had an average age of 48. Of the fourteen recipients of the requisition suggesting the formation of a society, nine were members of the stock exchange, eight were involved in insurance and nine were involved in bankruptcy work. As far as social background is concerned, there was little difference between the two groups with, if anything, a slightly stronger commercial background being found amongst the older of the two groups (See Table VI).

TABLE IV *Analysis of professional interests of early Glasgow chartered accountants*

Significant Events	No.	Bankruptcy %	Insurance %	Stock Exchange %
September 1853 Signatories of invitation	27	85	63	26
Recipients of invitation	14	64	57	64
October 3, 1853 steering committee	9	67	44	67
Committee of elder members	3	100	33	100
November 9, 1853 Committee and office bearers	9	56	44	67
November 14-18, 1853 Signatories of constitution	13	69	62	77
May 16,1855 Charter signatories	49	71	67	35

Source: *The Alphabetical Compendium of Scotch Mercantile Sequestrations,* 1851; *Glasgow Post Office Directory 1853-54,* pp. 557-561; *Records of the Glasgow Stock Exchange Association 1844-1926,* Appendix I.

As a result of the requisition and the response to it, one of the signatories, McClelland, called a meeting on October 3, 1853, which was attended by nine of the fourteen accountants approached, who could be viewed as a steering committee. The strongest link between them was that six had been founding members of the Glasgow stock exchange and could presumably be expected to put this experience to good use in ensuring that efforts to form a society would finally be successful. Since the business center of Glasgow was extremely compact in the 1850s, the nine were probably well known to one another, particularly since four were involved in insurance work and six in bankruptcy. In addition, three of them had trained with McClelland who was also on the committee, who is credited with having been the prime motivator behind the society and who was appointed its first President. The steering committee appointed a small sub-committee of three named the Committee of Elder Members, to progress the detail of the plan. Since the average age of this group was forty, the term "elder" must have referred to experience rather than age. All of them were involved in bankruptcy work, all were founder members of the stock exchange, and two of them had trained with McClelland [Stewart, 1977, pp. 123, 125].

On November 9, 1853, a committee and office bearers were appointed, not one of whom had been a signatory of the original requisition, but all of whom had been recipients. At a general meeting on November 15, 1853, the Constitution was signed by all but one of the 14 accountants approached to form the society. Thus the Glasgow Institute came officially to life, fulfilling the objective of the younger practicing accountants in Glasgow who had recognized that the experience and reputation of the older, established members of the accounting community was essential for the society to achieve its objectives. [Institute of Accountants in Glasgow, *Minute Book*, No. 1, p. 1].

It was not until July 4, 1854, that the Council of the Glasgow Institute resolved to apply for a Royal Charter. The lapse of time between societal formation and the consideration of a charter can be explained by examining the main issues concerning the society in the interim period. Apart from their initial determination of entry barriers such as work experience, acceptability to founding members and entry fees, the members were concerned with only one matter - the proposed changes in bankruptcy legislation, which they were determined to petition against. The first action taken by them on December 2, 1853, was the formation of a committee to monitor these proposals, to suggest changes, and to co-operate with other interested bodies. This committee was the first example of a joint action between the two original groups involved in the Institute's formation and consisted of four established accountants and five younger members. On March 21, 1854, the committee called a Special General Meeting to discuss the proposed changes in the nomination procedure for Interim Factors and the election of trustees on bankrupt estates and determined to discuss a course of action with the Society of Accountants in Edinburgh. This meeting was reported at the reconvened special general meeting on March 29 at which the petition was presented to the members. The argument put forward by the accountants was that it would be "injurious to the interests of the Mercantile Community of Scotland" [Institute of Accountants in Glasgow, *Minute Book*, No. 1, p. 33] to proceed because there was, at the same time, a Commission of Enquiry investigating the improvement of some areas of Mercantile Law including Bankruptcy Law. The Commission had not yet reported and it was argued that it would be better to deal with the changes as a whole rather than on a piece meal basis. By April 28, 1854, the two societies of accountants had reached agreement on their tactics and submitted their views to the Lord Advocate.

Once this urgent threat had been dealt with, the Institute began to discuss the possibility of applying for a Royal Charter. By July 4, 1854, the membership had increased to almost 50 and the contact that several members had experienced with the Edinburgh accountants perhaps encouraged them to apply for the elevated status assumed to come with a successful charter application. Out of a total population of approximately 150 accountants practicing in Glasgow in 1855, 49 signed the charter application, the first to sign were the recipients of the original requisition proposing the formation of the society. Thirty-five percent of the signatories were also members of the stock exchange but the two strongest common areas of interest were insurance, with 67 percent of membership involvement and bankruptcy, with a 71 percent involvement. Given this last figure, it is little wonder that a charter application was considered of less immediate importance than attempting to prevent financially damaging changes in bankruptcy legislation. The strong involvement with insurance and the undoubted desire to signal to the business community their intention to retain this considerable interest explains the title of the Institute of Accountants and Actuaries in Glasgow.

Society comparison

The most obvious difference between the work undertaken by the two groups of accountants is the total absence of stockbroking activities in Edinburgh compared with a significant interest in Glasgow, a reflection of the fact that Glasgow was at the center of a large industrial and commercial area. In addition, the records of the

Glasgow society make it clear that it was not uncommon for accountants to be employed by companies [Institute of Accountants in Glasgow, *Minute Book,* No. 1, p. 37] and several of the early accountants are noted as having been involved in the formation and running of railway and utility companies [Stewart, [1977] p. 17].

Both groups were strongly involved in insurance in their respective cities. There were differences, however, in the kind of involvement. In Edinburgh, it was much more likely to be as an auditor or director; whereas in Glasgow, it was often as an agent and less likely as a director.

Social origins

The fact that the men who formed and were early members of the first Scottish accounting societies were broadly involved in the same areas of work might lead to the expectation that they would have come from broadly similar family backgrounds. However, this is not the case although the differences became less obvious as the societies developed.

Edinburgh

Table V confirms that the early members of the Edinburgh society were predominantly upper to upper-middle class with the most significant group coming, in all cases, from a legal background. It is perhaps not surprising to find this to be the case in Edinburgh which was the center of the Scottish legal system. Different sections of the legal profession, such as advocates and writers to the signet,[2] had long standing professional associates with which the Edinburgh accountants would be familiar. In addition, many early members trained in legal offices and much of the work eventually carried out in accounting offices was previously performed in legal offices. Since the accounting profession in Edinburgh had for many years been viewed as a section of the legal profession, this preponderance of legal parentage is not surprising, particularly in the pre-charter period. The strong legal ties would be significant in establishing the social status of the members of the new society since "The real leaders of Edinburgh Society, however, were not to be found among merchants and tradesmen but among professional men: and among the professions there were none, in numbers, wealth or prestige, to equal the lawyers" [Smout, 1969, p. 375].

Other significant groups among the charter signatories were the Church, landowners and government and armed services. What is also important is that none of the early members came from a commercial background and very few from manufacturing or trade. The social origins of members were such that the Edinburgh society could not fail to gain immediate social status which was then imputed to subsequent members.

TABLE V *Social origins of significant groups of early Edinburgh chartered accountants*

	Original Letter %	First Meeting %	Rules and Regs. Meeting %	Council & Officers %	Charter Signatories %
CA	--	--	--	--	1.6
Other accountants	6.7	12.5	--	--	4.9
	6.7	12.5	--	--	6.5
Legal profession	26.7	25.0	33.3	27.3	18.0
Banking & insurance	6.7	12.5	8.3	18.2	4.9
Church	13.3	-	16.7	18.2	16.4
Government & armed service	13.3	12.5	8.3	9.1	9.8
Landowner	13.3	25.0	16.7	9.1	16.4
Other profession	-	-	-	9.1	3.3
	80.0	87.5	83.3	91.0	75.3
Merchant	-	-	-	-	-
	80.0	87.5	83.3	91.0	75.3
Manufacturer	-	-	*	-	1.6
Craftsman/ tradesman	6.7	12.5	8.3	-	4.9

TABLE V *Continued*

	Original Letter %	First Meeting %	Rules and Regs. Meeting %	Council & Officers %	Charter Signatories %
Miscellaneous	-	-	-	-	-
Unknown	13.3	-	8.3	9.1	18.0
	100	100	100	100	100
(N)	15	8	12	11	61

Source: Scottish Records Office: Certificates of Birth. Marriage and Death; *Census of Population Records* 1841, 1851.

Glasgow

It is clear from Table VI that the social background of the early chartered accountants in Glasgow was significantly different from that of those in Edinburgh. The largest group in all cases in Glasgow came from a mercantile background, reflecting the fact that Glasgow was an industrial city, while the representation of a manufacturing background was negligible in Edinburgh. The legal profession, the Church, and landowners were also represented, but at a lower level than in Edinburgh, and the overall impression that emerges from Glasgow is a society with a lower proportion of upper and upper-middle class members.

TABLE VI *Social origins of significant groups of early Glasgow chartered accountants*

	Sigs. of Reqn.	Recipients of Reqn	Steering Committee	Const. Sigs	Charter Sigs.
CA	-	-	-	-	-
Other Accountants	7.4	14.4	11.1	7.7	8.2
	7.4	14.4	11.1	7.7	8.2
Legal profession	11.1	7.1	11.1	7.7	8.2
Banking & insurance	3.7	7.1	-	7.7	4.1

TABLE VI *Continued*

	Sigs. of Reqn.	Recipients of Reqn	Steering Committee	Const. Sigs	Charter Sigs.
Church	7.4	14.4		15.4	8.2
Government & armed service	-	-	-	-	-
Landowner	18.5	7.1	11.1	7.7	12.2
Other professions	7.4	-	-	-	4.1
	55.5	50.1	33.3	46.2	45.0
Merchant	3.7	35.7	44.5	38.4	16.3
	59.2	85.8	77.8	84.6	61.3
Manufacturer	14.9	7.1	11.1	7.7	8.2
Craftsman/tradesman	-	-	-	-	2.0
Miscellaneous	3.7	-	-	-	4.1
Unknown	22.2	7.1	11.1	7.7	24.4
	100	100	100	100	100
(N)	27	14	9	13	49

Source: Scottish Records Office: Certificates of Birth, Marriage and Death; *Census of Population Records* 1841, 1851.

Society concerns

The distinct differences in the social origins of the founder members of the two societies and the different emphasis in the work undertaken by them might lead to an expectation that they would have developed in different directions. As professional bodies, however, their concerns were very similar.

The first area to be tackled by both groups was that of professional closure. Several instruments were utilized to ensure that the societies were elitist and therefore of high professional and social reputation. Entry to the societies was initially limited to those who had been approached personally to join and who were generally in the same social class as the small groups of organizers. Subsequently, membership for practicing accountants depended on their ability to convince existing members of their suitability for admission. For apprentices, the barriers were the necessity to find a member to whom he would be indentured; the cost of paying for his indenture, which amounted to an average of one hundred guineas in 1853; and the ability to pass the informal or formal examinations. Both societies adopted very similar systems of entry as a means of controlling their quality and size.

Because both groups of chartered accountants had an involvement in bankruptcy and insurance work that was higher than the average for all accountants in either city, they were anxious to increase their proportion of available work, or at least prevent its decrease. The first example of their activities in this area was in April 1854 after the new Bankruptcy (Scotland) Act came into operation, when both societies provided the Lord Advocate's clerk with a list of members, described as a list of the accountants in the two cities who were experienced to deal with sequestrations from the Court of Session. This obvious attempt to exclude from this work accountants who were not members of the two societies was successful in the long run: by 1900, Edinburgh chartered accountants had a virtual monopoly of Edinburgh bankruptcy work and Glasgow chartered accountants dealt with the majority of cases in their area.

The exclusivity of the new societies led to the formation of rival institutions. Two such institutions emerged in Scotland, the Scottish Institute of Accountants in 1880 and the Corporation of Accountants in 1891. Both were formed by accountants who were not eligible for entry to the chartered societies [Stacey, 1954, p. 33]. The Corporation of Accountants encouraged its members to designate themselves CA - corporate accountants. Since the members of the Edinburgh and Glasgow societies had agreed in 1855 to use the same designatory letters, and had done so with some consistency, they were concerned at the confusion that might be caused by the Corporation's directive. The Corporation, however, refused to desist from using the designation until the chartered bodies raised a successful action against them in the Court of Session.

Similar concern had been raised in 1880 on the formation of the Institute of Chartered Accountants in England and Wales. Some Glasgow accountants who were debarred from membership of the Scottish chartered bodies were admitted to the English Institute and henceforth designated themselves as 'Chartered Accountants' as contained in the Institute's Charter. The Edinburgh and Glasgow societies co-operated on dealing with this problem and took legal advice on the matter. Interestingly, they were advised not to pursue the matter since they were unlikely to succeed [Institute of Accountants in Glasgow, *Minute Book*, No. 2, p. 131].

Conclusion

This study has highlighted the social differences that existed between the men responsible for the formation of the Edinburgh and Glasgow chartered accountants' societies, two of the founder members of the Institute of Chartered Accountants of Scotland. Similarly, it has indicated the difference in the involvement of each group in the main areas of professional work at that time.

The distinct differences in pre-societal formation were of secondary consideration when the new societies faced any outside threat, however, for such threats were often responded to jointly. The matters of joint concern to them were similar to those facing any new professional body. Primarily, they wished to ensure that the new societies had a recognized status in their respective communities, which they accomplished by inviting membership only from men of proven social and professional standing. Once the societies had achieved the desired status, it would be imputed to future members. It was necessary, also, to prevent the societies from overly rapid growth which might have diluted the quality of performance and the amount of work for each member. This was achieved by restricting entry to those who had the proper social background and the money and education that usually accompanied that background.

The other common threat to the chartered societies was that posed by other accounting societies being formed and by the members of one of them adopting the designatory letters 'CA'. Again the societies acted together to repel these problems. Thus, while the societies remained separate for about a century, probably because of the different social characteristics of Edinburgh and Glasgow, in times of adversity the social differences were submerged and common interests successfully pursued.

Notes

1. *A History of the Chartered Accountants of Scotland,* Edinburgh (1954)
    p. 11. Advertisement dated 1778 for John Gibson of Glasgow offering to

act as accountant on "Settling of Copartnery or Other Disputes, Making Out Accounts of the Rankings of Creditors, and the Division of Subjects."
2. An advocate is the Scottish equivalent of a barrister. A writer to the signet is a member of an ancient Scottish society of law agents similar to an attorney.

Bibliography

The Alphabetical Compendium of Scotch Mercantile Sequestrations 1851, London, Longman, Brown, Green & Longmans (1851).

Bradshaw's Railway Almanac, Directory, Shareholders' Guide and Manual, 1848, etc. [An annual directory of British and Foreign Railway Companies giving details of each company's capital structure, office bearers and significant financial events.]

BPP 1847 (597) LXIII, 101; 1849 (249) LI, 101; 1850 (165) LIII, 277; 1851 (102) LI, 255; 1852 (153) XLVIII, 395; 1852-53 (253) XCVII, 229; 1854 (105) LXII, 559; 1854 (495) LXII, 599; 1854-55 (511) XLVIII, 631,

Brown, R. (ed.) *A History of Accounting and Accountants*, T. C. and E. C. Jack, Edinburgh (1905).

Edinburgh and Leith Post Office Directories, 1853 etc.

Gibb, Sir A., *The Story of Telford: The Rise of Civil Engineering*, Glasgow: Maclehose (1935): 186-7.

Glasgow Post Office Directories, 1853 etc.

Hadfield, C., "Sources for the History of British Canals", *Journal of Transport History* (1955): 84.

Hadfield, C., *The Canal Age*, London: Pan Books Ltd. (1971): 22-25.

History of the Chartered Accountants of Scotland, Edinburgh, Institute of Chartered Accountants of Scotland (1954): 11.

Institute of Accountants of Edinburgh Sederunt Book, Council Minutes, No, I.

Institute of Accountants in Glasgow, Minute Book, No. 1, [No. 2, 131].

Lewis, R. and Maude, A., *Professional People*, London: Phoenix House Ltd. (1952): 48.

Lindsay, J., *The Canals of Scotland*, Newton Abbot: David & Charles (1968): 210-13.

Michie, R. C., *Money, Mania and Markets*, Edinburgh: John Donald Ltd. (1981): 17.

Records of the Glasgow Stock Exchange Association 1844-1926, Glasgow: Jackson, Wyllie & Co. (1927): Appendix I.

Scottish Records Office: Annual Report of the Accountant of Bankruptcy in Scotland.

Census of Population 1841, 1851.

Certificates of Birth, Marriage and Death.

Smout, T. C., *A History of the Scottish People 1560-1830,* London: Collins (1969): 375.

Stacey, N. A. H., *English Accountancy 1800-1954,* London: Gee and Company (1954): 33.

Stewart, J. C., *Pioneers of a Profession,* Edinburgh: Institute of Chartered Accountants of Scotland (1977): 17, 18, 123, 125.

Tyson, R. E., "The Failure of the City of Glasgow Bank and the Rise of Independent Auditing" *The Accountants' Magazine* (1974): 126.

A Review Essay: Professional Foundations and Theories of Professional Behaviour

Thomas A Lee

Introduction

The accountancy profession is nearly one hundred and fifty years old. Formally organized in Scotland in the mid 1850s, it has expanded rapidly worldwide to become one of the leading professions in terms of the number of people it employs, the quantity and variety of services it offers and renders, the size and pervasiveness of its public firms, the extent of its provision and use of educational and research resources, the degree of influence it has in its relations with the state, and the social status and economic rewards enjoyed by its members. Yet, it still must cope with persistent and seemingly intractable problems such as the dubious meaning of reported accounting figures, inconsistencies in accounting rules, education orientated solely to training for current practice, a lack of research influence on practice, and managing the ethical behavior of practitioners.

For these reasons, and more than ever before, there is a need to explore the origins and development of the accountancy profession - that is, to discover the reasons why it came into existence, and the means by which it has prospered despite its long-standing problems. Hopefully, such historical studies will not only provide the profession's current and future members with an understanding of their roots, but will also signal clues as to possible resolutions of at least some of its problems.

Reproduced from *The Accounting Historians Journal*, Volume 18, Number 2, December 1991, pp 193-203, with kind permission from the Editor.

With these thoughts in mind, this review essay is intended to provide some historical perspective on the modern accountancy profession by critiquing the recent study of Dr. Kedslie into the origins of the earliest professional accountancy bodies formed in Scotland in the mid 1850s [Kedslie, 1990].[1] It would be arrogant to claim that these bodies were necessarily different in character, origin or purpose from other bodies formed at about the same time in England and elsewhere. Nevertheless, there is a curious fascination about the founding fathers of any enterprise. For example, consider the attention given to Pacioli regarding the introduction of double-entry bookkeeping despite knowledge of its existence prior to the date of his publication [see de Roover, 1974].

Given this natural curiosity about 'beginnings,' what is most surprising with respect to the Kedslie text is that it represents one of a very few scholarly studies of the Scottish origins of the modern accountancy profession. One of the earliest and often-quoted texts is that of Brown [1905], a leading Scottish chartered accountant at the beginning of this century, who wrote very generally of the origins of the profession in Scotland, the establishment of the first societies, the first chartered accountants, and the work and problems of these early professionals [pp. 181-231 and 314-42]. Pre-professional accounting in Scotland is covered in a detailed study by Mepham [1988] of eighteenth century accounting and accountants, the main feature of which is the considerable intellectual capacity of the men behind the accounting ideas which were part of the Scottish Enlightenment [pp. 381-3].

Post-professionalization in Scotland has also been studied by accounting historians, and in a number of ways. First, there is an anonymous general history of the early development to 1954 of the main Scottish professional body, described within a context of accounting activities and leading Scottish accountants of the period [ICAS, 1954/1984]. Second Stewart [1977/1986] produced a historical review of Scotland's professional beginnings in accounting in the form of a series of brief biographical sketches of the original Scottish chartered accountants to 1879. Third, Winsbury [1977] has written a history of a leading international public accountancy firm which originated in Scotland. Fourth, Lee [1984] has edited a book of papers which were delivered over a seventy-year period to Scottish accounting student societies by leading accountants, revealing the type of persistent issues which were brought to the attention of Scottish accounting practitioners and their apprentices over several decades. Fifth, Walker [1988] recently wrote an extensive empirically-based social history of recruitment to the earliest Scottish accountancy body, with specific references to the social mobility of the recruits.

Kedslie's text touches on most of the activities and issues covered in these earlier studies. It is particularly related to that of Walker [1988], in the sense that both historians have observed and interpreted the main factors which they perceive to have comprised the origins of the earliest Scottish accountancy bodies. However, lest any reader feel that there is duplication between these two recent studies, it should be stated at the outset that Kedslie's study provides a broad observation and commentary on a multiplicity of connected issues. It establishes what Carr [1987, p. 104] has described as one of the essential roles of history – "a rational and logical quilt of knowledge." In this case, knowledge concerns the origins of professional accountancy in Scotland. Walker, on the other hand, has produced a more socio-scientific study of certain specific variables which he argues determined the nature and size of the recruitment and self-recruitment to one of the founding professional bodies in Scotland. In particular, his study is of developments from the origins of professionalization, with specific emphasis on the openness of professional accountancy in Edinburgh to the phenomenon of upward social mobility.

Plea for knowledge

Kedslie's study of the early Scottish accountancy profession must be seen in the context of several recent pleas for more and better knowledge of the origins of accounting generally, and the accountancy profession particularly. The particular motivations behind these urgings are the need to understand the role of accounting and accountants within the context of significant organizational and societal change; not to study these phenomena as if they were static and neutral; and, more specifically, to observe accounting (and presumably the accountant) becoming what they were not [see Burchell *et al.*, 1980; Willmott, 1986; and Hopwood, 1987]. Kedslie's text is compatible with these ambitions for the study of accounting history, although it is not necessarily faithful to them all and at all times. The purpose of this review is to identify the compatibilities and incompatibilities between Kedslie's thesis and prior historical prescriptions, remembering the warning of Carr [1987, p. 22] that history is not just about facts; it is also about the historian, and the problem he or she has in separating fact from interpretation, and the unique from the general. It is also perhaps relevant to note the view of Collingwood [1974, p. 37] that the proper task of historians is to penetrate the minds of those persons they seek to study historically. Each of these points will be touched on at appropriate parts of this review. But, first, a summary of Kedslie's thesis with, where relevant, comparisons to that of Walker.

Content of Kedslie (1990)

Kedslie's study is of the origins and events surrounding the formation of three Scottish professional accountancy bodies in the mid 1850s (chronologically, in Edinburgh, Glasgow and Aberdeen). What is fascinating about these developments is not the formations themselves, but why they took place in Scotland at that time. Kedslie's careful research has provided some interesting answers, and she has managed to present them (both in her book and related paper) in a way that is accessible not just to the accounting historian, but also to the practitioner and the student of accounting. Indeed, her study provides a data base for further research as much as definitive conclusions on the issues concerned. In this respect, and as will be explained later in this review, arguably its main weakness is its failure to use such a data base to support or reject hypotheses which could be specified with respect to familiar models of professional behavior.

Kedslie's study begins with an examination of the accounting and accounting-related activities with which identifiable accountants were involved prior to professionalization in Scotland. She reveals evidence of these accountants as connected in a variety of ways, and to different degrees, with such businesses as canals and railways [pp. 15-28]; banking, insurance and stockbroking [pp. 28-39]; and, most particularly, bankruptcy [pp. 39-54 and 114-34]. In general, Kedslie discovered from data gathered from directories, court records, and other relevant sources, there were significant differences in pre-professional activities in the three geographical locations researched, depending on the nature and preponderance of different businesses in different regions. For example Edinburgh was a legal and financial center, whereas Glasgow had an industrial and stockbroking focus. These inevitably led to the founding fathers of chartered accountancy in Scotland having different social backgrounds, and being involved and specializing in different accounting and related activities depending on the city in, which they did business. For example, Edinburgh accountants entering the new profession were more likely to have family connections with the legal or financial communities than were their colleagues in Glasgow [p. 82]. At least within the context of Edinburgh, these findings are consistent with those of Walker [1988, p. 265].

One thing above all others is clear from Kedslie's thesis. Pre-professionalization, accountants as a social grouping were significantly involved in bankruptcy work and this was the principal factor leading to the formation of the three Scottish professional bodies [pp. 50-77 and 114-34]. Indeed, a threat of change in bankruptcy law at the time, which would have led to lawyers rather than accountants undertaking such work, was the indisputable catalyst for action to form the Edinburgh body [p. 59], and then the Glasgow and Aberdeen bodies. In the end, the legal change did not take place, but it was sufficient to create the beginnings of modem professional accountancy. Involvement in bankruptcy and related legal work continued to be a major source of business for the early Scottish chartered accountants, to the point that they appear to have established a near-monopoly of such activity during the decades following the founding of the three professional bodies - that is, until a decline at the end of the nineteenth century [p. 134]. Indeed, Walker [1988, p. 34-40] provides data in the Edinburgh context from which a similar conclusion can he drawn. The main change in the mix of business appears to have been to company auditing - for example, in relation to Scottish banks [Kedslie, 1990, p. 145] and railway companies [Kedslie, 1990, p. 166]. Walker [1988, p. 40] confirms this trend with more general corporate data.

Kedslie examines the social origins of the early Scottish professional accountants [pp. 78-113]. When compared with the work of Walker [1988], the analysis is not as statistically detailed and argumentatively complex as his interwoven themes of recruitment factors [pp. 30-193], and his self-recruitment demographic model [pp. 203-64]. Kedslie's conclusions, however, are no less clear and concise. For example, her evidence indicates that the earliest recruits to the Scottish profession tended at first to come from an upper to middle class background [pp. 79-81]. This varied, however, between Edinburgh, and Glasgow and Aberdeen. Edinburgh's earliest recruits tended to be more upper to upper-middle class than their colleagues elsewhere. Later recruits in all three regions tended to come from a more uniform middle class background [pp. 81-96]. This matches the specific Edinburgh findings of Walker [1988, pp. 83-9]. Kedslie [1990, pp. 96-104] also found the earliest recruits usually had a sound education at fee-paying schools, with some having university education [pp. 101-4]. Walker [1988, pp. 89-95] presents similar data for Edinburgh recruitment. Finally, Kedslie [1990, pp. 110- 12] also demonstrates the earliest chartered accountants in Scotland were active in public life and so-called 'good works' in the community.

In other words, these early accounting professionals were predominantly members of an elite grouping in their communities prior to entry to membership of their professional bodies, and later members tended to come from reasonably similar backgrounds - with some differences over time and between bodies. Coming together at this time in such an organized way is a clear signal of some form of self-protection involving economic employment and social status. Kedslie reveals the several post-professionalization actions of Scottish chartered accountants which evidence such self-protection. Interestingly, despite differences in the composition and background of members of the three bodies, this evidence reveals unanimity of attitude and purpose over the issues concerned.

The first matter centers on the expansion and then decline in the second half of the nineteenth century in the involvement of Scottish chartered accountants in legally-driven work such as bankruptcies, and a compensating expansion of their involvement in other areas in which they had previous connections (such as auditing banks, insurance companies and railways [Kedslie, 1990, pp. 114-34 and 135-7]. Kedslie clearly reveals the adaptability and success of the early chartered accountants in capturing significant areas of accounting-related activity - to the point at which they occupied a near-monopoly position (as in the audit of railways) [p. 71].

The second example of protectionism cited by Kedslie [1990, pp. 179-217] is the increasingly explicit use by the three Scottish professional bodies of methods of restricted entry. This started with entry by invitation to a selected few with an appropriate background and experience. Then to indenture, apprenticeship and informal examinations. And, finally, to a unified national examination system. Several things above all others evidence deliberate barriers to entry - the high financial cost of entry to membership and the length of training prior to entry [for example, pp. 184-8]; and the rapid stiffening of educational and examination standards designed to provide chartered accountants with a knowledge which was directly relevant to their involvement in practice [for example, pp. 188-97].

Legal conflicts with rival accountancy bodies to prevent them receiving a charter of incorporation, and thus protect the exclusive use of the label of chartered accountant, comprises Kedslie's [1990, pp.

218-9] third example of professional closure. These protectionist actions were successful, although the rival bodies survived to be later absorbed into larger bodies in England. This defending of what amounted to a professional monopoly has been well documented and discussed by Walker [1991], with the particular conclusion that its success rested on appeals to the public interest being best served by restricting the title of chartered accountants to the then existing Scottish chartered bodies [p. 279].

The final example provided by Kedslie [1990, pp. 239-61] of early Scottish chartered accountants attempting to establish professional closure concerns the issue of registration of such accountants as the only ones licensed to practice as such. This was intended to be achieved by legislation and, over several years, numerous unsuccessful attempts were made by the Scottish and other UK bodies to do just that. As Kedslie [1990, p. 260] remarks, these attempts appeared to be deliberately explicit displays of national and inter-organizational rivalry. The Scottish activities have been extensively explored by MacDonald [1985].

A theory of professional behavior

The value of Kedslie's work is in its provision of a "quilt" of related topics which, when gathered together, give the reader a sense of how the Scottish bodies came into being in the mid 1850s, and then proceeded to restrict their membership and capture specific work for their members. In this respect, however, the quilt tends to lack a pattern which would help explain why these developments took place when and where they did. In other words, there is little or no specification of a general model or individual hypotheses of professional behavior with which to relate the data and derive explanatory conclusions of the type desired by writers such as Burchell *et al.* [1980], Willmott [1986] and Hopwood [1987]. Kedslie [1990, pp. 262-74] does attempt briefly at the end of her book to provide such a scenario - in the sense that she discusses various views of the attributes of a profession and its members. These include such well-known writers on the subject as Carr-Saunders and Wilson [1933] and Hall [1969].

Kedslie uses each of these studies to describe attributes or characteristics of professionalism such as a theoretical body of knowledge; social prestige through charters of incorporation; training,

examination and licensing; independence from the client and a code
of ethics; the use of rituals, symbols and specialist languages; a legal
monopoly; and the power and authority given to self-regulate. These
are used briefly by Kedslie [1990, pp. 270-4] with reference to her
findings on the Scottish bodies - that is, to evidence that, because
these attributes could be demonstrated to have existed in the formation
of these bodies, then each such body clearly had the characteristics of
a professional body [p. 273].

Such a conclusion is logical and necessary in such a historical
study. However, it limits the latter in its potential to explain the
rationale of the professional accountancy body and its Scottish origins.
Kedslie provides considerable data to make such a case. She fails to
take the opportunity - despite having access to several authorities
which could have assisted her. For example, she refers to
Carr-Saunders and Wilson [1933] in terms of professional
characteristics, but does not present this study as an example of the
functionalist approach to the study of professionalism. This is the
view that the professional exists to provide a functional service within
the public domain, and that his actions are primarily guided by
altruism - of putting service to the public before economic or social
self-interest. Kedslie [1990, p. 262] also makes brief and incidental
reference to Larson [1977], a principal advocate of the alternative
critical school of professionalism - but without mentioning his model
of the professional as a person seeking market control over needed
services and upward social mobility by a process of public
legitimation of his actions.

In other words, the evidence provided by Kedslie of the emergence and development of professionalized accountancy in mid to late
nineteenth century Scotland is presented without a formal theoretical
framework. In particular, the extensive and valuable data which she
has gathered have not been discussed or interpreted from either a
functionalist or critical perspective. For example, there is a
considerable literature on the power-knowledge relationship in the
context of professional activity - that is, where there is a body of
knowledge, there is the exercising of power, and vice versa. Johnson
[1972, pp. 41-7] discusses this concept in terms of a profession
creating a structure of uncertainty [p. 42-3] which can be both
threatening and exploitative [p. 44], and thereby exercising
occupational control [p. 45]. Bledstein [1976] argues in similar terms
- of the professional having power through command of his discipline
[p. 90], special rituals reinforcing the mystery of his power [pp. 93-4],
invoking disasters to increase client dependency [pp. 99-100], and

cultivating irrationality by uncovering anomalies [p. 102]. Larson [1977], also writes of the ideology of (professional) competence creating a societal image that subconsciously fuses power with superior ability and self-development [p. 241], but which uses the work ethic, universal service and *noblesse oblige* as components of a marketable commodity [p. 220]; professionalism as a means of controlling educated labor and co-opting elites [p. 237]; professionals constructing reality on their terms, thus obtaining a minimum of social authority [p. 231]; and professionals having a monopoly of competence as well as practice in terms of authority over a body of knowledge [p. 231].

Putting these ideas in the context of professional accountancy, Kedslie could have hypothesized that the early Scottish professional accountants acted in a concerted way to monopolize a body of knowledge or competence which they could exclusively practice; created an atmosphere of dependency for such services by pointing out the need for altruistically-driven superior abilities to successfully remove observable uncertainties to maintain the public interest; and reinforced such superiority by explicit signs of elitism and status. The evidence provided by Kedslie is certainly consistent with this model. For example, attempting to achieve professional monopoly in the areas of bankruptcies [pp. 50-77 and 114-34] and company audits [pp. 135-71]; involving a need for skilled professionals to deal with complex issues in bankruptcies and audits [p. 57, 62, 75, 141-2, 156, 160-1 and 168]; creating an image of elitism and status in terms of specific entry standards including apprenticeships, entry and membership fees, and education and examination [pp. 188-217]; and using the idea of the public interest to exclude other bodies from the domain of public accounting [pp. 218-39], protect the title of chartered accountant [pp. 239-49], and attempt to register only chartered accountants [pp. 249-61].

Kedslie does make some oblique references to these issues and interpretations, but her thesis is weakened by a lack of explicitness. In particular, she fails to provide her reader with a strong flavor of the ultimate challenge for the early Scottish chartered accountants - that is, what Montagna [1974, pp. 4-5] has described as the conflict between public interest and self-interest, and the need to balance these opposing responsibilities. In addition, because of her lack of a theoretical framework, she has neglected to relate her findings explicitly to the research of other writers in the same area - for example, the factors relating to recruitment and self-recruitment in the Scottish bodies [Walker, 1988]; the use of the examination process to create occupational control [Hoskin and Macve, 1986]; the standardizing of knowledge and the institutionalizing of training to gain social rewards [Richardson, 1988]; and social closure through occupational registration [Macdonald, 1985]. She has presented facts about actions without necessarily attempting to clearly "get behind" the thinking behind the actions as recommended by Collingwood [1974, p. 37].

Conclusions

As stated at the beginning of this review, there is a need to know how professional accountancy came to be what it was not. However, much of this process of investigation and explanation is subject to the constraint of the historian. In this case, Kedslie has provided much useful material to describe the emergence of professionalism in accountancy in Scotland. What is still required is an interpretive approach to such data to provide explanation and understanding. As she reveals in her preface [Kedslie, 1990, p. xiii] and conclusion [p. 274], recent events in the history of The Institute of Chartered Accountants of Scotland suggest that the process of professionalization is a continuing affair which will require further investigation and explanation. Dr. Kedslie is to be encouraged to continue that process as part of the larger task of understanding the role of professional accounting and public accountants in society.

Note

1. It should be noted that Kedslie's book appears in summarized form in a recently published paper which was awarded the 1990 Manuscript Award of the Academy of Accounting Historians [Kedslie, 1990a].

Bibliography

Bledstein, B. J. *The Culture of Professionalism*, W. W. Norton and Co. (1976).
Brown, R., *A History of Accounting and Accountants*, T. C. and E. C. Jack (1905).

Burchell, S., Clubb, C., Hopwood, A., Hughes, J. and Nahapiet, L. "The Roles of Accounting in Organisations and Society," *Accounting, Organizations and Society*, Vol. 5, No. 1 (1980): 5-27.

Carr, E. H., *What is History?*, Penguin Books (1987).

Carr-Saunders, A. and Wilson, P. A., *The Professions*, Oxford University Press (1933).

Collingwood, R. G., "Human Nature and Human History," in Gardiner, P., *The Philosophy of History*, Oxford University Press (1974): 17-40.

de Roover, R., "The Development of Accounting Prior to Luca Pacioli According to the Account Books of Medieval Merchants," in Kirshner, J. *Business, Banking and Economic Thought in Late Medieval and Early Modern Europe*, The University of Chicago Press (1974): 119-80.

Hall, R. H., *Occupations and the Social Culture*, Prentice-Hall (1969).

Hopwood, A. G., "The Archaeology of Accounting Systems," *Accounting, Organisations and Society*, Vol. 12, No. 3 (1987): 207-34.

Hoskin, K. W. and Macve, R. H., "Accounting and the Examination: A Genealogy of Disciplinary Power," *Accounting, Organisations and Society*, Vol. 11, No. 2 (1986) :105-36.

Institute of Chartered Accountants of Scotland, *A History of the Chartered Accountants of Scotland from the Earliest Times to 1954*, Garland Publishing (1954/1984).

Johnson, T. J., *Professions and Power*, Macmillan (1972).

Kedslie, M. J. M., *Firm Foundations: The Development of Professional Accounting in Scotland 1850-1900*, Hull University Press (1990).

Kedslie, M. J. M., "Mutual Self-Interest - A Unifying Force; the Dominance of Societal Closure Over Social Background in the Early Professional Accounting Bodies," *The Accounting Historians Journal* (December 1990a): 1- 19.

Larson, M. S., *The Rise of Professionalism: A Sociological Analysis*, University of California Press (1977).

Lee, T. A., *Transactions of the Chartered Accountants Students' Societies of Edinburgh and Glasgow: A Selection of Writings 1886-1958*, Garland Publishing (1984).

Macdonald, K. M., "Social Closure and Occupational Registration," *Sociology* (November 1985): 541-56.

Mepham, M. J., *Accounting in Eighteenth Century Scotland*, Garland Publishing (1988).

Montagna, P. D., "Public Accounting: The Dynamics of Occupational Change," in Sterling, R. R., *Institutional Issues in Public Accounting*, Scholars Book Co. (1974): 3-24.

Richardson, A. J., "Accounting Knowledge and Professional Privilege," *Accounting, Organisations and Society*, Vol. 13, No. 4 (1988): 381-96.

Stewart, J. C., *Pioneers of a Profession: Chartered Accountants to 1879*, Garland Publishing (1977/1986).

Walker, S. P., *The Society of Accountants in Edinburgh, 1854-1914: A Study of Recruitment to a New Profession*, Garland Publishing (1988).

Walker, S. P., "The Defence of Professional Monopoly: Scottish Chartered Accountants and 'Satellites in the Accountancy Firmament' 1854-1914," *Accounting, Organisations and Society*, Vol. 16, No. 3 (1991): 257-83.

Willmott, H., "Organising the Profession: A Theoretical and Historical Examination of the Development of the Major Accountancy Bodies in the UK," *Accounting, Organisations and Society*, Vol. 11, No. 4 (1986): 555-80.

Winsbury, R., *Thomson McLintock & Co. - The First Hundred Years*, Thomson McLintock & Co. (1977).

CHAPTER 6

The Genesis of Professional Organization in Scotland: A Contextual Analysis

Stephen P Walker

The causes of the formation of the first modern organizations of professional accountants which took place in Scotland in 1853 are the focus of the present analysis. It is contended that the existing explanations offered for the emergence of the Society of Accountants in Edinburgh (SAE) and the Institute of Accountants and Actuaries in Glasgow (IAAG) 17 years before the first organization of accountants in England, are either misdirected, speculative or generalized.

In part, such deficiences derive from the insular, teleological and evolutionary approaches of traditional accounting history recently questioned by Miller & Napier (1993). As an alternative, Miller & Napier advocate a genealogical approach to historical investigation which identifies the interplay of the "multiple and dispersed surfaces of emergence" of accounting phenomena (p. 633), assumes permeable disciplinary frontiers and examines "the outcomes of the past, rather than a quest for the origins of the present" (p. 631). Such a *modus operandi* has a potentially revelational impact on current understandings of the emergence of the accountancy profession (Loft, 1986) and the structure of accounting practice (Walker, 1993).

The conventional explanations for professional formation in Scotland suffer from such a decontextualized approach to the processes and motivations underlying professionalization. In particular, the nature of the contemporary social structure and political discourse have not featured significantly in the literature. Yet, as Willmott has rightly stated, "the organization of the profession cannot be adequately understood independently of an appreciation of the political, economic and legal circumstances that have supported and constrained its development" (1986, p. 556).

It has been shown recently that the success of the post-formation closure practices adopted by the Scottish chartered societies during the nineteenth century can be understood only in the context of theunderlying socioeconomic and political factors which sustained professional monopoly. In particular, it depended on the articulation of self-interested objectives through the medium of prevailing ideologies in support of occupational claims (Walker, 1991, pp. 276-279). The tendency to adopt a piecemeal approach to the historical investigation of the institutionalization of the accountancy profession in Scotland has resulted in the neglect of vital source material and a consequent inability to provide compelling explanations of why accountants north of the border organized earlier than their English counterparts.

The significance of professionalization in Scotland

The predecessor organizations of The Institute of Chartered Accountants of Scotland have attracted disproportionate attention in the professionalization literature (see Lee, 1991). Interest was engendered initially by the reputation of the Edinburgh and Glasgow societies as the first organizations of professional accountants. However, the nature of professional organization in Scotland is of a much broader import which transcends its antiquarian novelty. It is contestable that, in the following ways, events in 1853 had a formative impact on the organization of the accountancy profession outside Scotland as the successful professionalization project of accountants north of the border was emulated elsewhere.

The locally structured societies of Edinburgh and Glasgow were to be mirrored in the predecessor organizations of the ICAEW (in Liverpool and London (1870), Manchester (1871) and Sheffield (1877)). The exclusion from the Scottish societies of those not engaged in public practice and the equating of public practice with *professional* accountancy was imported by the associations later formed in England (Howitt, 1966, pp. 18-25), and effectively created a pool of accountants with employee status who would later form separate competitive societies and thereby create the fragmented configuration of the British profession (Robson & Cooper, 1990, pp. 380-382; Edwards, 1989, p. 277). The acquisition of charters of incorporation and the invention in Scotland of the "chartered accountant" with the requisite status enhancing credentials of "CA" became the quest of the professional organizations which were established in England and Ireland during the 1870s and 1880s (Howitt, 1966, p. 5; Robinson, 1964) and became the cause of much internecine strife (Walker, 1991). Furthermore, as will be shown later, once the explanation for professional formation in Scotland is disclosed, new insights into organizational developments in England are revealed.

A critical-conflict approach to the study of professional organization

The orthodox structural-functionalist framework for the analysis of professional organizations in which institutionalization was perceived as the first attribute in the acquisition of a catalogue of discriminating traits (Greenwood, 1957; Caplow, 1954; Wilensky, 1964) has been largely displaced. Recent commentators have recognized that explanations for professional formation founded on macro-theories of group behaviour (Durkheim, 1957) or generalized abstractions based on the collective experience of professional groups (Carr-Saunders & Wilson, 1933; Millerson, 1964) fail to accommodate the multiplicity of professional experiences given the peculiar occupational, historical and spatial contexts in which organization took place (see Robson & Cooper, 1990, pp. 367-379). As Saks commented, the traditional taxonomic perspective "was obscuring the social and historical conditions under which occupational groups became professions - including the power struggles involved in the process of professionalisation" (1983, p. 2).

The limitations of functionalist analysis encouraged the development of a critical-conflict oriented approach to the study of professional behaviour and organization founded particularly on Weberian concepts of social closure (see, for example, Parkin, 1979; Murphy, 1988). Critical research indicates that professional formation is a sociopolitical process which may be motivated by the desire for economic rewards and occupational ascendancy. Foremost among the revisionist writers of the 1970s was Larson (1977) who considered that professional organization comprised an integral part of attempts by an occupation to define and control the market for services and to achieve the collective social mobility of practitioners (pp. 66-78): "the professional project is an organizational project: it organizes the production of producers and the transaction of services for a market; it tends to privilege organizational units in the system of stratification; it works through, and culminates in, distinctive organizations - the professional school and the professional association" (p. 74).

Critical writers have increasingly recognized that professionalism is most usefully investigated at the level of particular occupations (Freidson, 1983; Parry & Parry, 1977). Collins has asserted that one reason why the sociology of professions is currently being revitalized is the emphasis on "historical variation" (1990a, p. 14) and that the investigation of the emergence of specific occupational groups offers the prospect of the development of broad multi-dimensional theories of professions which are grounded in historical comparisons: "all professions do not go through the same pathways, nor do they arrive at the same outcomes. We have instead a kind of family resemblance among different professions and current work is concerned with charting those multiple paths" (p. 15). The emphasis on historical comparisons necessarily involves an examination of "external dynamics" (Robson & Cooper, 1990, p. 374) - locating professionalization in the context of contemporary socioeconomic and political developments and utilizing an array of pertinent primary and secondary sources (Davies, 1983, p. 182; Jarausch & Cocks, 1990, p. 4).

Some commentators have also recognized the potential offered by conflict theory as a paradigm for the analysis of the behaviour of professional organizations (Collins, 1975, pp. 340-346; 1990b). Though usually applied to the analysis of macro-collectivities such as social classes (as in the work of Marx, Weber and Dahrendorf, for example) and states (see Collins, 1975, pp. 56-61; Rex, 1981, pp. 75-101) conflict models of social interaction may also be utilized to examine meso-collectivities such as occupations and allied institutions.

Hostility between collectivities may be precipitated when established market or property relationships are challenged by a group seeking material advantage or when traditional authority structures are threatened (ibid., p. 27; Neale, 1972, pp. 7-9). In conflictual encounters between collectivities the hostile groups engage in a process of political bargaining in an attempt to achieve desired outcomes. Ultimately, resolution may be achieved by violent means though the initial stages of conflict are usually characterized by discourse involving claims and counterclaims founded on pertinent legitimating ideologies (Rex, 1981, p. 14). Arguments are directed at internal constituents, opponents, potential supporters, opinion formers and actors within those institutions which may act as a forum for deliberation in the dispute.

Van Doorn asserted that "it is an accepted fact that conflict creates associations and increases the internal cohesion of social systems" (1966, p. 124). As applied to the story of professional formation contained in this paper, conflict theory provides a number of important insights. Conflictual models of stratification reveal that the outcome of encounters between collectivities is largely dependent on the ability of the combatants to mobilize their capabilities, marshall their resources and engage in concerted political action (Collins, 1975, pp. 60-61; Rex, 1981, pp. 90-92). A number of imperatives may be noted. Formal organization is essential for effective mobilization, the encouragement of internal allegiances and for the development of group consciousness. A collectivity remains passive until it becomes organized; thereafter its energy potential is transformed from latent and static to active and kinetic (Etzioni, 1968, pp. 103-104). For the collectivity engaged in macroscopic political contest institutionalization provides a framework for the emergence of group cohesion and control.

The degree of motivation towards participation in conflict and the development of group consciousness is also enhanced by the existence of articulate spokespersons, leadership, normative bonds between group members and the identification of a common opponent. Organized collectivities also augment their resources in conflict situations by mobilizing the support of other groups outside their formal memberships. Appeals to unifying and prevailing ideologies encourage internal cohesion and consciousness and also reveal the dispute as being more than privatized (Neale, 1972, pp. 9-10).

Studying professions as organized collectivities with the capacity to engage in conflict also suggests the redundancy of the attribute-trait approach with its narrow, insular focus and excessive emphasis on certain rigidly defined perceptions of professionalism. Turner and Hodge, for example, advocated the development of a broader analytical framework in which occupations rather than professions alone could be compared and contended that "in setting out to examine the crystallization and operation of occupational organization ... it is necessary to consider the form of organization, the ideologies advanced, and the activities carried out, and to attempt to relate these to the wider social structure" (Turner & Hodge, 1970, pp. 35-36).

A conflict-centred approach to the study of occupational groups was advanced by Krause (1971) whose analysis combined elements of

Weber-derived pluralism and Marxian concepts of class consciousness. Societies are characterized by the struggle between different interest groups for power and rewards. The effective advancement or protection of collective interests in the political arena is dependent on a developed occupational consciousness – "a code word for the degree to which an occupational group is fighting as a group in its own interest" (p. 88). Occupational consciousness is strengthened by organization (as a profession or trades union, for example) and adherence to unifying, articulated ideologies. Ideologies which comprise "texts, theories, doctrines, phrases, or concepts which are proposed by an interest group (proponent) with a target group in mind" (p. 89). Group ideologies are changed to accommodate new objectives or to react to competitive ideologies and may be developed in order to encourage "cross-occupational complexes" or alliances with other groups in order to assist the achievement of a mutual interest (pp. 88-93).

The approach taken in this paper is to investigate the formation of occupational organizations within a critical-conflict based analytical framework. The emphasis placed by critical writers on the extent to which professions seek market control and are engaged in the pursuit of their economic self-interest explains why Scottish accountants were motivated to organize in 1853. Conflict theory as applied to collectivities provides insights into the circumstances which compelled institutionalization; how the resources and strategies employed by a threatened occupational group were utilized; and, how the organizations of accountants which were formed in Scotland in 1853 to defend job monopolies were moulded by encounters with hostile outsiders. Further, the paper seeks to accommodate the demands of the "post-revisionist" sociologists of the professions for historical investigations of a rigorous, contextual character. The latter is largely absent from prevailing analyses of the emergence of organizations of accountants in Scotland.

Explanations for professional organization in Scotland

Existing explanations for the formation of the institutes of accountants in Edinburgh and Glasgow in 1853 are founded on one or more of three primary phenomena. Firstly, early professionalization in

Scotland is perceived as a symptom of the differences between the English and Scottish systems of jurisprudence and legal institutions, particularly in respect of the law of bankruptcy. Secondly, organization was grounded in the development and maturation of an urban-industrial society and the increased demand for accounting labour which was engendered by the expansion of capitalist enterprise. Thirdly, professional formation in Scotland was induced by the need for accountancy practitioners to achieve social closure and collective social mobility.

Brown's (1905) account of the formation of the SAE and IAAG falls into the first of the aforementioned categories. Brown contended that the background to the organization of the profession in Scotland was the difference between Scottish and English law which encouraged the early recognition of accountancy as a separate occupation north of the border (p. 232). Although the specific causes of professional organization were not addressed directly, Brown's detailed (though insular) description of events includes a recognition that, in Glasgow at least, proposed changes to the Scots law of bankruptcy was one reason for societal formation in that city in 1853 (pp. 203-211).

Brown's account of professional organization in Scotland substantially coloured subsequent analyses such as those of: Littleton (1933, p. 286) who provided a more detailed narrative of the importance of the Scottish bankruptcy statutes in creating work for accountants; Carr-Saunders & Wilson (1933, pp. 209-210); ICAS (1954, pp. 20-24); Jones (1981, pp. 79-83) and Parker (1986, pp. 14-20).

Stacey (1954) also recognized the potential significance of bankruptcy law as a causal factor in the development of the profession of accountancy in Scotland and, like Brown, noted that changes in the law in 1853 were heavily discussed by the newly formed societies in Edinburgh and Glasgow (p. 22). However, Stacey also drew attention to the economic circumstances in which the organization of the profession in Britain took place. The vast expansion of trade, transportation, manufacturing and financial institutions during the first half of the nineteenth century increased the demand for the services of accountants as bankruptcy practitioners, auditors and as financial and cost accountants:[1] "no wonder that some three associations were formed in Scotland, quickly in succession at the commencement of the second half of the nineteenth century" (p. 20).

Stewart's (1975, 1977) explanations for the early professionalization of accountants in Scotland also integrated the economic determinist and differential legal system approaches. The vast expansion of industrial and financial activity required the services of skilled accountants by the mid-nineteenth century. The new industrial capitalism produced economic failures as well as successes and in Scotland bankruptcies were administered primarily by accountants, unlike the situation in England. Stewart's commentary draws attention to the need to consider the long-term economic and legal background to professional organization (1975, p. 113). However, like Stacey, he failed to identify any specific developments in the contemporary context which induced institutionalization in 1853 and concluded that "the movement was entirely spontaneous. There was no legislative pressure nor even any official encouragement" (1977, p. 8).

An alternative analysis of professional formation in Scotland was offered by Macdonald in 1984. Macdonald applied the concepts of collective social mobility and social closure to Stewart's collective biography of Scottish CAs to 1879 in order to explain the circumstances which induced their organization. Macdonald hypothesized that the process of professionalization differed in Edinburgh and Glasgow. In Edinburgh, the respectable social origins of accountants and their close proximity to the landed proprietor-lawyer nexus in local society conferred a high occupational status on a large proportion of accountancy practitioners. This, and the contents of the Edinburgh Institute's charter application of 1854 suggest that "an important impetus came from the need to establish both equality with and distinctiveness from the legal profession" (Macdonald, 1984, p. 185) by the institution of a separate professional organization of accountants.

In Glasgow, the fact that younger practitioners took the initiative to form an association reveals that "somewhat different forces were at work" (ibid.). The lower respectability of younger Glaswegian accountants and the recent organization of professional competitors in Edinburgh probably induced "this competent but less well endowed generation" (ibid., p. 186) to lobby the senior accountants of Glasgow to form an association so that the juniors might "acquire some of the ascribed and inherited characteristics of their seniors. By this means they could achieve a 'closure' and create a distinction between themselves and those of even lower attainment and background" (ibid).

It will be shown later that Macdonald's deductions concerning professional formation in Glasgow have some credibility but that his observations for the Edinburgh case are more questionable. The fact that the professional status of Edinburgh accountants largely derived from their association with the lawyers is likely to have constituted a disposition averse to organizational and occupational differentiation lest the status ascribed by association with the legal fraternity be fractured. Further, contemporary evidence suggests that Edinburgh accountants did not require organization in order to achieve "equality" of status with the lawyers. During the mid-nineteenth century the legal profession comprised a gradation of occupational and social statuses ranging from the advocate to the writer. Accountants were regarded as equal in status to qualified solicitors (who were located in the middle ranges of the stratification of lawyers) well before 1853 (see Walker, 1988, p. 15).

Edinburgh accountants did not require organization in order to achieve collective professional status as that also had been acquired previously without the need for institutionalization. Evidence of the early professional standing of accountants is provided by the eminent Scots commercial lawyer Bell who attested in 1826 that "in this country we have a set of professional accountants, possessing a degree of intelligence, and a respectability of character, scarcely equalled in any unincorporated body of professional men" (p. 491). Similarly, in 1834, the Society of Writers to the Signet referred to Edinburgh accountants as "a most respectable body of professional gentlemen" (see Walker, 1988, pp. 14-15). The "first stirrings of professionalism" (Bryer, 1993, pp. 671-672) did not, therefore, commence with the institution of professional organizations during the 1850s. Finally, as with the technological determinists, Macdonald's hypotheses cannot explain why the need for collective action arose specifically in 1853 and his conclusions are inevitably speculative given their reliance on secondary sources.

Macdonald's inferences were disputed by Briston & Kedslie (1986). On the basis of an examination of the minute books of the SAE and IAAG, Briston and Kedslie contended that the catalyst for the formation of both the Edinburgh and Glasgow societies in 1853 was impending alterations to the Scots law of bankruptcy which posed a threat to the principal source of income of accountants (p. 125) – "it was a purely economic stimulus which had nothing to do with respectability or collective social mobility" (p. 128). This thesis, which advanced the differential legal infrastructure explanation for early professionalization in Scotland, was expanded upon by Kedslie (1990a,b). To date Kedslie's work comprises the most convincing account of professional organization in Scotland and has been recognized by other writers (Lee, 1991, p. 197; Napier and Noke, 1992, p. 35).

Kedslie showed that those accountants who were instrumental in forming the SAE and IAAG in 1853 had a substantial pecuniary interest in bankruptcy work (1990a, pp. 39-48; 1990b, pp. 6-7). Hence, when it was proposed in the Bankruptcy (Scotland) Bill, 1853 (the Lord Advocate's Bill), that the office of Interim Factor (the official appointed to preserve the bankrupt's estate until a trustee was elected by the creditors) be abolished and the duties transferred to local sheriff clerks, accountants were induced to constitute societies to protect this source of income. Professional organization commenced in Edinburgh on 17 January 1853 "between the introduction of the Bill to Amend the Laws relating to Bankruptcy in Scotland and the subsequent Act which came into force on 4 August 1853" (1990a, p. 53). It was also contended that the new Bankruptcy Act was the principal motivation behind professional organization in Glasgow in September 1853 (1990a, p. 66). Kedslie concluded that "without any doubt, the catalyst for the formation of these two societies was the proposed changes in Scottish bankruptcy legislation" (1990a, p. 77).

Although Kedslie's recognition of the importance of bankruptcy legislation is correct, the emphasis on the Bankruptcy (Scotland) Bill, 1853, is misplaced. There are a number of difficulties with the thesis that the Bankruptcy (Scotland) Bill induced the organization of Scottish accountants. The first problem concerns the office of Interim Factor which was to be abolished by the Bill. Although their appointment as Interim Factors was important to Scottish accountants because it often resulted in their election to lucrative trusteeships (Bell, 1826, p. 332), it was not in itself an important source of remuneration. Interim factorships were so insignificant that one group of Scottish accountants concluded in 1853 that: "we cannot, after the most patient and searching consideration, see any particular use or advantage of an Interim Factor, or any reason why the office should not be altogether abolished" (A Scotch Accountant, p. 12). In 1856 the Bankruptcy (Scotland) Act, which had been devised following consultations with representatives of the SAE and IAAG (Brown, 1905, p. 213), eradicated the office of Interim Factor.

Secondly, the Bankruptcy (Scotland) Bill, 1953, was an unlikely instigator of professional organization. Brown described the Bill as of "a limited and tentative nature" (ibid.). The sponsor of the Bill, the Lord Advocate, considered it "not of any great extent" and comprised an attempt to smooth some of the rough edges in bankruptcy administration (*The Law Magazine*, 1853, pp. 331-332). Thirdly, the chronology of the Bill's progress is inconsistent with the timing of the formation of the SAE. The Edinburgh society was constituted in January 1853 yet the Bankruptcy (Scotland) Bill was not ordered until April and received its First Reading in May (Alphabetical List of Public Bills, 1852-3, p. 2). The Institute of Accountants and Actuaries in Glasgow was instituted in September 1853 - after the Bankruptcy (Scotland) Act had entered the Statute Book.

Fourthly, Kedslie's thesis is founded primarily on quantitative evidence that discloses the substantial pecuniary interest of Scottish accountants in bankruptcy which was threatened by the Bankruptcy (Scotland) Bill, 1853. Investigation of the work mix of contemporary accountancy practices suggests that sequestration was an important but not always the most significant source of fee income (Walker, 1993, pp. 134-135). The winding-up of insolvent estates under voluntary trusts (as opposed to judicial bankruptcy) was also a lucrative area of work for accountants in Scotland during the nineteenth century (ibid., pp. 135-138). As early as the 1820s it was suggested that creditors should choose a professional accountant as a trustee under a voluntary trust because "the regularity of conduct, the clearness of accounts, the perfect system of administration, according to which these gentlemen manage their trusts, afford an admirable instrument in the arrangement of insolvent estates" (Bell, 1826, p. 491).

Another important branch of the Scottish accountant's practice was judicial factory work (Walker, 1993, pp. 138-140). That significance was never more apparent than in 1834 when one of the previously unidentified antecedent organizations of Edinburgh accountants was founded to lobby Parliament concerning an Accountant-General Bill. The Bill threatened to place the audit of judicial factories - a practice which accountants had "been exclusively accustomed under the employment of the Court, to discharge" (Report by the Committee named at a Meeting of Accountants, p. 4) - in the hands of an Accountant-General. An *ad hoc* 10-man Committee of Accountants Practising Before the Court of Session (chaired by James Brown, the first president of the SAE), successfully fought against the offending legislation.

It will be shown in this paper that occupational organization in Edinburgh and Glasgow in 1853 was induced primarily by proposals which would have posed a massive, rather than a marginal threat to the *whole insolvency practice* of Scottish accountants. The nature of the threat required that accountants strengthen their competitive position in the political arena by instituting protective organizations and by devising a compelling counter-ideology to that propounded by their opponents. Such imperatives acted not only to enhance the occupational consciousness of accountants in Edinburgh and Glasgow but also assisted in the establishment of cross-sectional alliances capable of repelling the demands of a powerful antagonistic interest group. The source of the antagonism was The London Committee of Merchants - an organization whose ideological discourse was founded on the ascendent economic philosophy of mid-Victorian Britain: free trade, and the related concept of the assimilation of commercial laws. The product of The London Committee's labours and the menace to Scottish accountants was the Bankruptcy and Insolvency (Scotland) Bill, 1853 - legislation which has been overlooked by previous writers as a cause of the formation of the SAE and IAAG.

In order to comprehend the intimidatory nature of the Bankruptcy and Insolvency (Scotland) Bill, 1853, to Scottish accountants, it is necessary to understand the power and motives of its devisors and sponsors and the political context in which the Bill emerged.

The emergence of a threat to the interests of Scottish accountants: the London Committee of Merchants, 1851-1852

The defects in the system of administering insolvent estates in Scotland were discussed frequently during the early 1850s. In April 1851, for example, a group of wholesale merchants and traders in Edinburgh, alarmed by an increase in fraudulent and reckless trading which tarnished the reputation of the whole commercial community, formed a Mercantile Protection Association (later the Edinburgh and Leith Trade Protection Association and the Scottish Trade Protection Society) to investigate and prosecute offenders (*The Edinburgh Courant*, 3 April 1851, p. 2; also 15 May 1851, p. 3). By February 1853 the Association boasted 253 members.

During the autumn of 1851, a more vociferous and powerful interest group was formed. Following their sustaining of what were perceived as heavy losses as creditors of a bankrupt in Glasgow, a group of (mainly cloth) warehousemen trading with Scotland located in the City and Cheapside districts of London formed the London Committee of Merchants and Others Associated for the Improvement of the Commercial and Bankruptcy Laws of Scotland, and the Assimilation of Those Laws in England and Scotland.[2]

By September 1852 the London Committee comprised 22 merchants, 4 Liberal MPs, 6 lawyers and was chaired by Robert Slater of the largest mercantile house in Britain (Hansard, 1856, Vol. 140, p. 1395). Having suffered as creditors of a Scottish bankrupt the members of the London Committee attempted to identify the reasons for their meagre dividends. They were astonished to discover that 5% of the bankrupt's estate was paid in commission to the trustee - a percentage which was deemed "enormous and out of all proportion to the amount of service rendered for it" (*Trade Protection Circular,* January 1853, p. 201).

During the first year of its existence the London Committee undertook extensive inquiries into the state of the bankruptcy law of Scotland. A series of "Queries" on the subject was circulated to a wide audience of businessmen and lawyers and articles on the defects of the Scottish system of insolvency administration were printed in the Committee's mouthpiece - *The Mercantile Test.*

The fruits of the London Committee's labours were produced in a 'Report and Suggestions Addressed to the Mercantile Community of the United Kingdom' in October 1852 which listed a miscellany of evils under the current Scottish law of insolvency. Delays in the appointment of Interim Factors and in the realization and distribution of the bankrupt's estate were highlighted. The principal grievance, however, concerned the Scottish system of vesting the management of the bankrupt's estate in the hands of a trustee. The judicial powers of the trustee were considered as excessive, the system of election by the creditors encouraged litigious and time-consuming competitions for trusteeships and the payment of "exorbitant" levels of commission disadvantaged creditors. Although it was conceded that "there are many professional trustees who are excellent men of business" (*Report*, 1852, p. 19), "many hundreds of trustees in sequestrations are mere tradesmen and mechanics, who have no knowledge whatever either of commercial jurisprudence, or the rules of evidence, or even of the most simple branches of judicial procedure" (ibid).

The reforms suggested by the London Committee to remedy the evils of the Scottish system of insolvency administration were sweeping. It was proposed to impose the English process of bankruptcy on Scotland. So far as the accountants of Edinburgh and Glasgow were concerned - remunerative sequestration trusteeships (see Kedslie, 1990a, pp. 39-49) would be supplanted by the administration of bankrupt estates by a small number of judicial officers and the hitherto unregulated and lucrative system of voluntary trusteeships would be placed under the supervision and scrutiny of the courts.

The unorganized accountants of Scotland had every reason to fear the realization of the London Committee's proposals. The fact of their emanation from significant merchants located in the nation's business capital was threat enough.[3] In addition, the London Committee had zealously set about developing cross-occupational alliances by mobilizing the support of mercantile, manufacturing and legal groups. The Edinburgh based *Trade Protection Circular* warned that the London Committee "have an object to carry, and that for the carrying of that object their chief dependence is on the parliamentary power possessed by the commercial interests of England" (8 January 1853, p. 210). The London Committee's Report was distributed to the chambers of commerce, merchant companies, town councils and law societies of all the major towns and cities in Britain (*Report*, 1852, pp. 5-6). Public meetings, lecture tours and personal lobbying of organized commercial interests were planned to highlight the national importance of the issue. The London Committee's Report concluded that: "it appears almost impossible to over estimate the importance of this movement to the commercial interests of this great empire ... The movement is national, and should be nationally supported: the London Committee, connected as they are with the greatest commercial city in the world, have, they hope, not improperly ventured to lead it" (ibid., p. 40). More importantly, the London Committee commissioned its Secretary to draft an insolvency bill for Scotland in the expectation that its proposals would become enshrined in the Statute Book.

The emergence of a group ideology antagonistic to Scottish accountants: free trade and assimilation

In order to excite contemporary opinion and cultivate cross-sectional alliances, the London Committee's reforms were advanced on the basis of an ideological discourse constructed around the ascendent philosophies of free trade and the assimilation of commercial law. In order to comprehend the threat to Scottish accountants posed by this strategy, it is necessary to show how the allied concepts of free trade and assimilation had come to dominate economic thought and the attention of law reformers by the early 1850s.

Free trade

The idea of maximizing national wealth through the removal of obstacles to trade and the creation of the most favourable conditions for the free play of market forces is rooted in the classical economics of Adam Smith and Ricardo. The extent to which free trade became the prevailing economic doctrine in Britain during the mid-nineteenth century has been well documented (see Mathias, 1969, pp. 293-303; Grampp, 1987, pp. 107-112). According to Neale "if there was any axiom of political economy entering the psyche of Victorian men and women it was this: free trade - Cobden and Bright were the culture heroes of mid-nineteenth-century England not Marx" (1972, p. 130). The evidence for the conversion of policy makers from protectionism to free trade is usually presented as a series of landmarks from Huskisson's tariff reforms of the 1820s, to the repeal of the Corn Laws in 1846 and the Navigation Acts in 1849 and culminating in Cobden's Commercial Treaty with France in 1860. Grampp has identified the decision by Parliament to adopt Free Trade in 1820, following a petition from an earlier Committee of London Merchants, as the climacteric in the re-orientation of British commercial policy (1987, pp. 86-106).

Richard Cobden and other adherents to the Manchester School philosophy considered that free trade comprised more than a crusade for the removal of restraints on the exchange of goods. Free trade would also bind nations, reduce international discord and secure universal peace (Edsall, 1986, p. 228). One impediment to these ambitious ideals was the disparate and often conflicting nature of the mercantile laws within which free international trading was to be conducted. The solution to the lack of consistency in the commercial laws of nations was considered to be their assimilation.

The assimilation of commercial laws

Demands for the assimilation, or homogenization of the mercantile laws of individual states during the late 1840s and early 1850s had their intellectual foundations in the work of Jeremy Bentham. Bentham recognized the incoherent and inconsistent nature of English statute and common law and in its place prescribed a more comprehensible "Pannomion", or, a unified set of constitutional, civil and penal legal codes (Dinwiddy, 1989, pp. 54-65). Although some customization would be required to take account of the peculiar circumstances of individual nations, universal legal codes were considered by Bentham to be an attainable objective because human nature and needs were largely congruous across territories (ibid., pp. 70-71). Britain's domination of world trade, improved communications and the increasing internationalization of business by the mid-nineteenth century engendered renewed interest in the development of national and international codes of commerce. The most notable manifestation of the mood was the work of an associate of Cobden, Leone Levi (1821-1888) (*Dictionary of National Biography*, XI 1917, pp. 1035-1037).

The publication of Levi's four volume treatise *Commercial Law: its Principles and Administration* (1850-2) has been described as "an international event" and its author was "showered" with gold medals and prizes (Palgrave, 1986, Vol. 2, p. 598). Levi compiled a synopsis of the merits and conflicts of the mercantile laws of 59 nations in an attempt to identify universal principles upon which a general conformity of commercial jurisprudence might be based (Levi, 1850-2, Vol. 1, pp. vii-ix). In a Cobden-like vein, Levi envisaged that the development of an international code on subjects such as the laws of contract, bills of exchange and bankruptcy would improve the circulation of capital and encourage the development of international business. The results would "cement peace between all countries, extend commerce and promote morals and justice" (Levi, 1851, p. iii).

Levi's treatise and a supporting series of lectures in 1851 resulted in the formation of committees in London. Birmingham, Edinburgh and Glasgow (consisting primarily of merchants) to consider the best means of carrying out his proposals.[4] Levi's mission also excited considerable interest because of the concordance of his objectives with those of the Great Exhibition of May-October 1851. The Exhibition was "calculated to promote and increase the free interchange of raw materials and manufactured commodities between all the nations of the earth" (Babbage, 1851, p. 42) - it was a celebration of "peace and international understanding through Free Trade" (Fay, 1951, p. 9). The effects of the Great Exhibition were envisaged as being an expansion of trade and the liberalization of commercial transactions (*The Illustrated London News*, October 1951, p. 458). Levi's proposal that a conference of commercial men from around the world should meet during the Exhibition to discuss "one Universal Code of Laws, regulating commercial transactions under whatever clime or position" (1851, p. 19) received some support from Prince Albert and other influential personages (Levi, 1850-2, Vol. 1, p. ix).

Although the unification of the mercantile laws of all nations was considered to be an unrealistic objective made in the excitement of the Great Exhibition (*The Law Magazine*, Vol. XIV, 1851, pp. 60-61), the potential advantages of at least assimilating the separate mercantile laws of England, Scotland and Ireland in order to extend commercial relations within the Kingdom was recognized to be an attainable objective (*Trade Protection Circular*, September 1852, p. 118). One area of difference in the commercial laws of England and Scotland which was singled out for close scrutiny by assimilationists was the law of bankruptcy.

The London Committee embraced free trade and assimilation as the ideological justification for its proposals for reform. The bankruptcy law of Scotland was considered to be an impurity in commercial relations (*Report,* 1852, p. 40) and an impediment to the internal trade of Britain because the commercial community in England could not rely on Scottish legislation which was perceived to render credit insecure. The Committee considered that:

> at this momentous era, when the established principles of free trade, and the recent discoveries of gold, hold out the prospect of a grander development of British commerce than it has yet attained, every impediment, from whatever quarter proceeding which may tend to hinder its progress should be removed out of the way. Such on the most mature consideration, they are constrained to regard the present bankruptcy laws of Scotland (*Second Address*, 1853, p. 16).

A great effort was required from the mercantile interest "to free the internal commerce of this country from a most unquestionable evil" (ibid., p. 30) and replace existing Scottish bankruptcy law with a unified law having "one weight and one measure throughout the United Kingdom" (ibid., p. 17).

The national political arena, November 1852-January 1853

The pressure on Scottish accountants to protect their interest in insolvency work became more urgent during the late autumn of 1852 owing to a confluence of developments which enhanced the position of the London Committee on the wider political scene. Firstly, the public profile of assimilation was raised. On 16-17 November the Law Amendment Society successfully organized Levi's major conference of "deputations from the principal trading and commercial towns in the United Kingdom, as well as several law societies" (*The Scotsman*, 20 November 1852, p. 4) to consider the propriety of assimilating the mercantile laws of England, Scotland and Ireland. The attendees drew particular attention to the often antagonistic nature of English and Scottish commercial law which tended "greatly to restrict and embarrass commerce, by producing uncertainty, perplexity and delay" (ibid). The conference determined that progress on assimilation would best be served by a Royal Commission on the subject and it was resolved to despatch a deputation immediately to represent its collective views to the Prime Minister. The Earl of Derby concurred that the issue was of great importance and saw no objection to the institution of a commission[5] on assimilation (*Hansard*, 7 March 1853, p. 2034).

Secondly, free trade was confirmed as the guiding principle of British commercial policy. On 26 November, following the "great free trade debate", the House of Commons voted for the maintenance and extension of financial and administrative reforms based on free trade (Connacher, 1972, pp. 151-159). *The Edinburgh Courant* reported that the cause of protectionism was lost - free trade is now "accepted without further protest: it is safe; it is triumphant" (18 November 1852, p. 2).

Thirdly, the causes of free trade and law reform were further advanced by the fall of Derby's Conservative administration on 16 December and its replacement by the Aberdeen Coalition (see Stewart, 1971, pp. 206-215). In late December the new Peelite Prime Minister stated that the mission of his Government would be the preservation and advancement of free trade policies (Connacher, 1968, p. 33) and his ministerial team emphasized the "necessity of vigorous measures of Law Reform" (*Edinburgh Courant*, 6 January 1853, p. 2).

Given the increasingly liberal and reformist political environment of November 1852-January 1853 the London Committee's threatened bill to overhaul the Scottish system of insolvency administration, which posed a substantial threat to the interests of Scottish accountants, had a chance of success. The accountants of the principal cities of Scotland were bound to respond. They did so by establishing protective occupational organizations and by devising a potent counter-ideology to free trade and assimilation.

The emergence of counter organizations: Scottish accountants, January-October 1853

Conflict theorists reveal that collectivities such as occupational groups who are engaged in conflict situations require organization, articulation and leadership for the effective engagement of their opponents. The initial response of Scottish accountants to the agitation for bankruptcy law reform which had emanated from London took the form of the publication of a series of pamphlets by a number of leading practitioners who were to form the SAE. The first and most influential of these was *Reform of the Bankruptcy Law of Scotland* by Samuel Raleigh which appeared at the end of 1852.

Raleigh considered that in the current climate of reform the bankruptcy law of Scotland was likely to be the subject of legislation in the Parliamentary Session of 1852-53. Although he provided a convincing rebuttal of the London Committee's allegations, Raleigh did recognize that the London Committee's concerns about the qualifications of trustees had some validity. Although he showed that 75% of bankrupt estates in Scotland were managed by "professional trustees" (of whom the majority were accountants), there was a need to secure "the exclusion of all unqualified and incompetent parties" (1852, p. 25). This might be achieved by the compilation of public certified lists of suitably qualified individuals eligible for selection as trustees. These trustees might become organized "as a separate professional body" (ibid., p. 26). The determination of the membership of such an institution was to be subject to discussion but Raleigh had no doubts that an organization could be formed (ibid., Appendix).

Raleigh's ideas were supported by a group of Edinburgh accountants who, in their *Remarks on The Revision of the Bankruptcy Laws of Scotland*, also rejected the London Committee's proposals (1853). It was considered that Raleigh's suggestion "that a qualified body of Trustees should be organized, and a certified list of such drawn out, thereby constituting them as a separate professional body, and excluding incompetent and interested parties from the charge of bankrupt estates, would, we think, be found highly beneficial" (ibid., p. 18). Further, it was argued that "the active part of the movement should no longer be left entirely in the hands of our thorough and energetic London reformers" (ibid., p. 20).

The Institute of Accountants in Edinburgh

It was in the context of the imminent threat to their bankruptcy and insolvency practice and demands for the organization of qualified trustees that the first move was made on 17 January 1853 for "uniting the professional Accountants in Edinburgh" (Society of Accountants in Edinburgh, Sederunt Book, p. 1). Whereas other individuals acting as sequestration trustees, such as lawyers, bankers and merchants, had established institutions to defend their interests, the occupational group which occupied most trusteeships - accountants - were unorganized.

The Minute Books of the Institute of Accountants reveal that organization was an urgent political expedient. By 22 January 1853 a draft constitution was discussed and attempts were made to enrol suitable members "with as little delay as possible" (ibid., p. 4). Such exigency was necessitated by the fact that the London Committee's promised Bill to overhaul the Scottish system of bankruptcy administration was now drafted - on the same day as the Institute of Accountants discussed its draft constitution, the London Committee's Chairman was explaining the merits of the Bill to the Edinburgh Chamber of Commerce (Alexander, 1853, p. 21).

The progress of the Bankruptcy and Insolvency (Scotland) Bill

The offending Bill (House of Lords, *Sessional Papers*, 1852-3, Vol. 3, 100) consisted of 266 clauses and was designed to consolidate the insolvency law of Scotland, improve the collection and division of sequestrated estates, prevent delays in the winding-up of bankruptcies and place all insolvency proceedings under judicial control (ibid., 100a, *Paper of Observations*, p. 1). The guiding principles of the Bill were to assimilate and codify the law of bankruptcy, protect creditors and produce "the soundest and truest Economy" in insolvency administration (ibid., pp. 32-33). These objectives were to be achieved by removing the exclusive power of the Court of Session in Edinburgh to award sequestrations and by reposing administrative power in new local Courts of Bankruptcy and Insolvency throughout Scotland. The management of bankrupt estates would be vested in five Official Assignees for Scotland rather than in the 862 trusteeships currently filled by accountants (60%), lawyers (10%), bankers (4%), merchants and others (26%) and which cost creditors a total of £90,702 in trustees' commission (Report by the Sub-Committee of the Edinburgh General Committee on Bankruptcy-Law Reform, 1853, p. 2). Voluntary trusts for behoof of creditors - a highly lucrative source of income for accountants and lawyers which were currently outwith the public gaze and judicial control - were to be supervised by the new Courts of Bankruptcy and Insolvency to which trustees were to be made accountable for their actions.

The parliamentary progress of the Bankruptcy and Insolvency (Scotland) Bill was unpredictable in a legislature of shifting allegiances and comparatively weak party discipline (Beales, 1967; Woodward, 1962, pp.160-166). However, the London Committee claimed that the Bill was received by the Government "in a friendly manner" (*Second Address*, 1853, p. 21). The Bill's chances of success were further advanced when its parliamentary sponsor was revealed as Henry, Lord Brougham (1778-1868) (*Dictionary of National Biography*, Vol. II, pp. 1356-1366). Although he had only once held a major office of state (as Lord Chancellor 1830-34), Brougham remained a powerful political figure in the mid-1850s. As an acquaintance and sympathizer of Bentham (Stewart, 1985, p. 234), Brougham was a noted instigator of law reforms. He had been instrumental in formulating the English Bankruptcy Laws of 1831 and 1849 and in 1844 had founded the Law Amendment Society and chaired its conference on the assimilation of mercantile laws in November 1852 (Hawes, 1957, p. 201). As an advocate of reform and free trade (Aspinall, 1939, p. 250), Brougham was a champion of middle class causes in a legislature dominated by aristocratic representatives (Perkin, 1969, p. 316; Rubinstein, 1993, pp. 145-148). Hence, when the Bankruptcy and Insolvency (Scotland) Bill received its First Reading in the House of Lords on 15 March 1853, Brougham stressed that the "great mercantile body" in Britain felt "deeply anxious" on the need for reform on this subject (*Hansard*, 1853, Vol. 125, p. 196).

The appearance of Lord Brougham's Bill galvanized a cross-occupational alliance of accountants, lawyers and merchants in Edinburgh into vigorous lobbying of the principal Government representative in Scotland -the Lord Advocate (see Report by the Sub-

Committee of The Edinburgh General Committee on Bankruptcy-Law Reform, 1853). The result was the framing and introduction into the House of Commons of the Bankruptcy (Scotland) Bill on 4 May 1853. The Lord Advocate's Bill contained a mere 18 clauses designed to remedy the most obvious defects of Scottish bankruptcy administration and thereby negate the necessity for the radical reforms proposed in Brougham's Bill.

The appearance of the Lord Advocate's Bill resulted in an intensification of effort by the London Committee. A series of petitions in favour of its Bankruptcy and Insolvency (Scotland) Bill were raised including one from over 200 merchants in London whose trade with Scotland amounted to £5m (*Hansard*, 19 July 1853, p. 433). The assault on bankruptcy administration in Scotland, and particularly the system of trusteeship, became more venomous. In July 1853 Brougham stated that for trustees: "no qualification was required. He ought to be both an accountant and a judge. Instead of this, however, he was required to possess no learning whatever - no qualification of any sort" (*Hansard*, 4 July 1853, p. 1145). Brougham's Bill passed its Second Reading in the House of Lords on 22 July 1853. The Government measure - the Bankruptcy (Scotland) Bill - was passed in August with little parliamentary discussion. The new Act failed to quell the agitation of the London Committee.

Within one week of the Second Reading of its Bankruptcy and Insolvency (Scotland) Bill the London Committee reassembled at the Guildhall Coffee House. It was resolved that the Lord Advocate's Bill was "utterly inadequate" (*Second Address*, 1853, p. 20) and "in no way alters the state of the question" (ibid., p. 21). The campaign was to be escalated in order to further interest the mercantile community "in a matter of such vast importance to the welfare of our internal commerce" (ibid., p. v). A *Second Address to the Mercantile Community of the United Kingdom* was prepared and widely circulated during the summer of 1853 in order to encourage petitioning of Parliament against the system of insolvency administration in Scotland. The Secretary of the London Committee - John Gilmour - was remitted to lobby the mercantile and law organizations located in all the major commercial and manufacturing centres of Britain (ibid., p. vi). The 'second city of the Empire' was singled out for particular attention.

The Institute of Accountants and Actuaries in Glasgow

If the London Committee's message was to find a sympathetic ear in Scotland it was likely to find it in Glasgow. Many Glaswegian merchants and industrialists were persuaded by assimilationist measures intended to enhance trade with England and support could be found among Glasgow lawyers for measures which would reduce the hegemonic position of Edinburgh in the Scottish legal system (Hutchison, 1986, pp. 93-95). The London Committee's proposals to unify the law of bankruptcy and increase local judicial control over the administration of bankrupt estates together with ancillary measures relating to small debt procedures, were looked upon favourably by the Glasgow Law Amendment Society and the Glasgow and West of Scotland Society for the Protection of Trade which had petitioned in favour of Lord Brougham's Bill (*Second Address*, 1853, pp. 18-19).

Until the autumn of 1853 the agitation against Brougham's Bill was Edinburgh-centred. The reactionary Bankruptcy (Scotland) Act, 1853 had reflected the interests of Edinburgh accountants, lawyers and merchants. That Act failed to dampen the enthusiasm of the London Committee which promised the pursuit of its objectives with renewed vigour. In late September 1853 further parliamentary debate on the bankruptcy laws of Scotland seemed inevitable. John Gilmour had organized a public meeting in Glasgow for October to discuss Brougham's Bill. The younger accountants of Glasgow needed to organize to protect their pecuniary interests particularly as they practised in a city where many of their fellow citizens were in favour of law reform and assimilation.

Hence, 27 accountants who commenced practice after 1841 requisitioned their more senior colleagues to meet to consider the formation of an organization of professional practitioners in Glasgow. The requisition stated that organization was necessary now because of "the late changes and *contemplated* alterations in the Bankrupt Law of Scotland", and "in order that the practical experience of those parties who have hitherto been entrusted with the management of Bankrupt Estates in the West of Scotland may be properly represented, and have due weight in determining what changes require to be made upon the existing Bankrupt Law (Institute of Accountants and Actuaries in Glasgow, Minute Book, 1853, p. 1).

Two to three hundred attended the "great" public meeting in Glasgow to discuss Brougham's Bill in late October (*Hansard*, 15

May 1854, p. 299). Among the speakers was David McCubbin, one of
the requisitionists of the new Institute of Accountants. McCubbin
made a vigorous defence of the prevailing system of bankruptcy
administration in Scotland but like Raleigh had done a year
previously, conceded that it "is an evil in our current system, and a
great one too, that any man, whatever may be his abilities or
qualifications, may be elected trustee" (*Trade Protection Circular*,
October 1853, p. 25). McCubbin's solution was to compose a certified
list of experienced trustees eligible for election (presumably the members of the Glasgow Institute) and those with lesser experience might
enter the list following examination and by finding security for their
intromissions as evidence of respectability.

The emergence of a counter ideology: Scottish nationalism

The organization of accountants in Edinburgh and Glasgow was
insufficient by itself to challenge the likely re-introduction of Lord
Brougham's Bill in the parliamentary session of 1853-54. Conflict
models reveal the importance of developing group ideologies in order
to enhance collective consciousness and to elicit the support of other
interests. Hence, the occupational groups with a vested interest in the
maintenance of the existing system of Scottish insolvency
administration had to present a convincing case against the proposals
which had emanated from the London Committee of Merchants. A
rhetorical discourse founded on self interest - the deleterious
pecuniary consequences of Brougham's Bill for insolvency trustees -
was incapable of penetrating the utilitarian banners of free trade and
assimilation. Rather, the accountants reverted to what has been
described as "the most successful political ideology in human history"
(Birch, 1989, p. 3); the antithesis of the harmonization of
international law and the removal of institutional hindrances to
cross-border trade: nationalism. In order to comprehend the seductive
value of appeals to patriotic sympathies during the 1850s, the relevant
political context must be sketched.

Scottish nationalism in the 1850s

The period from 1850 to 1855 witnessed "one of the first flickers of modern Scottish nationalism" (Hutchison, 1986, p. 91). According to Hanham, the mid-century national movement, which persisted until attention was deflected to the Crimean War, was both romantic and radical. The patriotic upsurge was inaugurated in 1849 by the neglect of Scottish measures in the English-dominated legislature (Hanham, 1969, pp. 151-153). From 1850 to 1852 agitation against English hegemony in the machinery of government and the provincialization of Scotland were compounded by complaints against the irregular use of Scottish heraldic symbols. In May 1853 a National Association for the Vindication of Scottish Rights was formed and by November of the same year claimed 6000 members. In its first *Address to the People of Scotland,* the Association resolved that the national laws and institutions of Scotland should be preserved and that attempts "to subvert or place those institutions under English control, and under the pretence of a centralizing economy to deprive her of the benefit of local action" (1853, p. 33), should be strenuously resisted.

The centralization of governmental functions in London and the attempts to assimilate the laws of Scotland with those of England were deeply held grievances particularly in Edinburgh. One member of the National Association for the Vindication of Scottish Rights stated at its first public meeting that "Our manners and our customs may assimilate, but our laws and our religion are essentially different, and our own" (*Justice to Scotland,* 1853, p. 32). Hanham has concluded that "the main function of the national movement was to remind the nation that Scotland was a cultural and political entity, and to fight against the more blatant forms of assimilation with England" (1967, p. 177).

The leaders of the mid-century Scottish nationalist movement were primarily Tory protectionists who were marginalized by the confirmation of free trade and reformist policies in 1852-53 (Hutchison, 1986, pp. 91-92). Among the supporters of the National Association for the Vindication of Scottish Rights were those directly threatened by assimilationist pressures: accountants. One of the principal agitators, John Grant, was allegedly an accountant (Hanham, 1967, p. 159). The membership lists of the General Committee of the National Association include the names of five members of the SAE and IAAG (see *Address to the People of Scotland,* 1853, 1st and 2nd editions). The secretaries of the

Edinburgh and Glasgow branches of the National Association - Frederick H. Carter, CA, and George Wink, CA - were "leading spirits" of the movement (Hanham, 1967, p. 170). Robert Christie, senior, who mysteriously resigned as a member of the Institute of Accountants in Edinburgh shortly after its formation, wrote a scathing pamphlet on the inequitable distribution of government expenditure between England and Scotland (Christie, 1854).

The nationalist retort to assimilation

In the increasingly patriotic atmosphere of the early 1850s, Scottish accountants and their allies who were confronted by assimilationist measures in insolvency law, embraced the nationalist pennant. In addition to highlighting the specific technical defects of the London Committee's proposals, the accountant pamphleteers of 1852-53 expressed considerable resentment at the attempted imposition of the English system of bankruptcy administration on Scotland.

Samuel Raleigh argued that the assimilation of the bankruptcy laws ignored the peculiarities of the Scottish character and the indigenous legal system which would not readily accommodate "imported methods and foreign systems of procedure" (1852, p. 5). The "violent and wholesale substitution" (1854, p. 18) of the Scottish system of bankruptcy by the English and the consequent introduction of alien legal institutions with no tradition in Scotland would disrupt the whole judicial process north of the border. Further, it was argued that such contentions were not motivated by a selfish desire to protect the income of trustees: "the question is not whether professional interest shall give way to public good, but whether what has grown up among us -what adapts itself in many ways to our means and existing institutions, - instead of being improved and perfected, should be at once abolished, and a system demonstrably worse put in its stead" (1854, pp. 22-23). Raleigh was offended that demands for the overhaul of the Scots bankruptcy laws had emanated from London and not from those north of the Tweed who had an intimate and practical knowledge of their own national laws and institutions (1852, p. 30).

Another original member of the SAE, Christopher Douglas, also prepared a pamphlet in 1853 which advocated a nationalistic defence of the Scots bankruptcy law. Douglas argued that although in many respects England and Scotland were a single country, on the law of bankruptcy "no two countries scarcely can bear less resemblance to each other" (p. 4). Despite the Union of 1707 the Scots had deep affection for their independent laws and were firmly resolved not to have unsuitable English jurisprudence thrust upon them (ibid.).

Cross-occupational alliances

The nationalist ideology became a rallying call to other collectivities such as merchants and lawyers who (as trustees) had a direct interest in the maintenance of the Scottish bankruptcy procedure. The result was the formation of a cross-sectional coalition of accountants and other organized occupational groups which succeeded in mobilizing public opinion north of the border against the London Committee's proposals.

A patriotic ideology was advanced by the mercantile community in Scotland. The *Trade Protection Circular* considered that the assimilation of commercial laws might prove advantageous but not when "always, and in every instance, made at the expense of Scottish interests" (13 November 1852, p. 163). The *Circular* protested that it "could not conceive a greater evil falling upon any nation than an attempt, rashly to overturn its fundamental laws, and the principles of its judicatories" and their replacement by "a blind and indiscriminate imitation or adoption of English principles or practices" (26 March 1853, p. 278). The mercantile interest was particularly aggrieved by the apparent intent to use Scots bankruptcy law as an early test of assimilation. The Edinburgh Chamber of Commerce objected that the London Committee was attempting to make Scotland "a sort of experimental garden of legislation for England, on a bill prepared by English parties" (Alexander, 1853, p. 21).

In order that the initiative for bankruptcy law reform should shift to Scotland and that any legislation would not simply reflect the interests of English merchants, Samuel Raleigh suggested in late 1852 that "the parties chiefly interested and best informed on our bankruptcy administration, should themselves take this subject into their own hands" (1852, p. 30) and devise their own proposals for reform. The result was The Edinburgh General Committee on Bankruptcy Law Reform which met on 18 February 1853. The General Committee comprised a forum for the cross-occupational alliance which fought the London Committee's proposals under the ideological banner of the protection of national interests. The General Committee immediately appointed a 34 man sub-committee (chaired by Raleigh) containing bankers, merchants, lawyers and four accountants (who were particularly active in the affairs of the early Edinburgh institute) to investigate the bankruptcy laws in Scotland, suggest "sound practical reform" and to watch any measures brought into Parliament on the subject (Report by the Sub-Committee, 1853, p. 1). The resulting report, which made many suggestions later incorporated into the Bankruptcy (Scotland) Act, 1856, was agreed on 31 March 1853 and remitted to the Lord Advocate (ibid., p. 6).

The appeal to patriotism also enlisted the support of Scottish Members of Parliament and policy-makers, the most important of whom was the Lord Advocate, James Moncreiff. During the legislative progress of his Bankruptcy (Scotland) Bill, 1853, Moncreiff displayed an anti-Anglo streak which surprised contemporaries (*The Law Magazine*, August-November 1853, p. 328). He conceded that assimilation might prove advantageous but not if it meant merely imposing the laws of one country on another (ibid., p. 324). The Lord Advocate stressed the superiority of Scottish jurisprudence, chastised the amateurish nature of the proposals from the London Committee of Merchants and urged those "anxious to preserve the nationality of Scotland" to exert themselves in order to "prevent our legal system from being . . . altogether upset by crude and rash importations from the other side of the Tweed" (ibid., p. 327).

It is testimony to the extent to which Scottish opinion was mobilized on the issue that commentators in England were astonished by the public interest shown north of the border in the apparently mundane subject of assimilation (*The Law Magazine*, 1854, p. 119). Whereas mercantile law reform in England was the exclusive domain of lawyers, in Scotland, with its jealously guarded separate legal system, such issues "have a more general and stirring effect" and the lawyers "are not left alone, but the people individually, collectively, and under various forms of organization, offer their sentiments" (ibid.). Hence Brougham's insolvency Bill "is all but universally condemned" (ibid.) not only by groups with a direct professional interest in the subject but also by chambers of commerce, local authorities and at public meetings.

The defeat of the assimilation of bankruptcy law, 1854-56

Having received the support of the Lord Advocate and successfully enlisted a majority of interested public opinion against the assimilation of bankruptcy law, the coalition of professional and commercial groups in Scotland were advantageously placed to confront the re-introduction of Lord Brougham's Bill in the House of Lords on 10 March 1854.

Parliamentary debate on the Bill during the spring of 1854 centred on Brougham's claim that "the Bill had the sanction of all classes both in England and Scotland, who were interested in the question" (*Hansard*, 10 March 1854, p. 588) and, in particular, that the Bill was universally supported by the mercantile interest. By 1854, however, the appeal of a nationalist-based ideology had ensured that the proponents of the Bill were almost exclusively from England. In 1853 six petitions in relation to Brougham's Bill were presented to Parliament by organized interests in Scotland: three supported the measure and three were opposed to it. By contrast, in 1854, 16 petitions were presented from Scotland of which only one was in favour of the Bill.

Despite such evidence to the contrary, Brougham argued that there was wide support for his Bill among the commercial community in Scotland, that opposition was restricted to, and driven by, self-interested accountants and lawyers (*Hansard*, 15 May 1854, pp. 301-302) and that the lack of support from the Lord Advocate could be disregarded as an inevitable symptom of that official's natural affinity with the Edinburgh-Parliament House view (ibid., 11 April 1854, p. 822).

Although Brougham's Bill passed its Second Reading in the Lords in April 1854, the weight of Scottish opposition and the lukewarm response of the Government, ensured that it proceeded no further in 1854. The subsequent progress of the Bill was effectively scuppered by the Lord Advocate who, later in 1854, requested the Faculty of Advocates to prepare a report on the Scots bankruptcy laws. The resulting document, following extensive discussion with interested organizations in Scotland, engendered the Bankruptcy (Scotland) Act, 1856, which subsisted as the primary insolvency statute north of the border until 1913.

Assimilation and professional formation in England

The Bankruptcy (Scotland) Act, 1856, does not mark the conclusion of the assimilation debate and its consequences for the organization of the accountancy profession in Britain. Paradoxically, the assimilation of bankruptcy law was to be achieved in 1870 not by the imposition of English laws on Scotland but by the adoption of Scottish insolvency practice in England via the Bankruptcy Act, 1869.

The English procedure of vesting bankrupt estates in the hands of official assignees under the aegis of courts of bankruptcy, which persisted after 1831, was criticized for its departure from the fundamental principle that the creditors should occupy the central role in the realization and distribution of the debtor's estate (Littleton, 1933, pp. 278-280). The deficiency was remedied by the Bankruptcy Act, 1861, which placed administration in the hands of a 'creditor assignee' elected by the creditors. In practice, the legislation of 1861 served only to increase the expense of bankruptcy administration as unpaid and inexperienced 'creditor assignees' tended to delegate the management of insolvent estates to knowledgeable and remunerated solicitors.

In 1864 a House of Commons Select Committee conducted an extensive inquiry into the working of the Bankruptcy Act, 1861, and concluded that economy and efficiency in winding-up would be secured by the introduction into England and Wales of the Scottish system of paid, creditor-elected trustees which had been successfully defended by accountants and their allies in 1853-54. Several witnesses to the Select Committee attested that the administration of insolvent estates by competent trustees would be of considerable benefit to accountancy practitioners in England who at present assumed a comparatively limited role (compiling the debtor's balance sheet) in the bankruptcy process compared with lawyers (Minutes of Evidence, pp. 171, 263, 308). The reforms suggested by the Select Committee were incorporated in the Bankruptcy Act, 1869. In introducing the Bankruptcy Bill to the House of Commons, the Attorney-General conceded that "the English system of bankruptcy had substantially failed" and "the Scotch system of bankruptcy had substantially succeeded. The conclusion naturally pointed to the adoption of the Scotch system" (*Hansard*, 5 April 1869, p. 780).

The Bankruptcy Act, 1869, made no provisions concerning the qualifications of trustees. As in Scotland the choice of trustee and his remuneration was to be a matter for the creditors. The extent to which this unregulated environment might attract canvassing and touting for trusteeships from a host of doubtful characters was considered less important than the potential advantages of competition for producing greater economy in bankruptcy administration.[6] Further, the Select Committee of 1864 had recognized that the potential dangers of open trusteeships had been mitigated in Scotland by the appointment of respectable professional accountants to trusteeships. The Attorney-General expressed the hope that in England the effect of introducing the Scottish system would "be to create a similar profession, so that there would be no difficulty in the way of creditors in the choice of able and efficient trustees" (*Hansard*, 5 April 1869, p. 781).

Demands for the institution of professional associations in England based on the Scottish model had also been made in *The Times* in 1867 and 1868 following public concern over the appointment of liquidators. Although 47% of liquidations under the Companies Act, 1862, were awarded to six eminent firms of public accountants (see Report of the Select Committee on the Limited Liability Acts, 1867, Minutes of Evidence, p. 59) a large number of the remainder were in the hands of men who had been attracted by the potential to make "very large fortunes" (ibid., p. 84) and comprised "a swarm of pettifoggers whose only qualification for the duties of accountants has been obtained by a series of personal experience of failure in every occupation they have tried" (*The Times*, 28 December 1867, p. 28). The remedy advocated by *The Times* to prevent the further encroachment into accountancy of the unqualified and financially immoral was the formation in London of a professional organization to emulate the successful professionalization project of the accountants of Edinburgh (ibid., 9 January 1868). The passing of the Bankruptcy Act, 1869, offered the prospect of a substantial expansion in the "herd of disreputable persons" (ibid.) offering their services as public accountants.

On 1 January 1870 the new Bankruptcy Act came into force and in the same month the first of the local English societies of accountants was formed in Liverpool. The extent to which accountants in England organized during the 1870s in order to protect their occupational status and gain socioeconomic advantage over the expected (and realized) influx of unqualified applicants for trusteeships following the introduction of the 'Scotch system' of bankruptcy administration is deserving of further investigation and indicates the potential limitations of histories of the English profession which commence in 1870 and fail to take cognizance of earlier developments north of the border (Kirkham & Loft, 1993, p. 524).

Commentators in the late nineteenth century certainly considered that the 1869 Act was the principal inducement to the organization of accountants in the major commercial and industrial centres of England. In 1895 it was asserted that following the Bankruptcy Act, 1869, established practitioners viewed with "alarm and disgust" the "great influx of men into the ranks of accountancy who had little or no capacity and fitness for the duties they assumed" (*A Guide to the Accountancy Profession*, p. 5). Respectable accountants were induced to combine in order to protect "the public and themselves from a recurrence of such evils" (ibid). Similarly, Dicksee (1897) claimed that the 1869 Act encouraged those devoid of morals and good conduct to enter the occupation to the detriment of reputable public accountants: "the presence of a black ship the midst of the body naturally resulted in the more respectable Accountants, forming various Associations for mutual protection, and for the purpose of affording to the public some sort of guarantee as to the standing of those whose services they employed" (p. 3).

If, as seems probable, the Bankruptcy Act, 1869, was instrumental in the formation of the first societies of accountants in England (and Boys has recently suggested as much (1994, p. 10)), then the successful preservation of the Scottish process of insolvency administration in 1853 assumes a more than parochial significance in the history of professionalization in Britain[7] - it comprises a common theme which links professional formation in England and Wales with previous developments in Scotland.

Conclusions

It has been shown in this paper that a critical-conflict based analysis of occupational organization which examines institutional developments in their historical, socioeconomic and political contexts offers new insights into the motives for professional formation. The institution of the SAE and IAAG in 1853 constituted organizational responses to the activities of a London-based group whose proposals, if enacted, posed a substantial threat to the interests of accountants in Scotland. Further, the ideological justifications for the law reforms advocated by the opponents of Scottish accountants were founded on the dominant economic philosophy of mid-Victorian Britain (free trade) and required that the accountants devise an equally mesmeric counter-ideology (nationalism) as a basis for mobilizing cross-occupational support for the engagement of antagonistic interests in the political arena.

Scottish accountants were compelled to participate in a political conflict precipitated by a challenge to what was perceived as their occupational property. Their organization was not based on functionalist imperatives, it was necessary for the mobilization of an occupational collectivity and its potential allies for engagement in a clash of ideologies. The events which resulted in the formation of the first organizations of accountants in Scotland and later in England suggest that institutionalization was essentially motivated not to achieve collective social mobility or to promulgate job monopolies but to protect established economic and social statuses from assaults by exogenous parties such as the London Committee of Merchants (as in Scotland) or occupational usurpers (as in England).

The explanation for the organization of the SAE and IAAG related above does not, however, result in the total redundancy of the traditional explanations for professional formation in Scotland. Rather, the foregoing analysis provides a connecting threat which weaves together certain pertinent tenets of the conventional histories.

In so far that the essential backdrop to the assimilation movement was the maintenance of separate laws and institutions in Scotland after the Act of Union, then the traditional explanation for the early professionalization of accountants in Scotland based on the different legal systems north and south of the border is relevant.

A connection between structural economic change and the organization of accountants in Scotland can also be found. Industrialization and commercial expansion ensured Britain's economic supremacy (Perkin, 1969, p. 408) and the existence of an increasingly numerous and wealthy middle class (Rubinstein, 1993, p. 147). During the early 1850s the energetic commercial, financial and manufacturing communities sought the affirmation and further extension of those Free Trade policies which had underpinned British economic hegemony. For a group of powerful London merchants aggrieved at losses suffered under the Scots law of bankruptcy, those laws were advocated as being part of "the huge, heterogeneous, in-efficient, and expensive pile of institutions and institutional gaps which clogged the road of progress" (Hobsbawm, 1968, p. 228). In the intoxicating days of the Great Exhibition of 1851 one prescription for the further creation of the optimum conditions for the operation of international capitalism was the assimilation of commercial law. In attempting to defend their pecuniary interests by the maintenance of existing laws and institutions, Scottish accountants came into conflict with the prevailing spirit of liberalizing commercial relations and law reform.

The analysis of events which resulted in the formation of societies of accountants in Edinburgh and Glasgow in 1853 also partly concords with the contention that organization was induced by attempts by practitioners to achieve social closure. The central objection of the London Committee of Merchants was the expensive administration of sequestrated estates in Scotland by trustees. The London Committee argued that many trustees were educationally unfit for office and were of questionable social standing. Further, those practitioners who were reputable had no formal professional qualification to justify their election as trustees. The necessity of distinguishing the professional from the non-professional trustee was recognized by the opponents of the London Commitee. The accountant pamphleteers of Edinburgh, the Edinburgh General Committee on Bankruptcy Law Reform and activist accountants in Glasgow, concurred that all unqualified and incompetent parties should be excluded from the office of trustee. The offensive by the London Committee against the competence of insolvency trustees was utilized by Scottish accountants as a justification for the imposition of closure practices. It was proposed that the creditors should choose their trustee from an approved list of qualified practitioners. One means of ensuring that the unorganized occupational group which filled most trusteeships - accountants in public practice - could claim evidence of professional respectability, fitness for office and appearance on a register, was membership of a qualifying association.

The evidence suggests, however, that initially, the formation of *qualifying* associations by accountants was a secondary objective. The accountants of Edinburgh had fleetingly organized in 1834 and, together with their professional brethren in Glasgow, associated on a more permanent basis in 1853 in order to form protective occupational groups geared for a political contest. As instituted in 1853, the Edinburgh and Glasgow organizations of accountants were agencies for the mobilization of participants engaged in a conflict to preserve collective socioeconomic interests. Hence, the first constitution of the Edinburgh Institute was chastised in legal circles for its absence of contemporary 'professional' attributes. Provisions relating to education and qualification were omitted and the constitutional arrangements as a whole were considered to be "hastily and crudely concocted" (see Walker, 1988, p. 301). Once the challenge to their dominance in the market for the provision of insolvency services had been repelled, and on the acquisition of Royal Charters, the SAE and IAAG began to assume the persona of qualifying associations by the establishment of structures for the testing of professional knowledge in 1855 (Walker, 1988, pp. 312-317; Kedslie, 1990a, p. 200) and by operating other closure strategies based primarily on credentialism. (Walker, 1991).

This paper has confirmed the heuristic value of examining professional formation and behaviour within critical-conflict models and the need to investigate the organizational development of occupations as opposed to the narrow profession-centred frame of reference which characterizes functionalist-based analysis. It has revealed the dynamic and political nature of the organizational objectives of the SAE and IAAG and confirms the fluid nature of professional ideologies. Moreover, the foregoing reiterates that "organizations are the outcome of struggles, reflect the social relations of wider society, and are thoroughly permeated by the inequalities and contradictions of that society" (Davies, 1983, p. 181).

Notes

The author is grateful for the constructive comments of two anonymous referees, Anthony Hopwood and members of the Scottish Committee on Accounting History. The helpful comments of participants at the Accounting, Business and Financial History Conference, Cardiff, September 1993, and members of the Manchester Accounting Group at a presentation in January 1994 were also much appreciated.

1. The difficulties inherent in identifying a nebulous causal link between industrialization and the emergence of specific qualifying associations was recognized by Millerson (1964) who contended that "To expound reasons for formation in terms of broad general factors is too approximate. It is as unrealistic as any attempt to suggest that the discovery of the wheel 'caused' the invention of the steam locomotive" (p. 51).
2. The Scots law of bankruptcy had long been a concern of merchants in London who traded with Scotland. In 1813, for example, a committee had been formed to prevent the passing of a Bankrupt (Scotland) Bill and to complain of the level of commission paid to trustees in sequestrations (see *Report of the London Committee on the Scotch Bankrupt Bill*, 1814). It is possible that the London Committee of

Merchants was related to The Committee of Merchants and Traders of the City of London which reported in 1851 that it had "for some time past endeavoured, with varying success, to improve the Laws relating to Bankruptcy and Insolvency" (p. 3).

3. For the significance of London and its 'commercial based' elite in British economy and society see Rubinstein (1986, p. 34; 1993, pp. 25-32, 157-160; also Briggs, 1968, pp. 311-360).

4. The Honorary Secretary of the London branch of the Association for Promoting an International Code of Commerce was the Scot, John Gilmour, a barrister who was also the Secretary of the London Committee.

5. A Royal Commission on the assimilation of the mercantile laws of the U.K. was later established in June 1853 by the Aberdeen Government (Robert Slater of the London Committee of Merchants was a commissioner). The recommendations of the Assimilation Commission (1854, 1854-55) resulted in legislation (Mercantile Law Amendment Act, 1856, and the Mercantile Law (Scotland) Amendment Act, 1856) which removed the most obvious discrepancies between English and Scottish commercial law. Bankruptcy was excluded from the work of the Commission (see *Hansard*, 26 February 1856, pp. 1393-1401).

6. Expectations of greater economy and efficiency in English insolvency administration following the implementation of the Bankruptcy Act, 1869, were soon disappointed. In 1877 the Comptroller in Bankruptcy was remitted to investigate the escalating expense of bankruptcy administration. The Comptroller reported a chaotic state of affairs in which costs had risen as bankruptcy had been placed "in the hands of some 20,000 scattered trustees" (Supplemental Report, p. 19). Canvassing was rife: "I believe that accountants, quite as frequently as solicitors, canvass on their own account, and that from the increased numbers of the lowest class of "touts" there is an infinitely greater amount of 'touting' than under any former system" (ibid., p. 10). The Bankruptcy Act, 1883, re-introduced judicial control.

7. The surviving minute books of the local societies of accountants which formed the ICAEW in 1880 state that organization was primarily induced for the protection and preservation of occupational status (Incorporated Society of Liverpool Accountants, 1870; Manchester Institute of Accountants, 1871; Sheffield Institute of Accountants, 1877; or for the elevation of occupational status (Institute of Accountants in London, 1870) (Habgood, 1994, pp. 201-205).

Bibliography

Address to The People of Scotland and Statement of Grievances by The National Association for the Vindication of Scottish Rights (Edinburgh: Johnstone & Hunter, 1853).

A Guide to the Accountancy Profession (London: Gee & Co., 1895).

Alexander, W., *Report to the Chamber of Commerce and Manufactures of Edinburgh Relative to the Amendment of the Bankrupt Act of Scotland* (Edinburgh: R. & R. Clark, 1853).

Alphabetical List of Public Bills Introduced into the House of Commons during the Session 1852-53, *British Parliamentary Papers* Vol. 83 (1852-3).

Aspinall, A., *Lord Brougham and The Whig Party* (Manchester: Manchester University Press, 1939).

Assimilation Commission. First Report of the Commission appointed to inquire and ascertain how far the mercantile laws in the different parts of the United Kingdom of Great Britain and Ireland may be advantageously assimilated, *British Parliamentary Papers* Vol. XXVII (1854) p. 455.

Assimilation Commission. Second Report of the Commission appointed to inquire and ascertain how far the mercantile laws in the different parts of the United Kingdom of Great Britain and Ireland may be advantageously assimilated, *British Parliamentary Papers* Vol. XVIII (1854-55) p. 653.

Babbage, C., *The Exposition of 1851* (London: John Murray, 1851).

Bankruptcy and Insolvency (Scotland) Bill, 1853, with Paper of Observations, House of Lords, *Sessional Papers* Vol. 3, 100-100a (1852-3).

Beales, D. E. D., Parliamentary Parties and the "Independent" Member, 1810-1860, in Robson, R. (ed.), *Ideas and Institutions of Victorian Britain* (London: G. Bell, 1967).

Bell, G. J., *Commentaries on the Laws of Scotland and on the Principles of Mercantile Jurisprudence,* 5th Edn (Edinburgh: Bell & Bradfute, 1826).

Birch, A. H., *Nationalism and National Integration* (London: Unwin Hyman, 1989).

Boys, P., The Origins and Evolution of the Accountancy Profession, in Habgood, W. (ed.), *Chartered Accountants in England and Wales. A Guide to Historical Records* (Manchester: Manchester University Press, 1994).

Briggs, A., *Victorian Cities* (Harmondsworth: Penguin, 1968).

Briston, R. J. & Kedslie, M. J. M., Professional Formation: the Case of Scottish Accountants - Some Corrections and Some Further Thoughts, *British Journal of Sociology* (1986) pp. 122-130.

Brown, R. (ed.), *A History of Accounting and Accountants* (Edinburgh: T. C. & E. C. Jack, 1905).

Bryer, R. A., The Late Nineteenth-century Revolution in Financial Reporting: Accounting for the Rise of Investor or Managerial Capitalism?, *Accounting, Organizations and Society* (1993) pp. 649-690.

Caplow, T., *The Sociology of Work* (Minneapolis: University of Minnesota Press, 1954).

Carr-Saunders, A. M. & Wilson, P. A., *The Professions* (Oxford: Clarendon Press, 1933).

Christie, R., *Injustice to Scotland Exposed* (Edinburgh: T. Constable, 1854).

Collins, R., *Conflict Sociology. Toward an Explanatory Science* (New York: Academic Press, 1975).

Collins, R., Changing Conceptions in the Sociology of the Professions, in Torstendahl, R. & Burrage, M. (eds), *The Formation of Professions. Knowledge, State and Strategy* (London: Sage, 1990a).

Collins, R., Market Closure and the Conflict Theory of the Professions, in Burrage, M. & Torstendahl, W. (eds), *Professions in Theory and History. Rethinking the Study of the Professions* (London: Sage, 1990b).

The Committee of Merchants and Traders of the City of London, appointed to promote the Improvement of the Law relating to Debtor and Creditor, *Replies from Foreign Countries to Questions Relating to the Law of Debtor and Creditor and to the Law of Partnership* (London: W. Clowes & Sons, 1851).

Connacher, J. B., *The Aberdeen Coalition 1852-1855* (Cambridge: Cambridge University Press, 1968).

Connacher, J. B., *The Peelites and the Parly System 1846-52* (Newton Abbot: David & Charles, 1972).

Davies, C., Professionals in Bureaucracies: the Conflict Thesis Revisited, in Dingwall, R. & Lewis, P. (eds), *The Sociology of the Professions* (London: Macmillan, 1983).

Dicksee, L. R., *The Student's Guide to Accountancy* (London: Gee & Co., 1897).

Dictionary of National Biography (Oxford: Oxford University Press, 1917).

Dinwiddy, J., *Bentham* (Oxford: Oxford University Press, 1989).

Doorn, J. A. A. van, Conflict in Formal Organizations, in de Reuck, A. V. S. & Knight, J. (eds), *Conflict in Society* (London: J. & A. Churchill, 1966).

Douglas, C., *Review of Recent Publications Regarding the Proposed Reform of the Bankruptcy Laws of Scotland* (Edinburgh: Bell & Bradfute, 1853).

Durkheim, E., *Professional Ethics and Civic Morals* (London: Routledge & Kegan Paul, 1957).

The Edinburgh Courant (1851-3).

Edsall, N. C., *Richard Cobden. Independent Radical* (London: Harvard University Press, 1986).

Edwards, J. R., *A History of Financial Accounting* (London: Routledge, 1989).

Etzioni, A., *The Active Society. A Theory of Societal and Political Processes* (London: Collier-Macmillan, 1968).

Fay, C. R., *Palace of Industry* (Cambridge: Cambridge University Press, 1951).

Freidson, E., The Theory of the Professions: the State of the Art, in Dingwall, R. & Lewis, P. (eds), *The Sociology of the Professions* (London: Macmillan, 1983).

Grampp, W. D., How Britain Turned to Free Trade, *Business History Review* (1987) pp. 86-112.

Greenwood, E, Attributes of a Profession, *Social Work* (1957) pp. 45-55.

Habgood, W. (ed.), *Chartered Accountants in England and Wales. A Guide to Historical Records* (Manchester: Manchester University Press, 1994).

Hanham, H. J., Mid-century Scottish Nationalism: Romantic and Radical, in Robson, R. (ed.), *Ideas and Institutions of Victorian Britain* (London: G. Bell, 1967).

Hanham, H. J., *Scottish Nationalism* (London: Faber & Faber, 1969).

Hansard's Parliamentary Debates, 3rd Series, 125-141, 193-196 (London: Cornelius Buck, 1853-6, 1868-9).

Hawes, F., *Henry Brougham* (London: Jonathan Cape, 1957).

Hobsbawm, E. J., *Industry and Empire* (Harmondsworth: Penguin, 1968).

Howitt, H. Sir, *The History of The Institute of Chartered Accountants in England and Wales 1870-1965* (London: Heinemann, 1966).

Hutchison, I. G. C., *A Political History of Scotland 1832-1924* (Edinburgh: John Donald, 1986).

The Illustrated London News (March-November, 1851).

Institute of Accountants and Actuaries in Glasgow, Minute Books (1853-4) (Glasgow: ICAS).

Institute of Chartered Accountants of Scotland, *A History of The Chartered Accountants of Scotland From the Earliest Times to 1954* (Edinburgh: ICAS, 1954).

Jarausch, K. H. & Cocks, G., Introduction, in Cocks, G. & Jarausch, K. H. (eds), *German Professions 1800-1950* (Oxford: University Press, 1990).

Jones, E., *Accountancy and the British Economy 1840-1980. The Evolution of Ernst & Whinney* (London: Batsford, 1981).

Justice to Scotland. Report of the First Public Meeting of the National Association for the Vindication of Scottish Rights (Edinburgh: Paton & Ritchie, 1853).

Kedslie, M. J. M., *Firm Foundations. The Development of Professional Accounting in Scotland, 1850-1900* (Hull: Hull University Press, 1990a).

Kedslie, M. J. M., Mutual Self-interest - a Unifying Force; the Dominance of Societal Closure Over Social Background in the Early Professional Accounting Bodies, *The Accounting Historians Journal* (1990b) pp. 1-9.

Kirkham, L. M. & Loft, A., Gender and the Construction of the Professional Accountant, *Accounting, Organizations and Society* (1993) pp. 507-558.

Krause, E. A., *The Sociology of Occupations* (Boston: Little, Brown and Company, 1971).

Larson, M. S., *The Rise of Professionalism. A Sociological Analysis* (Berkeley: University of California Press, 1977).

The Law Magazine or Quarterly Review of Jurisprudence (London, 1851-4).

Lee, T. A., A Review Essay: Professional Foundations and Theories of Professional Behaviour. *The Accounting Historians Journal* (1991) pp. 193-203.

Levi, L., *Commercial Law: its Principles and Administration or, The Mercantile Law of Great Britain Compared with the Codes and Laws of Commerce of the Following Mercantile Countries* (London: William Benning & Simpkin Marshall, 1850-2).

Levi, L., *International Code of Commerce in Connection with the Law of Nature and Nations: A Lecture* (London: Simpkin Marshall, 1851).

Littleton, A. C., *Accounting Evolution to 1900* (New York: Russell & Russell, 1933).

Loft, A., Towards a Critical Understanding of Accounting: the Case of Cost Accounting in the UK, 1914-1925, *Accounting, Organizations and Society* (1986) pp. 137-169.

The London Committee of Merchants and Others Associated for the Improvement of the Commercial and Bankruptcy Laws of Scotland, and the Assimilation of Those Laws in England and Scotland, *Report and Suggestions Addressed to the Mercantile Community of the United Kingdom* (London: Longman, Brown, Green & Longmans, 1852).

The London Committee of Merchants and Others Associated for the Improvement of the Commercial and Bankruptcy Laws of Scotland and the Assimilation of Those Laws in England and Scotland, *The Second Address to the Mercantile Community of the United Kingdom* (London: Longman, Brown, Green & Longmans, 1853).

Macdonald, K. M., Professional Formation: the Case of Scottish Accountants, *British Journal of Sociology* (1984) pp. 174-189.

Mathias, P., *The First Industrial Nation* (London: Methuen, 1969).

Miller, P. & Napier, C., Genealogies of Calculation, *Accounting, Organizations and Society* (1993) pp. 631-647.

Millerson, G., *The Qualifying Associations* (London: Routledge & Kegan Paul, 1964).

Murphy, R., *Social Closure. The Theory of Monopolization and Exclusion* (Oxford: Clarendon Press,1988).

Napier, C. & Noke, C., Accounting and Law: an Historical Overview of an Uneasy Relationship, in Bromwich, M. & Hopwood, A. (eds), *Accounting and the Law* (Hemel Hempstead: Prentice Hall,1992).

Neale, R. S., *Class and Ideology in the Nineteenth Century* (London: Routledge & Kegan Paul, 1972).

Palgrave, R. H. Inglis (ed.), *Dictionary of Political Economy* (London: Macmillan, 1986).

Parker, R. H., *The Development of the Accountancy Profession in Britain to the Early Twentieth Century* (Academy of Accounting Historians: Monograph 5, 1986).

Parkin, R, *Marxism and Class Theory: a Bourgeois Critique* (London: Tavistock, 1979).

Parry, N. & Parry, J., Social Closure and Collective Social Mobility, in Scase, R. (ed.), *Industrial Society: Class, Cleavage and Control* (London: George Allen and Unwin, 1977).

Perkin, H., *The Origins of Modern English Society 1780-1880* (London: Routledge & Kegan Paul, 1969).

Raleigh, S., *Reform of the Bankruptcy Law of Scotland* (Edinburgh: A. & C. Black, 1852).

Raleigh, S., *Letter to Lord Brougham Regarding his Lordship's Bankruptcy and Insolvency Bill for Scotland and the Assimilation of the Scotch to the English System* (Edinburgh: A. & C. Black, 1854).

Report by the Committee named at a Meeting of Accountants practising in the Court of Session, held at Edinburgh on 2nd July 1834, regarding the Bill in progress for the appointment of an Accountant General in the said Court (1834) (ICAS Library, Queen Street, Edinburgh).

Report by the Sub-Committee of The Edinburgh General Committee on Bankruptcy-Law Reform (1853). (Lord Advocate's Department Papers (AD 56/83), Scottish Records Office, Edinburgh).

Report from the Select Committee on the Limited Liability Acts, *British Parliamentary Papers*, Vol. 10 (1867).

Report of the London Committee on the Scotch Bankrupt Bill (London: W. & S. Graves, 1814).

Report of the Select Committee to Inquire into the Working of the New Bankruptcy Act, *British Parliamentary Papers* Vol. 5 (1864).

Rex, J., *Social Conflict. A Conceptual and Theoretical Analysis* (London: Longman, 1981).

Robinson, H. W., *A History of Accountants in Ireland* (Dublin: ICAI, 1964).

Robson, K. & Cooper, D. J., Understanding the Development of the Accountancy Profession in the United Kingdom, in Cooper, D. J. & Hopper, T. M. (eds), *Critical Accounts* (Basingstoke: Macmillan, 1990).

Rubinstein, W. D., *Wealth and Inequality in Britain* (London: Faber & Faber, 1986).

Rubinstein, W. D., *Capitalism, Culture and Decline in Britain 1750-1990* (London: Routledge, 1993).

Saks, M., Removing the Blinkers? A Critique of Recent Contributions to the Sociology of Professions, *Sociological Review* (1983) pp. 1-21.

A Scotch Accountant, *Remarks on the Revision of the Bankruptcy Laws of Scotland* (Edinburgh: Bell & Bradfute, 1853).

The Scotsman (1852-3).

Society of Accountants in Edinburgh, Sederunt Books (1853) (ICAS, Queen Street, Edinburgh).

Stacey, N. A. H., *English Accountancy. A Study in Social and Economic History* (London: Gee & Co., 1954).

Stewart, J. C., The Emergent Professionals, *The Accountant's Magazine* (1975) pp. 113-116.

Stewart, J. C., *Pioneers of a Profession: Chartered Accountants to 1879* (Edinburgh: Scottish Committee on Accounting History, 1977).

Stewart, R., *The Politics of Protection. Lord Derby and the Protectionist Party 1841-1852* (Cambridge: Cambridge University Press, 1971).

Stewart, R., *Henry Brougham 1778-1868 His Public Career* (London: Bodley Head, 1985).

Supplemental Report on the Expenses of Bankruptcy Administration. General Report by the Comptroller in Bankruptcy. For the Year ending 31st December 1876, *British Parliamentary Papers* Vol. 69 (1877).

The Times (1867-8).

Trade Protection Circular and Mercantile Remembrancer (Edinburgh: William Hill, 1852-3).

Turner, C. & Hodge, M. N., Occupations and Professions, in Jackson, J. A. (ed.), *Professions and Professionalisation* (Cambridge: Cambridge University Press, 1970).

Walker, S. P., *The Society of Accountants in Edinburgh 1854-1914. A Study of Recruitment to a New Profession* (New York: Garland, 1988).

Walker, S. P., The Defence of Professional Monopoly: Scottish Chartered Accountants and "Satellites in the Accountancy Firmament" 1854-1914, *Accounting, Organizations and Society* (1991) pp. 257-283.

Walker, S. P., Anatomy of a Scottish CA Practice: Lindsay, Jamieson & Haldane 1818-1918, *Accounting, Business & Financial History* (1993) pp. 127-154.

Wilensky, H. L., The Professionalization of Everyone?, *American Journal of Sociology* (1964) pp. 137-158.

Willmott, H., Organising the Profession: a Theoretical and Historical Examination of the Development of the Major Accountancy Bodies in the U.K. *Accounting, Organizations and Society* (1986) pp. 555-580.

Woodward, L. Sir, *The Age of Reform 1815-1870* (Oxford: Clarendon Press, 1962).

CHAPTER 7

Identifying the Founding Fathers of Public Accountancy: The Formation of The Society of Accountants in Edinburgh

Thomas A Lee

Introduction

The purpose of this paper is to examine the 1853 formation of the Institute of Accountants in Edinburgh (IAE), and its 1854 incorporation under royal charter as the Society of Accountants in Edinburgh (SAE). These events signal the origins of sustained institutionalized professional accountancy, and therefore have considerable historical significance in helping to explain the professionalization process in public accountancy since the mid-nineteenth century. The formation of the IAE/SAE has been briefly described in detailed histories of the early Scottish professional accountancy bodies (e.g., Brown, 1905; Walker, 1988; Kedslie, 1990a), and there have been several studies which debate reasons for the event (e.g., Stewart, 1977; Macdonald, 1984; Walker, 1988, 1995; Kedslie 1990a, 1990b). However, with the exceptions of Stewart (1977) and Kedslie (1990a), little has been published which specifically identifies the men who formed the IAE/SAE, and their individual involvement in the institutionalization of professional accountancy in mid-nineteenth century Edinburgh.

As historians persistently remind us (e.g., Collingwood, 1974; Carr, 1987), history is about individuals comprising events in time. This paper therefore focuses on the 1853 formation of the IAE, and the sixty-four individuals who were the founding members of its successor body (the SAE) in 1854. In particular, the study seeks to identify the men who, in a self-interested way, organized within an institutional framework.[1] The paper is structured as follows. First, pre-formation

Reproduced from *Accounting, Business & Financial History*, Volume 6, Number 3, December 1996, pp 315-35, with kind permission of Routledge.

events are reviewed in the context of a Victorian middle class. Second, four meetings to plan and form the IAE are identified and discussed (including the establishment of its first Council). Third, several IAE Council and general meetings are examined to observe the process of petitioning for a royal charter for the SAE. Fourth, post-formation SAE Council decisions to create significant committees are discussed. Finally, the individual participants in each of the foregoing stages are reviewed to identify key players and roles in the institutionalization process.

Pre-formation events

The history of professional accountancy in Edinburgh extends back well beyond the granting of a royal charter to the SAE on 23 October 1854. Brown (1905) identifies several influential accountants in business in the city prior to the emergence of institutionalized accountancy (e.g., George Watson [1645-1723], the first accountant of the Bank of Scotland; James Balfour [1735-95], accountant and socializer; and William Paul [1786-1848], master to many of the accountants who became managers of banks and insurance companies at the beginning of the nineteenth century). The number of these early professional accountants was small. For example, Brown (1905: p. 183) notes that seven accountants were listed in the first Edinburgh *Directory* of 1773, and seventeen in the 1805 *British Almanack and Universal Scots Register*. Mepham (1988: 49-60) identifies thirty-nine Edinburgh accountants at the end of the eighteenth century. In 1853, however, Kedslie (1990b: 8) reports that the *Edinburgh and Leith Directory* listed 132 accountants. This suggests a critical mass had been achieved for purposes of formal organization at that time.

Sixty-four individuals were founding members of the SAE in 1854 (sixty-one signed the petition for a royal charter, and a further three were added later in 1854). Fifty-four of the founding members were sole practitioners or partners in public accountancy firms. The remaining ten formed a mix of insurance company managers, court officers and one senior government employee. However, consistent with the wording of the petition for a royal charter, all sixty-one signatories claimed to be professional accountants. These figures suggest the SAE formation in 1854 was not an event involving all Edinburgh professional accountants. Indeed, it is reasonable to suggest that approximately one half of the Edinburgh accountants publicly listed at that time were not invited to join the SAE. Its formation was therefore based on an elitism which is clearly demonstrated in later sections of this paper.

Corfield (1995) offers a detailed analysis of the history of professionalization in the UK from 1700 to 1850. She therefore provides a relevant environmental context in which to place the activities of a small number of professional accountants in Edinburgh in 1853 and 1854. Corfield identifies the fundamental idea of economic class emerging in the eighteenth and early nineteenth centuries, particularly that of a middle class socially positioned between landed and working-class interests. Eighteenth and nineteenth-century professionals challenged the powerful position of the gentry by forming a significant element of what was an untitled and unlanded middle class. Professionals put into operation the idea of owning knowledge rather than titles, land and other forms of wealth. Ownership of knowledge provided power in Foucault's (1980) sense of invisible social disciplining by means of a 'mystery' created by owned knowledge available for purchased service. As is the case today, the early professionals were compensated by a combination of high monetary reward and social status.

The general need for formal organization by means of professional associations emerged as a result of increased competition for professional services, and the persistent existence of 'quacks' claiming a professionalism which inevitably invited criticism and satire. The specific professions of medicine and law had organized in such a way by the eighteenth and nineteenth centuries. In Edinburgh, for example, the Royal College of Surgeons was founded in 1503, the Faculty of Advocates in 1532, the Writers to the Signet in 1564, and the Royal College of Physicians in 1681. These associations were initially run as exclusive clubs, but gradually developed self-regulating organizational structures involving admission, training, examination and disciplining procedures. It should not be surprising, therefore, that, when forming their association, Edinburgh professional accountants used the model of legal practitioners centuries before.[2]

According to Corfield (1995: 32), the 1851 *Census* in Scotland reported 32,181 professionals, of which 4,204 were in the well-established trinity of professions (i.e., church, medicine and law), and 852 were described as accountants. These figures illustrate the broad interpretation given then (and today) to the term 'professional' (data included, for example, government officials, farm managers, army and navy officers and engineers, as well as artists, authors, actors and musicians). The *Census* thus covered all occupations offering expert services based on specialist knowledge. Without formal organization to bring social closure, however, eighteenth and early nineteenth-century professions were open to all individuals claiming ownership of relevant knowledge. Professional associations provided a means of regulating memberships of professions, limiting professional services in response to growing demand and, most importantly, control over the bodies of knowledge underpinning professional activities (Freidson, 1986). In other words, monopoly economics raised the monetary price of professional services, and self-regulation improved non-monetary prestige and reward for the professionals (Larson, 1977).

Although organized because of a specific threat to their economic self-interest (Kedslie, 1990b; Walker, 1995), it would be surprising if Edinburgh accountants had not been generally influenced by these matters by mid-nineteenth century. An important key to professional respectability was a royal charter to incorporate a professional association. Medical and legal practitioners in Edinburgh had achieved this mark of social respectability prior to the nineteenth century. For example, the Writers to the Signet were chartered in 1797. Thus, once institutionalized in 1853, sixty-one IAE members petitioned for a royal charter of incorporation as the SAE in 1854 (Brown, 1905: 8). At this time, there were 132 individuals described as accountants in Edinburgh (Kedslie, 1990b: 208). In 1853, forty-three Glasgow accountants formed the Institute of Accountants and Actuaries in Glasgow (IAAG) (Brown, 1905: 210). In 1854, forty-nine IAAG members petitioned for a royal charter. The total accountant population in Glasgow at that time was approximately 150 (Kedslie, 1990b: 12). As both the IAE/SAE and IAAG formations and petitions were by invitation, and given the known number of accountants locally and nationally, it is reasonable to deduce that exclusivity was practised by the mid-nineteenth-century Scottish accountancy professionals seeking their royal-chartered status.

An overview of the IAE and SAE institutionalization process is given in Table I. It reveals a steady progression from an original group of fifteen invitees in 1853 to one of sixty-four SAE founding members. These data were derived directly from IAE and SAE Council Sederunt and Minute Books (1853-5).

In 1853, the initial group of fifteen invitees (eight of whom attended the first meeting) expanded to eighteen (thirteen attending the second meeting), then to forty-eight (forty-seven at the third meeting) and, finally, to sixty-five suggested and originating IAE members. During 1854, eleven IAE members left the organization, and seven individuals joined it. This resulted in sixty-one IAE members signing the petition for a royal charter to incorporate the SAE. A further three members were admitted after the signing of the petition, which gave the SAE its sixty-four founding members. The following sections describe this sequence in greater detail and, by relating the social and occupational characteristics of the key individuals, reveal the elitist nature of the participants.

TABLE I *The IAE/SAE institutionalization events*

	Invitees	Meetings 1	Meetings 2	Meetings 3	IAE Member	1854 Change	SAE Petition
Sent letter	15						
Attended		8					
Additional invitees	3						
Attended			13				
Additional invitees*	30						
Attended				47			
Additional invitees*	17						
Suggested IAE members					65		
Removed or resigned						(11)	
Additional members						7	
SAE petitioners							61
Additional members							3
SAE members							64

*Given eighteen individuals invited to the first two meetings, and sixty-five proposed members, an additional forty-seven men must have been invited. Thirty of them attended the third meeting.

The formation meetings

An important commentary to the IAE/SAE formation events was written by Richard Brown (1905). Brown was indentured in 1872 to Kenneth Mackenzie, an invitee to the initial IAE meetings, a founder member of the SAE, its Treasurer from 1853 to 1863 and, twice, an SAE Council member previous to 1879. Brown was SAE Secretary and Treasurer from 1892 to 1916. However, all relevant facts described in his text have been verified from relevant IAE/SAE Council and general meeting minutes.

On 17 January 1853, Alexander W. Robertson, a sole practitioner of accountancy, wrote a letter inviting fourteen other accountancy practitioners in Edinburgh to a meeting in his chambers on 20 January to consider the formation of an association of professional accountants. Aged 35, Robertson came from a well-known Edinburgh legal family (his uncle was a judge, and his father was a Writer to the Signet and a director of the Scottish Widows Fund). He had started his public accountancy practice in 1842, and much of his work related to the courts (e.g., sequestrations, bankruptcies and trusts) and managing insurance companies. The wording of Robertson's letter suggests prior planning. He stated that 'several gentlemen connected with our profession have resolved to bring about some definite arrangement for uniting the professional accountants in Edinburgh' (Brown, 1905: 203). Table II identifies the invitees and attendees at the first meeting. It is debatable whether all of the 'several gentlemen' mentioned in his letter were invited to or attended the meeting on 20 January.

TABLE II *The first meeting*

Individuals	Invitations	Meeting 1	Council	Petition
Borthwick, A.	*	*	*	*
Dickson, J. J.	*			*
Dickson, T. G	*			*
Esson, G. A.	*			*
Horne, A.	*		*	*
Martin, T.	*	*		*
Mackenzie, K.	*	*	t	*
Meldrum, G.	*	*		*
Moncreiff, J. S.	*	*	*	*
Moncreiff, W.	*			*
Pearson, C.	*			*
Raleigh, S.	*	*		*
Robertson, A. W.	*	*	s	*
Scott, T.	*		*	*
Wood, W.	*	*		*

s secretary; t treasurer

The average age of the fifteen invitees was 42.6 years. T.G. Dickson was the youngest at 34, and A. Horne was the oldest at 57. Each individual was an established accountancy practitioner but, as later events reveal and with the exception of Horne, none could be described as among the most senior professional accountants in Edinburgh at that time. Ten of the fifteen, however, were partners in accountancy firms, indicating established and successful practices.

Eight of the fifteen invitees met in Robertson's chambers in Dundas Street. Their average age was 40.3 years, and four were partners. C. Pearson sent his apologies. His senior partner was James Brown who, although not involved in the original invitation, later became the IAE's first President. G. A. Esson was invited and also failed to attend the first meeting. His senior partner, D. Lindsay, was not invited but, like Brown, became a founding IAE Council member. Thus, two of Edinburgh's most respected accountancy firms in 1853 were invited to be represented in the IAE's formation, did not participate, but had senior partners as founding IAE Council members. Six of the fifteen invitees became originating IAE office-bearers (four Council members, the Secretary, and the Treasurer). All eight attendees were petitioners for an SAE royal charter.

Archibald Borthwick chaired the meeting on 20 January 1853, and it is reasonable to assume that he, as chairman, and Robertson, as the host, were two of the 'several gentlemen' mentioned in the invitation letter. Borthwick was descended from titled landowners. His father was the first manager of the National Bank of Scotland. Borthwick trained as a lawyer and had been in accountancy practice since 1834. Two of his (separate) partners, T. Martin and S. Raleigh, were invitees and attendees at the 20 January meeting. Another likely member of the pre-invitation group was Kenneth Mackenzie who became the IAE's first Treasurer (Robertson was its first Secretary). Mackenzie was the son of an Edinburgh Writer to the Signet who had been Deputy Keeper of the Signet, and brother of the owner of a large landed estate near Edinburgh. Through previous and current partnerships, Mackenzie was connected to two other accountants who became IAE members (H. Ivory and G. Todd).

The meeting on 20 January discussed and revised a draft constitution and rules for a professional association to be called the IAE. A second meeting was held on 22 January with thirteen attendees (Table III). The average age of the thirteen attendees was 41. Five were partners and eight sole practitioners. The thirteen included seven of the original eight attendees (Raleigh did not attend the second meeting), other original invitees (J.J. Dickson, W. Moncreiff and T. Scott), and three new invitees (R. Gordon, J. M. Macandrew and J. S. Ogilvy). Of the six new attendees, Moncreiff was the best connected. He was the son of the current Lord Advocate, and was appointed Accountant of Court in 1865. His father and father-in-law were landowners. In practice from 1842, Moncreiff had a former partner who was Treasurer of the Bank of Scotland. Moncreiff and Scott became originating IAE

Council members, and each served in that capacity for several terms. Gordon, Macandrew and Ogilvy never achieved office in the IAE or SAE, but were petitioners for the royal charter. Gordon was a landowner and sole practitioner. Macandrew was the son of a lawyer, sole practitioner and founding member of the Faculty of Actuaries. Ogilvy was the son of an accountant and sole practitioner.

TABLE III *The second meeting*

Individuals	Invitations Meeting 1	Meetings 1	Meetings 2	Council	Petition
Borthwick, A.	*	*	*	*	*
Dickson, J. J.	*		*		*
Dickson, T. G.	*				*
Esson, G. A.	*				*
Gordon, R.			*		*
Horne, A.	*			*	*
Martin, T.	*	*	*		*
Macandrew, J. M.			*		*
Mackenzie, K.	*	*	*	t	*
Meldrum, G.	*	*	*		*
Moncreiff, J. S.	*	*	*		*
Moncreiff, W.	*		*	*	*
Ogilvy, J. S.			*		*
Pearson, C.	*				*
Raleigh, S.	*	*			*
Robertson, A. W.	*	*	*	s	*
Scott, T.	*		*	*	*
Wood, W.	*	*	*		*

s = Secretary; t = Treasurer

At the meeting of 22 January, further revisions were made to the draft constitution and rules for the IAE and, with one exception (W. Moncreiff wished to think further on the matter), it was agreed to form into sections to invite other Edinburgh professional accountants to become founding members. Thus, with the planning stage complete, the next step was to recruit a group of accountants who were deemed suitable to join the proposed IAE. As Macdonald (1995: 192) states: 'So the initial move in crystallizing the membership is similar to the creation of an exclusive club: the founding coterie then select those whom they believe have the necessary qualities and qualifications to match up to themselves.' In the case of the eighteen accountants identified in the planning phase (fourteen of whom attended at least one of the two planning meetings), it is reasonably certain that they knew who they were going to recruit. Forming into sections to do this suggests it was undertaken on the basis of personal knowledge and existing relationships within the accountancy community. Table IV incorporates the main features of the third meeting on 31 January 1853 at which agreement was reached to form the IAE now that the recruitment phase was complete (new entrants to the process are given in italic script).

As a result of the recruitment effort, forty-seven individuals met under the chairmanship of James Brown on 31 January 1853, and agreed to form the IAE and eventually seek a royal charter.[4,5] An initial IAE membership of sixty-five individuals was tabled. It comprised forty-eight ordinary members (accountancy practitioners) and seventeen honorary members (former accountants who were managers of life assurance companies or court appointees). Of the forty-seven attendees, thirty-three ordinary and ten honorary individuals met for first time in this process. Eleven of the sixty-five proposed members

TABLE IV *The third meeting*

Individual	Invitation Meeting 1	Meetings 1	2	3	Proposed Members	Nominating Committee	Council	Petition
Baillie, J. M.				*	o			*
Balfour, R.				*	h			*
Barron, J.				*	h			*
Barstow, C. M.				*	o	*		*
Borthwick, A.	*	*	*	*	o	*	*	*
Borthwick, J.				*	h			
Brown, J.				*	o	*	*	*
Brown, J. A.				*	o			*
Callender, H.					o			*
Carter, F. H.				*	o			*
Chaplin, T. R.					o			*
Christie, R.				*	h			
Christie, R. jun.				*	o			*
Cormack, D.					o			*
Dickie, H. D.					h			
Dickson, J. J.	*		*	*	o			*
Dickson, T. G.	*			*	o			*
Douglas, C.				*	o			*
Dundas, G.				*	o			*
Esson, G. A.	*			*	o			*
Finlay, J. L.				*	h			
Fraser, J.					h			

TABLE IV *Continued*

Individual	Invitation Meeting 1	Meetings 1	2	3	Proposed Members	Nominating Committee	Council	Petition
Gibson, A.				*	o	*		*
Gordon, R.			*	*	o			*
Grant, T.					h			*
Grieve, J.					o			
Horne, A.	*				o	*	*	*
Howden, J.				*	h			*
Hunter, J.					o			*
Ivory, H.					h			
Jamieson, A.					o			*
Lindsay, D.					o	*	*	*
Low, W.					o			*
Macandrew, J. M.			*	*	o			*
Mackenzie, J.					h			
Mackenzie, K.	*	*	*	*	o	*	t	*
Maclagan, D.				*	h			*
Maitland, J.					h			*
Mansfield, T.					o	*	*	*
Martin, T.	*		*	*	o	*	*	*
Meldrum, G.	*		*	*	o	*		*
Mitchell, G. T.					o			*
Moncreiff, J. S.	*	*	*	*	o			*
Moncreiff, W.	*		*	*	o	*	*	*
Murray, G.				*	o	*		*
Ogilvy, J.				*	o	*		*
Ogilvy, J. S.			*	*	o			
Pearson, C.	*			*	o			*
Peddie, D. S.				*	o			*
Raleigh, S.	*		*	*	o			*
Ramsay, G.				*	h			*
Robertson, A. W.	*		*	*	o	*	s	*
Russell, W.				*	o			*
Scott, R. E.				*	o	*	*	*
Scott, T.	*		*	*	o	*	*	*
Smith, W.				*	h			
Souter, D. R.				*	o	*		*
Spottiswoode, R.				*	o			*
Thomson, C. W.				*	o			*
Thomson, W. T.					h			
Todd, G.				*	o			*
Watson, H. G.				*	o	*	*	*
Watson, J.					h			
Wilkie, J.				*	o			*
Wood, W.	*	*	*	*	o			*

h honorary; o ordinary; s secretary; t treasurer

attended none of the three meetings. These included D. Lindsay and T. Mansfield who, despite their lack of attendance, were appointed to a committee to nominate IAE office bearers and Council members. Indeed, of the seventeen members of the nominating committee, six attended at least one of the two earlier meetings, eight were attending their first meeting, and three never attended any meeting to organize the IAE.

The above description of attendees at the third meeting to form the IAE suggests that the participants in the first two meetings had been laying the groundwork for the later entry of several key players. A major clue to this development is the composition of the nominating committee. Eleven of its seventeen members were not involved directly in the two previous planning meetings. The first IAE President, Secretary, Treasurer, and all eight Council members were members of the nominating committee. The President (J. Brown) and five Council members (A. Horne, D. Lindsay, T. Mansfield, R. E. Scott and H. G. Watson) were elected without being present at the planning meetings. In contrast, the Secretary (K. Mackenzie), Treasurer (A. W. Robertson), and one Council member (A. Borthwick) attended all three meetings to form the IAE. The remaining Council members (W. Moncreiff and T. Scott) attended two meetings.

Of the six nominating committee members who were not elected to office in 1853, the most prominent was C. M. Barstow. He was descended from landed gentry, an apprentice of J. Brown, a sole practitioner specializing in court remits, and became SAE President in 1869. A. Gibson was aged 60 years, the son of a lawyer, and a sole practitioner. T. Martin was a future partner of S. Raleigh and elected twice to the SAE Council. G. Murray was a son of the manse, and was elected to the SAE Council in 1876. J. Ogilvy was descended from landed gentry and is thought to have left Edinburgh for Dundee soon after the 1853 formation. D. R. Souter was also descended from landed gentry, and worked in the area of estate accounting and management. He was later elected to the SAE Council. Thus, with the exception of Gibson (perhaps on the grounds of age) and Ogilvy (because of relocation), all members of the nominating committee of 1853 achieved SAE office.

At a fourth meeting on 4 February 1853, the first IAE Council (as stated above) was proposed and approved. Council had, in fact, already met on 1 February to arrange for the printing of the IAE constitution, and to determine accommodation for IAE meetings. There were twenty-one attendees on 4 February, all of whom had attended the previous meeting on 31 January. Five of the eleven office-bearers and Council members elected did not attend (i.e., A. Horne, D. Lindsay, T. Mansfield, W. Moncreiff and T. Scott). This meant that Horne, Lindsay and Mansfield had not been present at any of the four formation meetings. Horne (aged 57 years) was descended from landowners and had a well-established Edinburgh practice. He was a director of the Royal Bank of Scotland, and had been in partnership at various times with two other IAE founding members (R. Christie and J. J. Dickson [who was an original invitee]). Lindsay (aged 57 years) was the son of a landed gentleman, trained as a lawyer, and an established practitioner (auditor of the Scottish Widows Fund and director of the Royal Bank of Scotland). He was in partnership with G. A. Esson, another of the invitees to form the IAE, and later assumed G. A. Jamieson (a founding SAE member). T. Mansfield (aged 53 years) was the son of a banker and landowner, and in partnership with Robert Spottiswoode (one of the IAE founding members who joined the process at the third meeting). He became SAE President following the death of James Brown in 1864.

Three of the founding Council members (R. E. Scott, T. Scott and H. G. Watson) have not been biographically described to this point in the paper. R. E. Scott was a sole practitioner and director of insurance companies who jointly audited the North British Railway with Watson. He became SAE President in 1879. T. Scott was a son of the manse and son-in-law of a Writer to the Signet. H. G. Watson was the son of a naval captain and partner to T. G. Dickson.

The average age of the eleven office-bearers and Council members was 50.6 years, ranging from 35 (A. W. Robertson) to 67 (J. Brown). The average age of the five men who had been involved in the planning phase was 42.4 years. That of the six individuals introduced at the third meeting was 57.5 years. Eight individuals were partners in public accountancy practices, eight had strong connections to the legal profession, eleven to the insurance industry, and eight to the landed gentry. More specifically through family connections, six individuals (Borthwick, Lindsay, Mansfield, Mackenzie, W. Moncreiff and Robertson) had strong ties to the landed gentry and the legal profession, one (J. Brown) to the landed gentry and the ministry, one (Horne) to the landed gentry, one (R. E. Scott) to the legal profession, one (T. Scott) to the ministry and one to the navy (Watson). This would suggest, consistently with Macdonald's (1995) thesis, that the founding Council and office-bearers formed an upper-middle-class grouping in Edinburgh society.

Six of the fifteen original invitees became founding office-bearers or Council members of the IAE. Of the nine who were not appointed, J. J. Dickson (son of the manse and former partner of A. Horne) attended three meetings but never achieved SAE office); T. G. Dickson (son of a lawyer, a partner of H. G. Watson, and who married into the aristocracy) attended two meetings and became SAE President in 1889; T. Martin (a former partner of S. Raleigh) attended four meetings, and twice became an SAE Council member; J. S. Moncreiff (the son and father of Edinburgh accountants) attended three meetings and became an SAE Council member in 1868; C. Pearson (partner of J. Brown, and whose father was Secretary of the Scottish Board of Excise) attended one meeting and became SAE President in 1876; and W. Wood (whose father was Auditor of Excise, and partner of J. Maitland who became Accountant of Court) attended four meetings and thrice became an SAE Council member, and its Treasurer in 1879. G. A. Esson (trained as a lawyer, was a partner of Lindsay at the formation, and was appointed Accountant in Bankruptcy in 1856), G. Meldrum (a sole practitioner since 1842) and S. Raleigh (a partner of Borthwick, and who was appointed Manager of the Scottish Widows Fund in 1859) never a held office in the SAE, although each had roles in the initial committees of the SAE dealing with by-laws and bankruptcy legislation. Indeed, Raleigh convened the bankruptcy committee and was an SAE examiner for twenty-seven years.

The first IAE President, James Brown, was a son of the manse whose grandfather was Moderator of the General Assembly of the Church of Scotland in 1777. He was descended from and married into landed gentry. Commencing his accountancy practice about 1813, he was probably the most respected Edinburgh accountant in 1853. His practice was largely focused on legally-related work such as bankruptcies and trusts, and estate management. He was auditor and then director of the Edinburgh Life Assurance Company, and a director of the Bank of Scotland. He was President of the SAE until his death in 1864 aged 78 years. The SAE *Council Sederunt and Minute Book* (1864) merely notes his death, and records a Council expression of the need to ensure a reasonable rotation of Presidents. This suggests that, by 1864, Brown's occupancy of the Presidential office had outlived its initial usefulness of 1854. His successor, T. Mansfield, was 64 years of age when entering office and died in it four years later.

The royal charter

The formation of the IAE took a very brief period of eighteen days to complete (i.e., from the initial planning meeting on 17 January 1853 to the approval of the IAE Council on 4 February 1853). This further suggests a great deal of pre-planning by a relatively few individuals. Obtaining a royal charter as a means of creating an authoritative and credible professional association took somewhat longer (i.e., from agreeing to seek a charter at the general meeting of 31 January 1853 to its granting on 23 October 1854), The formal history of the IAE covered twenty-three months, beginning on 31 January 1853 and ending on 29 December 1854 with the formation of the SAE. The meetings of the IAE Council held during this period of transition are summarized in Table 5.

The work of Council following the general meeting on 4 February 1853 was initially concerned with providing input to the Lord Advocate on proposed changes to the law of bankruptcy. Such actions provide a basis for the thesis of writers such as Kedslie (1990a, 1990b) that the IAE formation was a response to a threat to Scottish accountants' monopoly in bankruptcy work.[6] The Council meeting on 8 April 1853 also dealt with the collection of membership subscriptions and the resignations of several members (i.e., R. Christie, H. D. Dickie, J. Grieve, H. Ivory and W. T. Thomson). Neither Christie nor Grieve paid a subscription.

TABLE V *Council meetings 1853-4*

Attending	1	2	3	Meetings 4†	5	6	7
Barstow, C. M.					*		
Borthwick, A.	*	*	*	*	*	*	*
Brown, J.	*	*	*	*		*	*
Horne, A.			*				*
Lindsay, D.							
Mackenzie, K.	*	*	*	*	*	*	*
Mansfield, T.	*						
Moncreiff, W.	*			*			
Robertson, A. W	*	*	*	*	*	*	*
Scott, R. E.	*	*	*	*		*	*
Scott, T.	*	*	*	*	*	*	
Souter, D. R.					*		
Watson, H. G.		*				*	*

1 1.2.53; 2 8.4.53; 3 11.5.53; 4 19.4.54; 5 29.5.54; 6 15.6.54; 7 18.12.54

† Lindsay and Mansfield were replaced by Barstow and Souter on 1 February 1854.

The next IAE activity was its first annual meeting of 1 February 1854. At this time, it was agreed that Council members would retire in rotation, two every year. The order of rotation was decided by ballot - i.e., D. Lindsay, T. Mansfield, W. Moncreiff, A. Horne, T. Scott, A.

Borthwick, H. G. Watson and R. E. Scott. Particularly for the earliest rotations, this order coincides reasonably with the level of activity of the individuals concerned at general and Council meetings. Lindsay, Mansfield, Moncreiff and Horne had little or no involvement in the early IAE Council meetings. Indeed, as Table 5 demonstrates, Council activity in 1853 and 1854 was largely in the hands of a small group, i.e., A. Borthwick, J. Brown (President), K. Mackenzie (Treasurer), A. W. Robertson (Secretary), R. E. Scott and T. Scott.

At the meeting of 1 February 1854, six new members were proposed and admitted without examination (i.e., J. C. Fraser, G. A. Jamieson, J. M. Liddell, P. Morison, A. M. Paterson and A. T. Niven). Given the five resignations earlier, there were now sixty-six IAE members (fifty-three ordinary and thirteen honorary). The meeting also unanimously agreed to petition for a royal charter, and Council then proceeded to work on this with the assistance of the IAE law agents Gibson, Craigs, Dalziel and Brodie. The latter was paid £204.9s.6d for this service.

As Table V reveals, Council met four times during 1854, and was largely preoccupied with the petition. However, the meeting on 19 April 1854 was a joint one with the Council of the IAAG to discuss the omission of Glasgow accountants from the court-maintained lists of interim factors on sequestrated estates. At a Council meeting on 18 December 1854 a letter was approved to the Lord President of the Court of Session concerning the need to include members of both the IAE and IAAG on the interim factor list.

The Council meeting of 29 May 1854 agreed to a draft petition for a royal charter prepared by its law agents. A general meeting of twenty-three members of the IAE on 30 May 1854 (at which D. Marshall was admitted without examination) discussed and approved the draft. It was signed by all fifty-four ordinary members. At a Council meeting on 15 June 1854, however, the inconsistency of an IAE constitution permitting honorary members with a draft petition and charter to protect professional accountants in public practice was considered. As a result, the remaining thirteen honorary members of the IAE were communicated with and asked if they wished to translate to ordinary membership or resign from the IAE. Seven individuals agreed to transfer (i.e. R. Balfour, J. Barron, T. Grant, J. Howden, J. Maitland, D. Maclagan and G. Ramsay), and six ceased to be members (i.e. J. Borthwick, J. L. Finlay, J. Fraser, J. Mackenzie, W. Smith and J. Watson) (see Walker, 1988; Kedslie, 1990a). Sixty-one IAE members therefore signed the petition which was eventually granted by Queen Victoria on 23 October 1854.

The petition particularly emphasized the 'long standing and great respectability' of professional accountants, and their involvement in a variety of accounting work which required actuarial and legal knowledge. Insolvencies, bankruptcies, property rights, trusts, sequestrations and court remits were specifically mentioned. Court-related work was likened to that of the Masters in Chancery in English courts. The petitioning strategy was undoubtedly to place the profession of accountancy, on a level with that of lawyers, and to imply the indispensable nature of accounting work to the functioning of the legal system in Scotland. Indeed, the petitioners went so far as to compare part of the work of professional accountants as equivalent to that of senior court officials in England. The benefits of the proposed SAE were identified as 'public'.[7]

The petition's heavy emphasis on law suggests that the petitioners were concerned to be connected with the well-established profession of lawyers. It is therefore unsurprising to find it reported that 62 per cent of the sixty-one petitioners were involved in legal work, and that the formation of the IAE/SAE was part of a deliberate process of monopoly protection with respect to bankruptcy and other court-related legal work (Kedslie, 1990a, 1990b). The more general emphasis in the petition was on the identification of a unique and respected profession of public accountants with an identifiable body of knowledge.[8]

The difficulty over ordinary and honorary memberships in the signing of the petition for a royal charter suggests a change in the IAE/SAE institutionalization process, whereby public accountancy became the single focus (see Walker, 1988; Kedslie, 1990a). Presumably because of prior and existing relationships in 1853 between public accountants and well respected former accountants involved in insurance and court work, it was expedient to include the latter in the IAE on an honorary basis at a reduced fee. Honorary members were presumably believed to enhance the credibility and reputation of the new IAE. However, in 1854, the charter petition had to be written more narrowly in order to emphasis the SAE objective of ensuring the 'proper performance' of public accountancy work. This amended focus immediately conflicted with the wider membership structure of the draft charter. Allowing only the fifty-four ordinary members to sign the petition was not a legally sound option. Consequently, the draft charter was amended to exclude honorary memberships. This meant that, when the petition was signed, seven petitioners (R. Balfour [Insurance], J. Barron [court], T. Grant [banking], J. Howden [Insurance], J. Maitland [court], D. Maclagan [insurance] and G. Ramsay [Insurance]) who were not then in public practice.

The royal warrant of incorporation of the SAE was presented to twenty-two SAE members in general meeting on 29 December 1854. The institutional process was thus complete, less than two years from A. W. Robertson's initial letter of invitation. A final comment, however, needs to be made regarding the men involved in the SAE petition and charter.

As noted above, there were sixty-one petitioners and, therefore, founding members of the SAE. However, at the 29 December 1854 meeting, it was recorded that one petitioner (C. Douglas) resigned in order to pursue a career in London, and three other individuals were approved to become founding SAE members. This meant that the initial membership was sixty-four, dropping to sixty-three with the resignation of Douglas. The three additional accountants were J. Moinet (aged 49 years and manager of the Caledonian Insurance Company); D. Murray (aged 66 years, a sole practitioner and former Deputy Controller of Excise for Scotland); and W. Myrtle (a sole practitioner aged 36 years). These memberships were approved without examination by the SAE on 29 December 1854. The applications of Moinet, Murray and Myrtle were made by petition from the Lord Advocate, father of Council member W. Moncreiff. The reason for this petition is reasonably clear in correspondence between Myrtle and the Lord Advocate (Lord Advocate's Department, 1854). Along with seven other Edinburgh accountants excluded from the SAE charter, Myrtle pleaded a case to be included and, in doing so, threatened to publicly expose what he saw as bias in the selection process. The Lord Advocate appears to have bowed to this pressure, and supported the cases for SAE admission of Moinet, Murray and Myrtle. Moinet was removed from membership in 1855 for failure to pay the required membership fee. He believed he had no need to pay, and sustained a protracted correspondence on the issue with the Secretary, A. W. Robertson.

Post-formation events

The meeting of 29 December 1854 also agreed to several other matters which ensured the SAE was to be founded on a strong basis. The two main concerns were to determine specific rules and regulations by which to govern the organization and its membership (consistent with what is now accepted as professionalization theory), and to provide effective comment to the Lord Advocate on proposals to change the bankruptcy laws. Two committees were created for these tasks, each with a sub-committee to presumably lay the groundwork. Table VI outlines the memberships of these committees.

These committees and sub-committees provide evidence of where particular SAE members' talents were put to work. Twenty-two of the sixty-three existing members were involved - twelve former or current office-bearers (only H. G. Watson was not involved) and ten other members (five of whom were original invitees to the first meeting on 17 January 1853). In fact, on both sub-committees, five of the six members were original invitees. Thus, ten of the fifteen invitees were members of one or other of the sub-committees (which presumably did most of the work for the main committees). Two of the invitees convened the subcommittees (A. Borthwick [by-laws] and S. Raleigh [bankruptcy]). This suggests that the invitee group continued to do what it had been doing since the original invitation, i.e., lay out, discuss and present issues, proposals, and solutions. The most heavily involved individuals appear to have been A. Borthwick, T. Martin, K. Mackenzie, S. Raleigh, A. W. Robertson and R. E. Scott.[9]

TABLE VI *By-laws and bankruptcy*

Members	By-laws Committee		Bankruptcy Committee	
	Main	*Sub*	*Main*	*Sub*
Barstow, C. M.	*		*	
Borthwick, A.	*	*	*	
Brown, J.	*		*	
Dickson, T G.			*	*
Esson, G. A.	*		*	*
Gibson, A.	*			
Horne, A.	*			
Lindsay, D.	*			
Mansfield, T.			*	*
Martin, T.	*	*	*	
Mackenzie, K.	*	*	*	
Macandrew, J. M.	*			
Meldrum, G.			*	*
Moncreiff, J. S.	*			
Moncreiff, W.	*		*	
Peddie, D. S.	*			
Raleigh, S.	*		*	*
Robertson, A. W.	*	*	*	*
Scott, R. E.	*	*	*	
Scott, T.	*	*		
Souter, D. R.	*		*	
Wood, W.	*		*	

The issue of specific rules and regulations for admission of members had arisen at the general meeting of 29 December 1854. Nine individuals had applied at that time (i.e., J. Coventry, T. Dall, J. Latto, R. Murray, A. Paterson, D. Scott, T. Scott jnr, A. B. Tawse and R. Wilson). Their admission was left to the Committee on By-Laws to decide. Council approved this committee's rules for admission and training on 7 February 1855. The rules stipulated that all applicants be time-served and discharged apprentices of SAE members (with exceptions for those trained with lawyers or with sufficient experience outside apprenticeship), and examined on specific subjects by examiners in whatever form the latter felt necessary. At a Council meeting on 13 February 1855, C. Pearson, S. Raleigh and W. Wood were appointed as examiners. It was also decided to admit the outstanding applicants without examination. A Committee of Examinators was then formed, and met for the first time on 22 March 1855 (also including A. Borthwick, J. Brown and A. W. Robertson). They passed a further eight applicants (i.e., J. H. Balgarnie, G. T. Chiene, A. Craig, A. Henderson, D. C. Kerr, J. Ogilvy, C. Robertson and A. G. Smith). These individuals were admitted to membership on 29 March 1855.

Major players

The previous analyses review the institutionalization process of forming the SAE in 1854. From the letter of invitation on 17 January 1853 to the first SAE general meeting on 29 December 1854, there were three IAE planning meetings, four IAE/SAE general meetings and seven IAE/SAE Council meetings (i.e., a total of fourteen meetings). Attendance by the IAE/SAE participants varied. An overall summary is given in Table VII. The data relate to the sixty-one petitioners for an SAE royal charter (ignoring the three late additions because of the Lord Advocate's petition), and are divided between Council and non-Council petitioners.

TABLE VII Overall involvement in the institutionalization process

Participants		Meetings attended			Total
	n	*0-4*	*5-9*	*10+*	
Council members*	13	5	2	6	14
Non-Council members	48	42	6	0	14
Total	**61**	**47**	**8**	**6**	**14**

* Including the offices of President, Secretary, and Treasurer.

The data in Table VII reveal interesting differences (significant at < .01 using the chi square test of significant association). For Council members (including office-bearers), the distribution is bi-modal, i.e., either Council members were heavily involved through the process or they were not. The most involved individuals were A. Borthwick, K. Mackenzie and A. W. Robertson (with attendance of 13 or 14 meetings), followed by J. Brown (the President), R. E. Scott and T. Scott (with attendance of 10 or 11 meetings). Seminar accountants with little or no attendances were A. Horne, D. Lindsay, T. Mansfield, W. Moncreiff and H. G. Watson. Indeed, with a possible maximum sixty-six man-meetings for these latter individuals, they had 24 per cent attendance. Lindsay attended no meetings, Mansfield two, and Horne four. Although joining Council at a late stage, C. M. Barstow and D. R. Souter restricted their attendances to three of the nine meetings available to them.

For non-Council members, the skew of the distribution is towards little or no involvement. However, there was a group of involved individuals, all of whom were invitees to the first two formation meetings. J. J. Dickson, J. M. Macandrew, T. Martin, G. Meldrum, J. S. Moncreiff, J. S. Ogilvy, S. Raleigh and W. Wood attended at least four of the seven meetings available to them. The remaining participation ranged from zero to three meetings. In fact, eleven of the forty-eight non-Council members did not attend any meeting.

Reasons for the variability in IAE/SAE involvement can only be speculated upon. Twelve of the most heavily involved individuals came from the eighteen person group invited to the initial two planning meetings. They were well-established and reputable public accountants with an age range from 35 to 47 years. With the exceptions of J. Brown and R. E. Scott, the most senior Council members tended to participate only occasionally. This suggests that they were elected to Council more to provide respectability to the IAE/SAE than work-related effort. In contrast, the non-Council members who made little or no contribution to IAE/SAE meetings tended to be younger, less-established accountants. Of the forty individuals involved, sixteen were less than 35 years of age at the IAE formation, and six were over 50 years of age. The average age of the group as a whole was 33 years.

Adding the three Lord Advocate nominees to the sixty-one petitioners, it is reasonable to split the founding group of sixty-four individuals into two main groupings, each of two sets. The first grouping comprises fourteen reputable and established public accountants who were the 'workers' in the formation process. They can be classed as such because of their potential to influence the formation process at meetings they attended. In turn, such a grouping can be divided into two sub-groups - the first and most senior was composed of six men elected to Council (including particularly, A. Borthwick, K. Mackenzie and A. W. Robertson), and the second comprised eight others, four of whom later joined the SAE Council. Twelve of the fourteen were elected to join the important By-Laws and Bankruptcy Committees of the SAE on 29 December 1854, and seven were elected to the Committee of Examinators in 1855 (including five of the six Council members).

The second main grouping comprised fifty other accountants, of whom seven were Council members (who were typically very senior in the Edinburgh profession), and with the remaining forty-three typically less experienced and containing all those members not in public practice. Ten of these individuals (six of whom were Council members during 1853-4) were elected to the By-Laws and Bankruptcy Committees. Two became examiners in 1855. These important SAE positions were principally occupied by the most senior members of this second main grouping.

From this overall analysis, it is clear that the IAE/SAE formation and initial functioning was successfully implemented with the primary use of approximately twenty-one key players. The 'inner cabinet' appears to have comprised thirteen Council members and office-bearers, six of whom were regularly and actively involved in the detailed administration. With the exception of H. G. Watson, a 62-year-old partner of T. G. Dickson, all of these individuals were named to the initial SAE committees. As previously determined, the most obvious key players in this group were A. Borthwick, K. Mackenzie and A. W. Robertson, i.e., all experienced but not the most senior public accountants. They were involved in almost every activity associated with the IAE/SAE. An 'outer cabinet' comprised eight individuals in public practice who were non-Council members. Six joined the initial SAE committees. Each person was an original invitee to the formation. Prominent among this group was S. Raleigh, a key figure in the bankruptcy movement of the time (Walker, 1995) and a partner of A. Borthwick.

Conclusions

The formation of the IAE/SAE was effectively the organization of a very special type of club. It was formed by stages in a very elitist way. A small number of influential individuals laid the groundwork and introduced a further few persons of considerable stature within the Edinburgh accounting community to form the governing elite. The initial membership was restricted to approximately one half of the total community of accountants. Selection appears to have been based on a mixture of social background, legal connection, and professional reputation, i.e., particularly with respect to the planners and eventual Council members and office-bearers. Thus, the formation of the IAE/SAE, so often characterized as the creation of a work monopoly with respect to court-related work, can also be characterized as the creation of a social elite. What requires more research in this respect is identification of the crucial relationships which assisted in such a creation, i.e., school, university, master/apprentice, partner and work. This research is the subject of a second paper. Meantime, this paper provides the first detailed accounting of the individuals who characterized the events of 1853 and 1854.

Notes

1. For a historical review of this process, see Lee (1995).
2. Walker (1988) and Kedslie (1990a) particularly emphasize the family and geographical proximity of early public accountants to other professionals such as lawyers.
3. It is useful to reveal the post-1853-4 offices of key individuals in the IAE formation as these provide proxy indicators of their pre-1853-4 status.
4. The urgency of IAE formation is explained in Walker (1995).
5. Brown chaired an 1834 group of Edinburgh accountants who unsuccessfully attempted to organize as a professional association in response to a proposed change in the law dealing with judicial factories (Walker, 1995).
6. Given the existence of an independent Edinburgh General Committee on Bankruptcy-Law Reform (comprising IAE members such as Borthwick and Raleigh) to consider the latter, the reasons for the formation are better explained in the broader argument of Walker (1995) concerning free trade and the merging of Scots and English law.
7. A more detailed analysis of this strategy is contained in Macdonald (1984).
8. The petition therefore fits the argument of Freidson (1986) that professions are dependent on the institutionalization of a formal body of knowledge.
9. Four of these individuals (Borthwick, Martin, Mackenzie and Raleigh) were members of the Edinburgh General Committee on Bankruptcy-Law Reform of 1853.

Bibliography

Brown, R. (ed.) (1905) *A History of Accounting and Accountants*, Edinburgh: Jack.

Carr, E. H. (1987) *What is History?*, London: Penguin.

Collingwood, R. H. (1974) 'Human nature and human history', in R. Gardener (ed.) *The Philosophy of History*, Oxford: Oxford University Press.

Corfield, P. J. (1995) *Power and the Professions in Britain 1700-1850*, London: Routledge.

Friedson, E. (1986) *A Study of the Institutionalization of Formal Knowledge*, Chicago, IL: University of Chicago Press.

Foucault, M. (1980) *Power/Knowledge: Selected Interviews and Other Writings 1972-7*, Brighton: Harvester.

Kedslie, M. J. M. (1990a) *Firm Foundations: The Development of Professional Accounting in Scotland 1850-1900*, Hull: Hull University Press.

Kedslie, M. J. M. (1990b) 'Mutual self-interest - a unifying force: the dominance of societal closure over social background in the early professional accounting bodies', *The Accounting Historians Journal*, December: 1-20.

Larson, M. S. (1977) *The Rise of Professionalism: A Sociological Analysis*, Berkeley, CA: University of California Press.

Lee, T. A. (1995) 'The professionalisation of accountancy: a history of protecting the public interest in a self-interested way', *Accounting, Auditing & Accountability Journal*, 8(4): 48-69.

Lord Advocate's Department (1854) *Papers on The Society of Accountants in Edinburgh Petition*, Edinburgh: Scottish Record Office, AD 56/29 and 81.

Macdonald, K.M. (1984) 'Professional formation: the case of Scottish accountants', *British Journal of Sociology*, June: 174-89.

Macdonald, K. M. (1995) *The Sociology of the Professions*, London: Sage.

Mepham, M. J. (1988) *Accounting in Eighteenth Century Scotland*, New York: Garland.

Society of Accountants in Edinburgh (1853-5, 1864), *Council Sederunt and Minute Books*, Edinburgh: Institute of Chartered Accountants of Scotland.

Stewart, J. C. (1977) *Pioneers of a Profession: Chartered Accountants to 1879*, Edinburgh: Institute of Chartered Accountants of Scotland.

Walker, S. P. (1988) *The Society of Accountants in Edinburgh 1854-1914: A Study of Recruitment to a New Profession*, New York: Garland.
Walker, S. P. (1995) 'The genesis of professional organization in Scotland: a contextual analysis', *Accounting, Organisations and Society*, 20(4): 285-312.

PART 2

POST FOUNDATION EVENTS

The Defence of Professional Monopoly: Scottish Chartered Accountants and "Satellites in the Accountancy Firmament" 1854-1914

Stephen P Walker

> There appears now to hover over the Scotch chartered bodies a cloud at present no bigger than a man's hand which may either disappear or eventually overspread and darken the sky (*The Accountant*, 5 January 1889, pp. 1-2).

Macdonald (1985) has provided a valuable overview of the unsuccessful endeavours of British accountants since 1870 to gain social closure by the most comprehensive and exclusionary device available to professional organizations - a legal monopoly secured by state registration of the occupation. By way of contrast, the first objective of this paper is to analyse a success story - how Scottish chartered accountants (CAs) were able to nurture and defend a monopoly of practice founded not on registration (as in the medical profession) but on the sole possession of Royal Charters of Incorporation - a monopoly acquired before the state assumed a major role in regulating the appointment of auditors which was the source of the *de facto* monopoly subsequently gained by chartered accountants south of the border (ibid., pp. 553-554). This is an account of collective entrenchment and status maintenance, of the preservation of an almost complete monopoly in the provision of accountancy services established on the basis of continuous and exclusive usage of the designation "chartered accountant" and its abbreviate "CA".

Reproduced from *Accounting, Organizations and Society*, Volume 20, Number 4, pp 257-283, Copyright 1991, with kind permission from Elsevier Science Ltd., The Boulevard, Langford Lane, Kidlington, OX5 1GB, UK.

The second aim of the paper is to examine, in the context of mainstream sociological theories of professions, how challenges to the chartered monopoly by two aspirant and tenacious organizations were successfully repelled. The justifications advanced before state institutions for the maintenance of professional privileges are considered in relation to the 'functionalist' analysis of professionalization. The ideological foundations of the attack on the chartered monopoly and the underlying objectives of the chartered societies in defending their domination of the supply of accountancy services, are revealed as evidence of the wider 'critical' approach to the study of the professions.

In addition to the aforementioned primary objectives of the paper, other significant issues are touched upon. The paper is responsive to demands for a more thorough insight into the development of organized accountancy (Burchell *et al.*, 1980; Willmott, 1986), current understandings being poor in relation to the significance of the profession in modern economies and lacking when compared with the wealth of research into the longer-established professions, particularly medicine. One characteristic of the U.K. accountancy profession which renders its study complex and challenging is its representation by a succession of separate organizations. This disunified structure reflects spatial factors, the emergence of specialisms and, as will be illustrated, is a result of the development of local monopolies among the early associations of professional accountants. The socio-economic advantages acquired by the founder organizations resulted in the emergence of aspirant associations of excluded practitioners who demanded and fought for equality of status with the established professionals - challenges which perpetuated inter-organizational discord.

The relationship between accounting knowledge and professional privilege analysed by Richardson (1988) is also relevant. The most potent single justification advanced by the Scottish chartered societies for the maintenance of monopolistic control (and the concomitant economic rewards to their memberships) was the unequal inter-organizational distribution of "pure" accounting knowledge. The singular attempts of the chartered societies to codify, institutionalize and control that knowledge prior to the organization of other practitioners, enabled them to advocate the existence of a major gulf in professional status between themselves and their competitors. The introduction of the examination as a device for testing the acquisition of the knowledge required for practice and in the professionalization of accounting organizations (Hoskin & Macve, 1986) is also revealed as having been significant for the acceptance of professional monopoly.

Before discussing the nature of the chartered accountants' monopoly, some background narrative is provided.

The protagonists - organizational responses to the emergence of a professional monopoly

The defenders of professional monopoly comprised the three organizations which merged to form the Institute of Chartered Accountants of Scotland in 1951: the Society of Accountants in Edinburgh (constituted in 1853 and chartered in 1854), the Institute of Accountants and Actuaries in Glasgow (formed in 1853 and chartered in 1855) and the Society of Accountants in Aberdeen (founded in 1866 and chartered in 1867) (Brown, 1905; Stewart, 1977; Jones, 1981; Walker, 1988).

The three local chartered societies were the sole organizations of professional accountants in Scotland until the autumn of 1880 when the Scottish Institute of Accountants was founded in Glasgow. The impetus to the formation of the Scottish Institute (which boasted 33 original members) was the granting of the first 'national' charter to a British society of accountants - the Institute of Chartered Accountants in England and Wales (ICAEW) in May 1880. The Scottish Institute of Accountants comprised the principal challenger to the chartered monopoly until the mid-1890s when the mantle of leading agitator passed to the Corporation of Accountants, Ltd. The Corporation was registered under the Companies Acts and was constituted during November 1891 by seven radical members of the Scottish Institute who had become disillusioned with the Institute's failure to break the CA monopoly (*The Corporate Accountants' Yearbook*, 1936, p. 505).

The Corporation was to adopt a more direct and provocative approach by concentrating its efforts on the central contention - the chartered societies' claim to exclusive usage of the notation "CA": the Corporation's title could be abbreviated to CA and its articles of association encouraged members to emulate that professional designation (Corporate Accountants, Ltd., Articles, 2230/2, p. 6).

Until the emergence of the rival Scottish Institute of Accountants in 1880, the three locally organized chartered societies were characterized by an envious detachment (*The Accountant,* 1885, p. 4). The Edinburgh society was considered dominant in membership and prestige (Walker, 1988, pp. 16-18). With the challenge to their control of the profession in Scotland, the geographical and status demarcations of the CA societies were superceded by a unity of purpose necessary to resist the threat to their paramount mutual interest: the defence of the monopolized supply of professional services north of the border. The new found commonality of the Edinburgh, Glasgow and Aberdeen societies was epitomized by institutional federation during the 1890s: in 1893 a uniform education system was introduced under a General Examining Board, a directory of members was published in 1896, *The Accountants' Magazine* first appeared in 1897 and members of the three societies were to be referred to henceforth under the collective title of "Chartered Accountants of Scotland" (Privy Council, 1896, Opponent's Case, pp. 7-8; Woolf, 1912, p. 166).

The professional arena

Whereas the protagonists in the debate on the registration of the accountancy profession fought before the legislature by formulating and opposing a succession of private bills (of which 17 were presented to Parliament from 1891 to 1912 according to Woolf (1912, p. 185)), those in the Scottish professional arena during the 1854-1914 period fought their major battles before institutions performing judicial functions - *ad hoc* committees of the Privy Council constituted for hearing applications for Royal Charters and the highest court in Scotland, the Court of Session.

The emphasis on litigious activity was symptomatic of several factors. From the perspective of the three chartered societies, gaining statutory ratification for their monopoly was unlikely given the demonstrable failure of legislation for the profession which, on each occasion after 1890, was opposed by one or more of the many contending and disparate organizations of British accountants. Editorials in *The Accountants' Magazine* frequently questioned the prudence of expending time and money on draft legislation given that the whole profession was unlikely to agree to it (January 1898, pp. 1-2). Hence, when Scottish registration bills were presented to the legislature (as in 1896-1898) they were essentially a response to, or supplementary to, activities before the Privy Council and designed to maintain sectional interests during the peak of the debate on British registration (see *The Scottish Accountant*, April 1896, pp. 90-91).

From the viewpoint of the challengers to the chartered monopoly - the Scottish Institute and the Corporation - litigation was preferred as the chartered societies' claim to exclusive use of the "CA" designation was based on contestable legal foundations. Further, it was necessary for the competing organizations to gain identical "CA" status and thus ensure equality of treatment in any proposed regulatory legislation emanating from one of the British accountancy organizations (see *The Scottish Accountant,* January 1893, p. 63).

Sociological approaches to the study of the professions and professional monopoly

The emergence and defence of the monopoly acquired by Scottish CAs during the second half of the nineteenth century and the arguments advanced for its devolution are analysed here in the context of two of the mainstream theoretical approaches to the sociology of the professions summarized by Willmott (1986).

The functional approach is rooted in Durkheim's theory of social solidarity which is maintained by the division of labour and occupational differentiation in industrial societies (Durkheim, 1933). The professional association, in regulating the conduct and behaviour of its members and by instilling primary orientation to the public interest, is the example to the rest of society as to the means of preserving moral order (see also Halmos, 1970). The identification of professions and the attainment of professional status is conditional upon the exhibition of organizational and membership traits as evidence of the performance of their fundamental function in society. The identification of the definitive set of professional characteristics has proved elusive though most commentators enumerate: an intellectual basis to practice acquired by specialist training and education –"the distinguishing mark of the professional" according to Carr-Saunders and Wilson (1933, p. 200); a code of ethical behaviour; professional autonomy; and altruism as opposed to self-interest (Greenwood, 1962; Gross, 1958; Hughes, 1963).

Functionalists contend that the high rewards gained by professionals and the privileges attained by their associations are legitimated by their provision of essential services to the community (Barber, 1963). Through the imposition of formalized systems of recruitment and training, the professional organization ensures that only the competent gain access to the occupation. Income differentials and status rewards provide the necessary inducement to those with appropriate abilities to undergo the rigours of vocational preparation and to occupy the functionally important professional positions in the division of labour (Davis and Moore, 1945).

Claims about the acquisition of such functionalist professional traits by the defenders of, and challengers to, professional monopoly constituted the central 'public' arguments before the Privy Council and the Court of Session. The success of the Scottish Institute of Accountants and the Corporation depended on the exhibition of the professional characteristics previously attained by the established local chartered societies. Conversely, the most persuasive arguments employed by the chartered societies for the maintenance of their monopoly rested on the functionalist concept that their privileges had been sanctioned by the community as the fair reward for the provision of essential accountancy services by competent practitioners.

Two early students of the profession whose analysis was to become associated with the functionalist school, Carr-Saunders and Wilson (1933), elucidated the concept of "institutional monopoly" which also underpinned the chartered accountants explanation for the source of their domination of the supply of professional services. According to Carr-Saunders and Wilson, a professional organization could gain market control in the absence of statutory regulation of practice on the basis of "institutional advantages":

> Some degree of monopolistic advantage may be won by a particular group of practitioners in an unregistered profession. In that it accrues, not to the registered since there is no register, but to the members of an association of practitioners, and it does so whenever the association succeeds in making membership as much a hall-mark of qualification as admission to the register in a state-regulated profession (1933, p. 358).

The extent to which a professional organization achieves an institutional monopoly depends on the existence of favourable circumstances such as a limited and wealthy clientele (as in the actuarial profession) or, the adoption and legal recognition of an exclusive professional title which becomes equated in the consciousness of the clientele as a testimonial of superior qualifications (as in the CA profession). Such arguments had been advanced by the Scottish chartered societies during the 1880s and 1890s - their economic dominance was symptomatic of 'CA' becoming established as a mark of exceptional professional proficiency and service compared with lesser accountants.

The critique of the chartered monopoly offered by the Scottish Institute and the Corporation of Accountants, challenging the underlying objectives and behaviour of the chartered societies in defending their privileges, is most usefully analysed in terms of an alternative critical approach to the study of professions.

The critical approach examines the broader economic and political conditions necessary for the achievement of professional status. Successful professionalization is not dependent on societal recognition of the functional significance of the provision of necessary services but "upon recognition and acceptance of the claims of aspiring professionals by powerful others (e.g. agents of the state) and, in particular, their capacity to 'responsibly' and 'reliably' regulate the quality of their valued services" (Willmott, 1986, p. 538).

The professional association is not instigated to ensure the efficient and competent discharge of professional functions but is a means to the achievement of the collective social mobility of practitioners (Macdonald, 1984, 1987). Through the imposition of a series of closure practices motivated by self-interest, the organization asserts, maintains and protects monopolistic control of professional services (Parry and Parry, 1977). Closure is achieved by the introduction of recruitment systems to restrict entry and by state recognition of the exclusive practice of a vocation or sanction of acquired restrictive privileges. It was one such means of attaining social closure which formed the central focus of the challenge to the Scottish chartered accountants - the adoption, exclusive usage and subsequent legal protection of the professional title – 'CA'.

Such a closure mechanism was recognized by Weber who noted the increasing use of credentials in the formation of privileged groups and in legitimating the socio-economic rewards derived from advantaged status (Gerth and Wright Mills, 1948, pp. 240-244). The institution of examinatory testing imputed valued to diplomas, restricted access to the certified elite and thus encouraged the continuation of the privileged stratum. According to Parkin, such credentialism - which he defines as "the inflated use of educational certificates as a means of monitoring entry to key positions in the division of labour" (1979, p. 54) - comprises a particularly effective exclusionary device "for protecting the learned professions from the hazards of the market place" (p. 56; see also Larson, 1977, pp. 239-240).

Before investigating the defence of their privileges, the development and extent of the chartered accountants' monopoly is described.

The adoption of distinctive professional credentials

Most likely, it was in emulation of their close occupational associates, the legal profession (where notations such as WS-Writer to the Signet - and SSC-Solicitor to the Supreme Courts - had long been used), that 35 members of the Society of Accountants in Edinburgh resolved on 30 January 1855 "that members of the Society do assume the abbreviate letters 'C.A.' and attach the same to their names" (Interdict Case, Print of Documents, p. 3). Following its acquisition of a Royal Charter in 1855, members of the Glasgow Institute determined likewise, on 29 January 1856, to designate themselves as chartered accountants and CAs. The Aberdeen Society, on receiving its charter in 1867, conformed and announced in the local press that its members would adopt the same professional title.

Although use of the terms 'chartered accountant' and 'CA' was reputedly immediate and universal among members of the Glasgow and Aberdeen societies (Interdict Case, Proof, p. 47), there was some apparent initial reticence in Edinburgh. In the *Edinburgh and Leith Post Office Directory, 1856-7,* 27 of the 68 members of the Society for whom an occupation is provided were not referred to as 'CA' in any section of the directory. Archibald Borthwick, Donald Lindsay (senior partner of the then largest accountancy firm in Edinburgh) and James Brown (President of the Edinburgh Society 1853-1864) who comprised "about the most leading professional accountants in Scotland at the time" (Interdict Case, Proof, p. 38), habitually continued to designate themselves as "accountant" or, the more ancient, "accomptant", until their retirements during the 1860s. By 1892, however, the President of the Edinburgh Society could assert that "as time went on, and the older men dropped off, the name became more generally used", and that now "there is nobody in our society who shows a disposition to object to the letters 'C.A.'" (Interdict Case, Proof, p. 31).

The distinctive professional designations adopted by the members of the three chartered societies were rapidly recognized among their clientele - the legal, commercial and manufacturing communities. Charles B. Logan, Writer and Deputy Keeper of the Signet, confirmed, in 1892. that the nomenclature 'CA' was well known:

> I have no doubt that my professional brethren. and persons engaged in business generally, understand these letters in the same way as I do, as designating members of the three bodies. I have to do with banks and insurance companies, as well as mercantile matters in connection with the management of estates, in all those branches of my business I find that "chartered accountant" and "CA" designate what I have described, and are understood by others in that way (Interdict Case, Proof, p. 16).

In addition to the continuous usage of the professional titles, the members of the Scottish chartered societies could also claim their exclusive usage for 36 years until the Corporation of Accountants, Ltd was formed in 1891. Previous instances of non-members poaching the designations were rare and consisted mainly of members of the English and Welsh Chartered Institute (incorporated in 1880), of whom there were 18 in Edinburgh, Glasgow and Aberdeen in 1890, duplicating 'chartered accountant' and in a few cases, affixing to their names 'CA' rather than the conventional 'ACA' or 'FCA'.[1]

The mere use of a peculiar professional credential was, by itself, insufficient foundation upon which to gain market control. The prime source of the monopoly constructed by the Scottish chartered accountants was to increase the currency of the notations by ensuring their recognition as a mark of professional and academic superiority over unorganized and unqualified accountants. Proponents of the chartered societies' cause utilized a functionalist interpretation of the development of their monopoly. Whereas the letters 'CA' "when originally used, merely expressed the simple fact that the person using them was a Member of a Body or Society of Accountants Incorporated by Royal Charter" (Privy Council, 1890, Appendix, pp. 76-77), following the institution of increasingly sophisticated systems of professional education by the chartered societies, particularly from the 1870s (see Walker, 1988, ch. 4), they came to represent an "appreciated guarantee to the public of professional efficiency and good standing and conduct" (Privy Council, 1890, Appendix, pp. 76-77).

By thus retaining the exclusive and continuous use of the designation 'CA' and by nurturing it as a hallmark of the provision of superior professional services for over 30 years, the Scottish chartered accountants succeeded in creating a status dichotomy between themselves and competing accountants. In evidence of this achievement, a succession of senior lawyers and businessmen testified in 1892 to the high public esteem of those who could attach to their names 'CA' and declared their preference for employing CAs due to their unique professional status, thorough education, high character and respectability (Interdict Case, Proof, pp. 6-65). By contrast, members of the Scottish Institute of Accountants who had been recently admitted as CAs, confessed to previously having lost appointments through not being entitled to the designation (pp. 57, 59). As *The Accountant* was to state in 1893 "if numerical majority and public esteem go for anything - the terms 'Chartered Accountants,' and 'the Accountancy Profession' are practically synonymous" (15 July, p. 634).

Not surprisingly, the CAs themselves were fully cognizant of the significance of their designation in the competition for the provision of professional services. In 1892 Richard Brown, Secretary of the Edinburgh Society, was asked the rhetorical question:

Have you found that the fact of a man being a member of one of three
Chartered Societies and designating himself "CA" helps to get
business? (A.) No doubt of it. I know that in making appointments,
not only in competition with private employment but for auditorships
or other *quasi* public offices, that is looked to (Interdict Case, Proof,
p. 34).

The extent of the chartered monopoly

On the basis of their institutional advantages, the Scottish chartered
accountants succeeded in creating a differentiated market in which they
gained an almost complete monopoly of the most lucrative accountancy
appointments while the unchartered and unorganized contested the less
remunerative business. In 1884, the Edinburgh Society claimed that "at
least nine-tenths" of the whole business of accountants was, and had
been for many years, conducted by CAs (Privy Council, 1890,
Appendix, p. 93). In 1890 the chartered societies jointly asserted that
95% of the important business outside the Courts was handled by their
members and that the workload of non-CAs consisted mainly of minor
sequestrations (Privy Council, Opponent's Case, p. 12). In 1896, in
opposition to a third application of the Scottish Institute of Accountants
for a Royal Charter, the chartered societies presented the most
comprehensive analysis of the registered business of accountants in
Scotland for the previous year. The statistics, which are summarized in
Table I, revealed the extent of concentration particularly in the
increasingly voluminous and lucrative branch of auditing.

The Scottish Institute of Accountants objected that such analyses
of registered business were misleading and unrepresentative due to the
exclusion of smaller, private audits which, it claimed, constituted "the
greater mass of accounting business by which the profession lives, and
makes its money" (Privy Council, 1896, Speeches, pp. 92-93). The
evidence, however, proved the existence of a differentiated market for
professional services and how the CAs were increasingly dominant at
its upper, most remunerative end.

Given this fact and the increasing intervention of the state in
regulating the appointment of public auditors by the last third of the
nineteenth century, it was vital, in order to increase their memberships
and ensure organizational survival, that the sub-class of accountants in
Scotland gain a share of the superior workload. To achieve that
objective they required equal privileged status by use of the
professional designation that was the source of the chartered monopoly
- the letters 'CA'.

TABLE I *Distribution of accountancy appointments in Scotland, 1895*

Occupation of appointee	Nature of appointments (%)			
	Public audits	Judicial factories	Estates wound-up*	Total
Scottish CA	85.4	29.4	45.0	44.9
SIA member	4.0	2.8	10.7	5.2
Accountant	3.1	2.9	8.3	4.4
Non-accountant	7.5	64.9	36.0	45.5
N	483	1267	666	2416
Capital value (where known £m)	227.5	0.3	5.8	233.6
Percentage of accountants' business held by CAs				
Number	92.3	83.8	70.4	82.3
Value	98.9	93.0	92.5	98.8
Percentage of total business held by CAs				
Number	85.4	29.4	45.0	44.9
Value	98.7	35.6	48.2	97.4

*Includes statistics for companies liquidated 1892-5 and cessios and sequestrations for the year ending 31 October 1895.

The objective: CA

That the principal aim of the Scottish Institute of Accountants and of the Corporation of Accountants was to acquire equal 'CA' standing was to become abundantly clear from their contests with the chartered societies before the Privy Council and the Scottish Courts. In 1892, an ex-President of the Scottish Institute admitted that "To my mind, the chief object in applying for a charter was to enable the other members seeking it, and myself to call ourselves chartered accountants, and to use the initial letters 'C.A.'" (Interdict Case, Proof, p. 74). At the hearing concerning the Scottish Institute's application for a charter in 1890, the chartered societies proposed to withdraw their opposition provided that members of the new incorporated society used an alternative designation such as 'PA' - Provincial Accountant - and were prohibited from using 'chartered accountant' and 'CA'. The Scottish Institute refused. Similarly, at the subsequent hearing before the Privy Council in 1896, counsel for the Scottish Institute of Accountants responded in the affirmative to the comment from a committee member that "The inference is that you are exceedingly anxious under any pretext to call yourselves Chartered Accountants; that is really the long and short of it" (Speeches, p. 51).

The Corporation of Accountants, Ltd was unashamedly created and constituted to advance the mimetic objective of its members to designate themselves as CAs - Corporate Accountants - and thereby "identify themselves with the members of the corporations, and to share that amount of reputation and public confidence which the latter, in virtue of their membership, enjoy" (*Cases Decided in the Court of Session*, 1892-3, p. 754). As *The Scottish Accountant* remarked in 1894, "The *raison d'etre* of this Society's existence cannot he disguised or denied, was to appropriate to those who might join its membership any benefit which the use of the letters 'C.A.' might be supposed to confer" (April, p. 182).

It was feasible for the Scottish Institute and the Corporation to endeavour to attain equality of professional status due to the fact that the Scottish chartered societies had no codified legal foundation for their claim to exclusive usage of the term 'chartered accountant' and its abbreviate 'CA'. As a correspondent to *The Glasgow Herald* noted in 1892, it was the societies in Edinburgh, Glasgow and Aberdeen that received charters and not their members, hence, the expression 'CA' is an anomaly, as strictly speaking, no such individual exists" (*The Accountant*, 13 February 1892, p. 141). Furthermore, whereas the charter of the English and Welsh Institute of 1880 contained a provision for its members' use of professional titles, the earlier Scottish charters did not and the names of their organizations were also devoid of the term 'chartered accountants'. Although the Edinburgh Society adhered to the tenuous assertion that 'chartered accountant' was recognized by Parliament in the Act of 1887 establishing its annuity fund, a former President in 1892 admitted the following in Court:

> (Q) When did you get the exclusive privilege of using the name "chartered accountant" or the initials C.A.? (A.) We did not get it by Act of Parliament or by charter. . . it was done by resolution of our own body. (Q) You have no other title to it except that? (A.) No (Interdict Case, Proof, p. 28).

In the absence of codification, the chartered societies were compelled to advance their right to sole use of the 'CA' credentials on the contentious grounds of prior possession and continuous usage or 'long use and wont' which invited legal verification. The claim to exclusive use was also contestable as the chartered societies had exhibited toleration of the adoption of 'chartered accountant' and 'CA' by the members of successively incorporated organizations. The Edinburgh Society did not object to the Glasgow Institute assuming the designations in 1856, neither contested the resolution of the Aberdeen Society to do likewise 12 years later, and all three organizations failed to examine the legality of members of the English and Welsh Institute who practised in Scotland under the 'chartered accountant' title (Interdict Case, Proof, pp. 2, 13, 29-30, 47). The chartered societies justified their inactivity by claiming that each of these organizations had received a charter thus entitling their members to the same designation. Why then, should aspiring organizations of Scottish accountants not attempt to gain incorporated status or adopt the 'CA' credential in the expectation that their use would be similarly tolerated by the existing societies. Figure I outlines their determined attempts to acquire the 'CA' title and thus break the chartered societies' monopoly.

FIGURE I *Chronological listing of challenges to the chartered monopoly*

Year and disputant	Strategy and outcome
1884 Scottish Institute of Accountants	Petition for a Royal Charter (first) which proposed that Institute members use the 'CA' notation. Opposed by the chartered societies and rejected without a hearing before the Privy Council following the submission of report by the Lord Advocate (John B. Balfour).
1886 Scottish Institute of Accountants	Sought consensus with the CA societies for a joint application to incorporate a united Scottish profession. The chartered societies refused to co-operate.

FIGURE I *Continued*

Year and disputant	*Strategy and outcome*
1889-1890 Scottish Institute of Accountants	Petition for a Royal Charter (second) as 'The Incorporated Society of Accountants in Scotland'. The petition was opposed by the CAs and rejected by the Privy Council following a three day hearing.
1891 Scottish Institute of Accountants	Application for Incorporation under The Companies Act, 1867 as 'The Incorporated Society of Accountants in Scotland'. The CA societies lodged a successful objection on the grounds that the title implied representativeness of the whole profession in Scotland.
1891-1893 Corporation of Accountants, Ltd.	Incorporation under the Companies Acts with articles containing a provision that members designate themselves 'Corporate Accountant' or "any initial or abbreviation thereof". The CA societies raised an action in February 1892 indicting the Corporation from using the 'CA' notation which was granted by Lord Kyllachy in the Court of Session in January 1893 and upheld on appeal in May. The Corporation's use of 'CA' was considered an invasion of the Royal Charters and the appropriation of the status and pecuniary benefits by individuals not bound by the charters constituted a legal wrong. (*Cases Decided in the Court of Session,* 1892-3, pp. 750-759; *The Scottish Law Reporter,* 1892-1893, pp. 667-684; *The ScotsLaw Times,* 3 June 1893, pp. 41-42).

FIGURE I *Continued*

Year and disputant	Strategy and outcome
1895-1896 Scottish Institute of Accountants	Petition for a Royal Charter (third) as 'The Scottish Provincial Institute of Accountants' craving use of the designation CPIA (Chartered Provincial Institute of Accountants). The chartered societies attempted to override this potentially successful petition by presenting The Accountants (Scotland) Bill to Parliament in March 1896 which proposed that only existing CAs could use that designation in the future. The petition was also opposed and rejected following a Privy Council hearing in May 1896. The Bill was consequently withdrawn in July of Accountants (*The Scottish Accountant,* July 1896, p.103).
1896-1898 Scottish Institute of Accountants	Incorporation via Accountants (No. 2) Bill introduced in July 1896 and 1897-1898 session. The chartered societies responded by re-introducing the opposing Accountants (Scotland) Bill. Both bills were withdrawn or obstructed before a second reading.
1900-1903 Corporation of Accountants, Ltd.	Company resolution to adopt the designation 'MCA' in November 1900. The Corporation sought a declarator from the Court of Session to confirm their entitlement to use 'MCA' and prevent the CAs object "to crush the Corporation out of existence" (*The Accountants' Magazine,* January 1903, p. 46). Lord Kincairney adjudicated in November 1903 that 'MCA' infringed the decision in the 'CA case' of 1893 (*The Accountant,* 1903, pp.143-145,1433-1448, 1475-1476; *The Scots Law Times,* 28 November 1903, pp. 424-426).

FIGURE I *Continued*

Year and disputant	Strategy and outcome
1905 Corporation Accountants, Ltd	Company resolution to adopt the designation of 'FCRA' (Fellow of the Corporate Registered Accountants). The CA societies offered no formal objection (Corporation of Accountants, Ltd 2230/22, p. 14).

The 'MCA case' was final confirmation that the chartered societies had gained legal protection for their exclusive use of the professional credential that underpinned and represented their monopoly. On the strength of the Scottish decisions of 1893 and 1903, cases were brought before the English courts in 1906-1907, the outcome of which provided legal protection for the designations of English and Welsh chartered and incorporated accountants (see Stacey, 1954, pp. 75, 77-78, 84; *The Accountant*, 1906-1907; *The Incorporated Accountants' Journal*, 1906, 1907).

The major threats to the Scottish CA's privileges were the applications of the Scottish Institute of Accountants for a Royal Charter and the litigation that emanated from the activities of the Corporation of Accountants.

At the public proceedings where the economic domination of the CAs was placed on trial, the Scottish Institute and the Corporation argued that the chartered monopoly contradicted several strands of prevailing socio-political philosophy and adopted a 'critical' interpretation of the CAs' privileges - revealing the motives of the chartered societies as essentially self interested. The CAs successfully repelled their opponent's case by constructing a more alluring defence based upon a functionalist perspective of the role and characteristics of the professions in the nineteenth century context.

The functionalist defence of professional monopoly

Monopoly vs the public interest

The Scottish CAs were compelled to justify the existence of their monopoly given its contradiction of free market liberalism (see Berlant, 1975, pp. 145-167). According to James Martin (1844-1935) (see *The Corporate Accountants' Year Book*, 1936, pp. 504-506), the founder and Secretary of the Corporation of Accountants, the opposition of the chartered societies to the demands of the aspiring organizations of Scottish accountants was a selfish design to "protect and extend their own monopoly" (*The Accountant*, 8 July 1893, p. 631), to destroy their competitors and "secure all professional business for themselves" (1908, p. 8). Martin claimed that their dominance in the supply of accountancy services inevitably resulted in CAs imposing exhorbitant fees on an apathetic public and that this, together with a host of other consequential malpractices, constituted "the systematic robbery and plunder of the public" (1896a, p. 23). Similarly, at the hearing before the Privy Council on the Scottish Institute's 1889 application for a charter, the opposition of the chartered societies was described as "purely professional opposition, prompted by professional exclusiveness and a desire to maintain for themselves that monopoly which they have up to the present enjoyed" (Speeches, 1890, p. 90).

In an unapologetic defence of their monopoly, the chartered societies assumed a functionalist retort and appealed to higher, service orientated values. They denied that their three organizations positively strived for economic domination and asserted that their monopoly was, in fact, the outcome of free competition between individual CAs and other accountants. The accountants begin, claimed counsel for the chartered societies in 1890, with a "perfectly fair field; the business is open to one as to other". Yet, on the basis of over 30 years of "public experience and public comparison", CAs had received the bulk of appointments (Privy Council, Speeches, pp. 77-78). The monopoly was a monopoly "in the sense that to a very large extent the public themselves, whose interests I am now speaking of, have selected the members of the Chartered Societies as against gentlemen, particularly the members of the Scottish Institute" (p. 62). Monopoly was the CAs' reward for the efficient discharge of accountancy services to the community.

The chartered monopoly and its maintenance were absolved on the grounds that it was the public - the protection of whose interests was the paramount consideration - who had freely determined to employ CAs rather than other accountants. Dismantling the monopoly would thus constitute an interference with the public will, with the process of public selection and would not be conducive to the efficient discharge of professional services which the public considered were most competently performed by CAs.

The chartered societies were also to succeed in demonstrating that the removal of the source of their market control - the exclusive use of the 'CA' initials - would render great harm to the public.

Professional vs non -professional

In order to gain a Royal Charter or right to use the CA notation, the Scottish Institute of Accountants and the Corporation of Accountants were confronted with the major problem of proving that their memberships *deserved* equality of status with the CAs - that their success and the creation of a national chartered profession would not result in the existence of two classes of CAs in Scotland. Essentially, the aspiring organizations were required to demonstrate that they were *professionals* and to achieve this they attempted to display the acquisition of professional characteristics by their organization and memberships. The exploitation of a status dichotomy between themselves and their competitors constituted the chartered societies' most potent weapon in favour of maintaining their monopoly and was one which they utilized to maximum advantage at each contest with the opposition.

Under the conditions of professional status determination prevalent during the late nineteenth century, the paramount professional trait was the acquisition of a professional *respectability*, which derived from the provision of expert service on the basis of tested esoteric knowledge. As Perkin has stated, this was the justification for the professions' receipt of state-conferred privileges such as incorporation (1969, p. 259). Entry to the professions was increasingly based upon proven abilities and expertise, attributes which were tested by examinations. The existence of comprehensive written tests of knowledge came to validate organizational claims to professional status and autonomous control over practice (see Hoskin & Macve, 1986, pp. 132-133). As Reader (1966) has explained:

> Between 1855 and 1875 the old official world of patronage, purchase, nepotism, and interest was turned upside down. . . Examinations, both qualifying and competitive, came into the centre of the stage for

the classes which looked for a living either to the public service or to the open professions (1966, p. 98; see also Elliott, 1972, pp. 43-52).

To prove their professional status, the Scottish Institute and the Corporation were required to demonstrate that their organizations provided for the recruitment and training of a respectable group of learned practitioners. The competing societies set about this task in three ways. Firstly, they sought to establish a social cognizance supportive of their claim to respectability by formulating, for public consumption, expressions of their laudable objectives and self-satisfying descriptions of the honourable and competent practitioners who comprised their memberships. Secondly, they sought status by association - by pursuing the corroboration of those in existing respectable occupations. For instance, in 1889 the Scottish Institute backed its application for a Royal Charter with a public petition signed by 3,228 senior individuals "engaged in professional, commercial and mercantile enterprise" (Privy Council, Petitioner's Case, p. 2) and in 1896 submitted a petition containing the names of nearly 5,700 men of influence in Scotland. Thirdly, the Scottish Institute at least, sought pedagogical legitimation by attempting to emulate the esteemed systems of professional education instituted by the chartered societies and thus illustrate that it too had attempted to codify and institutionalize accounting knowledge and participated in its control and distribution. In October 1892, for example, the Institute introduced a revised structure of examination and training which it considered "not inferior to that of any other Society or Institute in the Kingdom" (*The Scottish Accountant*, October 1892, p. 50).

Despite such efforts, throughout the formal proceedings of the 1880s and 1890s, the chartered societies advocated the existence of a great divide in professional status between their memberships and those of the competing societies. In 1889, for example, the CAs argued, with reference to the Scottish Institute, that "neither in numbers, nor in professional estimation or standing, are they entitled to place themselves on a par with the three bodies of Chartered Accountants in Scotland" (Privy Council, Opponent's Case, p. 71).

The chartered societies also presented derogatory evidence to illustrate that their competitors were not professionals but were engaged principally in commercial occupations - pursuits which were accorded a lower status in Victorian society (due to moral judgements deriding the egoistic profit-making orientation of businessmen compared with the adherence to the public service ideal and autonomy of the professional) (see Dennis and Skilton, 1987, pp. 70-71; Walker, 1988, pp. 58-64). By contrast to the high proportion of CAs in practice as "pure" and independent accountants, the majority of members of the Scottish Institute were also public officials, house factors, valuators, insurance agents or mercantile clerks. In 1889 an investigation of local directories by the chartered societies revealed that the true occupational distribution of the members of the Scottish Institute was as shown in Table 2.

Whereas only 34.4% of members of the Scottish Institute were occupied solely as accountants or accountant's clerks, the Institute's own analysis revealed that 83.8% of CAs in Edinburgh were either in practice or clerks to CAs as were 67.7% of CAs in Glasgow (a large proportion of the residual were stockbrokers). Similarly, in the 'CA case' counsel for the chartered societies called witnesses who also revealed that several corporate accountants did not practice as accountants: among their members were house factors in Glasgow and a coal importer in Stromness (Interdict Case, Proof, p. 57). In the 'MCA case', the chartered societies claimed that the "great majority" of corporate accountants in Scotland "do almost no real accountancy business, but are primarily estate agents, insurance agents, or the like" (*The Accountant*, 24 January, 1903, p. 145). Such 'accountants', claimed the chartered societies, were not comparable in occupation and standing with their own members who predominantly practised the *profession* of accountant.[2] It was iniquitous and against the public interest that the sub-class of quasi-accountants should be accorded "a status which has been hitherto applied to pure Accountants" (Privy Council, 1890, Speeches, p. 52).

TABLE II *Occupations of 151 members of the Scottish Institute of Accountants in 1889*

Occupation	N
Accountant/accountant's clerk only	52
Occupied solely or in combination with accountancy as:	
House or property agent/factor	32
Assurance/insurance agent, secretary, or manager	18
Stock or share broker	9
Clerk or cashier (non-accountants)	8
Solicitor/solicitor's clerk	6
Bank employee	5
Company/association secretary or manager	5
Town or city chamberlain	4
Railway company employee	2
Collector of poor rates	1
Official in stamp and tax office	1
Law stationer	1
Commission agent	1
Merchant and insurance agent	1
Sanitary and ventilating engineer	1
No description	4
Total	151

In addition to labelling their opponents as non-professional due to the commercial orientation of their clientele and employee status, the chartered societies also accused them of inferior ability. This defect was deemed a consequence of the Scottish Institute and Corporation's non or partial institutionalization of the structures required for imparting and testing the acquisition of the knowledge considered by the CAs as necessary for the practice of the *profession*.[3] By the year of the formation of the Scottish Institute, the Edinburgh, Glasgow and Aberdeen CA societies were in the advantageous position of having constructed and refined systems of professional education which, although separate, each had the "same object, viz., the exaction and maintenance within the societies of a high standard of education, conduct and professional capacity" (*Cases Decided in the Court of Session, 1892-3*, p. 752). By 1880 the three chartered societies had uniquely institutionalized a process for the transmission of the mysteries of "pure" accounting knowledge required for the provision of specialized professional services. They had well-established regulations regarding a four or five year formal apprenticeship, compulsory attendance at university law classes and entrance based upon a series of written and oral examinations. As stated earlier, in 1893 the structure of professional education was strengthened by the introduction of uniform arrangements for the three societies under the auspices of a General Examining Board (see Brown, 1905, pp. 211-212; Walker, 1988, pp. 330-336) which comprised an attempt to emulate the medical and legal professions by placing vocational education under the supervision of a regulatory council (*The Accountant's Magazine*, August 1919, p. 405).

By contrast to their own sophisticated examinations, the chartered societies asserted that those of the Scottish Institute of Accountants were mediocre and produced accountants of lesser aptitude. Consequently, their members did not deserve equal chartered standing. In 1889, for example, it was alleged that:

> It is well known that the papers set at the Institute's examinations are much simpler than those at the examinations of the Chartered Societies; and it is believed that the percentage exacted is lower. It is further worthy of note that, since the formation of the Institute in 1880, only two sets of papers had been used. It is obvious that, in some at least of the subjects, such a practice is clearly unjustifiable and improper (Privy Council, Opponent's Case, p. 32).

Even following the introduction of an improved examination system in 1892 modelled on that of the chartered societies, the CAs continued to denigrate the intellectual foundation of the qualifications acquired by Scottish Institute members. At the 1896 hearing before the Privy Council, the Institute's members were described as having been admitted without examination or of having passed an examination "of a merely perfunctory character" (Privy Council, 1896, Opponent's Case, p. 8).

The disparity in professional status and qualifications between the CAs and other accountants was most apparent in the contest with the corporate accountants in 1892-1893. The Corporation's lenient and ingenuous recruitment regulations induced *The Accountant* to comment in 1891 that entry was "thrown open to persons who are distinctly not public accountants in any sense of the term" (5 December 1891, p. 846). Following a relaxation of admission regulations, *The Scottish Accountant* in 1894 declared that "The Corporation invites all and sundry, without reference to qualification to join its membership" (April 1894, p. 182).

Consequently, when proof was allowed in the 'CA case' in December 1892, the senior office bearers of the chartered societies, supported by a succession of eminent lawyers and businessmen as witnesses, affirmed that CAs were recognized as erudite professionals. By contrast, the chief protagonists of the corporate accountants - James Martin and James L. Addie - and the accountant witnesses who testified on their behalf, were easily discredited as uninstructed practitioners (Interdict Case, Proof, pp. 66-90). Martin admitted that the Corporation had failed to institute arrangements for professional examinations and also that he had received no formal training as an accountant - his practical experience was gained as an employee for 18 years with the City of Glasgow Bank, advancing from office boy to branch agent. Addie disclosed that he had been a solicitor's apprentice but had failed the law examinations and was subsequently an estate agents clerk, accountant's cashier and, partner in a firm of writers before commencing business as an accountant in Glasgow (Interdict Case, Proof, pp. 83-90). The Corporation of Accountants, Ltd was not to introduce examinatory entrance until 1899, consequently, by the 'MCA case' in 1903, the chartered societies could assert that many corporate accountants, in not having served apprenticeships and not having passed any examinations, "are not properly qualified accountants" and that the examinations that were introduced were inferior "and form no satisfactory test that the person passing them is a properly qualified accountant" (*The Accountant*, 24 January, 1903, p. 145).

On the basis of such evidence, the chartered societies contended that so great was the divergence in the standard of professional education received by CAs and non-CAs, that to permit the lesser qualified to gain use of the identical CA notation would induce a host of deleterious consequences. The general standard of attainment among accountants would be lowered and efficiency thereby reduced, the public would be confused and damaged if they erroneously employed 'CAs' who had not received instruction under the regulations of the three established societies and overall, the impact would he to "bring down the character of the profession and of the name C.A." (Interdict Case, Proof, p. 27).

Exclusion and privilege vs guarantee of competence and efficiency

Although the chartered societies could justifiably claim to be the single adherents in Scotland to the professional ideal of preparing academically certified accountants, their recruitment regulations also seemingly contradicted prevailing social philosophy in not being objectively meritocratic and universalistic. The Victorian recipe for social advancement was self-help - individual industry and perseverance would secure a degree of upward mobility (see Altick, 1973, pp. 255-258). Implicit in the new positive social liberalism of the late nineteenth century was the supplemental principle that state intervention was tolerable when designed to remove institutional hindrances and material disabilities to individual improvement (see Fraser, 1973; Thane, 1982). The aspiring organizations of Scottish accountants employed these increasingly potent aspects of democratic ideology to reveal that entry to the chartered societies was conditional upon the ability to surmount exclusionary barriers rather than on individual merit. *The Scottish Accountant* declared with reference to the chartered societies that:

> Obstacles of an insurmountable kind bar the entrance to these societies of the young man of limited means, how ever keen of intellect, and this is altogether at variance with the spirit of the times. . . The whole tendency of modern legislation is in the direction of liberalizing our institutions, breaking down monopolies and privileges, and making the highest position in every walk of life accessible to the humblest subject who by individual merit have himself qualified to efficiently discharge his duties (January 1894, p. 181).

The alleged obstacles were threefold. First, the imposition of apprenticeship and entrance fees by the chartered societies ensured that entry to "their ranks are closed to any but the sons of the wealthier classes" (Privy Council, 1890, Appendix, p. 16). Although an apprenticeship under the rules of the Glasgow Institute did not require a fee, the Edinburgh society charged 100 guineas and the Aberdeen society imposed an indenture fee of 25 guineas. Admission to the chartered societies on qualification cost 50, 100 and 40 guineas, respectively. Second, only those formally apprenticed to a CA were eligible to sit the examinations of the chartered societies and qualify as members. Third, the localized organization of the chartered societies in Edinburgh, Glasgow and Aberdeen and their requirement of university attendance effectively closed the chartered profession to sons from the provinces. Essentially, the grievance propounded was not only had the chartered societies privately monopolized the distribution of the accounting knowledge required for professional practice by institutionalizing and codifying the means of its transmission (and thereby closing access to all but their own recruits), but they had also prevented the acquisition of that knowledge by many potential practitioners through self-imposing artificial barriers to entering their systems of vocational preparation. Consequently, recruitment was unfairly selective according to individual socio-geographical circumstances.

By contrast to the exclusionary recruitment regulations of the chartered societies, the Scottish Institute proposed entry purely on the basis of meritorious attributes, to "open up the profession in Scotland to well educated and deserving men all over the country" (Privy Council, 1890, Petitioner's Case, p. 16). The Institute set admission fees at 10 guineas (equal to the ICAEW - The Corporation of Accountants imposed entry fees of 10 guineas in 1891 and one guinea from June 1893) and envisaged that in the event of incorporation, facilities for vocational training in the provincial towns would be established.

The chartered societies strenuously denied the charge of social exclusivity and again advanced a functionalist defence. The imposition of barriers to recruitment was unavoidable if the overriding altruistic consideration of ensuring that only qualified, learned and reputable professionals supply accountancy services to the public was to be maintained. Entry regulations "are exclusive in the sense of insisting on special qualifications as a condition of membership, and in the sense of excluding incompetent persons from their ranks" (Privy Council, 1896, Opponent's Petition, p. 8). The doors of the chartered societies were open to those with the necessary attainments. As Thomas G. Dickson, President of the Edinburgh Society declared in 1892:

> We are willing according to our rules to admit any person into our Society of good character, who complies with the course of training and the requirements and qualifications of the Society. We do not exclude persons otherwise, who satisfy what we regard as essential to the proper practice of the business (Interdict Case, Proof, pp. 30-31).

As evidence of their commitment to unlimited recruitment of the qualified, the chartered societies revealed their rapidly expanding memberships (see Table IV).

The specific accusations of fostering exclusion due to the imposition of high fees was answered by the chartered societies in a manner designed to highlight their more distinguished and professional standing. It was argued that entry to "any of the learned professions cannot be obtained free of expense" (Privy Council, 1896, Brief, p. 3) and besides, costs were low in comparison with other branches of the established legal profession. During the 1890s entrants to the Scottish Bar paid over £350 and indenture and entrance fees for Writers to the Signet amounted to just under £485 (see *The Parliament House Book*, 1892-3, pp. 2-6).

The denunciation of the chartered societies' recruitment regulations on the grounds that they excluded aspiring accountants resident in the provinces was countered in similar terms:

> it is for the benefit of the profession and the public that Accountants in Scotland should receive their education and training in the University towns, where the great bulk of the legal and general business of the country is conducted, and where the education and training are more varied and efficient than in small provincial towns (Privy Council, 1890, Appendix, p. 73).

A national vs a local profession

One of the most pursuasive arguments advanced by the competing organizations in favour of breaking the chartered monopoly and one which was particularly exploited by the Scottish Institute was based on the atypical structure of the chartered profession north of the border. Whereas the English and Welsh, and Irish Institutes were incorporated as national organizations, the three societies in Scotland had individually received local charters (see Parker, 1986, pp. 14-15) and subsequently progressed within their respective municipalities as essentially separate institutions (until threatened by the Scottish Institute). This idiosyncrasy permitted the Scottish Institute to assert itself as the custodian and representative of the interests of the *national* profession in Scotland and to claim that the three chartered societies had proved insufficient agencies for the supply of practitioners in all districts of the country. In 1889, the Institute declared that the *raison d'etre* of its formation was to complete the organization of accountants in Scotland as the existing chartered societies "are strictly local in character, and can only be regarded as professional organizations for the three cities - Edinburgh, Glasgow and Aberdeen to which they respectively relate" (Privy Council, 1890, Petitioner's Case, p. 1). James Martin of the Corporation of Accountants declared also that his organization had been established for the same laudable objective "to get the whole accountants in Scotland into one body . . . It would be for the advantage of accountants in Scotland, if instead of being split up into small Societies, they were associated together into one general body; and that would also be for the advantage of the public" (Interdict Case, Proof, p. 88). By equalizing the status between CAs and organized non-CAs, it was envisaged that a national, amalgamated society of Scottish chartered accountants would ultimately result to supply the requirements of the whole nation.

The competing organizations claimed that objectionable consequences emanated from the localized structure of the Scottish chartered profession: accountants in urban centres with a significant industrial or commercial infrastructure such as Paisley, Greenock and Dundee were unorganized; and the city based organization was conducive to the creation of artificial scarcity in the supply of locally trained provincial accountants.

As evidence of the localization of the chartered societies compared with its own national status, the Scottish Institute revealed in 1896, for example, that in Scotland "the practising members of the Chartered Societies are confined to 7 towns, leaving 26 burghs in which the Institute alone is represented" (Privy Council, Petitioner's Case, p. 6). Members of the Scottish Institute, it was asserted, were dispersed over the whole country. To emphasize its national composition and objective of uniting provincial accountants, the Scottish Institute launched *The Scottish Accountant* in 1892 - the first accountancy journal in Scotland, the declared intention of which was to advance "the interests of the Accountancy profession throughout Scotland," and to furnish "a medium of communication between members of the Scottish Institute of Accountants who are to be found practising in almost all the principal towns" (April 1892, p. 10).

The Scottish Institute supported its claim for incorporation on the foundation of its nationality by stressing two factors. The Institute referred firstly to precedent. The local organization of the chartered societies in Scotland was anomalous - in 1880 the English and Welsh Institute received a national charter as did the Irish Institute in 1888 - why should not the Scottish Institute, which "has had a standing since 1880 coeval with the English Chartered Institute" (*The Scottish Accountant*, January 1893, p. 97) be likewise incorporated? The proposed charters of the Scottish Institute were constructed closely on the model of the successful ICAEW charter with the added intention to "fill up the blanks in Scotland caused by the three old charters being purely local . . . bringing it to an equality with that obtained for England and Ireland under their general charters" (*The Scottish Accountant*, July 1895, pp. 21-22).

Secondly, the Scottish Institute asserted that the volume of accountancy business outwith the cities was increasing and it was in the public interest that this should be conducted by practitioners of recognized (incorporated) status. In January 1893 *The Scottish Accountant* declared:

> The day is long past when a monopoly of accounting business could be kept in the metropolis. Commerce has demanded in every centre

of industry the professional services of accountants. Each year brings further development in their work, and legislation is constantly increasing the need for accountants in remote places (p. 64).

The Scottish Institute drew particular attention to a number of statutes during the 1880s and 1890s permitting the appointment of judicial factors by Sheriff (local) Courts and the audit "by fit persons" of county, burgh and parish councils which expanded the workload of accountants outside the major cities.[4] In 1896, for example, the Institute declared that 13 of its members resident in eight different towns had received parish council auditorships whereas 42 of the 46 auditorships awarded to CAs were conferred upon practitioners in the three cities.

The chartered societies refuted the nationalist pretensions of their competitors by revealing that the allegedly extensive geographical diffusion of their memberships was fictitious. At the 1896 application of the Scottish Institute for incorporation, the chartered societies showed that a large majority of Institute members practised not in the provinces but in the city bases in which they were themselves numerically dominant. Information on the respective geographical distribution of members is given in Table III.

TABLE III *Geographical distribution of CAs and members of the Scottish Institute of Accountants in 1896 (%)*

Location	CA	SIA
Edinburgh, Glasgow and Aberdeen	75.0	61.5
Rest of Scotland	5.3	34.8
England and Ireland	13.9	2.2
Abroad	5.8	1.5
Total	100.0	100.0
N	585	135

The CAs observed further, regarding the Institute's claim to represent the national profession and its ability to fill the deficiencies in the supply of competent accountants in the provinces, that "out of 110 towns in Scotland having a population of over 3000, the Scottish Institute has Members in only 23" (Privy Council, 1896, Opponent's Case, p. 21), that most Institute members outside the cities practised in small towns which were in close proximity to the principal centres of population and of 427 non-CA accountants in Scotland, only 123 were members of the Scottish Institute. Statistics such as those presented in Table III also reveal that far from being purely local, the chartered societies were positively international:

> There is nothing local about these Societies. There are Members only too glad to go wherever business is to be found. In the Edinburgh Society there is an immense number of young men. If they do not find scope for carrying on their business in Edinburgh or Glasgow, they go to England or to the Colonies, and if they do not go to country places in Scotland, it is simply because they do not think there is work for them (Privy Council, 1890, Speeches, p. 8).

Not surprisingly, the chartered societies claimed, on the basis of constituting the original and solitary organizations of accountants in Scotland from 1853 to 1880 and containing the most eminent practitioners, that they were the authentic representatives of the profession in Scotland. The Edinburgh Society provided accountants for the East of Scotland, the Glasgow Institute served the west and the Aberdeen Society supplied accountancy services in the north.

In explicating their concentration in the cities, the chartered societies contended that their highly qualified memberships of independent professionals found limited scope for the practice of 'pure' accountancy in the provinces: "the profession of an accountant does not in reality exist as a distinct profession in the provincial towns in Scotland, other than in the five or six largest" (Privy Council, 1890, Opponent's Case, p. 45). Practitioners outside the major urban centres necessarily combined accountancy with an additional "business" occupation and were, by implication, of less than professional status. Hence, in defending the structure of the Scottish profession, the local societies explained that:

> The system of separate Societies with separate charters had been deliberately preferred to the English system of one National Society. Each system has its advantages; but the circumstances in Scotland, where substantially the whole business of accounting proper is done at the great centres, seemed to render the system of separate Societies most expedient (Privy Council, 1890, Opponent's Case, p. 27).

Self interest vs identity of professional and
public interests

Given that altruism was accorded primacy over the pursuit of profit
in the professional ideal (Duman, 1979, pp. 124-129), it was inevitable
that the opposition of the chartered societies to the demands of the
competing organization's aspirations for equality of status would be
alleged to be an attempt to preserve narrow selfish monetary interests.
Indeed, in the 'CA case' it was incumbent on the CAs to testify that the
activities of the Corporation of Accountants would cause patrimonial
and pecuniary loss to the societies and their memberships.

The chartered societies argued that in the event of the Scottish
Institute receiving a charter or the Corporation gaining sanction to use
the 'CA' notation and, the consequent breakdown of the distinctions
between them, their organizations would suffer a decline in recruitment
and membership. The President of the Glasgow Institute declared, in
1892, that the exclusive acquisition of 'CA' constituted "a substantial
element in inducing young men to join our body" and pay the necessary
entrance fees (Interdict Case, Proof, p. 41). Individual CAs would also
suffer loss through an abstraction of business should members of the
Scottish Institute and Corporation acquire the 'CA' or 'chartered
accountant' title due to a consequent influx of competitors trading
under previously restricted professional designations.

In admitting that their exclusive use of the 'CA' designation
constituted "a professional mark of high pecuniary value" (Interdict
Case, Condescendence for Pursuers, 2), the chartered societies provided
valuable ammunition to their opponents such as James Martin:

> it is a strange commentary upon the whole of the claims put forward
> by the chartered societies to prove their superiority over other
> accountants that the only one which has a vestige of truth in it shows
> that by their own confession their grandest conception of the nobility
> of their profession reaches no higher than the breeches pocket (1896a,
> p. 7).

As it was patently impossible to deny self interest yet vital to
present an altruistic exterior, the chartered societies replied to their
critics with two arguments. The first was that the public interest was
inextricably linked to their own private interests. The public had
illustrated their confidence in chartered accountants, their superior
abilities and provision for the efficient discharge of accountancy
services, by vesting in them the great bulk of important business. By
virtue of dominating the profession in Scotland and assuming

responsibility for its nurture and status, the chartered societies, claimed their counsel in 1890, "are really representing not merely their own interests but also the interests of the Scottish public in the matter of the services of Accountants" (Privy Council, Speeches, 17). Thus, by damaging the private interests of the chartered societies and their members, the demands of the rival organizations were deleterious to the more important public interest.

Second, it was relatively simple for the chartered societies to illustrate that the competing organizations were also primarily motivated by selfish interests - their design, in attempting to secure the 'CA' designation was to expand their clientele. As one Glaswegian witness in the 'CA case' related:

> (Q) Does any reason occur to you why people should form themselves into a company and take the use of the letters "C.A." except one? (A.) I can imagine no reason, except a pecuniary one - to get business, perhaps by the use of these letters (Interdict Case, Proof, p. 25).

The chartered societies argued not only that it was inequitable that their competitors should appropriate business on the basis of acquiring a designation whose currency was the result of their own endeavours, but also the utilitarian philosophy that an action is right only if its consequences produces the greatest happiness for the greatest number. As is shown in Table IV, of the two sets of contending interests, the chartered societies represented by far the majority at each of the major conflicts with the Scottish Institute and the Corporation.

TABLE IV *Memberships of competing organizations of Scottish accountants*

	Year of contest				
Organization	*1884*	*1890*	*1893*	*1896*	*1903*
Society of Accountants in Edinburgh	184	247	267	310	372
Institute of Accountants in Glasgow	115	140	195	244	373
Society of Accountants in Aberdeen	21	21	25	32	49
Total CAs	320	408	487	586	794

TABLE IV *Continued*

	Year of contest				
Organization	1884	1890	1893	1896	1903
Scottish Institute of Accountants	122	160		143	
Corporation of Accountants, Ltd			22		276*

*Only 43 of these practised in Scotland.

In addition to the consequences for their larger memberships, the chartered societies also drew attention to the detrimental effects that the success of their opponents would have on the future supply of competent practitioners. In 1884 the Edinburgh Society revealed that it had 93 apprentices deeply interested in the maintenance of its organizational status "who in the aggregate have invested in apprentice fees, stamp duty, &c., a sum exceeding £10,000" (Privy Council, 1890, Appendix, p. 93). If to the total members are added the number of associates and apprentices of the chartered societies, the scale of their dominant interest is more apparent. In 1890 that total was 667 and in 1903 was 1,285, statistics which, in the former year, precipitated the CAs to declare astonishment that the Scottish Institute:

> Seriously proposed to incorporate into a National Institute under an all inclusive aim a society whose whole membership does not amount to a third of the membership of the existing Chartered Societies, and many of whose members have had no proper training for the practice of the profession (Privy Council, Opponent's Petition, p. 31).

The defence of professional monopoly in its broader context

Adherents to the critical approach have acknowledged the significance of investigating professionalization projects and the maintenance of restrictive closure practices in their wider economic and political contexts (Friedson, 1983). In his comparative study of monopolization in the medical profession, Ramsey asserted that the extent to which a monopoly develops, is tolerated and protected depends on changes in the relative power of interested parties, the structure of political institutions and the contemporary "political climate" (1984, pp. 226-227). Willmott (1986, pp. 559-561) has asserted that professional organizations must be regarded as political bodies and that their activities are more suitably considered in their broader politico-economic setting.

The attempts of the Scottish Institute and the Corporation to achieve equal status with the chartered societies and the CAs' efforts to defend their monopoly, must be investigated beyond the public proceedings at the Privy Council and the Court of Session. Several underlying economic, social and political factors assisted the chartered societies' cause.

Economic and social domination

On the basis of their comparatively long existence, high admission fees and expanding memberships, the chartered societies were able to amass greater resources than their competitors with which to finance the defence of their interests. At the time of the second application of the Scottish Institute of Accountants for a Royal Charter in 1889, the Edinburgh, Glasgow and the Aberdeen societies had total funds amounting to £29,500. By comparison, the activities of the younger, low-fee accountancy organizations appear to have been impeded by fewer assets. Although the Corporation of Accountants, for example, survived the payment of £750 costs in the 'CA case' in 1893 by relaxing entry requirements and admission fees and by expanding its non-Scottish membership, the chartered societies at the 'MCA case' in 1903 sought assurances that a corporation with funds of only £385 could finance costs that might be imposed by the Court (see *The Accountants' Magazine*, February 1903, p. 86).

It was the leading corporate accountant and principal agitator in the 'CA case', James Martin, who detected a series of socio-cultural assets which also assisted the chartered societies in their disputes with the competing organizations. Martin responded to the lack of success of the Scottish Institute and the Corporation by preparing a series of scathing articles and pamphlets after 1893. Initially, he argued that the structure of the accountancy profession in Scotland and the chartered monopoly was against the public interest (1896a), that reform was vital and, that the decision in the 'CA case' had been a "misapplication of the law" (1896b). From the late 1890s, however, Martin's tone and the nature of his grievance shifted from the validity of the judgement to the circumstances which encouraged it (1897a, 1897b) - in 1908 he asked "Were the Law Courts Bribed?"

Martin alleged that in 1892-1893 the chartered societies, by claiming that they had a sole and exclusive right to use the 'CA' designation, had lied to the Court - the charters had conferred no such prerogative. Given that the judges did not concede that the chartered societies had a legal monopoly of the letters yet still found in their favour, Martin claimed that the explanation for this extraordinary decision was that their Lordships had been corrupted. Although he hesitated to pronounce that the judges in the 'CA case' had been overtly bribed: "I do suggest that they were influenced by other considerations than those connected with, or belonging it the case" (1897a, p. 1) and that through "backstairs influence and crawling" (1908, p. 28) the CAs had "a complete understanding with the judges as to the result of the case" (1897a, p. 13).

Martin believed that he discovered the source of contamination of the Scottish bench as being the close kinship and social connections between the Edinburgh centred CA and legal professions. He noted that "Judges and CAs mix in Edinburgh society" (1908, p. 19), and further that "the C.A.s in Scotland are wealthy and influential. I do not say the Glasgow body have much influence, but the influence is strong elsewhere. I was not, when the case was raised, aware of the family relationships between C.A.s in Edinburgh and the Court" (1897a, p. 31).

Although Martin's polemical observations were prejudiced by his frustration as an unsuccessful litigant and his allegations that the CAs influenced the judges in 1892-1893 are not substantiated, his revelation of the connections between them was well founded. Among the Senators of the College of Justice and Crown Officers at the time of the 'CA case', the head of the Second Division was Lord Welwood, brother of Francis J. Moncreiff, CA whose sister married John B. Balfour, the Lord Advocate in 1877 (who, it will be recalled, recommended the refusal of the Scottish Institute's charter application of 1884); Lord Kyllachy was a close friend of David Pearson, CA (*The Scotsman*, 11 December 1918, p. 4); William H. Smith, CA was an "old and valued friend" of Lord Kingsburgh, the Lord Justice Clerk (*The Scotsman*, 10 May 1919, p. 8) and sons of Lord Low and the Lord Advocate were later to become CA apprentices. Although there is no evidence that such connections resulted in the corruption of the court, the existence of strong filial and social associations with lawyers (the latter were often founded on mutual attendance at Edinburgh Academy) indicate that the chartered societies had access to legal services and to the senior legal profession which surpassed that of their opponents.[5]

There had always existed a close occupational relationship between the accountancy and legal professions in Edinburgh. Indeed, it may be claimed that the former developed as an offshoot of the latter (Brown, 1905, p. 198; Jones, 1981, p. 80). Occupational connections between the two vocations were compounded by kinship ties: 27.5% of all recruits to the Society of Accountants in Edinburgh to 1874 were the sons of lawyers (Walker, 1988, p. 85); several of the younger sons of Court of Session judges entered chartered accountancy.[6] A recruitment custom developed whereby the elder sons of lawyers entered their father's profession while a younger son became a CA and conversely (p. 86), the elder sons of several eminent CAs became advocates or Writers to the Signet (p. 241).

The development of a law-accountancy kinship nexus in nineteenth-century Edinburgh ensured that the senior office bearers of the Society of Accountants could exploit the resources of their lawyer relatives when threatened by competing organizations. Of the six counsel who pleaded before the Privy Council and the Court of Session for the chartered societies, three were related to Presidents of the Society of Accountants in Edinburgh. The senior counsel in 1890 was Charles J. Pearson (1843-1910, later Lord Advocate, Dean of the Faculty of Advocates and judge) (see *Dictionary of National Biography*) who was the second son of Charles Pearson, President of the Edinburgh Society 1876-1879 and brother of David Pearson, President from 1898-1901; senior counsel in 1896 was Richard B. Haldane (1856-1928, later Viscount Haldane, Lord Chancellor) (see Haldane, Sommer, Maurice, *DNB*) a pleader of repute before the Privy Council in charter applications and nephew of James Haldane, President of the Edinburgh Society 1895-1898; and counsel in all cases was Charles R. A. Howden (1862-1936) (see *Who's Who),* the second son of James Howden, President of the Edinburgh Society 1892-1895. The significant point is that these advocates defended not only the chartered organizations but also the future financial security and status preservation of their own relatives who were partners in the largest firms of CAs in Edinburgh.

Political conditions conducive to the maintenance of professional monopoly

The Scottish Institute and Corporation of Accountants were also disadvantaged by political circumstances in their conflicts with the chartered societies. The cause of the aspirant organizations was clearly identified in contemporary party politics as reformist Liberal whereas the underlying creed of the CA defence of privilege was Conservatism. In the 'CA case' the leading counsel for the Corporation of Accountants was the Liberal Solicitor-General Alexander Asher

(1835-1905) (Orr, 1923, p. 136; *DNB*) whereas the senior advocate for the CAs was the Dean of the Faculty of Advocates, Charles J. Pearson (1843-1910), the foremost Conservative of the Scottish Bar.

The 'CA case' of 1892-1893 was heard before Lord Kyllachy (William Mackintosh, 1842-1918) whose ideological sentiments did not augur well for the Corporation. Kyllachy, a declared Liberal-Unionist "would probably have referred to he described as an old Whig, which as much as to say that he was more conservative than many professing Tories . . . all William Mackintosh's instincts, prejudices, and convictions were strongly enlisted upon the side of the status quo" (*The Scotsman*, 11 December 1918, p. 4).

The ideological complexion and judicial temperament of the majority of the four Second Division judges who heard the Corporation's appeal in May 1893 may also have proved unfavourable to its liberal cause. Lord Kingsburgh was a "stalwart Conservative" (*The Scotsman*, 10 May 1919, p. 8; *DNB*), Lord Rutherford Clark, an "old-whig", gave opinions which "were decidely, though rationally conservative" (*The Scotsman*, 31 July 1899, p. 7; *DNB*), Lord Trayner, though a Liberal was an impatient judge who took a side in a case before it was heard (*The Scotsman*, 4 February 1929, p. 9; *Who's Who*), and Lord Young - a reforming Liberal and potential sympathiser with the intentions of the Corporation - was wayward and unpredictable in his judgements (*The Scotsman*, 23 May 1907, pp. 6-7; *DNB*).

The Scottish Institute was also confronted by structural and political hindrances implicit in the process of applying to the Privy Council for a Royal Charter. The first problem was that following the Companies Act, 1867 (which permitted incorporation by the Board of Trade without the word "Limited") and up to 1896, only two Scottish professional organizations received a Royal Charter (the Faculty of Actuaries in 1868 and the Society of Law Agents in 1884). Further, as Carr-Saunders and Wilson have remarked, though certain procedural conventions were adopted for dealing with petitions for incorporation, these were uncodified and based upon tradition and precedent (1933, p. 332). During the late nineteenth and early twentieth centuries, applications for charters were considered by *ad hoc* committees of five Privy Councillors headed by the current or an ex-Lord President of the Council (Fitzroy, 1925, vol. 1, p. 110; de Smith, 1971, p. 148). In the selection of committee members (a function of the Privy Council itself) the attainment of a political balance was secondary to securing the services of councillors with a background pertinent to the subject of the petition under consideration (Fitzroy, 1928, p. 309). Hence, in 1890 and 1896 the committees which heard the Scottish Institute's applications included the Secretary of State for Scotland and others with a Scottish connection by birth, education, occupation or title and all but one of the ten members were Conservatives. Furthermore, only in 1896 did the committee include two members of the non-political judiciary - the remainder were senior statesmen with high political profiles.[7] Neither committee, in comprising members of the Conservative landed and professional political elite, can be considered to have constituted an ideally neutral tribunal for hearing the Scottish Institute's radical cause.

That political allegiences were relevant to decisions of the Privy Council to grant Royal Charters was suggested by *The Accountant* in 1895. While discussing the Scottish Institute's third petition for incorporation, it noted that greater success might be possible on this occasion "as a good deal depends upon the party in office" (11 May, p. 444) and a senior member of the governing Liberal Party had signed the petition (which contained the names of 37 Scottish Liberal MPs and 23 Conservatives or Unionists - 36 and 25, respectively, in 1890). Unfortunately for the Institute, by the time that the committee was formed to hear the application in 1896, the Conservatives, who had governed when the 1890 petition was considered, had been decisively returned to power (Hutchison, 1986, p. 192).

Conclusion and epilogue

It has been shown in the paper that the successful public defence of professional privilege in the Scottish accountancy profession depended on the adoption of a functionalist analysis of the role of the profession in late nineteenth- and early twentieth-century society. As an ideological basis for justifying monopoly before state institutions, functionalism was so potent as to override tenets of prevailing socio-political philosophy and the admission of self interest. The underlying motives and behaviour of the professions, are however, only revealed by a wider critical analysis of the activities of the professional association. The successful defence of domination in the supply of professional services is also dependent on underlying, more hidden circumstances not disclosed by a simple historical investigation of proceedings in Parliament, the courts or the Privy Council. Contemporary political conditions and economic dominance were essential perquisites of the maintenance of the CA's privileges.

The development and preservation of the Scottish chartered monopoly of practice in the 1854-1914 period is also instructive in revealing the process of professionalization, which partly explains the disunified structure of the accountancy organizations in modern Britain. Events in the profession north of the border had interesting parallels in

England. In common with the findings of Loft (1986, pp. 152-153) and to some extent of Willmott (1986, pp. 566-567), it is suggested that the early organized accountancy profession was characterized by the following series of events.

Accountants in major financial, commercial or manufacturing centres (such as Edinburgh, Glasgow and London) formed associations and embarked upon attempts to establish professional status by adopting the traits exhibited by the traditional professions (particularly those of the legal profession). Following the achievement of professional standing, the attendant privileges and improved market position, practitioners excluded from the original organizations (such as the Scottish Institute, the Corporation of Accountants, the Society of Accountants in England) desired access to the same status and economic rewards. This was attempted by establishing organizations which necessarily emulated the successful professionalization project of the established associations (the Scottish Institute, the Corporation and Institute of Cost Accountants endeavoured to use the designations of Scottish and English chartered accountants respectively) and by presenting a unique characteristic as justification for their separate existence (the 'national' status of the Scottish Institute, the new specialism represented by organizations of cost accountants).

As emulation posed a likely threat to the market position of the established professional accountants, the aspirant organization was confronted by obstruction and attempts to denigrate its members' occupational and social status. The resultant intra-professional altercation was not conducive to the organizational integration of the profession.

The longer term disunification of the profession was to be reflected in the subsequent history of the organizations which had contested in the Scottish professional arena from 1854 to 1914.

Following its unsuccessful attempts to become chartered, 123 of the existing 140 members of the Scottish Institute joined the Society of Accountants and Auditors in 1899 (eight others were already members) as its Scottish branch. *The Scottish Accountant* was discontinued in the same year. Despite the amalgamation with the incorporated accountants, membership of the Scottish branch remained static at 129 in 1910 and 142 by 1935. The *Incorporated Accountants' Journal* reported that competition from CAs and greater opportunities overseas encouraged the emigration of younger Scottish members (April 1911, p. 188; Garrett, 1961, p. 24).

The Corporation of Accountants, Ltd, in Scotland at least, suffered a similar fate. Following the 'CA case', the Corporation made successful attempts to expand its membership outside Scotland so that by 1903 only 15.4% of members were resident north of the border (12.2% in 1935). The Corporation became, in effect, an English organization with headquarters in Glasgow. The inevitable internal conflict arising from this imbalance, occurred over the 'MCA case' when the obsessions of the Scottish leadership appeared as provincial irrelevancies to its London board which:

> Finding further controversy or connection with the Glasgow council useless . . . decided to form a distinct and independent society in the interests of the English and other members leaving the Corporation of Accountants free to conduct their own affairs in Scotland in their own manner (*The Accountants' Magazine*, January 1904, pp. 2-4).

The Institution of Certified Public Accountants was the resulting splinter organization.

The Corporation of Accountants did, however, prosper outside Scotland during the inter-war period by conforming to the standards set by its former chartered competitors and basing entrance on comprehensive examination. The reward of Parliamentary recognition was gained in 1931, and in 1933, ironically, the Corporation was granted an injunction preventing non-members from using the designations 'Corporate Accountant' and 'TRCA' (see *The Corporate Accountants' Year Book*, 1936, pp. 510-511). In 1939 the 2,100 members of the Corporation amalgamated with the London Association of Certified Accountants, Ltd, as the Association of Certified and Corporate Accountants with offices in London (*The Accountant*, 17 December 1938, p. 829; 11 March 1939, p. 318). The Association of Certified Accountants received a Royal Charter in 1974.

On 24 October 1904, the Society of Accountants in Edinburgh celebrated its 50th jubilee as a chartered organization (as did the Glasgow Institute in 1905) (see Brown, 1905, pp. 401-449). The grand scale of this act of self-congratulation was justified: not only had the chartered societies developed expanding, high standing professional organizations, they had also gained domination of the practice of their vocation, secured judgements which provided legal protection for the source of that dominance and, witnessed the demoralization and ineffectiveness of their competitors who had been weakened by unsuccessful challenges to that domination. The cloud which hovered over the Scottish chartered societies from the 1880s, had all but disappeared.

Notes

1. The most notable example was Thomas S. Lindsay, an original member of the ICAEW and chairman of the Edinburgh branch committee of the Scottish Institute of Accountants. He practised as an accountant in Edinburgh and later in London.

2. The ICAEW advanced an identical argument in opposition to the attempts of the Institute of Cost and Works Accountants to gain a Royal Charter in 1922 (see Parker, 1986, p. 42).

3. What constituted the *practice of the profession* in Scotland (and consequently, the subject disciplines tested in CA examinations) was self-defined by the chartered societies. In 1892, the President of the Edinburgh Society from 1889 to 1892 considered that: "the work done by an accountant consists of acting as trustee on bankrupt estates, dealing with remits from the courts in regard to accountings, acting as judicial factor, or factor *loco tutoris* or *curator bonis,* dealing with actuarial business to some extent, investigating the accounts of commercial concerns. . . auditing the funds of public companies and private undertakings, and similar business, and also explaining how accounts ought to be kept generally. What I have described seems to me to cover what is usually regarded as the business of an accountant" (Interdict Case, Proof, p. 26).

4. These were the Judicial factors (Scotland) Acts, 1880 and 1889; Local Government (Scotland) Acts, 1889 and 1894, and the Burgh Police (Scotland) Act, 1894.

5. The formation of connections within elite educational institutions and the consequent creation of an inter-organizational network of alumni has been discussed in a different context by Hoskin and Macve (1988) in their identification of the significance of engineering graduates of West Point in the dissemination of cost and management accounting knowledge among manufacturing concerns in nineteenth-century America.

6. In 1868-1869 alone, sons of Lords Kinloch, Moncreiff and Neaves were contracted as apprentices to the eminent CA firm of Lindsay, Jamieson & Haldane.

7. In 1890, the Committee of the Privy Council that heard the Scottish Institute's application consisted of: the Lord President of the Council - Lord Cranbrook (Gathorne Gathorne-Hardy); The Duke of Richmond and Gordon - Secretary of State for Scotland 1885-1886 (Charles H. Gordon Lennox); the Secretary of State for Scotland - The Marquis of Lothian (Schomberg H. Kerr); Sir Francis Richard Sandford; The Lord Advocate (James Patrick Bannerman Robertson). In 1896, the committee consisted of: The Duke of Richmond and Gordon; The Earl of Kintore (Algernon H. Thomond Keith-Falconer); the Secretary of State for Scotland - Lord Balfour of Burleigh (Alexander Hugh Bruce); a Lord of Appeal - Lord Watson (William Watson); the Lord Justice-General - Lord Robertson (James Patrick Bannerman Robertson). For biographical details and

references see *DNB, Who's Who*, and obituarial notices in *The Times* and *The Scotsman*.

Bibliography

The Accountant (1880-1914, 1938-1939).

The Accountants' Magazine (1897-1914).

Altick, R. D., *Victorian People and Ideas* (New York: Norton, 1973).

Anderson, R. D., *Education and Opportunity in Victorian Scotland* (Oxford: Clarendon Press, 1983).

Barber, B., Some Problems in the Sociology of the Professions, *Daedalus* (Fall 1963).

Berlant, J. L., *Profession and Monopoly. A Study of Medicine in the United States and Great Britain* (London: University of California Press, 1975).

Brown, R., Recent Proposed Legislation Relating to the Profession, *Transactions of the Chartered Accountants Students' Society of Edinburgh* (1894) pp. 31-42.

Brown, R. (ed.), *A History of Accounting and Accountants* (Edinburgh: T. C. & E. C. Jack, 1905).

Burchell, S., Clubb, C., Hopwood, A., Hughes, & Nahapiet, J., The Roles of Accounting in Organizations and Society, *Accounting Organizations and Society* (1980) pp. 5-27.

Carr-Saunders, A. M. and Wilson, P. A., *The Professions* (London: Oxford University Press, 1933).

Cases Decided in the Court of Session, Court of Justiciary and House of Lords 1892-3 (Edinburgh).

Checkland, S., *British Public Policy 1776-1939* (Cambridge: Cambridge University Press, 1983).

Checkland, S. and Checkland, O., *Industry and Ethos, Scotland 1832-1914* (London: Edward Arnold, 1984).

The Corporate Accountants' Year Book (Glasgow: Corporation of Accountants, 1929-1938).

Corporation of Accountants, Ltd, Dissolved Company File BT.2/2230. Scottish Record Office, Edinburgh.

Davis, K. and Moore, W., Some Principles of Stratification, *American Sociological Review* (1945) pp. 242-249.

de Smith, S. A., *Constitutional and Administrative Law* (London: Longman, 1971).

Dennis, B. and Skilton, D. (eds.), *Reform and Intellectual Debate in Victorian England* (New York: Croom Helm, 1987).

Dictionary of National Biography (Oxford: Oxford University Press).

Duman, D., The Creation and Diffusion of a Professional Ideology in Nineteenth Century England, *Sociological Review* (1979) pp. 113-138.

Durkheim, E., *On the Division of Labour in Society* (New York: Macmillan, 1933).

Eddington, A., *Contemporary Biographies. Edinburgh and the Lothians at the Opening of the Twentieth Century* (Edinburgh: W. T. Pike, 1904).

The Edinburgh Academy Register (Edinburgh, privately, 1914).

Edinburgh and Leith Post Office Directory, 1856-7 (Edinburgh, 1856).

Elliott, R., *The Sociology of the Professions* (London: Macmillan, 1972).

Fitzroy, Sir A., *Memoirs* (London: Hutchinson, 1925).

Fitzroy, Sir A., *The History of the Privy Council* (London: John Murray, 1928).

Fraser, D., *The Evolution of the British Welfare State* (London: Macmillan, 1973).

Freidson, E., The Theory of the Professions: State of the Art, in Dingwall, R. & Lewis, P. (eds), *The Sociology of the Professions* (London: Macmillan, 1983).

Garrett, A. A., *History of the Society of Incorporated Accountants* (Oxford: Oxford University Press, 1961).

Gerth, H. H. & Wright Mills, C., *From Max Weber: Essays in Sociology* (London: Routledge & Kegan Paul, 1948).

Goldstein, J., Foucault among the Sociologists: the "Disciplines" and the History of the Professions, *History and Theory* (1984) pp. 170-192.

Green, W. L., *History and Survey of Accountancy* (New York: Standard Text Press, 1930).

Greenwood, E., Attributes of a Profession, in Nosow, S. and Form, W. E., *Man, Work and Society* (New York: Basic Books, 1962).

Gross, E., *Work and Society* (New York: Thomas Y. Crowell, 1958).

Haldane, R. B., *An Autobiography* (London: Hodder & Stoughton, 1929).

Halmos, P., *The Personal Service Society* (London: Constable, 1970).

Harrison, J. F. C., *Early Victorian Britain 1832-51* (London: Fontana/Collins, 1979).

Hopwood, A. G., The Archaeology of Accounting Systems, *Accounting, Organizations and Society* (1987), pp.207-234.

Hoskin, K.W. and Macve, R.W., Accounting and the Examination: A Genealogy of Disciplinary Power, *Accounting, Organizations and Society* (1986), pp. 105-136.

Hoskin, K.W. and Macve, R. W., The Genesis of Accountability: The West Point Connection, *Accounting, Organizations and Society* (1988) pp. 37-73.

Hughes, E. C., Professions, *Daedalus* (Fall, 1963).

Hutchison, I. G. C., *A Political History of Scotland 1832-1924* (Edinburgh: John Donald, 1986).

The Incorporated Accountants' Journal (1899-1914).

I.C.A.S., *A History of the Chartered Accountants of Scotland from the Earliest times to 1954* (Edinburgh: Blackwood & Sons, 1954).

Interdict Case. The Chartered Accountants of Scotland against The Corporation of Accountants, Ltd, 1892-1893. I.C.A.S. Collection, National Library of Scotland, Edinburgh.

Jones, E., *Accountancy and the British Economy 1840-1980* (London: Batsford, 1981).

Kellas, J. G., The Liberal Party in Scotland 1876-1895, *Scottish Historical Review* (1965) pp. 1-16.

Knight, W., *Some Nineteenth Century Scotsmen* (Edinburgh: Oliphant, Anderson & Ferrier, 1903).

Larson, M. S., *The Rise of Professionalism. A Sociological Analysis* (Berkeley: University of California Press, 1977).

Loft, A., Towards a Critical Understanding of Accounting: The Case of Cost Accounting in the U.K., 1914-1925, *Accounting, Organizations and Society* (1986) pp. 137-169.

Macdonald, K. M., Professional Formation: the Case of Scottish Chartered Accountants, *British Journal of Sociology* (1984) pp. 174-189.

Macdonald, K. M., Social Closure and Occupational Registration, *Sociology* (1985) pp. 541-556.

Macdonald, K. M., Professional Formation: A reply to Briston and Kedslie, *British Journal of Sociology* (1987) pp. 106-111.

Martin, J., *The Accountant Profession: A Public Danger,* 2nd Edn (Glasgow: Wm Hodge & Co., 1896a).

Martin, J., *The Accountant "CA" Case. Was there a Misapplication of the Law?* (Glasgow: Wm Hodge & Co., 1896b).

Martin, J., *Did the Devil win the Toss? or, The Lie Triumphant in the Law Courts. An Exposure* (Glasgow: Carter & Pratt, 1897a).

Martin, J., *The Sanctification of the Lie Grace, grace unto it! A Tribute to the Queen's Sixty Years' Reign* (Glasgow: Carter & Pratt, 1897b).

Martin, J., *The Accountant Squabble. The Government and the CA Case. Were the Law Courts Bribed? A Scathing Exposure* (Glasgow, 1908).

Maurice, Sir F. B., *Haldane 1856-1928* (London: Faber & Faber, 1937 & 1939).

Millerson, G., *The Qualifying Associations: A Study of Professionalization* (London: Routledge & Kegan Paul, 1964).

Omond, G. W. T., *The Lord Advocates of Scotland Second Series 1834-1880* (London: Andrew Melrose, 1914).

Orr, R. L., *Lord Guthrie. A Memoir* (London: Hodder & Stoughton, 1923).

Parker, R. L., *The Development of the Accountancy Profession in Britain to the Early Twentieth Century* (Academy of Accounting Historians, Monograph 5, 1986).

Parkin, F., *Marxism and Class Theory: A Bourgeois Critique* (London: Tavistock, 1979).

The Parliament House Book, 1892-3 (Edinburgh: Burness, 1892).

Parry, N. & Parry, J., Social Closure and Collective Social Mobility, in Scase, R. (ed.), *Industrial Society.Class, Cleavage and Control* (London: George Allen & Unwin, 1977).

Perkin, H., *The Origins of Modern English Society 1780-1880* (London: Routledge & Kegan Paul, 1969).

Portwood, D. and Fielding, A., Privilege and the Professions, *Sociological Review* (1981), pp. 749-773.

Privy Council. In the Matter of the Petition of the Scottish Institute for Incorporation by Royal Charter (1890). (Scottish Dept, Edinburgh Central Library).

Privy Council. In the Matter of the Petition of the Scottish Institute for Incorporation by Royal Charter (1896). (Scottish Dept, Edinburgh Central Library).

Privy Council. Speeches by Counsel (1890). In the Matter of the Petition of the Scottish Institute of Accountants for Incorporation by Royal Charter. (Scottish Dept, Edinburgh Central Library).

Privy Council. Speeches by Counsel (1896). In the Matter of the Petition of the Scottish Institute of Accountants for Incorporation by Royal Charter. (Scottish Dept, Edinburgh Central Library).

Ramsey, M., The Politics of Professional Monopoly in Nineteenth Century Medicine: The French Model and its Rivals, in Geison, G. L. (ed.), *Professions and the French State 1700-1900* (Philadelphia: University of Pennsylvania Press, 1984), pp. 225-305.

Reader, W. J., *Professional Men* (London: Weidenfeld & Nicolson, 1966).

Richardson, A. J., Accounting Knowledge and Professional Privilege, *Accounting, Organizations and Society* (1988) pp. 381-396.

The Scots Law Times (1893, 1903-1904).

The Scotsman (1892-1936).

The Scottish Accountant (1892-1899).

The Scottish Law Reporter (1892-1893).

Sommer, D., *Haldane of Cloan. His Life and Times 1856-1928* (London: Allen & Unwin, 1960).

Stacey, N. H. A., *English Accountancy, A Study in Social and Economic History* (London: Gee, 1954).

Stenton, M. and Lees, S., *Who's Who of British Members of Parliament* (Hassocks: Harvester Press, 1976-1981).

Stewart, J. C., *Pioneers of a Profession. Chartered Accountants to 1879* (Edinburgh: ICAS, 1977).

Taylor, A. J., *Laissez-faire and State Intervention in Nineteenth-Century Britain* (London: Macmillan, 1972).

Thane, P., *Foundations of the Welfare State* (London: Longman, 1982).

Unwin, D. W., The Development of the Conservative Party Organization in Scotland until 1912, *Scottish Historical Review* (1965) pp. 89-111.

Walker, S. P., *The Society of Accountants in Edinburgh 1854-1914. A Study of Recruitment to a New Profession* (New York: Garland, 1988).

Wark, J. L. (ed.), *Enyclopaedia of the Laws of Scotland* (Edinburgh: Wm. Green & Son, 1926).

Who's Who (London, A. & C. Black).

Willmott, H., Organising the Profession: A Theoretical and Historical Examination of the Development of the Major Accountancy Bodies in the UK, *Accounting, Organizations and Society* (1986) pp. 555-580.

Woolf, A. H., *A Short History of Accountants and Accountancy* (London: Gee, 1912).

Wright Mills, C., *White Collar* (New York: Oxford University Press, 1951).

CHAPTER 9

Scottish Chartered Accountants: Internal and External Political Relationships, 1853-1916

Ken Shackleton

Introduction

This article explores the internal and external political relationships which existed between the three societies of Chartered Accountants in Scotland during the period 1853 to 1916. The period covers the formation of the first chartered society, the Society of Accountants in Edinburgh (SAE) in 1853,[1] to the creation of the Joint Committee of Councils of the three Scottish chartered societies in 1915.

Thus, the article addresses directly a number of issues raised by Fleischman (1990), in his review of work cited in this article. Fleischman noted a shortage of information about the SAE's social and political activities and speculated that the minutes may have been "underutilized". He called also for information relating to the SAE's contribution to the evolution of professional accounting in Scotland (Fleischman, 1990, p. 147). Walker's (1988) research was essentially about recruitment to a profession. Political issues and relationships were outside the remit of the work and therefore require separate investigation.

This research reports on the political and administrative context of the times by reference to the considerations of, advice to, and decisions made by the Lord Advocate, the Secretary of State for Scotland and the Committee of the Privy Council on matters relating

---

Reproduced from *Accounting, Auditing and Accountability Journal*, Volume 8, Number 2, 1995, pp 18-46, with kind permission of MCB University Press.

to the Scottish chartered societies. These details were gained from perusal of official papers retained in the Scottish Record Office in Edinburgh and the Public Record Office in London, much of which has not been reported previously.

Members of the three Scottish societies assumed the nomenclature of chartered accountant and the designatory letters C.A., which theydefended vigorously on a number of occasions against rival nascent accountancy bodies during the late nineteenth century. The conventional view has been that, during this period, the three societies were united and co-operated when responding to all external threats and pressures (Kedslie, 1990a, p. 222; Walker, 1991, p. 274). However, other accounting groups, and contributors to contemporary journals, argued that the societies were not only independent but also antagonistic to one another (Scottish Institute of Accountants, 1885; *The Accountant,* 1885a, 1885b). Consideration of a number of primary records reveals that there were in fact significant underlying tensions within the tripartite relationship and in the association with the political and administrative establishment in Scotland.

The political relationships between the Edinburgh, Glasgow and Aberdeen societies began to undergo subtle shifts at the turn of the century, although legacies from these earlier relationships were to have implications for the development of accounting institutions in Scotland in subsequent years and perhaps still influence attitudes to merger proposals in modern times.

This article attempts to explain why the Scottish societies were able to obtain individual charters in the 1850s, whereas the position in England resulted in the successful application for a national charter in 1880. Thereafter, consideration is given to a number of attempts to form a national society in Scotland which repeatedly were frustrated by the behaviour and decisions of the Edinburgh Society, despite promptings from the Privy Council and the Secretary of State for Scotland. The article reviews the efforts of the Scottish chartered societies to open up membership ranks in response to criticism from politicians, advised by their own Civil Servants, and also examines the campaign to establish appropriate and acceptable federal institutions in the form of the General Examining Board in 1893 and the Joint Committee of Councils in 1915.

Research methodology

The records of the Scottish societies are unusual among world accounting societies owing to the organizational structures adopted during the nineteenth century, in that they provide high level validation through triangulation. This process normally is understood as "the combination of methodologies in the study of the same phenomenon" (Denzin, 1978, p. 291). In this study, the methodology was to identify multiple viewpoints in order to obtain greater accuracy (Jick, 1979). Consequently, cross-validation is provided by comparing and contrasting, on a chronological scale, the official records of the three Scottish chartered societies. Thus, it is possible to observe the official recording of matters which are brought to the attention of each Council and to note the various strands of argument on contentious issues.

At least one of the societies adopted a highly selective recording of its deliberations and decisions during this period, which would have rendered a one-dimensional view of events, had the other two societies not recorded a more precise record of matters under consideration. Therefore, it can be claimed that a comprehensive and correlated examination of the Scottish societies' records avoids the major limitations discussed by Previts *et al* (1990a, 1990b) that, in institutional research, there is a problem because of:

> ... the potential for the "selective survival" of archival sources that are incomplete or biased representations of original records.

The initial sources employed in this research began with an examination of the primary records of The Institute of Accountants and Actuaries in Glasgow (IAAG). Having access to these records did not resolve completely all issues. While it was possible to clarify the reasoning behind many decisions taken by the IAAG, it was obvious that this Society existed in a political and triangular relationship on many matters of common interest with the SAE and The Society of Accountants in Aberdeen (SAA). Consequently, the research widened progressively to encompass the records and minute books of the SAE, the SAA and the early records of the Joint Committee of Councils. On a number of other matters, additional primary records were located and consulted. These primary records were the papers of the Lord Advocate, the Secretary of State for Scotland and the Committee of the Privy Council during the period 1867 to 1910. By integrating these records into the chronological scale, it is possible to observe the manner and timing in which each of the societies responded to the political and administrative environment in which it operated. It is conceivable that many of the attitudes and convictions adopted during the latter half of the nineteenth century played an important part in the subsequent development of accounting institutions in Scotland. These in turn may have reinforced beliefs of professional exclusiveness (Hastings and Hinings, 1970) and national independence far beyond the numerical strength of the societies, either separately or jointly. In 1969 and 1989 Scottish accountants were to vote to maintain their independent status when given the opportunity to unite with other UK bodies in different organizational forms.

Political relationships

In the literature on the sociology of the professions, there appear to be a number of contrasting viewpoints which attempt to describe the reasons for the formation of professional associations and the attempts these societies make to secure and maintain control of their environments. Factors which require to be examined normally encompass the economic, political, social and intellectual spheres (Allen, 1991). For many years the functionalist school (Carr-Saunders and Wilson, 1933) considered that professions could be identified by their exhibition of certain attributes, e.g. specialist knowledge, independence and self-discipline, which were necessary for practice of the service (Barber, 1963; Goode, 1960). Thus, there was an assumption that, within a self-regulatory framework, society granted social and economic privileges to professional groups on the basis that these groups operated with ethical and non-exploitative standards of behaviour and knowledge and had formal training and examination requirements for entrance. However, as Saks (1983, p. 2) stated:

> It was increasingly clear that this perspective was obscuring the social and historical conditions under which occupational groups became professions - including the power struggles involved in the process of professionalization.

An alternative, more critical perspective, employs the work of Weber (1968) to explain professional activity and power. Allen (1991, p. 52) argues that for these theorists "profession, and the manner in which it is negotiated, created and sustained" becomes the problem to investigate. Professions, as interest groups, strive to convince others of the legitimacy of their claim to professional recognition. Consequently, the association acts as an organizational instrument for defining and securing a "respectable" and "valued" social identity. Nevertheless, the presence of competing coalition groupings within professional associations should be recognized. The professional society, being subject to these sectional and competing interests, may have difficulty in portraying itself as conducting its affairs in a unitary manner. These societies are not homogeneous bodies. Willmott (1986, p. 556) observed that:

> ... professional associations are primarily, but not exclusively, political bodies whose purpose is to define, organise, secure and advance the interests of their (most vocal and influential) members.

However, it is necessary to stress that the professional organization is constrained in policy and decision making by its own membership, within the terms of its constitution. Within the SAE and SAA, major constitutional changes required a two-thirds majority, while the IAAG threshold for change was three-quarters. Harmonization of constitutional reform was made even more difficult for the Scottish chartered accountants by the necessity to consult, debate and resolve issues between the societies. This article concentrates on the political relationships which existed between the three 'local' societies from their formation to the penultimate step towards eventual amalgamation in 1951 - the formation of the Joint Committee of Councils in 1915 - and also makes observations on the relationship with organs of the State such as the Lord Advocate and the Secretary of State for Scotland.

The rise of the Scottish chartered societies

There has always been some dispute on the reasons for the formation of Scottish societies during the middle nineteenth century. Brown (1905) saw formation being concerned with differences between Scottish and English law and this interpretation has been accepted subsequently by a number of writers (Carr-Saunders and Wilson, 1933; ICAS, 1954). Stewart (1977, p. 8) was unable to trace any specific reason for the formation of the societies and considered the development to be entirely spontaneous. Macdonald (1984) argued that reasons for the formations in Edinburgh and Glasgow were different. He asserted that the Edinburgh formation was motivated by a desire to place the accountants on parity with the legal profession. This view was disputed by Briston and Kedslie (1986) who contended that the motivation was purely economic and was brought about by a Bill on Bankruptcy in 1853. Subsequent research by Walker (1993) confirms that, while bankruptcy legislation was of paramount importance to contemporary Scottish accountants, the Bill quoted by Kedslie (1990b) was not the principal cause of organization and that the provisions would have had only a marginal economic consequence. Walker contends that the main threat was seen to be proposals which would have "posed a massive ... threat to the *whole insolvency practice* of Scottish accountants". The proposal to which he refers was the Bankruptcy and Insolvency (Scotland) Bill, 1853, which had its roots in the free trade debate of that time and pressure exerted by London merchants for the harmonization of commercial law between England and Scotland.

The three Scottish chartered societies were formed and obtained their charters between 1853 and 1867. At the time of their application for charters their membership numbers were as shown in Table I.

TABLE I *Membership numbers of societies on application for charters*

	Formed	*Charter granted*	*Members*
Edinburgh	1853	1854	61
Glasgow	1853	1855	49
Aberdeen	1866	1867	12

From the earliest days, the SAE assumed leadership of the profession in Scotland, acting out its role as the senior society based in the capital city. It is interesting to note that the official history of ICAS described the first 50 years of the societies as having various periods when tranquillity reigned and attendance (at meetings) was small. It was recorded that "there was a measure of joint consultation among the Societies on matters of common interest" (ICAS, 1954, p.

34). Furthermore, it was stated that there was some consideration given to federation or amalgamation of the three societies during the nineteenth century, but that "this feeling, far-sighted though it may have been, could not be said to have been a majority view in those days" (ICAS, 1954, p. 35).

Towards the end of the nineteenth century some concern was expressed that the accountancy profession in Scotland was overstocked, generating an editorial in *The Accountants' Magazine* which questioned whether there was sufficient professional work for the new entrants to the societies' membership (*The Accountants' Magazine*, 1898). However, the structure of professional work in accounting practices had begun to change. Towards the end of the nineteenth century, accounting practices began to become more involved in corporate auditing. Accordingly, during the last 20 years of the nineteenth century the societies' memberships grew significantly. The Companies Act, 1900 required all registered companies to conduct an audit, although there was no specification that the auditor should be a professionally qualified accountant and further audit work became available from banks, railway companies, Scottish burghs and councils (Kedslie, 1990b, Ch. VI).

In addition to specific expansions in accountancy practices, the growth and distribution of the societies' memberships also reflected the different economic structures in Scotland during the latter part of the nineteenth and early twentieth centuries. The city of Glasgow became the centre of an area of heavy manufacturing industry, with a strong emphasis on shipbuilding and engineering in addition to being a major commercial and trading centre (Daiches, 1977; Massie, 1989). Particular industries "increased their outputs in a spectacular fashion in the period 1870-1914" and Scottish engineering gained a worldwide reputation. The west of Scotland "derived great prosperity before 1920 from its very dependence on the production of capital goods". Steel production increased to 964,000 tons in 1900 from 241,000 tons achieved in 1885, while the proportion of the total shipbuilding output reached 35 per cent of the total UK output by 1902 (Lythe and Butt, 1975, pp. 202-23). The Scottish economy during this period operated as a dual economy with the major growth emanating in the West (Slaven, 1975). Edinburgh, by contrast was not a major manufacturing centre and did not benefit to the same extent. Between 1851 and 1911 there was a significant shift in the proportions of the population resident in the major cities in Scotland. The Edinburgh population doubled during this period, although there was only a small increase in the proportion from 6.7 per cent to 8.4

per cent. In Glasgow, by contrast, the population almost tripled and the proportion increased from 11.9 per cent to 21 per cent (see Table II).

TABLE II *Population of the principal towns (thousands) 1851-1911*

Year	Aberdeen	Edinburgh and Leith	Glasgow	Total
1851	72	194	345	2,889
	(2.5)	(6.7)	(11.9)	
1881	105	295	587	3,736
	(2.8)	(7.9)	(15.7)	
1911	164	401	1,000	4,761
	(3.4)	(8.4)	(21.0)	

Note: Percentage of total population in parentheses

Thus the increase in the number of Glasgow chartered accountants reflected local industrial, commercial and demographic transformations. Membership of the IAAG expanded at an annual rate of 10 per cent during the first five years of the twentieth century, (i.e. twice the rate of the Edinburgh increase), becoming the numerically larger society in 1902. While the outbreak of the First World War had a deleterious effect on membership numbers, by the time of formation of the Joint Committee of Councils in 1915, the membership numbers of the Scottish societies of chartered accountants showed that the IAAG was 40 per cent larger in membership than the SAE. The constitutional affairs of the societies were determined by the local members. Members who practised in English cities were not able to play any significant part in the deliberations of their society and enlargement of Council constituency was a twentieth century development.

Although the SAE played a leading role in the affairs of the Scottish societies throughout the period being reviewed, it is clear that the IAAG began to exert a major influence on Scottish professional affairs, no doubt influenced by its increasing numerical dominance. It remains for later research to demonstrate that the IAAG was able to develop as the dominant political influence, until the amalgamation (as The Institute of Chartered Accountants of Scotland) of the three Scottish societies in 1951.

The Scottish royal charters

The formation of the three chartered societies, in whole or in part, has been well documented (Brown, 1905; ICAS, 1954; Kedslie, 1990b; Stewart, 1977; Walker, 1988). Although it is often noted that the SAE was the senior grouping and held the oldest royal charter, the fact that the SAE charter was obtained in a manner which was *ultra vires* its own constitution has always been overlooked. It may be that the outline provided by Brown is responsible for this oversight. In his description of the process whereby the SAE obtained its charter, Brown is very specific on the dates of early meetings and yet he states that: "In May 1854 the Council approved of a draft Petition... and at a General Meeting ... held on 30 May 1854 this Petition was adopted" (Brown, 1905, p. 207).[2] Referring back to the primary record, it transpires that the Council meeting to consider the draft petition (prepared by John C. Brodie, WS.)[3] was held on 29 May and it was recorded that Mr. Brodie was travelling to London on other business and "would have the opportunity, if desired by Council, of forwarding the object in view" (SAE, 1854a). The Council, having approved the petition, and anxious to avail themselves of Mr Brodie's offer, called a Special General Meeting to be held *the next day*. While the underlying reason for calling the meeting can be understood, it has to be recognized that this meeting was in fact unconstitutional. Clause 12 of the original and prevailing Constitution and Rules required ten days' notice for the calling of a Special General Meeting (SAE, 1854b) and there was no time-waiver clause in the Constitution.

Before the SAE petition was prepared, the IAAG had called a Council meeting for the 17 May 1854 to consider an application for a royal charter. This was cancelled because the meeting was not quorate (IAAG, 1854a). Thus, when the IAAG meeting to proceed with an application was held in July 1854, the SAE Petition was already in process with the Privy Council. There is no record of any apprehension about the IAAG intentions in the SAE records, yet there must have been some concern because the IAAG minutes record that the SAE president had written to suggest that "it would be better to delay the presentation of the Glasgow Petition until the outcome of the Edinburgh Petition was known". Despite this plea by the SAE for a clear run, the IAAG Council resolved "to take immediately the requisite measures for making an application" (IAAG, 1854b).

The SAA application to the Privy Council was made in 1867. Following normal consultation the Lord Advocate proposed that a supplementary charter be granted to the SAE. The purpose of this supplementary charter was to provide the SAE with powers to grant diplomas to accountants in the various provincial towns of Scotland. It soon became clear that the Lord Advocate was not aware that a charter was held by the IAAG and, when he was apprised of its existence, declared that it would be necessary to widen the consultation process (SAE, 1867). However, there is no record of any formal discussion being held between the Lord Advocate and the IAAG nor any subsequent communication with the SAE. Kedslie (1990a, p. 76) speculates that:

> One can imagine the reaction that such an act would have had in the city of Aberdeen which almost certainly was not considered by its inhabitants to be a provincial town and whose accountants would have been appalled at an attempt to make them inferior members of the Edinburgh Society.

An alternative interpretation is that the Lord Advocate was attempting to establish the SAE as the national accounting body but that, ultimately, he had appreciated that the existence of the Glasgow charter constrained his ability to achieve such a logical objective. There is no evidence to suggest that the Lord Advocate consulted either the IAAG or the putative SAA on this matter. Such evidence as does exist records (in the Aberdeen charter) that the Lord Advocate's views had been sought. Evidence from a slightly later period suggests that the SAA was positively in favour of being a constituent member of a national organization.

A national society: the Scottish chartered societies

Although the three societies were formed and awarded charters on an individual basis, they attempted, retrospectively, to provide a rational explanation for this. In a statement made by them jointly to the Privy Council in 1890, while opposing a petition for a royal charter by The Scottish Institute of Accountants (SIA),[4] it was stated that:

> The system of separate Societies, with separate Charters, had been deliberately preferred to the English system of one National Society. Each system has its advantages, but the circumstances in Scotland, where substantially the whole business of accounting proper is done at the great centres, seemed to render the system of separate Societies most expedient (Privy Council, 1890, p. 27).

This proposition was advanced as a counterclaim to the SIA contention that the SIA could be regarded as a national body, while the Scottish chartered societies were merely local in character (Walker, 1991, p. 258). However, this argument is untenable chronologically. The reality was that a national system had not been specifically considered during the applications by the SAE and IAAG. Furthermore, the English charter of 1880 postdates the Scottish charters by many years and there is evidence that the ICAEW became a national society at the behest of the Privy Council rather than by deliberate choice of the English societies (ICAEW, 1966). It would appear that the Scottish societies were attempting to counter the SIA's claim to national status. Scottish Office officials advised the Minister that some form of "consolidation" in the form of a national society was desirable (Lord Advocate, 1890), and the societies had prepared the outline of a contingency plan. This contingency plan was no more than a vague intention to be activated if the Privy Council made recommendations for the formation of a national society.

Evidence exists that two of the chartered societies (the IAAG and the SAA) were prepared to contemplate a national organizational structure and in fact at various times both societies made proposals to accomplish this objective. There were four documented attempts to establish a national organization during the period 1883 to 1915. However, it proved impossible for the 'senior' society (SAE) to be convinced that this proposition was in the long-term interest of Scottish chartered accountants. It is a matter of concern that these proposals were not recorded in the minute books of this 'senior' society for reasons which are not specified but possibly arising from the relationship of that Council with its own members. A reasonable assumption is that the proposals were discussed among a small group of the Council and that this group concluded that advocating such proposals might not meet with universal approval from the SAE membership. Rather than raise the matter within the SAE for further debate and discussion, the issue was put to one side and not discussed formally. Evidence to support this assumption is provided below.

The first occasion on which one of the societies considered organizational change arose in 1883. At the 1883 Annual General Meeting of the IAAG a motion had been proposed to liberalize admission rules. In the ensuing discussion it was determined not to proceed with this resolution because, it was argued, a more laudable objective would be the creation of a national body. If the other societies were willing to discuss merging, it would facilitate the process if there was an approximate harmonization of the rules of the three societies. It is clear from this occasion that the IAAG always considered it advisable not to alter its own rules when possible amalgamation was being proposed or discussed.

Wyllie Guild, a past president of the IAAG, was delegated to meet the Edinburgh Secretary to discuss the resolution passed at the AGM which proposed "to have a General Institute for Scotland to be formed by amalgamation of the three Scottish Societies" (IAAG, 1883a). In the event Guild was unable to broach the subject of amalgamation as instructed, for he found the Edinburgh Council in session on his arrival, holding urgent discussions on the issue of the application for a royal charter by the Scottish Institute of Accountants. Guild reported back to the Council of the IAAG that he had proposed co-operation between the IAAG and the SAE in opposing this application. This offer of co-operation had been accepted, and Guild reported that he would "endeavour to accomplish that [the amalgamation proposal] shortly" (IAAG, 1883b).

However, there is no further record of the IAAG proposal being resubmitted and it has to be assumed that no immediate further opportunity arose. There is no doubt that the chartered societies found themselves actively defending their status and position against the SIA and later the Corporation of Accountants Limited (CofA),[5] for a number of years (Kedslie, 1990b; Shackleton, 1991; Walker, 1991).

In 1884, the SIA again petitioned for a royal charter to which the three chartered societies objected vigorously and with ultimate success. The chartered societies had prepared an article of objections for presentation to the Lord Advocate, although, during this preparation, the Council of the SAA sent a letter to the SAE suggesting "the propriety of the three societies endeavouring in some way to unite into one Incorporation" (SAA, 1884). There is no record of this approach being discussed formally by the Council of the SAE.

The next attempt to raise the issue of a national organization was in 1889 which again coincided with, and indeed was almost certainly motivated by, another petition for a royal charter by the SIA (under the title of The Incorporated Society of Accountants in Scotland[6]). Although the chartered societies were again unanimous in their opposition to the petition, it is clear that the SIA application prompted the Glasgow Council to reconsider the issue of uniting the Scottish societies. In 1889 the IAAG Council minuted that "some steps should be taken with a view to bringing the three Chartered Bodies in Scotland into closer connection with one another", and the Council resolved to make an approach to the SAE (IAAG, 1889a). Yet again there was no formal consideration of this approach being minuted by the SAE, although there must have been some discussion on this issue among a number of the SAE Council members, because in 1890 the secretary of the SAE was quoted (at the Aberdeen AGM as saying that:

> ... his Society quite concurred in the idea the time had now come for the proposal that there be a General National Society of Accountants in Scotland similar to that for England & Wales (SAA, 1890a).

This statement was made at the time of a further application by the SIA, when that society was emphasizing the local character of the three societies and effectively claiming that the SIA was capable of embracing all Scottish accountants. At a meeting held in Edinburgh on 14 February 1890, the three chartered societies had agreed to instruct Counsel to disclose to the Committee of the Privy Council that the adoption of a scheme of national co-operation was actively being contemplated. This 'offer' was to be made only if the issue was raised directly by the Committee of the Privy Council (SAE, 1890a). The exact position to be taken had been drafted for this meeting at a meeting of the SAE Council on 10 February which concluded that, in the event of the Judicial Committee finding the SIA application reasonable, then:

> ...Counsel should be instructed to say that, while there are many difficulties surrounding the question of the Societies extending their privileges beyond the limits of the three cities ... the matter was one which had already engaged the attention of the Societies and that they were prepared to consider carefully the whole question with a view of ascertaining whether such a suggestion could be carried into practical effect (SAE, 1890a).

The Aberdeen Council reacted positively to the apparently radical declaration of policy attributed to the secretary of the SAE. However, the Aberdeen representatives who attended the meeting of 14 February warned the Council, on their return from Edinburgh, that the SAE, while most anxious to oppose the application jointly, seemed unwilling to unite with the other chartered societies, whereas the Glasgow delegates appeared enthusiastic for an amalgamation and the establishment of a General Board of Examiners. Nevertheless, the Aberdeen Council submitted a letter to the Edinburgh society (with a copy to Glasgow) on 20 February. In this letter, the SAA claimed that opposition to the SIA application was not sufficient, and that the Aberdeen society was:

> ... disposed to admit (the) propriety of establishing a General Society for Scotland ... Such proposal ... should be that a new Charter be granted to a Society consisting of the members of the three present Societies, with instructions to them to form an Examining Board and to admit such of the petitioners (of the SIA) as are in practice on their own account and are found qualified and eligible (IAAG, 1890a).

The response from the other two societies is most revealing in reflecting Council procedures on sensitive discussions and issues. The Glasgow minute book records fully the receipt of this letter and its terms. It also records that the Glasgow Council wished to hold to the agreement reached at the 14 February meeting at that juncture in the Privy Council proceedings, as:

> ... we may be unable at once to condescend on the details of the proposed federation ... and [it] would weaken our position by showing the Privy Council that there were divergences of opinion among us (IAAG, 1890a).

Thus, on purely tactical grounds, it was thought that a change in the official defensive position was not advisable.

The SAE minute book contains no record of the Aberdeen letter having been either received or discussed, which is additional evidence that sensitive proposals were not always minuted. The salient issue is whether these issues were discussed within the SAE Council. One analysis would be that because these matters were not minuted they would not appear to have been discussed. However, this proposition seems inconceivable. Discussion must have taken place among some members of the SAE Council, even if only on an informal basis. Messages transmitted to Aberdeen and Glasgow were in no doubt about the Edinburgh position on amalgamation. A minute recorded at a meeting of the Aberdeen Council stated that:

> It is quite evident that the Edinburgh Society will consent to no amalgamation with other Societies *until they are compelled to do so* (SAA, 1890b, emphasis added).

Therefore it would seem reasonable to conclude, on the evidence from all three societies' records, that amalgamation was not considered explicitly through the formal decision process of the Council of the Edinburgh society, but was given consideration by a process of informal discussions within that Council.

Awareness of the Edinburgh position must have had some substantive basis, probably arising in the form of a message from an Edinburgh Council member or official. The problem for the SAE was that there was a body of opinion among its members which was opposed strongly to any scheme of national structure even in a federal form. A prominent Edinburgh member, James Walker, proposed an amendment at the 1891 AGM which stated that "The Chartered Societies are indisposed to Federation through the Constitution of a National Society", and this motion was added as an amendment to the President's motion. The President's motion had asked that the question of the status of the Edinburgh society in relation to other existing societies be referred back to the President and Council for more detailed consideration (SAE, 1891a).

It seems quite clear that the Scottish chartered societies united in the face of a definite threat to their professional monopoly in the form of the SIA applications to the Privy Council for a royal charter. Nevertheless, it is also clear that within their ranks there was considerable divergence of opinion concerning how to meet this threat. The SIA applications were the catalyst in forcing the societies to consider their organizational forms. Both the Glasgow and Aberdeen societies were amenable to proposals for a national society promulgated by agreed merger. The Edinburgh society, on the other hand, regarded fusion into a national society as something which would only be agreed under external duress (i.e. Government/Privy Council pressure). This attitude was probably a function of two factors. First, the SAE saw itself as the predominant and elder society, based in the capital, and with close links to the national legal and administrative institutions of that city. This was implied most clearly in the report on the 50th anniversary celebrations of the IAAG, which drew the comment in *The Accountants' Magazine* leader that:

> The Glasgow banquet, although it had the disadvantage of coming after that of Edinburgh... lacked nothing in enthusiasm, and considerably exceeded the Edinburgh meeting in numbers. *While the numerous guests who were present to do honour to the Institute were not perhaps as a whole so widely representative of Scottish national institutions or of the learning and dignity of the country as those who were present at Edinburgh,* they were fully representative of that for which Glasgow stands pre-eminent, viz. its manufacturing, commercial and financial interests (*The Accountants' Magazine,* 1905, emphasis added).

Second, members of the SAE were reluctant to accept any change to the constitutional position. The possibility that the SAE Council could propose and obtain support for constitutional change was very remote.

In order to place the pressures for a national society in its wider context, it is important to assess the considerations and attitudes of the political and administrative authorities. The applications of the SIA to the Privy Council were always referred to Scotland for advice and, by tracing the advice to Ministers, and the response of those in political power, it is possible to obtain a wider dimension of understanding about the position and status of the Scottish chartered accountants.

A national society: the political and administrative authorities

The relationships between the three chartered societies and political institutions in Scotland was in an evolutionary stage during the period 1880-1915, not only because of the recent formation of the societies, but also because, in 1885, the office of the Secretary for Scotland was created (Gibson, 1985). Prior to 1885 the Lord Advocate had performed a similar role but political feelings in Scotland had been assuaged by the appointment of the Secretary for Scotland, with a seat in the Cabinet, arising from the actions and support of Lord Rosebery (Gibson, 1985, p. 24).

The procedure for consideration of applications for a royal charter changed in Scotland during the period under review. Initially, the advice of the Lord Advocate was sought by, and was sufficient guidance for, the Committee of the Privy Council, which was established to proffer advice to the Monarch. However, the creation of the Secretary for Scotland in 1885 caused the Privy Council to seek his advice as the principal political government officer in Scotland. When the first SIA application for a royal charter was made in 1884, the Privy Council sought the opinion of the Lord Advocate. In defending their position, the chartered societies prepared a petition of objection for presentation to the Lord Advocate and the Privy Council. The chartered societies were able to put forward a sufficiently persuasive case such that, on the advice of the Lord Advocate, the SIA petition for a charter was rejected by the Privy Council in August 1884.

In his opinion on the 1884 application, the Lord Advocate made a comment which, in later years, was to allow a wider consideration of subsequent applications:

> ... if there was a large and important body of educated and skilled accountants in the other towns of Scotland outside Edinburgh, Glasgow and Aberdeen, who desire to be incorporated and who could show evidence of adequate qualification, a Petition for their Incorporation would deserve very serious consideration (Lord Advocate, 1890).

In subsequent applications the SIA laid great emphasis on the number of accountants practising in Dundee and claimed that these accountants and others were disadvantaged by the 'closed' memberships operated by the three chartered societies.

On the 1889 application by the SIA for a royal charter, the Privy Council sought the opinion of the Secretary of State. The Secretary for Scotland was advised by his officials that, if he advised against the petition, it would be refused but that, if he thought there were prima facie grounds at least for considering it, then a Committee of the Privy Council would hear the petition, and that the Secretary of State would be asked to sit on the Committee. He was therefore advised "not at present to give a decided opinion in favour of the Petition, although he may, with propriety, report decidedly against it" (Scottish Office, 1889).

On full consideration, the advice was that he would be justified in advising the Privy Council against that application, but that:

> ... it would evidently be for the public advantage if the existing Societies were to open their ranks, or in some way consolidate, and

any influence or pressure in this direction would... be properly applied (Scottish Office, 1889).

A further Civil Service minute in this set of articles supported this view and amplified the argument, stating that:

> A satisfactory solution would be the opening of the ranks of the existing bodies, but I go further and think that *if the existing bodies were to join together and add to their members all duly qualified persons in Scotland, so as to make one Society of Chartered Accountants for Scotland with the existing safeguards for efficiency and training and possibly a reconsideration of the very high fees existing in Edinburgh ... it would be the most satisfactory solution* (Scottish Office, 1889, emphasis added).

This minute is marked in red in the margin GOOD, presumably by the Secretary of State. The Lord Advocate was requested by the Secretary of State to advise on the petition and he reported that he was not prepared to recommend that the application be refused without a hearing, although it was noted that "the objections... are certainly most weighty and I do not see how they are to be got over" (Scottish Office, 1889).

The Lord Advocate summarized his fundamental objections as:

> 1. It is practically avowed that the petitioners propose, if a Charter is granted, to assume the designation CA. It is manifest that this would be an injustice, not merely to the other Chartered Bodies, but also to the public, who would be induced to believe men to be of equivalent status, who are not so.

> 2. While many of the petitioners are very good accountants, I am afraid this can hardly be affirmed of all, and yet it is proposed ... that they shall all be members without any test or examination.

> 3. The name proposed is misleading, having regard to the comparatively small proportion which the petitioners bear to their profession in Scotland (Scottish Office, 1890).

In 1893, the SIA made an unusual, and ultimately unsuccessful, plea direct to the Secretary of State for Scotland, requesting that the application rejected by the Privy Council in 1890 be reconsidered. The Minister was advised that he did not have any formal powers in the matter because the Privy Council offered the view that it was an irregular course for the petitioners to approach the Secretary for Scotland directly. The Scottish Office concluded that the petition was more of a remonstrance against the refusal of the Privy Council in 1890. The Scottish Office officials minuted that:

> The Memorialists would no doubt make a regular application to the Committee (of the Privy Council) if they now get any encouragement from the Secretary for Scotland. If the Secretary for Scotland, without giving any encouragement, simply refers them to the Council office, I should think the odds are that they do nothing further in the present.

In the event the Secretary for Scotland accepted this latter advice but requested that "the letter should be not an unfriendly communication ... I have seen these gentlemen more than once".

It is interesting to note that the advice of officials contained in this set of articles refers yet again to the "true" solution being the establishment of one Society of Chartered Accountants for Scotland:

> I think we go too far in reflecting the vested interests of those closed Corporations in Edinburgh, Glasgow and Aberdeen. If such respect leads to the refusal to allow cities so important as Dundee to have Chartered Accountants of its own and sooner than have a new Charter for every fresh town that wants one, I think that one Charter for Scotland would be better (Scottish Office, 1893).

It is a matter of record that by 1893 the Glasgow and Aberdeen societies had opened their ranks by making amendments to their admission requirements, although this was not to the complete satisfaction of the SIA, many of whose members were excluded from admission to the chartered societies. Nevertheless, the actions of the Aberdeen society, and Glasgow in particular, in 1890 (referred to below) limited the force of this particular argument about closed corporations. However, the failure of the SAE to make similar concessions weakened the Scottish societies' case to counter fully this criticism. The suggestions made by Scottish Office officials on forming a national society were repudiated effectively by SAE resistance.

Opening membership ranks

There were at least two fundamental differences between the Scottish societies on recruitment to membership. The first matter, which remained unresolved throughout their existence as independent societies, was the issue of indenture fees. From its formation, the SAE demanded that there be a substantial indenture fee payable by the apprentice to the master (Walker, 1988, p. 129).[7] The IAAG had no such requirement and pursued, as a matter of principle, a more egalitarian recruitment policy which did not require the payment of indenture fees. The SAE were often criticized for the high cost of entrance fees and made a number of attempts to harmonize the position among the Scottish societies in order to mitigate its specific exposure to criticism on this issue. However, in order to succeed it was necessary for the SAE to persuade the IAAG to modify its position. All these efforts failed, with the IAAG making abundantly clear its total opposition to imposing an indenture fee. The Council of the IAAG made a statement of principle on this matter in response to a formal request for harmonization on rates of indenture fees made by the SAE by stating:

> The feeling of the meeting was distinctly opposed to the proposal for the imposition of such an Apprentice Fee as would deter any large proportion of lads from which Glasgow Apprentices were principally drawn from entering into an Indenture with a member (IAAG, 1910).

The second difference which arose was the issue of opening the membership ranks to other accountants who were regarded as well qualified (usually by experience) and had been in public practice for a number of years. The IAAG Council came under pressure from its younger membership to open up the ranks to other accountants. The IAAG Council often deferred taking such steps on the declared grounds that sensitive discussions were being held with other UK accounting bodies and advanced the claim that the existence of differences among the societies' rules for admission precluded any steps to amalgamation or co-operation. However, when the IAAG did effect changes to open the membership ranks, this action prompted considerable criticism from the SAE (IAAG, 1892a).

The first attempt by the IAAG to alter admission regulations was in 1882. This proposal was deferred, as noted earlier, when Wyllie

Guild was delegated to discuss with Edinburgh the possibility of forming a national society (IAAG, 1883a). In the immediate aftermath of the rejection of the SIA approach to form a national organization in 1885, the IAAG considered another amendment to admission rules, so that the undernoted accountants could be admitted:

(a) gentlemen who had been in practice for a period of four years
(b) men who had been trained with other than a Glasgow member and
(c) members of the ICAEW (IAAG, 1885).

Throughout the 1880s and 1890s the Council of the IAAG was lobbied persistently by John Mann Jnr (later Sir John Mann) and a number of younger members, to admit accountants who had been in practice for many years. Mann pleaded that experienced accountants should be admitted without apprenticeship and without examination.

The IAAG Council procrastinated on this issue for a number of years, but the Council, while clearly unwilling to accede, was reluctant to reject outright the pleas of Mann (1951). Consequently, at the quarterly meeting, in April 1889, it was proposed that membership should be offered to those accountants who had been in practice for a number of years. However, this proposal was not put to members because at the October quarterly meeting it was decided that it was not expedient to proceed in view of moves for proposed negotiations for uniting the three Scottish societies. It was considered that controversial constitutional changes might undermine the more important issue of union into a national society (IAAG, 1889a).

After the rejection of the SIA petition in 1890, all three societies determined to counter criticism on entry policy by amending the rules of admission. The IAAG and the SAA were successful in obtaining members' approval but the SAE encountered extraordinary opposition, not only from the members but also from within the body of the Council.

The Glasgow Council first considered the issue of admitting experienced accountants to membership at a meeting on 8 July 1890 and, at the July quarterly meeting, President Walter Mackenzie moved:

. . . that now they could, *with a good grace,* open the door to admit some of those who were ineligible ... but whose position and qualifications fitted them for membership (IAAG, 1890b, emphasis added).

This amendment became known as the 'ten year' rule. Under the terms of the rule, the IAAG admitted 16 members of the SIA, including Thomson McLintock from Glasgow (who was also a member of the ICAEW), and David Myles (ex-president of the SIA) from Dundee. Aberdeen altered its rules in a similar fashion, although the only additional admission was Mr Cram, the Chamberlain of the City of Aberdeen (SAA, 1890c).

Consideration of the change in the Edinburgh rules did not proceed so smoothly, and it soon became apparent that the Council was split on the issue into at least three different factions, including outright opposition to the principle of admission (SAE, 1890b). The majority of the Council was able to propose at the 1891 Annual General Meeting that a modification should be passed which imposed no time restriction for implementation. However, the split in the Council was so fundamental that it became necessary, prior to the AGM, to announce that the Committee and Council were not bound by the terms of the resolution. At the AGM, a resolution "to consider the previous question" attracted such support from the members that defeat for the admission rules resolution was certain. In the face of such hostility from the members, the rules resolution was withdrawn (SAEGM, 1891). It should be noted that the Edinburgh members acted contrary to the statements made to the Privy Council on their behalf and the full-powers mandate given to their representatives in attendance at the 1890 Privy Council hearing. Furthermore, it could be argued that the SAE proved less gracious to the SIA members than the IAAG. It is a matter of record that from 1890, chartered accountants practising in the fourth Scottish city of Dundee (situated on the East coast) were almost entirely members of the IAAG (situated on the west coast) through to 1951.[8]

There is some evidence that the SAE considered that the actions of the IAAG were opportunistic and unacceptable. During negotiations with the IAAG over the formation of the General Examining Board (GEB), the Edinburgh Council indicated that the "ten year" rule posed problems. In a letter dated 19 November 1892, the SAE secretary stated:

> As regards the continuation of your rule admitting outside accountants under certain restrictions, I fear this proposal would give rise to considerable discussion in our Society and I should have

thought that you had already admitted as many under this rule as was desirable (IAAG, 1892a).

The Council of the IAAG was clearly not impressed by this viewpoint and indicated its intention to renew the rule. Eventually, this issue was resolved by a compromise which allowed the IAAG to maintain this admission rule, although formal admission of applicants had to be submitted for approval by the GEB. It was already apparent that the actions of the IAAG in admitting a significant number of ex-SIA accountants had reduced the effectiveness and credibility of the SIA as a political force in Scottish accountancy. Almost all the important senior accountants in the SIA were admitted to the IAAG and the principal objective of the proposals of John Mann and other younger members, which had been made with the intention of reducing external competition and bringing these accountants within the scope and discipline of the IAAG, was realized.[9]

General Examining Board

Until 1893 the Scottish chartered societies conducted examinations on an independent basis (Kedslie, 1990a; Shackleton, 1993; Walker, 1988). The first indication that the three societies might co-operate in the establishment of a joint examination body arose at a meeting in Edinburgh, on 14 February 1892, to consider the positions to be adopted by the Scottish societies in opposing an application for a royal charter to the Privy Council by the SIA. The meeting comprised representatives of the three societies and they resolved:

> To instruct Counsel, if the Privy Council indicate the necessity, in their opinion, of providing a qualification for practitioners in the smaller towns, and outside the existing Societies, to state that the three Societies are considering how these objections might be overcome by an affiliation or other arrangement between the existing Societies (SAE, 1890c).

Aberdeen had suggested to the SAE, in a letter dated 20 February 1890, that this proposal be activated. The SAE reaction to this overture had been ambivalent. The SAE Council at that time was struggling to reconcile different viewpoints within its own ranks and within its membership. There were substantial and vocal elements hostile to any forms of federal structure being created. However, external pressures, most particularly in the form of SIA and CofA made the position of separate and independent societies difficult to sustain, particularly in the relationship with the administrative and political authorities in Scotland and London. Thus, the SAE Council, in formulating a policy response to these external pressures, deduced that the formation of an examining board, comprising the three chartered societies, would be the maximum response to external criticism which would be acceptable to the coalition groups within its membership. As became clear later, it also provided the SAE with the opportunity to maintain its hegemony within the Scottish societies by prescribing the examination and training requirements for all Scottish societies, modelled on the Edinburgh system.

Consequently, the SAE revived the proposal for the creation of a General Examining Board at a Council meeting on 11 December 1891:

> ... the general opinion being that steps should be taken in the direction of forming a closer bond of union with the Scotch Societies, it was resolved to ascertain the views of these Societies on the subject of the formation of a General Board of Examination for Scotland (SAE, 1891b).

This proposal was contained in a letter to the IAAG dated 15 December 1891. A conference of delegates was held in the chambers of Alexander Sloan, the IAAG secretary, on 21 December, at which broad general agreement was reached to form a board to embrace the three chartered societies. The representatives of the SAE volunteered to draft an agreement. Sloan's report to the IAAG Council stated that the Glasgow delegates thought that "no difficulty of any importance would present itself in the way of assimilating examination" (IAAG, 1891).

However, when the committees met next in Edinburgh, in February 1892, the Glasgow representatives were surprised that, in addition to the scheme for the establishment of the board and a syllabus of examinations, the SAE had incorporated general regulations relating to admission to the societies. As this had "not formed part of the scheme agreed at the conference", the IAAG Council was unable to agree to the draft terms (IAAG, 1892b). The major problem was the insistence of the SAE that apprenticeship should be for a period of five years and under a proper form of indenture. The SAE wrote to the IAAG stating that they would not join in any regulations which would permit any society to dispense with the five-year apprenticeship. The IAAG conceded the principle of the indenture but resisted successfully the five-year term, preferring their own requirement of four years. (The IAAG revised this period to five years in 1898).

By September 1892, the IAAG Council appeared ready to confirm the draft agreement establishing the General Examining Board. However, by the Council meeting of the 25 October, some of the Council members expressed second thoughts, sufficient for the minute to record that:

> ... it having become apparent to certain members that the proposed alterations were more radical than had been contemplated, it was agreed, after considerable discussion, that it would be premature to submit to the quarterly meeting the proposed alterations (IAAG, 1892c).

The new major points of disagreement centred on the "ten year" rule, which the SAE wished to have abolished, and the appointment of the president and secretary of the SAE as chairman and secretary of the GEB respectively. The IAAG informed the SAE that the Council felt "very strongly the importance of retaining the power to meet exceptional circumstances in the admission of members" (IAAG, 1892d).

After considerable correspondence and further meetings, it was agreed that the IAAG position on special admissions be accepted, subject to approval by the GEB. Chairmanship rested with the president of the city in which the GEB meetings were held. In general the three societies co-operated throughout the life of the GEB to 1951.[10]

The Joint Committee of Councils

For many years from about 1890, the Scottish societies were involved in formulating, negotiating or objecting to various bills which were proposed to Parliament for the registration of the public accounting profession (Kedslie, 1990a; Kirkham and Loft, 1992; Macdonald, 1985). Many of these attempts were started on a UK basis, although, among the Scottish chartered societies, the major effort was undertaken by the SAE, with the fairly passive co-operation of the IAAG and the SAA (SAE, 1891a, 1891b). There was no satisfactory outcome to any of these attempts to obtain the highest level of monopoly status primarily because mutual understanding and agreement were required between all the accounting bodies and these proved impossible to obtain. The endeavour was, to an extent, satisfied partially many years later by the passing of the Companies Act, 1947 (later consolidated to the Companies Act, 1948).

In addition to these Registration Bills there were two other attempts to restructure the profession which affected the Scottish societies directly. The first attempt was in 1901 and involved the Institute of Chartered Accountants in England and Wales (ICAEW). The origins are to be found in a letter addressed to the IAAG by the Council of the ICAEW dated 10 December 1888 which expressed the desire "to bring about closer co-operation of English and Scottish chartered accountants" (IAAG, 1888).

These feelings were reciprocated by the Council of the IAAG and a conference was held in London where the Glasgow representatives anticipated that, although matters of mutual eligibility were to be discussed, "it was thought that the Conference might lead to some wider scheme of Incorporation being proposed" (IAAG, 1889b). After the meeting on 3 April 1901, the ICAEW undertook to contact the SAA and SAE. This approach was probably deferred for a period as the Scottish societies were involved heavily at that time in opposing the SIA application for a royal charter.

However, in January 1901, the SAE received a letter from London members complaining about disadvantages which they claimed to suffer and, in response, the SAE proposed writing to the ICAEW to formulate a scheme of mutual recognition and co-operation between the societies of chartered accountants in Britain (SAE, 1901). A conference was duly held in March in London, at which it was determined to form a Joint Committee of 20 members to consider practicable actions and to invite the Institute of Chartered Accountants in Ireland (ICAI) to join the committee. A meeting held in December constituted the Joint Committee but thereafter the arrangement faltered, primarily because the SAE took the view that:

> ... as the duties of the proposed Board are merely deliberative and no independent administrative powers are to be given to it, they do not consider the execution of a joint Agreement necessary *especially as such an Agreement would require to be submitted to a General*

Meeting of the Society before it could be effective (SAE, 1902; emphasis added).

This conclusion was communicated to the IAAG and the SAA. There were two difficulties for the SAE. The first was the fundamental problem that the SAE Council was unwilling to delegate administrative powers outside Council. The second problem was that the SAE Council was reluctant to resuscitate the considerable opposition in its own membership to any form of constitution based on a national society.

The IAAG noted the Edinburgh position but disagreed, stating that the Council was "of opinion that, in order to constitute aright the proposed Board, an Agreement would be necessary" (IAAG, 1902). Although this opinion was communicated to Edinburgh, it did not change the SAE position and, ultimately, the ICAEW confirmed that it would accept the SAE view. Thus, the Joint Committee did not have any executive powers, nor was it constituted by formal agreement. Eventually, the Joint Committee became ineffectual, holding its last meeting in 1905 (IAAG, 1913), and an opportunity to establish a British institute passed through the disinclination of the SAE to submit proposals for major constitutional reform to its membership in general meeting.

The second effort to restructure the Scottish profession arose from proposals made in 1915 to establish a Joint Committee of Councils of the Scottish chartered societies. The Scottish chartered societies had benefited in a number of ways from the establishment of the GEB. One advantage gained was the provision of a forum for discussion and co-operation between them. Another advancement was the demonstration of national co-operation through the activities of the GEB, which could be presented as evidence to deflect criticism from external sources. Therefore, it is surprising in retrospect that it took a number of years for these particular lessons to be absorbed fully.

By 1915 it was clear to the IAAG that issues of mutual interest to the Scottish societies raised in the early years of the twentieth century were difficult to resolve. This was attributed to the structures of governance within the Scottish societies. Decision taking, which involved discussion between the societies, was performed in an *ad hoc* manner, was time-consuming and often proved difficult to co-ordinate.[11] Consequently, the IAAG President, Mr Alexander Moore, proposed the formation of a permanent Joint Committee of the Councils of the Scottish societies for the consideration of matters of mutual interest (IAAG, 1915). The specific event that instigated this proposal was a letter in June 1915 from the Association of Scottish Chartered Accountants in London:

> ... calling the attention of the Council to certain English Private Bills now before Parliament containing an audit clause limiting the election of auditors to members of the English Institute and the Incorporated Society.

The Association asked that the Scottish societies should take immediate steps to have this clause altered so as to permit the election of Scottish chartered accountants (IAAG, 1915). Initially the SAE response had been to the effect that there would be considerable difficulties and, therefore, had proposed no particular actions. The IAAG responded in a more positive manner recording that:

> The President suggested that it was very desirable that a Joint Committee of the three Scottish Societies should be formed to deal with questions of this kind and other mutual interests and it was accordingly agreed to ask the SAE and SAA to confer as to the appointment of such a committee (IAAG, 1915).

The SAE and the SAA proved to be in full agreement with this proposal and during November and December 1915 a draft agreement was approved by the three societies. The agreement stated that the general objects were:

> ... the furthering and protecting the mutual interests of the Chartered Accountant Societies in Scotland, of maintaining the high standard of the profession, of considering all questions and matters relating to the profession that may come under their notice and reporting to the Councils of the several Societies thereon (Joint Committee of Councils, 1915).

The membership of this Committee comprised the three presidents plus three representatives from the SAE and the IAAG and one from the SAA. Expenses, however, were to be borne in proportion to the membership of each society. The original structure of the Joint Committee remained in force until 1951, although the membership proportions of the individual societies changed significantly throughout the first half of the twentieth century (see Table III).

TABLE III *Membership of the three Scottish chartered accountants societies 1900-1950*

Year	Edinburgh	Glasgow	Aberdeen
1900	351	330	39
1905	429	479	47
1910	497	666	61
1915	588	830	75
1920	630	975	81
1925	783	1,403	115
1930	1,005	1,964	169
1935	1,206	2,511	199
1940	1,342	2,986	228
1945	1,262	2,982	222
1950	1,373	3,447	251

Source: ICAS (1954)

While the duties of the Joint Committee were to consider issues and report back to each Council, there was no intention that it should have executive powers. It was explicitly stated in Clause 4 that:

> The Committee shall in no manner regulate or (except by way of report, advice, suggestion or recommendation to the Councils of the several Societies) interfere with the management or organization of any of the three Societies (Joint Committee of Councils, 1915).

The SAE justified the creation of this Committee to its members by referring to the fact that, in the past, a Special Committee had been required for each issue, whereas "the appointment of a Standing Committee ready to act at once will obviate some inconvenience which has been experienced" (*The Accountants' Magazine*, 1916a). The IAAG noted that the Committee was "only advisory" (*The Accountants' Magazine*, 1916b), but before long it was suggested that the Joint Committee be given "full powers to take whatever steps might be necessary in connection with the new Finance Act" (IAAG, 1916). The SAA was prepared to remit consideration of the Finance Act to the Joint Committee and confer full executive powers and stated that it was prepared for this remit to be widened beyond the Finance Act to encompass other legislation (SAA, 1916).

However, the SAE disagreed with these proposals, saying that, before the Joint Committee acted on any particular matter, it should, in the first instance, report the matter back to each respective Council (SAE, 1916). Thus, the SAE maintained its position of independence and unwillingness to become involved more closely in anything that corresponded to a national organization.

Summary and conclusions

The official history of the first 60 years of the three Scottish chartered societies suggests that their relationships were based on joint consultation on matters of common interest followed by unanimity in pursuing agreed policies. Some recent research (Kedslie, 1990b; Walker, 1991) appears to confirm that political differences between them were submerged and common interests pursued successfully in response to external threats. In an address at the Closing Plenary Session of the centenary celebrations of ICAS, Browning (1954, emphasis added) stated:

> Much is said ... of the antagonism between ... Edinburgh and Glasgow. It has a high local entertainment value and we would not be without it, *but, in so far as it applies to matters of importance, it is a truly magnificent fiction by which the outsider is not infrequently deceived.*

Browning was presenting a historical perspective only three years after the three societies had finally united in 1951. It is unlikely that a critical historical analysis of inter-society affairs would have been welcomed with acclamation. Close examination of the affairs of the three societies suggests that the reality was in some respects different from that portrayed by Browning. On certain important issues, such as establishing the closure of the profession against external threat, there was agreement on the objectives but there were also strong underlying tensions between the societies. Furthermore, it is clear that there were strong forces within the Edinburgh membership which were capable of wielding an influence much greater than their numbers in Scotland merited. They were able to exercise an effective control, not only on the affairs of the Edinburgh society, but also to frustrate the viewpoints of the eventually larger institute in Glasgow and the small society in Aberdeen.

It is clear from the foregoing that during the second half of the nineteenth century the Edinburgh society saw itself as the dominant force in Scottish accounting specifically and, thus, the major Scottish voice in British accounting circles. The SAE wished to prevail over the Glasgow and Aberdeen societies to the extent that the alternative views expressed by these 'junior' societies, often on matters of great principle, were not accorded formal consideration by its Council. The SAE adopted a highly selective recording of matters of concern in its official records and this becomes apparent when the researcher is able to cross-check against the contemporary records of the other societies.

Among the most important issues arising during this period were the numerous attempts by the SIA to obtain a royal charter and the efforts of the Corporate Accountants to adopt the nomenclature 'CA'. On this the Scottish chartered societies were united in opposition to the applications. However, it became clear that the concept of operating as independent 'local' bodies was under attack and it was suggested, on a number of occasions, that a national society be formed. The SAE was opposed to this and refused to contemplate such a structure until persuaded by counsel that the Scottish chartered societies should concede the principle before the Privy Council. Even after the successful appearance before the Privy Council, the SAE members refused subsequent efforts to alter its constitution to open membership ranks and found it difficult to discuss any form of union such as a Federation. A reasonable conclusion based on analysis of the primary records suggests that the SAE had significant schisms within its own membership and that this realization influenced the Council. It is conceivable that, as a consequence, the Council of the SAE was reluctant to disclose to the general membership that such matters were being given further consideration. A common phrase employed by the SAE to deflect consideration of contentious matters was to state that "it [i.e. contemplation of the problem] would present Council with great difficulties" (IAAG, 1892a). This phrase was employed on a number of occasions, most particularly addressed to the IAAG Council, stating effectively that the SAE did not wish to discuss the matter further.

The societies were also under pressure from the Secretary of State for Scotland, advised by his officials, that the real requirement in Scotland was for the formation of a national society which would incorporate all members of the accounting profession who could be regarded as properly qualified. This normative perspective did not recognize the considerable differences existing, not only between the three chartered bodies, but also among other accounting groups in Scotland. There is no evidence that the Secretary of State pursued actively the advice given to him and, as a consequence, the chartered societies were not strongly pressed on the issue from that quarter.

Towards the end of the nineteenth century the 'old' idea of forming a General Examining Board was resurrected by the SAE and indeed was seen by its Council as a means of accommodating some of the federalist ideas held by other societies. However, even this issue was controversial, primarily because of the manner in which the SAE attempted to dominate by administrative control. The IAAG was so concerned at the SAE tactics that the Council of the Glasgow Institute almost withdrew from the negotiations on at least two occasions before formal agreement was reached. This matter probably induced the realization within the IAAG that it was no longer a junior partner in the tripartite relationship. Thereafter, the IAAG began to be more assertive on a number of issues.

By the outbreak of the First World War, the IAAG expressed dissatisfaction with the decision-making system adopted by the Scottish societies and proposed that a Joint Committee of Councils of the Scottish Chartered Accountants be formed in 1915. The IAAG proposal was made in the knowledge of failure to achieve previously any significant advances in British accounting by the creation of a Joint Committee with the ICAEW and the ICAI. The Scottish societies were able to reach agreement on the principle of forming a Joint Committee quite quickly, although it is significant that the Scottish Joint Committee was not given executive powers. Eventually the IAAG and the SAA indicated that they would be willing to delegate such powers but they were frustrated by the SAE's unwillingness to accede to this proposal, thereby delaying the eventual union of the Scottish chartered societies for a further 35 years. Nevertheless, the structure of the relationship was altered fundamentally by the arrangements made between the societies by the formation of the General Examining Board and the Joint Committee.

It becomes apparent, from careful study of the internal and external political relationships of the three Scottish chartered societies, that *the catalyst for any major co-operative action was always exogenous to them*. If there had been no external pressure for change then there would have been little incentive for the SAE to accept any proposal from the two 'junior' societies of Glasgow and Aberdeen with which the Edinburgh members were in disagreement. This situation certainly prevailed during the second half of the nineteenth century. During this period, the SAE enjoyed leadership of the Scottish societies, a reflection of its seniority, status and connections to the administrative, political and legal establishments in the capital city. Furthermore, *the constitutional independence enjoyed by the three societies provided no mechanism for discussion and compromise.* At the turn of the century, Glasgow began to approach equality in numbers and, thereafter, proceeded to exceed the Edinburgh membership. This was primarily a function of the social and economic development of Glasgow. The IAAG became unwilling to accept the position of the SAE on a number of matters and effectively questioned its dominance. However, because there were no mechanisms in place to accommodate these aspirations, advancing new concepts of governance was dependent on being able to proceed by consensus, however difficult that was to achieve.

Future research on the political relationships of the Scottish chartered societies in the period 1916 to 1951 has to be traced in the accounts offered by the minutes of the three societies, enriched by the opportunity to cross-reference to the records of the General Examining Board and the Joint Committee of Councils.

Notes

This research was generously supported by Grant Thornton which operates nationally and internationally via 46 offices nation-wide and representation in 72 countries worldwide. Particular thanks are due to Stephen Foster, managing partner, Edinburgh and Professor Ian Percy, senior partner, Scotland. Ian Percy is an ex-president of The Institute of Chartered Accountants of Scotland and is convener of The Institute's Research Committee. Transcripts quoted from the minute books of The Society of Accountants in Aberdeen; the Society of Accountants in Edinburgh; the Institute of Accountants and Actuaries in Glasgow and The Joint Committee of Councils, are made with the permission of Peter Johnston, secretary and chief executive of The Institute of Chartered Accountants of Scotland. I wish to acknowledge the valuable advice and guidance of Dr Alan Borthwick, Scottish Record Office, West Register House, Edinburgh. Transcripts quoted from papers consulted at the Scottish Record Office, West Register House, Edinburgh, are made with the permission of the Keeper of the Records of Scotland. An earlier version of this article was presented to The British Accounting Association; Scottish Conference at the University of Aberdeen on 9 September 1991 and a modified version of the paper was presented to the 6th World Congress of Accounting Historians, Kyoto, Japan on 21 August 1992. I am grateful for comments made by the participants. I am grateful for the advice and comments on earlier versions of this article by Garry Carnegie; Clive R. Emmanuel; Richard K. Fleischman; David Flint; Patti Mills; Lee D. Parker, Stephen P. Walker and anonymous reviewers.

1. A further two Royal Charters of Incorporation were granted to Scottish accounting societies during this period, viz. The Institute of Accountants and Actuaries in Glasgow (IAAG), formed in 1853 and granted a charter in 1855, and the Society of Accountants in Aberdeen (SAA), formed in 1866 and granted a charter in 1867.

2. Richard Brown, who edited A *History of Accounting and Accountants* in 1905, was a very prominent member of the Society of Accountants in Edinburgh. He was secretary of the Society between 1892 and 1916 and was elected president for 1916-1918.

3. The designatory letters W.S. denotes a lawyer, a member of the Society of Writers to the Signet, organized in 1594. The Scottish legal profession was organized in a hierarchical structure ranging from Advocates at the top, through Writer to the Signet, Solicitor to the Supreme Court to solicitor (see Grant, 1936; Walker, 1988, p. 271).

4. The Scottish Institute of Accountants was formed in 1880, by accountants who found themselves excluded from admission to any of the Scottish chartered societies either by experience or by the admission rules operated by the three chartered societies (see Walker, 1991).

5. The Corporation of Accountants Limited was incorporated in Scotland in 1891. The members of the CofA were mainly ex-members of the SIA who were determined to acquire the nomenclature of CA. Frustrated by the failure of the SIA to obtain a royal charter, a breakaway section of the SIA membership established a limited company, which, because of its corporate title, 'enabled' the members to use the nomenclature 'CA' after their name. The Scottish chartered societies were successful in opposing this claim in an action before Lord Kyllachy in 1892.

6. The SIA was finally unsuccessful in obtaining a royal charter and, in 1899, the remaining 123 members voted to become the Scottish branch of the Society of Incorporated Accountants. In 1957, members of this society joined the ICAEW, ICAI or ICAS under a scheme of integration. Of 11,500 society members, 128 joined ICAS (Garrett, 1961).

7. Indenture fees were required by SAE members in the sum of 100 guineas. Glasgow had no requirement for an indenture fee, while the Aberdeen fee was 50 guineas.

8. An application on behalf of the Dundee members was received by the Edinburgh society, which was considered at a Council meeting dated 7 May 1891. The Dundee accountants were informed that their application "would not meet with favour among the members of the Society, generally" (SAE, 1891a).

9. The intentions of John Mann are often implied from the proposals made to the IAAG Council. However, in a letter addressed to Campbell Davies offering his condolences on the death of James Davies, John

Mann referred to the period 1880-1892. In this letter he stated: "I quietly and persistently, over some years, urged and pled and agitated - in and out of season - for alteration of the Rules for a limited time during which the Society men who had for years been established and respected practising (accountants) should be admitted ... My plea was partly based on decency and fair treatment but also upon the expediency of weakening the growth in Glasgow of the English Incorporated Society". Sir John Mann anticipates the union of the SIA with the English Incorporated Society (1899) in this letter (Mann, 1951).

10. There was one major disagreement after the First World War which almost brought about the withdrawal of the IAAG. This difference of view about the examinations to be taken by apprentices who were returning from military duties became a major issue to the Glasgow council and resulted in a motion being prepared calling for the withdrawal of the IAAG from the GEB. After considerable difficulties and many meetings, a compromise was eventually found and the motion was withdrawn.

11. Problems in co-ordinating inter-society affairs were exacerbated by differences in Council procedures for calling meetings. Glasgow held monthly meetings but it was only in June 1915 that the SAE resolved to hold its committee meetings on a regular monthly basis (SAE, 1915).

Bibliography

The Accountant (1885a), "The incorporation of the Scottish Institute of Accountants", Editorial, No. 537, 21 March, pp. 6-7.

The Accountant (1885b), "The incorporation of the Scottish Institute of Accountants", Editorial, No. 538, 28 March, pp. 4-5.

The Accountant' Magazine (1898), "Increase of Scottish Chartered Accountants", Editorial, Vol. II No. 19, November, p. 491.

The Accountants' Magazine (1905), "Fiftieth anniversary celebrations", Editorial, Vol. IX No. 84, April, pp. 189-90.

The Accountants' Magazine (1916a), "Report of the Society of Accountants in Edinburgh 63rd Annual General Meeting", Vol. XX No. 193, March, pp. 173-6.

The Accountants' Magazine (1916b), "Report of the Institute of Accountants and Actuaries in Glasgow 62nd Annual General Meeting", Vol. XX No. 193, March, pp. 180-2.

Allen, K. (1991), In pursuit of professional dominance: Australian accounting 1953-1985, *Accounting, Auditing & Accountability Journal,* Vol. 4 No. 1, pp. 51-67.

Barber, B. (1963), "Some problems in the sociology of the professions", *Daedalus,* Vol. 92 No. 4, pp. 669-88.

Briston, R.J. and Kedslie, M.J.M. (1986), "Professional formation: the case of Scottish accountants - some corrections and some further thoughts", *British Journal of Sociology*, Vol. 37 No. 1, pp. 122-30.

Brown, R. (Ed.) (1905), *A History of Accounting and Accountants*, T.C. and E.C. Jack, Edinburgh.

Browning, R. (1954), "The chartered accountants of Scotland, 1854-1954", *The Accountants' Magazine*, Vol. LVIII No. 578, August, pp. 453-65.

Carr-Saunders, A.M. and Wilson, P.A. (1933), *The Professions*, Clarendon Press, Oxford.

Daiches, D. (1977), *Glasgow*, Andre Deutsch, London.

Denzin, N.K. (1978), *The Research Act*, 2nd ed., McGraw-Hill, New York, NY.

Fleischman, R.K. (1990), "Review of The Society of Accountants in Edinburgh 1854-1914", by Walker, S.P., *The Accounting Historians Journal*, December, pp. 145-7.

Garrett, A.A. (1961), *History of the Society of Incorporated Accountants, 1885-1957*, University Press, Oxford.

Gibson. J.S. (1985), *The Thistle and the Crown: A History of the Scottish Office*, HMSO, Edinburgh.

Goode, W.J. (1960), "Encroachment, charlatanism, and the emerging profession", *American Sociological Review*, Vol. 25 No. 6, pp. 902-14.

Grant, Sir F.J. (1936), *History of the Society of Writers to his Majesties Signet*, Writers of the Signet, Edinburgh.

Hastings, A. and Hinings, C.R. (1970), "Role relations and value adaptation: a study of the professional accountant in industry", *Sociology*, Vol. 4 No. 4, pp. 353-66.

IAAG (1854a), *Minute Books of Council*, No. 1, 27 May, Institute of Accountants and Actuaries in Glasgow, pp. 39-40.

IAAG (1854b), *Minute Books of Council*, No. 1, 4 July, pp. 41-2.

IAAG (1883a), *Minute Books of Council*, No. 2,30 January, pp. 208-10.

IAAG (1883b), *Minute Books of Council*, No. 2,9 March, pp. 211-13.

IAAG (1885), *Minute Books of Council*, No. 2, 28 July, p. 282.

IAAG (1888), *Minute Books of Council*, No. 2,26 December, pp. 394-6.

IAAG (1889a), *Minute Books of Council*, No. 2,2 October, pp. 442-3.

IAAG (1889b), *Minute Books of Council*, No. 2,30 April, pp. 420-3.

IAAG (1890a), *Minute Books of Council*, No. 2, 24 February, pp. 466-73.

IAAG (1890b), *Minute Books of Council*, No. 2,8 July, pp. 500-2.

IAAG (1891), *Minute Books of Council*, No. 3,24 December, pp. 67-9.

IAAG (1892a), *Minute Books of Council*, No. 3,28 November, p. 116-21.

IAAG (1892b), *Minute Books of Council*, No. 3,22 June, pp. 87-8.

IAAG (1892c), *Minute Books of Council*, No. 3,25 October, pp. 107-8.

IAAG (1892d), *Minute Books of Council*, No. 3,5 December, p. 122.

IAAG (1902), *Minute Books of Council*, No. 3,16 September, pp. 143-4.

IAAG (1910), *Minute Books of Council*, No. 5,17 May, p. 117.

IAAG (1913), *Minute Books of Council*, No. 5,31 July, pp. 370-4.

IAAG (1915), *Minute Books of Council*, No. 5, 19 April, pp. 506-8.

IAAG (1916), *Minute Books of Council*, No. 6,17 April, pp. 21-2.

ICAEW (1966), *History of the Institute of Chartered Accountants in England & Wales 1880-1965 and its Founder Accountancy Bodies 1870-1880*, Institute of Chartered Accountants of England and Wales, London.

ICAS (1954), A *History of The Chartered Accountants of Scotland from the Earliest Times to 1954*, Institute of Chartered Accountants of Scotland, Edinburgh.

Jick, T.D. (1979), "Mixing qualitative and quantitative methods: triangulation in action", *Administrative Science Quarterly*, Vol. 24, December, pp. 602-11.

Joint Committee of Councils (1915), "Memorandum of arrangement between the councils of the SAE, IAAG and SAA, adopted at the first meeting held 28 December 1915", engrossed in *Minute Book No. 1*, pp. 1-5.

Kedslie, M.J.M. (1990a), "Mutual self-interest - a unifying force: the dominance of societal closure over social background in the early professional bodies", *The Accounting Historians Journal*, Vol. 17 No. 2, December, pp. 1-19.

Kedslie, M.J.M. (1990b), *Firm Foundations: The Development of Professional Accounting in Scotland*, Hull University Press, Hull.

Kirkham, L. and Loft, A. (1992), "Insiders and outsiders: intra-occupational rivalry in accountancy, 1880-1930", research paper presented at ABFH Conference, Cardiff Business School, September 1992.

Lord Advocate (1885), "Papers relating to the application of the Scottish Institute of Accountants for a royal charter", File Reference AD 56/81, Scottish Record Office, West Register House, Edinburgh.

Lord Advocate (1890), "Minute from the Lord Advocate to the Secretary for Scotland dated 8 January 1890", Papers reference S1345/2, File Reference HH.1/914, Scottish Record Office, West Register House, Edinburgh.

Lythe, S.G.E. and Butt, J. (1975), *An Economic History of Scotland 1100-1939*, Blackie, Glasgow and London.

Macdonald, K.M. (1984), "Professional formation: the case of Scottish accountants", *The British Journal of Sociology*, Vol. XXXV No. 2, June, pp. 174-89.

Macdonald, K.M. (1985), "Social closure and occupational registration", Sociology, Vol. 19 No. 4, November, pp. 541-56.

Macdonald, K.M. (1987), "Professional formation: a reply to Briston and Kedslie", *The British Journal of Sociology*, Vol. XXXVIII No. 1, pp. 106-11.

Mann, Sir J. (1951), Letter addressed to Campbell Davies dated 7 May 1951 on the occasion of the death of James M. Davies and also relating to the grandfather of Campbell Davies. This letter was discovered during research for the "History of Glasgow Chartered Accountants' Exhibition", October 1990.

Massie. A. (1989), Glasgow, *Portraits of a City*, Barrie & Jenkins, London.

Mitchell, B.R. and Deane, P. (1962), *Abstract of British Historical Statistics,* Cambridge University Press, Cambridge, pp. 24-7.

Previts, G.J., Parker, L.D. and Coffman, E.N. (1990a), "Accounting history: definition and relevance", *Abacus,* Vol. 26 No. 1, pp. 1-16.

Previts, G.J., Parker, L.D. and Coffman, E.N. (1990b), "An accounting historiography: subject manner and methodology", *Abacus,* Vol. 26 No. 2, pp. 136-58.

Privy Council (1890), *In the Matter of the Petition of the Scottish Institute for Incorporation by Royal Charter,* Scottish Department, Edinburgh Central Library.

SAA (1881), *Minute Books of Council,* No. 1, 14 February, Society of Accountants in Aberdeen, pp. 20-2.

SAA (1884), *Minute Books of Council,* No. 1, 13 February, pp. 30-2.

SAA (1890a), *Minute Books of Council,* No. 1, 17 February; pp. 56-7.

SAA (1890b), *Minute Books of Council,* No. 1, 20 March, pp. 58-9.

SAA (1890c), *Minute Books of Council,* No. 1, 26 December, pp. 436-8.

SAA (1916), *Minute Books of Council,* No. 2,19 April, pp. 78-9.

SAE (1854a), *Minute Books of Council,* No. 1, 29 May, Society of Accountants in Edinburgh, pp. 334.

SAE (1854b), *Minute Books of Council,* No. 1, "Constitution and Rules", pp. 11-15.

SAE (1867), *Minute Books of Council,* No. 1, 24 January, pp. 159-60.

SAE (1890a), *Minute Books* of *Council,* No.2, 10 February, pp. 80-2.

SAE (1890b), *Minute Books of Council,* No. 2,3 October, pp. 94-6.

SAE (1890c), *Minute Books of Council,* No. 2, 14 February, pp. 82-3.

SAE (1891a), *Minute Books of Council,* No. 2,7 May, pp. 119-20.

SAE (1891b), *Minute Books of Council,* No. 2, 11 December, pp. 127-8.

SAE (1901), *Minute Books of Council,* No. 2, 11 January, pp. 326-8.

SAE (1902), *Minute Books of Council,* No. 2, 23 January; pp. 339-41

SAE (1915), *Minute Books of Council,* No. 3,21 June, pp. 230-1.

SAE (1916), *Minute Books of Council,* No. 3,8 May, pp. 261-3.

SAEGM (1891), "Annual General Meeting", *Minute Books of General Meetings,* Society of Accountants in Edinburgh, 7 January.

Saks, M. (1983), "Removing the blinkers? A critique of recent contributions to the sociology of professions", *Sociological Review,* Vol. 31 No. 1, pp. 1-21.

Scottish Institute of Accountants (1885), "Letter addressed to the Lord Advocate, dated 18 February 1885", File AD 56/81, Scottish Record Office, West Register House, Edinburgh.

Scottish Office (1889), "Minute dated 10 December 1889", in articles reference S.1345/7, contained in File HH.1/914, Scottish Record Office, West Register House, Edinburgh.

Scottish Office (1890), "Papers reference S.1345/3 dated 22 September 1890", contained in File HH.1/914, Scottish Record Office, West Register House, Edinburgh.

Scottish Office (1893), "Papers reference S.1345/4 dated 17 March 1893", contained in File HH.1/914, Scottish Record Office, West Register House, Edinburgh.

Scottish Office (1895), "Papers reference S.1345/12 dated 28 October 1895", contained in File HH.1/914, Scottish Record Office, West Register House, Edinburgh.

Shackleton, K. (1991), "The Scottish Societies of Chartered Accountants and the Scottish Institute of Accountants, 1853-1907", research paper at Wards Research Seminar, University of Glasgow, 21 March 1991.

Shackleton, K. (1993), "The evolution of education policy within the Institute of Chartered Accountants of Scotland", in Kwabena Anyane-Ntow (Ed.), *International Handbook of Accounting Education and Certification,* Pergamon Press, Oxford, pp. 414-7.

Slaven, A. (1975), *The Development of the. West of Scotland: 1750-1960,* Routledge & Kegan Paul, London and Boston.

Stewart J.C. (1977), *Pioneers of a Profession. Scottish Committee on Accounting History,* The Institute of Chartered Accountants of Scotland, Edinburgh.

Walker, S.P. (1988), *The Society of Accountants in Edinburgh 1854-1914: A Study of Recruitment to a New Profession,* Garland Publishing, Inc., New York and London.

Walker, S.P. (1991), "The defence of professional monopoly: Scottish chartered accountants and 'satellites in the accountancy firmament' 1854-1914", *Accounting, Organizations and Society,* Vol. 16 No. 3, pp. 257-83.

Walker, S.P. (1993), "The genesis of professional organization in Scotland: a contextual analysis", research paper presented at the ABFH Conference, Cardiff Business School, 24 September 1993.

Weber, M. (1968), in Roth, G. and Wittich, C. (Eds), *Economy and Society: An Outline of Interpretative Sociology,* Vol. 1, Bedminster Press, New York, NY.

Willmott, H. (1986), "Organising the profession: a theoretical and historical examination of the development of the major accountancy bodies in the UK", *Accounting, Organizations and Society,* Vol. 11 No. 6, pp. 555-80.

CHAPTER 10

The Influence of the Individual in the Professionalisation of Accountancy: The Case of Richard Brown and The Society of Accountants in Edinburgh, 1892-6

Thomas A Lee

The purpose of this paper is to demonstrate the validity of the professionalisation proposition that, within the context of an institutional strategy to control markets for professional services by means of various functionalist activities, the role of an individual within the institutional elite is crucial to the strategy's success. The proposition was first enunciated explicitly in the accountancy literature by Lee (1996a) when introducing historical biographies of three early Scottish professional accountants. It is an extension of two well-accepted theories of professionalisation. The first is the conventional functionalist approach to professional behaviour which characterises the latter in terms of various social attributes of a professional (e.g. Carr-Saunders and Wilson, 1933). The second theory is an extension of the earlier one, and suggests that professional behaviour has a principal economic objective to control service markets (e.g. Larson, 1977). The Lee (1996a) theory extends the social and economic arguments by suggesting that neither works effectively without the intervention of key individuals within the ruling institutional elite of a profession.

Little research has been published on the role of the individual in the development of the accountancy profession. Most of what exists in this area can be labelled as biography. For example, Kitchen and

---

Reproduced from C.W. Nobes and T. Cooke (eds) *The Development of Accounting in an International Context*, 1997, pp. 31-48 with kind permission of Routledge.

Parker (1981) reviewed the achievements of six English accountants, and Zeff (1987) reported on fourteen American accountants who had 'made a difference' in the development of the US accountancy profession. Neither study, however, was set within a specific theoretical context, and neither examined beyond the broad influences each of the individuals had in their specific areas of expertise. The current study attempts to address these issues by, first, specifying a theory relating to the professionalisation of accountancy and, second, providing detailed evidence of the influence of an individual on the professionalisation process.

The individual used in this study is Richard Brown, who was Secretary and Treasurer of The Society of Accountants in Edinburgh (SAE) between 1892 and 1916. His biography has been recently published (Lee, 1996b), and the current study extends the general information about Brown into the specific area of the institutional process of professionalisation. The focus of the study is a series of events which took place between 1892 and 1896 (particularly between 1895 and 1896). These events were concerned with attempts by Scottish chartered accountants to create a professional service monopoly by means of the chartered designation 'CA', and involved a UK-wide strategy involving Scottish, English and Irish chartered accountants. As the chief executive of an established and respected professional accountancy body for twenty-four years, Brown was in a unique position to exercise direct influence over events and strategies such as these in the early history of professional accountancy.

Data for this study have been derived mainly from the early records of the SAE, particularly its Council Minute Books (designated 'CMB' here) and Letter Books (designated 'LB') kept by The Institute of Chartered Accountants of Scotland (ICAS).[1] Other data have come from published research on the SAE and other similar bodies (e.g. Kedslie, 1990; Macdonald, 1985; Walker, 1991). Each of these publications examines different aspects of the various challenges, defences and strategies concerning Scottish chartered accountancy in the late nineteenth and early twentieth centuries. None, however, reports research on the influence of individuals in these events. The current study redresses this imbalance and, by doing so, hopefully creates better insight into the professionalisation process of yesterday and today.

Richard Brown and the SAE

It would he inappropriate to study the actions of Richard Brown within the context of the SAE without briefly presenting some relevant biographical detail. Much of what follows is taken from a detailed biography of Brown (Lee, 1996b). Richard Brown had a remarkable life. He was born in 1856, the fourth and youngest son of a tenant sheep farmer located on the outskirts of Edinburgh. He also had two sisters. Brown was educated in the local parish school from 1860 until 1870. He then worked as a clerk for two years prior to entering an apprenticeship with Kenneth Mackenzie, an Edinburgh chartered accountant. Mackenzie was one of the original planners of the SAE and a founding member in 1853 (Lee, 1996c). He was the SAE Treasurer from 1853 to 1863, and on its Council from 1863 to 1873. Thus, when Brown signed his contract of indenture with Mackenzie in 1872, he was relating himself to a well-established and respected member of the SAE. Mackenzie was the son of the landowner for whom Brown's father was a tenant farmer. His partner, John Turnbull Smith, was also connected to Brown. Smith's father was Brown's schoolmaster.

Brown served his five-year apprenticeship uneventfully, and was satisfactorily discharged from it in 1877. He passed the final examinations of the SAE in first place in 1878, and was admitted to membership in 1879. He continued to work for Mackenzie and Smith for six years until the dissolution of that partnership in 1885 when Smith was appointed Manager of the Life Association of Scotland. Smith's audit clients were transferred to Brown, and he practised as a sole practitioner until 1893 when he admitted two partners (one probably related to a brewing client, and the other a nephew of Kenneth Mackenzie). This was the year immediately following Brown's appointment as Secretary and Treasurer of the SAE.

Brown's humble origins did not prevent him from progressing rapidly in a profession which was founded on elitism and closely connected to landowners and lawyers (Lee, 1996c). Much of his early success was obviously due to his good fortune in being connected to the Mackenzie and Smith families. Later success was due to a combination of intellectual ability, hard work and the earlier connections (particularly as these related to his accountancy practice and involvement in the SAE). The SAE was founded in 1853 and obtained its royal charter in 1854 (thus providing the designation of chartered accountant or CA). The Secretaryship of the SAE was its senior executive position and, *inter alia*, meant its holder was continuously working with a changing Presidency and Council. This mix of continuity for the Secretary and change for the office-bearers provided an ideal opportunity for the chief executive to shape events in the early history of the SAE.

Brown joined the Council of the SAE in 1891 aged 35 years and, in 1892, was elected to its Secretaryship. He held this office until 1916 when he was elected SAE President. He died in that office in 1918. During his tenure of the Secretary's office, Brown was responsible for a number of different and related tasks, all of which significantly influenced the organisation and determined its nature to the present day. There were 265 members and 93 apprentices when Brown became SAE Secretary in 1892. When he demitted office in 1916, the respective figures were 584 and 117. During that period, Brown acted as Secretary and Treasurer, worked with sixty-five Council members, and served eight Presidents. The position of Secretary and Treasurer entailed serving Council and other SAE meetings; maintaining financial, membership and indenture records; dealing with SAE investment of funds; purchasing and refurbishing the SAE headquarters in Edinburgh; establishing and maintaining the SAE library; the entire education and examination system (including SAE classes for apprentices and the secretaryship of the General Examining Board from 1893);[2] editing *The Accountants' Magazine* from 1897 onwards;[3] establishing educational links with the University of Edinburgh (eventually leading to the founding of a chair of accountancy in 1919, one year after his death); administering SAE responses to various pieces of Scottish and UK legislation affecting accountants (e.g. in bankruptcy); the effects of the First World War and the emergence of women accountants as a result; and the complex events to which the current study relates (involving competitive pressures and responses, protection of the CA designation, and attempts at registering professional accountants).

Thus, as well as managing a successful accountancy practice, Brown had what must have amounted to a full-time job as SAE Secretary. For his services, he was paid an annual fee of £100 from 1892 (increasing to £200 in 1909) and various *ad hoc* fees for specific services (e.g. with respect to various legal actions to protect the CA designation). Brown was also heavily involved in Church of Scotland affairs, and in various non-accounting bodies. He travelled extensively throughout the world, and wrote several contributions to the literature (of which his *A History of Accounting and Accountants* is the best known; Brown, 1905). Brown was very much a Victorian 'man of affairs', and a good example of the emerging professional middle class of that period in Scotland.

The SAE and competition

The SAE was well established by the time Richard Brown became its Secretary in 1892. It was the first professional accountancy body founded in Scotland[4] (and, indeed, the world) and, like most pioneering organisations, was advantaged and disadvantaged by that position. In particular, the SAE quickly found that obtaining a royal charter in 1854 was insufficient to create the work monopoly which was undoubtedly a major factor in the desire for its formation (Kedslie 1990; Walker 1995). The SAE was an elitist organisation (Lee, 1996c). It was formed by a small group of Edinburgh accountants in mid-century, and its initial membership was very deliberately chosen to mimic other well-established professional bodies. It therefore excluded accountants as well as including them. In addition, the Glasgow (IAAG) and Aberdeen (SAA) bodies were a constant source of irritation to it (Shackleton and Milner, 1996). This irritation appears to have arisen partly as a result of a long-standing rivalry between Edinburgh and other Scottish cities such as Glasgow, and partly because the IAAG (particularly) and SAA adopted different and apparently lower standards of membership than the SAE. Thus, the formation and development of the SAE not only created an 'external' schism between SAE members and other Scottish accountants, it also produced an 'internal' rivalry between competing Scottish bodies of chartered accountants. These divisions characterised a long-standing series of challenges to the superiority of Scottish chartered accountants, and the responses by the three chartered bodies. The responses were particularly difficult to sustain because of the 'internalised' disputations that persisted. This was the world of professional accountancy which Richard Brown entered in 1892. Events prior to this date described in this section are examined in greater detail by Kedslie (1990) and Walker (1991).

The first challenge to the privileged position of Scottish chartered accountants came in 1884 when a small body of accountants based in Glasgow petitioned Queen Victoria for a royal charter. The petitioning body was the Scottish Institute of Accountants (SIA) founded in 1880. The essence of its petition was a desire to permit SIA members to use the designation CA, thus appearing to be designated in the same way as chartered accountants. The three Scottish chartered bodies (led by the SAE) briefed the Lord Advocate on the matter, and the petition was rejected by the Privy Council without a hearing (following receipt of a report from the Lord Advocate). The main feature of this incident was the close cooperation between the senior law officer in Scotland and the SAE Council. Following rejection of the petition, the SIA attempted in 1886 to get the three chartered bodies to come to unify with it as one profession in Scotland with a national charter. This approach was firmly and immediately rejected by the chartered bodies.

The next SIA challenge to the Scottish chartered bodies came in 1889 with a further petition for a royal charter. The petition was supported by several thousand individual signatures of influential Scots. Opposition was organised by each of the three bodies with some attempt to ensure consistency and compatibility. For example, the SAE Secretary, James Howden, was instructed by his Council to ask the SAE law agent to draft a counter-petition (CMB, 2/2, 69) based on arguments concerning the educational superiority of chartered accountants and the inferiority of SIA members (most of whom were not employed in accountancy). The correspondence of the SAE Secretary in 1890 reveals that the Dean of the Faculty of Advocates and two colleagues were appointed to represent the SAE (LB, 78); a conference of the Councils of the SAE, IAAG and SAA was held to organise the opposition to the petition (LB, 79); Scots MPs were asked not to support the petition (LB, 90); and the petition was refused in July 1890 (LB, 92). The management of the opposition on this occasion was clearly in the hands of the individual Councils, although there were signs of an emerging unification on such matters with leadership from the SAE.

Several other events should be mentioned prior to the appointment of Richard Brown as SAE Secretary. They reveal that not all competitive events were regarded as important by the Scottish chartered bodies. For example, in 1890 and 1891, The Institute of Chartered Accountants in England and Wales (ICAEW) promoted the Chartered Accountants Bill which attempted to restrict the use of the CA designation to UK chartered accountants (with the caveat that the description should include the holder's professional body if he did not practise in the country of that body). The Bill failed to progress in Parliament, and there was no mention of it in the SAE Council Minute Books or Secretary's Letter Books.

In 1891, the SIA attempted to incorporate under the Companies Act 1867. The SAE Council suitably adjusted its previous counter-petition to the 1889 SIA petition, and submitted it to the Board of Trade (CMB, 2/2, 112-13). Incorporation did not take place. Also in 1891, a second Scottish rival to the chartered bodies (the Corporation of Accountants Limited (CAL), an offshoot of the SIA) attempted to incorporate as a body of corporate accountants with the explicit intention of using the designation CA. On this occasion, the three Scottish chartered bodies took joint court action to prevent such use in 1892. They were successful under appeal in 1893, and effectively obtained legal protection for the CA designation in Scotland from that time onwards.

The ICAEW made another attempt in 1892 to create a UK-wide monopoly of the CA designation. It promoted a further Chartered Accountants Bill which was defeated largely through the opposition of a rival English body, the Society of Accountants and Auditors Incorporated (SAAI). There is no mention of this Bill in the SAE Council Minute Books and Letter Books, indicative that the 1892 CAL court action was regarded by at least the SAE Council as sufficient to provide the monopoly use of the CA designation.

Finally, in 1892, the CAL made the first attempt in the UK to register or license accountants. Its Public Accountants Bill related only to accountants in Scotland. It failed in Parliament and, as with other similar legislation, did not prove to be sufficiently significant to warrant discussion by the SAE Council. This was not the case with later legislation dealt with by Richard Brown when he succeeded James Howden as SAE Secretary in 1892.

Richard Brown, competition and registration

The first legislation dealing with the registration of accountants, and which Richard Brown was required to monitor, was the SAAI's Public Accountants Bill (No. 1) in 1893 and 1894. This proposed statute suggested registration of members of five UK chartered bodies (including those in Scotland), the SAAI and the SIA. SAE Council minutes reveal that Brown was informed of this Bill early in 1893, and that Council decided at that point that legislation of this type was not required for its members (CMB, 2/2, 172-3). However, despite this decision, Brown wrote to the SAAI on 21 April 1893 suggesting amendments to the Bill, and informing it that the Bill would be supported in Parliament by Sir Charles Pearson MP (the SAE's Parliamentary adviser). It is unclear why there was this contradiction with respect to the actions of Council and Brown - particularly whether or not Brown was acting on the instructions of his Council. In the event, it mattered little as the Bill was defeated in Parliament.

The Council of the SAE took greater interest in a competing Bill on registration in 1893 and 1894. This was the Public Accountants Bill (No. 2), sponsored by the ICAEW, and covering the registration of ICAEW and SAAI members only. Thus, unlike the SAAI Bill, Scottish chartered accountants were excluded, and the issue arose of what would happen to Scottish chartered accountants working in England and Wales. Not surprisingly, the SAE Council Minute and Letter Books indicate the issue was taken seriously. On 6 February 1893, Brown wrote to his ICAEW counterpart to arrange a meeting to discuss the Bill (LB, 60). On his return by 11 February, he wrote in very general terms to the IAAG Secretary, Alexander Sloan, informing him of how the ICAEW and SAAI Bills were progressing through Parliament (LB, 64). He wrote more revealingly on 14 February to Walter Reid, the SAA Secretary, saying the SAAI Bill was 'harmless' whereas the ICAEW Bill was not (LB, 66).

On 17 March, Brown sent a copy of the ICAEW Bill to Sloan to allow the IAAG Council to discuss it (LB, 100).[5] The day before, he had written to his President, James Howden, expressing his major concern that all English accountants would be designated as CAs by the ICAEW Bill (LB, 102). The SAE Council met on 24 March to discuss the Bill (CMB, 2/2, 174-81). It disapproved of its exclusion of Scottish chartered accountants from practising as CAs in England. Brown was asked to instruct the SAE law agents to draft an amending clause to prevent such exclusion, and proceeded to London to discuss this and further amendments with Scottish MPs. Sir Charles Pearson MP opposed the Bill's reading, and it (and the SAAI Bill) were withdrawn.

Events of 1893 therefore witnessed significant changes in the approach of the Scottish chartered bodies to the issue of protecting the CA designation and to the registration of accountants. First, the SAAI approach to registration embraced all major UK accountancy bodies (including the SIA), and was presumably regarded as non-threatening by Richard Brown and his colleagues because of the inclusion of the SIA. The latter body had persistently been denied professional respectability by the Privy Council, the Board of Trade, and the Scottish courts. The ICAEW Bill, on the other hand, not only permitted SAAI members to be chartered, but also had the effect of preventing Scottish chartered accountants from practising as CAs in England. As a number of such individuals had been working in

England for a number of years, their interests required protection - hence the SAE intervention in the Bill's progress. The second change was the active involvement of Richard Brown in the legislative process. He appears to have become by 1893 the principal actor for the Scottish bodies in terms of gathering and disseminating information and activating policy. The third change was the realisation that there was a need to co-ordinate effectively responses to any challenges to Scottish chartered accountancy. On 18 November 1893, Richard Brown wrote to the Secretary of the ICAEW requesting him to send any future registration Bills to a special Joint Committee of the three Scottish chartered bodies. Thus, for the first time, these bodies formally acknowledged the potential consequences of registration as driven by the English bodies, and the need to act efficiently and effectively in response.

The Scottish chartered bodies did not have to wait long for the next round of proposed legislation. In 1894, the SAAI introduced a Public Accountants Bill similar to that defeated in 1893. The SAE Council noted it, instructed its law agents to continuously monitor such legislation, and decided to take no action (CMB, 2/2, 187-8). The Bill failed in October 1894. Richard Brown wrote to the ICAEW Secretary in January 1894 stating an SAE Council view that such legislation was not needed in Scotland but that the SAE should be informed of any proposed statutes (LB, 267). The scene was therefore set for the greatest and most complex challenge to the Scottish chartered bodies - the third petition of the SIA for a royal charter in 1895 and 1896. It was within the events surrounding this petition that Richard Brown can be seen to have had a major role.

The SIA petition of 1895

The 1895-6 petition of the SIA expressly asked that it be called the Scottish Provincial Institute of Accountants, and that its members be designated as CPIAs. Developments in the presentation of the petition extended over at least two years. Richard Brown was informed in 1893 of the SIA's intention to petition (its third). On 21 March 1893, he passed this news to his President (James Howden) and to the Secretaries of the IAAG (Alexander Sloan) and SAA (Walter Reid) (LB, 103). What the SIA had done was send a 'Memorial of Intent' to the Scottish Office prior to petitioning, and Brown was instructed by his Council on 24 March to write to the

Secretary of State for Scotland asking for a hearing on the matter (CMB, 2/2, 175). Brown, however, had already done so on 22 March pointing out previous failed SIA petitions) (LB, 105), and had written on the same day to Sloan asking him to write in similar terms to the Secretary of State, and to come with him to London to lobby Scottish MPs on the matter (LB, 107). Following his Council's meeting on 24 March, Brown wrote to Reid with the request to write to the Secretary of State but without the London invitation (LB, 108). He and Sloan also met with the ICAEW President in London, and reported this to Reid (LB, 110). Thus, competition and registration events appear to have been driven from Brown's SAE office, with subsequent ratification from the SAE Council and physical presence from the IAAG but not the SAA Secretary.

Nothing relevant appears to have occurred between early 1893 and late 1894. Then, on 10 November 1894, Brown informed Sloan of the emergence of the SIA petition, and asked whether it should be taken directly to the three chartered Councils or the Joint Committee formed in November 1893 as a result of the ICAEW and SAAI registration Bills of that year (LB, 384). Taking the matter to the Joint Committee appears to have been agreed by Brown and Sloan, and Reid was informed of this by Brown on 14 November (LB, 390). The SAE Council on 19 November received a letter from the SIA in which it informed the SAE of its intention to petition for a royal charter, and hoping that the three Scottish chartered bodies would join with it in a scheme to regulate Scottish accountants (CMB, 2/2, 198-214 and 222-31).[6] The SAE set up a subcommittee (including Brown) to organise opposition to the petition and to promote the idea of national registration.

A letter from Brown to Reid on 20 November outlines this tactic - that is, to oppose the proposed royal charter, and go for a Bill of registration similar to those which regulated legal and medical practitioners (LB, 399). A letter on the same day to Sloan informed him of the SAE subcommittee and the strategy which the SAA had agreed with Brown (LB, 401). The SIA was informed by Brown on 4 December of the opposition to its petition and the consensus regarding a Scottish registration scheme (LB, 410). A letter to Brown from the SIA on 24 December agreed to the registration idea (LB, 425). The SAE Council was informed by Brown on 4 January 1895 that the SIA would set its petition aside if legislation to register was introduced. Brown was instructed by his Council to proceed to draft such legislation. This was the Accountants (Scotland) Bill which was intended to restrict the use of the term 'accountant' in Scotland to those practitioners registered there.

Brown instructed the SAE law agent on 7 January 1895 to draft the Bill (LB, 434), and wrote to Sir Charles Pearson MP on 2 February inviting him to see the Bill through Parliament (LB, 463). Thus, as a result of the threat of a third SIA petition, the SAE generally, and its Secretary particularly, had taken charge of the issue by using the registration Bill tactic. The degree to which Brown felt he was in charge is evidenced by his letter to the SAA Secretary, Walter Reid, on 2 February 1895, in which he chastised Reid for mentioning the proposed Scottish Bill in the SAA annual report (LB, 466). Further amendments to the draft Bill were notified to the IAAG Secretary, Alexander Sloan, on 4 February (LB, 467) and, at the request of former SAE President, George Auldjo Jamieson, Brown informed the ICAEW President of the Bill (LB, 470). On 9 February, Brown acknowledged receipt from the ICAEW President of its Chartered Accountants Bill to register English, Welsh and Irish chartered accountants (LB, 476). The Scottish chartered bodies were therefore faced with three simultaneous issues: the proposed SIA petition dependent on Scottish registration legislation, draft Scottish registration legislation, and ICAEW-inspired non-Scottish chartered registration legislation. Richard Brown's hands were filling fast.

Brown wrote to Reid, the SAA Secretary, on 13 February 1895 regarding the ICAEW Bill (LB, 482). He stated that the IAAG Council wished to register all Scottish accountants who had been in practice for at least two years. In particular, he articulated the SAE objection to the ICAEW Bill (i.e. that only English CAs could be designated as CAs in England). He ended by warning Reid not to talk about these matters outside of the Joint Committee. On 19 February, Brown wrote to Reid, Sloan, the SAE President (James Haldane) and Sir Charles Pearson MP, enclosing his memorandum on the ICAEW Bill to the Joint Committee (LB, 487-90). He had received the Bill from Pearson. It was receiving its second reading in Parliament. Pearson was also notified by Brown that the drafting of the Scottish registration Bill was being held up by the IAAG Council (LB, 489). The letter to Haldane indicates that Brown rather than the SAE Council was the initiator of opposition to the ICAEW Bill (LB, 490).

A further letter from Brown to Pearson on 23 February gives the reason for objecting to the ICAEW Bill (i.e. the exclusion of Scottish chartered accountants from practising as CAs in England) (LB, 494). Brown stated that he had written on 23 February (LB, 496) to the ICAEW asking for removal of the exclusion in return for SAE support for the Bill. The IAAG and SAA were making similar overtures through their representative MPs. Brown then returned to the issue of the SIA. On 2 March 1895, he sent the SIA's lawyer a copy of the draft Accountants (Scotland) Bill (LB, 504). The SIA reply was communicated to the SAE Council by Brown on 28 March. The SIA wished to have the right to be designated as CAs, and rejected the proposed Bill. A letter was sent by Brown in response to the SIA indicating that the Scottish chartered bodies could not agree to a registration Bill which deprived them of their distinctive CA designation. The letter to the SIA had been drafted by the SAE law agent, and approved by the SAE President, James Haldane, and by Brown (LB, 528).

Brown's orchestration of opposition to the SIA petition can be evidenced in a series of letters from him in May 1895. He wrote to his President, James Haldane, on 1 May stating a need to fight the SIA, and to call a meeting of the SAE Council as soon as possible (LB, 534). Also on 1 May, he wrote to both his IAAG and SAA counterparts saying that, in the absence of Council meetings, there was an immediate need to send a circular letter to all Scottish MPs asking them not to sign the SIA petition (LB, 538-9). The SAE Council agreed to this idea on 9 May, and to revisiting the idea of a UK registration Bill. Writing to MPs appears to have been successful as it was reported to the SAE Council that names had been removed from the petition (CMB, 2/2, 227). Brown was empowered to travel to London with his President to lobby MPs (CMB, 2/2, 229), and also met Sir Charles Pearson MP in London with the objective of introducing a UK-wide Bill to Parliament (LB, 547 and 549). He was accompanied by the IAAG Secretary, Alexander Sloan.

The most immediate task for Brown at this time was organising a coherent and relevant case against the SIA petition. He did so in a number of ways. For example, on 4 June 1895, he wrote to SAE members in Dundee and Inverness asking them to research and inform him about the nature of the work they typically undertook in these locations (LB, 565). He wrote to Walter Reid, the SAA Secretary, on 5 June requesting that Reid inform Lord Provosts and Town Councils in the Aberdeen area of SAA opposition to the SIA petition (LB, 573). On 12 June, Brown wrote directly to the Lord Provost of Perth asking for his support against the petition. His main arguments were that the petition was delaying the Accountants (Scotland) Bill which would permit registration of eminent Perth accountants who were not chartered accountants, the SIA, did not represent the 'provinces', and the petition created confusion regarding use of the CA designation (LB, 581). Sloan and Reid were requested on 12 June to provide data on SIA members rejected for membership by the IAAG and SAA (LB, 583). Sloan was asked on 21 June to provide information on auditors appointed by Sheriffs under the Burgh Police Act 1892 (LB, 589). And Sloan and Reid were invited on 24 June to give Brown information on the business of SIA members in Glasgow and Aberdeen (LB, 591). Thus, Brown took responsibility for gathering a considerable amount of information to support a counter-petition to the SIA. On 28 June 1895 he informed the SAE President that the counter-petition had gone to the Privy Council on 22 June (LB, 605). This is somewhat surprising, given the data searches initiated by Brown subsequent to the delivery of the counter-petition. At the very least, it provides reason for speculating that the policy to involve the Secretaries of the IAAG and SAA was less than whole hearted. Alternatively, the information gathered would be of use at a later date if further challenges to the Scottish chartered bodies emerged.

It was reported at an SAE Council meeting on 29 July 1895 that James Haldane and Richard Brown had been to London to lobby MPs as part of the opposition to the SIA petition. In addition, Brown continued to rally support from non-accounting constituents (e.g. parish councils) (LB, 625). He also returned to the issue of registration legislation when he wrote to the Secretary of State for Scotland on 12 August 1895 asking that the Secretary and the Lord Advocate meet with him and the Presidents of the SAE and IAAG concerning such a matter (LB, 645). As no meeting took place, this tactic seems to have failed. However, Brown continued to orchestrate opposition to the SIA petition. Reid of the SAA was asked to write 'one or two' letters to Scottish MPs suggesting they were supporting the SIA petition on inadequate information (LB, 651). Sloan of the IAAG was asked by Brown to change the wording of the IAAG annual report regarding the SIA petition (presumably it was too conciliatory) (LB, 730).

The registration issue continued to develop. By 25 January 1896, Brown was able to report to Sloan that he, the SAE President, and the SAE law agent had met with the Lord Advocate, and that the latter person's advice was that registration legislation should not be seen as an argument against granting a royal charter to the SIA (LB, 738). In other words, whereas Brown and the other opponents to the SIA petition had attempted to use registration legislation as a ploy to defeat the petition, the senior law officer in Scotland was recommending that the two issues should be kept separate. On 29

January, Brown recommended to the SAE law agent further changes to the proposed Accountants (Scotland) Bill prior to a meeting of the Joint Committee (presumably in line with the Lord Advocate's advice) (LB, 740). Brown asked J. A. Campbell MP (now the SAE Parliamentary adviser) to ballot for the Bill on 5 February (LB, 758). Campbell agreed on 7 February, and Brown travelled to London to discuss tactics with him (LB, 761).

The Accountants (Scotland) Bill was intended to restrict the use of the term 'accountant' in Scotland to those individuals who were registered to practise as such. The register was to be similar to those maintained for legal and medical practitioners. The term 'chartered' was to be used only by members of the SAE, IAAG and SAA. There was to be a Registrar and Council appointed by the Lord President of the Court of Session. The Council's responsibility was to determine rules for educating, examining and training accountants for registration. Brown drafted a letter to go to members of the SAE, IAAG and SAA (enclosing a copy of the Bill) (LB, 781 and 782). However, a letter to Sloan on 28 February 1895 indicates that the IAAG Council was not happy with this procedure, wishing instead to examine the detail of the Bill before it went to members (LB, 783). Brown's advice was not to do this, particularly as the Bill was on its way to the Secretary of State for Scotland and Scottish MPs. This event further suggests that, despite a Joint Committee, co-operation between the three Scottish chartered bodies was not fully effective, and that Brown was a primary influence in events.

On 2 March 1895, Brown informed Sloan that the Privy Council wanted to know if the chartered bodies wished to appear before it in relation to the SIA petition (LB, 787). Brown stated the need to do so, and to prepare the appropriate case and immediately introduce the Accountants (Scotland) Bill. At the same time (5 March), Brown asked Reid, the SAA Secretary, to do nothing in London regarding the Bill or to let the ICAEW or SAAI know of its existence until he sent them copies (LB, 794). This suggests that Brown did not fully trust Reid's ability to remain a member of a team or to retain confidentiality. It also suggests that the English bodies were not being kept informed by Brown of Scottish registration developments in the same manner as he had requested the ICAEW to keep the Scottish bodies informed of English registration plans.

On 6 March 1896, the final version of the Accountants (Scotland) Bill went to J. A. Campbell MP, other supporting MPs, Sloan and Reid (LB, 797). The accompanying letters from Brown to the MPs stated the urgency of the Bill's introduction, and the need for their presence in Parliament when it was. On 12 March, Sloan was informed by Brown that there would he no meeting of members regarding the Bill, and he was sending it to the ICAEW and SAAI. *The Scotsman* and *The Glasgow Herald* (both with a small article), and all non-CA accountants in Scotland (LB, 811). He wrote to the ICAEW, ICAI (Institute of Chartered Accountants in Ireland) and SAAI on the same day, adding that, if similar legislation were introduced by them, the Scottish bodies would seek reciprocal arrangements for the various registers (LB, 814). The SAAI reintroduced its Public Accountants Bill in 1896 (including the three Scottish chartered bodies and the SIA). There was no mention of this legislation in the SAE Council minutes. The ICAEW also introduced its Accountants (No. 2) Bill in 1896. Like the SAAI Bill, it included all chartered bodies in the UK, the SAAI and SIA, and, for one year only, any other accountant approved by a General Council of Accountants. Three competing Bills therefore emerged in Parliament during 1896.

Meantime, the Scottish Bill was pursued by Brown. On 14 March 1895, he wrote to Reid of the SAA asking him to send the Bill to the *Aberdeen Press and Journal* (LB, 824). The Bill was also sent by Brown to *The Accountant* on 17 March, emphasising the desire of the Scottish bodies for reciprocation should the English Bills succeed (LB, 829). On 19 March, Brown reported to Sloan and Reid that the article he had sent to *The Glasgow Herald* was published, but that *The Scotsman* one was not (it was published several days later) (LB, 836). Brown also continued to seek more evidence of the frailties of SIA members (presumably for the Privy Council hearing). He sought from Sloan and Reid data on SIA members who had failed chartered accountancy examinations (LB, 836).

The strain of these events on Richard Brown must have been considerable. He was essentially running the show on his own, with occasional help from his IAAG and SAA counterparts. How much he was affected is clear in certain exchanges he had in the spring of 1896. For example, on 24 March, he wrote to the ICAEW Secretary (and J. A. Campbell MP) complaining about inaccuracies in *The Accountant* regarding the Scottish position over possible reciprocation on registration (LB, 861). He sent his *Scotsman* article to all Scottish CAs, and various letters to Scottish CAs in England reassuring them that, with reciprocation, they would he able to continue to practise in England. Brown was at his most testy in a letter to Reid on 21 April prior to the hearing with the Privy Council (which Reid would not attend) (LB, 899). He wrote that he would not be able to give Reid a copy of the minutes of the meeting, although he might have a spare copy of the Scottish bodies' case. By 22 April, he was complaining to Campbell about Parliamentary changes to the Bill which were destroying its intention and aiding the SIA and CAL (LB, 894). On 23 April, he bluntly refused the SIA's law agent access to SAE membership records (LB, 896).

The registration events affected organisations other than the professional accountancy bodies. Brown had to write to the Commercial Bank of Scotland to reassure its management that the Accountants (Scotland) Bill was not intended to prevent bank accountants being described as such (LB, 916). The more weighty problems affecting Brown, however, were those associated with the tactics of getting the proposed legislation through Parliament. For example, he wrote on 19 May 1896 to the Bill's sponsor, J. A. Campbell MP, informing him that the ICAEW was blocking all attempts to present registration Bills to a Select Committee of Parliament, and that he should present the Accountants (Scotland) Bill in the 'normal way' (LB, 919).

By this time, the SIA petition had been rejected for the third time by the Privy Council (CMB, 2/2, 248-9). Brown had attended the meeting at the beginning of May. The cost to the SAE of responding to the petition was £506 (CMB, 2/2, 254). Brown wrote a second letter to Campbell on 19 May seeking an amendment to the Accountants (Scotland) Bill which would permit cross-frontier reciprocation (this had been agreed with the ICAEW and SAAI and, in his opinion, would likely be agreed by the SIA because of its petition failure) (LB, 921). Brown's testiness was further demonstrated on 19 May when he wrote to, first, the Editor of *The Accountant* bluntly complaining of its misleading editorial on the failed SIA petition (LB, 923) and, second, the Secretary of the ICAEW (which he stated subsidised *The Accountant*) repudiating the article (LB, 936). The curious aspect of these letters is that Brown was authorised to write them on behalf of his Council at its meeting of 28 May - five days later (CMB, 2/ 2, 250). It is apparent that he was acting independently of his Council and seeking a retrospective approval of his actions. Whether SAE Council members were aware of this behaviour is unclear.

The Accountants (Scotland) Bill was sent in May 1896 to all SAE members for comment (CMB, 2/2, 247-8). However, it failed at its second reading in the same month (CMB, 2/2, 248). Despite this, Brown sent a further letter to J. A. Campbell MP on 8 June 1896 (LB, 944). In it, he stated that the Bill had received support from the Edinburgh Chamber of Commerce (by public report) and the

Solicitors to the Supreme Court in Edinburgh and Aberdeen (by petition). As a result of the Bill's failure, Brown's communications with the IAAG and SAA on the issue ceased for several months. Then Brown was authorised by his Council on 6 November 1896 to reintroduce the Bill. Alexander Sloan, Secretary of the IAAG, was informed of this intention on 10 November 1896 (LB, 52). Walter Reid, Secretary of the SAA, was not. Neither of these individuals had been written to by Brown on the issue of a Scottish Bill since mid-March 1896. This is not to say that there had been no other communications or meetings, merely that there is no record of them taking place.

The failure of the Accountants (Scotland) Bill meant that accounts required settling. Brown submitted his (undisclosed) fee note to the SAE law agent on 8 June 1896 (LB, 945). Several months later, on 16 December 1896, he asked the SAE law agent to submit his account for the Bill (LB, 102) and, on 24 December, wrote to Reid (for the SAA share of £9. 9s. 9d.) (LB, 111), and to Sloan for the (unstated) IAAG share. However, the Accountants (Scotland) Bill was not completely dead. On 29 December, Brown wrote to Reid asking for SAA permission for J. A. Campbell MP to ballot to reintroduce it to Parliament (LB, 116). A similar letter on 31 December was sent to Sloan regarding IAAG permission, with the following addendum which reflected that the action was regarded by Brown as political rather than practical:

> In reference to your letter of yesterday relating to the Accountants Scotland Bill. You may have an opportunity before Tuesday of pointing out to any members of your Council, that the use made of the Bill in the hearing before the Privy Council seems to us to impose a moral obligation to re-introduce the Bill in the forthcoming session of Parliament. It is not the least likely that our doing so will have any practical result, but as a matter of common honesty, we think we are bound to put it forward. In a matter of Policy also, unless we keep ourselves to the front regards legislation, there is a risk of Bills being passed at the instance of other bodies, which would be inimical to our interests, and in any event it is particularly desirable that our position should be made manifest. Yours very truly, Richard Brown.

Events after 1896

The proposed legislation was introduced as the Scottish Chartered Accountants Bill in March 1897 (CMB, 2/2, 264). It desired registration only for Scottish chartered accountants. Also in 1897, the ICAEW reintroduced its 1896 Accountants (No. 2) Bill, having failed to get its members to agree to a Chartered Accountants Bill which would have absorbed SAAI and ICAEW members into one body. On 18 January 1898, it was reported by Brown to the SAE Council that both the Scottish and English Bills had failed (CMB, 2/2, 281). The Scottish chartered accountants had one further attempt at registration in 1898, but this was blocked in Parliament on behalf of the ICAEW (CMB, 2/2, 286).

The registration issue persisted for some time into the twentieth century, and continued to involve Richard Brown as SAE Secretary. Although all proposed legislation failed in Parliament, its introduction meant a rapid and meaningful response from the Scottish chartered bodies generally and Brown particularly. The Scottish strategy was that Scottish chartered accountancy required separate registration as proposed in the Accountants (Scotland) Bill. For example, when the SAAI introduced a Bill in 1899, the Joint Committee responded with this argument (CMB, 2/2, 305-6). An ICAEW Bill was introduced and failed in 1905 with little comment from the Scottish chartered bodies (CMB, 2/3, 32 and 34). In 1909, a further ICAEW attempt at registration was made despite a lack of enthusiasm from the Board of Trade (CMB, 2/3, 104). In this case, the legislation was intended to include only England and Wales. Despite Scottish pressure to have UK-wide registration, the ICAEW would not amend it to include Scotland (CMB, 2/3, 111-12 and 114). The Bill failed, but the ICAEW introduced a further Bill in 1910, this time including Scotland (CMB, 2/3, 126). The Bill failed at the committee stage (CMB, 2/3, 144). It was followed by a further Bill by the SAAI which failed in 1912, and an ICAEW Bill in 1913 which was never introduced to Parliament. This was the last registration issue with which Richard Brown dealt during his secretaryship.

Conclusions

The early histories of the UK professional accountancy bodies include extensive discussions of the significant issues of competition between and registration of professional accountants (e.g. Kedslie, 1990; Macdonald, 1985; Walker, 1991 in relation to the Scottish chartered bodies). At the heart of these rivalries and disputes lay the right to the CA designation as a signal of professional respectability and status, and as a means of securing an economic monopoly over certain accountancy services. The issue was therefore a complex mix of social and economic factors. Previous research has not investigated the impact of individuals in these matters, particularly from the point of view of determining whether or not policy and action was influenced by either individuals (such as Richard Brown of the SAE) or groups (such as the SAE Council). Indeed, previous research implies that policy and action were group-induced matters.

This study argues to the contrary - that is, that the early professionalisation process in the UK was shaped in large part by the actions of a few key individuals. One of these men was Richard Brown of the SAE. Because of his position as chief executive of the SAE over a twenty-four year period in the early history of the UK accountancy bodies, Brown was able to shape events well beyond his proportional presence on the Council of one of five chartered bodies in the UK. Indeed, as evidence from the SAE Letter Books reveals, he influenced policy and practice in a number of important ways.

First, Brown became SAE Secretary during a period when Scottish chartered accountants were continuously challenged over their privileged economic and social position. The challenges were persistent and increasingly well managed. They needed to be responded to in an equally effective way. The SAE Council generally, and Brown particularly, appear to have taken the lead on these matters. The competition and registration events of the 1890s suggest that the IAAG and SAA were only supporting actors in the events. Often, the SAA did not appear to be involved at all.

Second, Brown took a lead role in these matters at a time when rivalries between the Scottish chartered bodies were as persistent as those with which the latter were attempting to cope *vis-a-vis* the SIA, ICAEW and SAAI. This is not to suggest that the Scottish chartered rivalries were as deep seated as the others. Despite the rivalries, Brown managed to fashion a unified Scottish approach to the royal charter petitions of the SIA, and the English-only registration attempts of the ICAEW. This was particularly the case in 1895 and 1896 when he had to deal with petitions and registration Bills at the same time. His major tactic appears to have been one of formulating policy and intended action (whether this was with the SAE Council is unclear at times), and then communicating these matters to the IAAG and SAA (and his President).

Third, Brown engineered events in such a way that he involved everyone who had to be involved without surrendering his position of leadership. In particular, despite the existence of a Joint Committee and three separate Councils, the responses to the charter petitions and registration Bills were skilfully orchestrated to allow others to participate without necessarily having significant involvement. For example, the IAAG and SAA Secretaries, Sloan and Reid, appear to have been reduced to gatherers of data and receivers of information on several occasions. Brown's correspondence to his counterparts in the IAAG and SAA suggest that the Joint Committee was not the primary source of policy and action with respect to petition and Bill responses. At times, Brown felt comfortable enough to put his counterparts in their place when he felt they were likely to stray from his designated strategy.

Fourth, despite his actions to include and exclude, Brown successfully managed the responses to the petitions and Bills without destroying other efforts at unifying the Scottish chartered accountancy profession, and relationships with the English and Irish bodies. For example, in Scotland several unification events took place during Brown's tenure as Secretary. The General Examining Board was formed in 1893 with Brown as its Secretary (CMB, 2/2, 152). A Joint Committee was constituted in 1894, also with Brown as Secretary. It met frequently without a constitution until its constituted formation in 1915 as the Joint Committee of Scottish Councils (CMB, 2/3, 244). *The Accountants' Magazine* was launched in 1897 largely as a result of Brown's efforts, and with him as its founding Editor (CMB, 2/2, 256). A Joint Committee *of* the Councils *of* the Chartered Bodies of Accountants in the United Kingdom operated from 1902 onwards (CMB, 2/3, 342-3).

It would be wrong to suggest that Richard Brown ran a completely 'one-man' show during his SAE Secretaryship. He obviously had to involve SAE, IAAG and SAA Council members and his Secretarial colleagues in Glasgow and Aberdeen. Also, there are no surviving records of the actions of the Joint Committee formed by the three Scottish chartered Councils. However, the correspondence of Brown with respect to the competition and registration events examined in this study overwhelmingly suggest that he was 'in charge'. Thus, when examining the early development of the Scottish professional bodies, it is important to look for the influence of individuals such as Brown on events as well as the events themselves. Such a lesson should be extended to research of other bodies and their policies and actions. To do otherwise is to cause their histories to be incomplete.

Notes

1. Permission by ICAS to access these sources is gratefully acknowledged.
2. The General Examining Board managed the complete examination system for the three chartered bodies in Scotland. It meant that, in one respect at least, Scottish chartered accountancy was a national system (Lee, 1996b).
3. *The Accountants' Magazine* was also a national effort to which each of the three Scottish chartered bodies contributed intellectually and financially. It appeared as a response to anti-Scottish accountancy sentiment expressed in the English-based *The Accountant* (Lee, 1996b).
4. The other bodies were The Institute of Accountants and Actuaries in Glasgow (IAAG) founded in 1855, and the Society of Accountants in Aberdeen (SAA) founded in 1867.
5. There is no evidence in the SAE records that the SAA was given the same opportunity.
6. The SAE Council's deliberations of the petition are captured in the Council Minute Book page references indicated. Individual events and comments are not separately referenced.

Bibliography

Brown, R. (1905) *A History of Accounting and Accountants,* Edinburgh: Jack.
Carr-Saunders, A. and Wilson, P. A. (1933) *The Professions,* Oxford: Clarendon Press.
Kedslie, M. J. M. (1990) *Firm Foundations. The Development of Professional Accounting in Scotland 1850-1900,* Hull: Hull University Press.
Kitchen, J. and Parker, R. H. (1981) *Accounting Thought and Education: Six English Pioneers,* London: Institute of Chartered Accountants in England and Wales.

Larson, M. S. (1977) *The Rise of Professionalism: A Sociological Analysis,* Berkeley, CA: University of California Press.

Lee, T. A. (1996a) 'Sociology of accountancy profession' in T. A. Lee (ed.) *Shaping the Accountancy Profession: The Story of Three Scottish Pioneers,* New York.

Lee, T.A. (1996b) 'Richard Brown, chartered accountant and Christian gentleman', in T. A. Lee (ed.) *Shaping the Accountancy Profession: The Story of Three Scottish Pioneers,* New York: Garland, pp. 153-221.

Lee, T.A. (1996c) 'Identifying the founding fathers of public accountancy: the formation of The Society of Accountants in Edinburgh', *Accounting, Business & Financial History* 6(3): December.

Macdonald, K. M. (1985) 'Social closure and occupational registration', *Sociology* November: 541-56.

Shackleton, J. K. and Milner, M. (1996) 'Alexander Sloan: a Glasgow chartered accountant', in T. A. Lee (ed.) *Shaping the, Accountancy Profession: The Story of Three Scottish Pioneers,* New York: Garland, pp. 81-151.

Walker, S. P. (1991) 'The defence of professional monopoly: Scottish chartered accountants and "Satellites in the accountancy firmament"1854-1914', *Accounting, Organisations and Society* 16 (3): 257-83.

Walker, S.P. (1995) 'The genesis of professional organisation in Scotland: a contextual Analysis', *Accounting, Organizations and Society* 20 (4): 285-310.

Zeff, S. A. (1987) 'Leaders of the accounting profession: 14 who made a difference', *Journal of Accountancy* May: 46-71.

CHAPTER 11

Anatomy of a Scottish CA Practice: Lindsay, Jamieson & Haldane 1818-1918

Stephen P Walker

Introduction

This paper seeks to anatomize or dissect the fee income of a major Scottish accountancy practice of the nineteenth and early twentieth centuries in an attempt to examine the postulate that contemporary accounting practice in Scotland was characterized by the early dominance of bankruptcy and its subsequent replacement by corporate auditing (Stewart, 1986: 13-15; Kedslie, 1990a: 12, 133-4). Further investigation of the work mix of early professional accountants in Scotland appears necessary because, for the following three reasons, assertions made in the existing literature rest on less than substantial foundations.

First, the bankruptcy-auditing thesis is not derived from the analysis of the records of accountancy practices extant during the nineteenth century. Research on the profession in England and Scotland has been largely frustrated by an apparent dearth of available primary source material generated by accounting firms. The increasing amalgamation of firms, the consequent evanescence of antecedent firms, the destruction of records (Chandley and Boys, 1991) and limitations on access to sensitive material (Stewart 1986: 15) have reduced investigative opportunities for the accounting historian. In the opinion of one reviewer, the absence of office records has resulted in recent commentators such as Kedslie (1990a) partly misconstruing the nature of the work conducted by chartered accountants (CAs) in the nineteenth century (Baxter, 1991: 384). The comments of the eminent business historian Peter Mathias are apposite:

Reproduced from *Accounting, Business & Financial History*, Volume 3, Number 2, September 1993, pp 127-54, with kind permission of Routledge.

the historical evolution of accountancy in the economy can only be provided through access to the archives of accountancy practices; the essential 'internal' documentation without which the full critical history of any profession, or firm, or trades union or any other institution can never be written. (Introduction to Jones, 1981: 12).

Second, as a result of the scarcity of quantitative data on the work undertaken by accountancy firms during the nineteenth century, several dangers in accounting history research identified by Napier (1989), such as generalizing on the basis of inadequate evidence and attempting to understand the past 'through the blinkers of the present' (p. 241), have materialized in this subject area. In the absence of the records of contemporary practices, descriptions of the sources of employment of early professional accountants have often been structured around headings which reflect the departmental organization of a modern large practice, or, track the changes in work which is common today and accord less priority to that which is unfamiliar (Stewart, 1986: 14). A teleological approach to history potentially results in the presentation of a distorted picture of nineteenth-century accounting practice as does a purely technological determinist perspective with its concentration on those changes in accounting practice which are explicable by economic and legislative developments.

Third, the lack of archival material on accountancy firms is not compensated for by published histories of firms, most of which are of limited utility for tracing changes in the work undertaken by accountants during the nineteenth century. The majority of histories of accounting practices are valuable launch pads to more intensive research, but are often defective from the perspective of the academic historian. Their creation is usually motivated by an anniversary and the desire to stress organizational continuity rather than by a recognition of the intrinsic values of historical inquiry. Consequently, published firm histories have usually provided an introverted and uncritical narrative of the work undertaken by their great founding fathers and abstain from the disclosure of data which reveal actual performance and the sources of fee income (Parker, 1981: 285).

It is testimony to the dearth of empirical primary source-based studies on the derivation of the fee income of early professional accountancy practices that so much use has been made of one of the few contextual studies of an accountancy practice. Jones' (1981) investigation of Ernst & Whinney 1840-1980 is relatively unique in analysing the development of a firm in its broader economic setting and providing detailed fee income data. The latter information has been quoted by several accounting historians, including Parker (1986:

22), Edwards (1989: 262) and Kedslie (1990a: 115-16) - the former lamenting that 'similar information is unfortunately not available for other firms' (p. 23). Recent important additions to the literature on English firms (Cornwell, 1991) have not been matched north of the border. No published histories are available which contain detailed quantitative material on the fee income of a nineteenth-century accountancy practice in Scotland.

It is anticipated that this paper, by providing an analysis of the clientele of a major firm during the nineteenth century and by revealing the significance of that clientele to other practitioners, will provide a deeper insight into the work conducted by Scottish CAs and supply a missing link in the history of their nascent profession.

Genealogy of Lindsay, Jamieson & Haldane

The practice for which primary records have recently become available is Lindsay, Jamieson & Haldane of Edinburgh.[1] The survival of a fragmentary selection of the records of a single firm necessarily raises questions concerning their use for drawing general conclusions about the contemporary profession in Scotland. Allowances must be made for particular specialisms in the workload of L, J & H (such as landed estate management), its location in a city dominated by financial and legal institutions and the firm's lack of involvement in areas of work which were important to other practices in the east and west of Scotland (such as insurance agency, stockbroking, company secretaryship, property factoring and the management of charitable institutions). However, evidence generated outwith L, J & H not only confirms the integrity of the surviving firm records but also reveals the general import of most of the work awarded to its partners. As one of the largest and most influential CA firms in Victorian Scotland, L, J & H earned fees from a broad range of the activities which were considered by contemporary commentators as comprising the mainstream clientele of professional accountants (Walker, 1991: 269).

Partners and profits

The *Edinburgh & Leith Post Office Directory* indicates that L, J & H originated in 1818 when Donald Lindsay (1796-1876) (Haldane, 1897) commenced practice as an accountant in Edinburgh.[2] Following his appointment as auditor of the Scottish Widows' Fund in 1837, Lindsay admitted George Auldjo Esson (1813-1888) (*Scotsman*, 14

March 1888: 6; Henderson, 1912: 393) as partner on 1 January 1838. The profit data (available from 1845) summarized in Table I and Figure I show that the practice's performance was relatively stable to the mid-1850s.

TABLE I *Lindsay, Jamieson & Haldane: business profits 1845-1918*

Period	Average annual profits	Standard deviation	Average annual profits price adjusted (Sauerbeck-Statist)
	£	£	£
1845-1855	2,361	456	2,504
1856-1867	4,913	920	4,421
1868-1878	7,799	2,256	7,156
1879-1890	14,237	4,326	16,759
1891-1900	9,922	1,579	13,418
1901-1918	7,857	623	8,385

Source: Profit Summaries 1845-91; Haldane (1954; 1955).
Note: profit data after 1905 are estimates based on known income less estimated expenses of 28.5 per cent.

Lindsay & Esson continued until 1855 when George Auldjo Jamieson (1828-1900) (*Accountants' Magazine*, 1900: 519-24; *Scotsman*, 20-5 July 1900; Henderson, 1912: 398), Esson's nephew, who had joined the practice about 1851, was admitted to partnership. Auldjo Jamieson was to become the firm's most eminent practitioner - a recent biographer stated that he 'was undoubtedly one of the most successful and influential accountants in Scotland during the last two decades of the nineteenth century' (Schmitz, 1990: 410; see also Society of Accountants in Edinburgh, Sederunt Book, 1900: 320; Brown, 1905: 221).

Esson left the partnership in 1856, on appointment as the first Accountant in Bankruptcy for Scotland; two years later James Haldane (1831-1906) (*Accountants' Magazine*, 1906: 544-9; *Scots Law Times*, 1906: 90-1) was assumed as a partner.

Figure I *Lindsay, Jamieson & Haldane business profits 1845-1918;
five-year moving average*

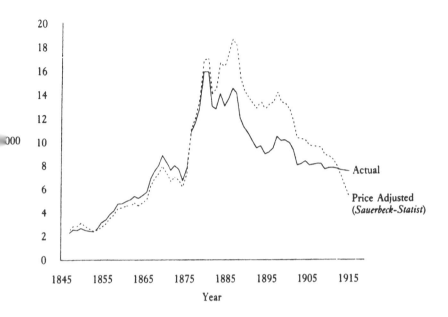

Figure I shows that a significant improvement in the profits of the
practice during the mid-1850s occurred contemporaneously with
partnership changes and that the period following the retirement of
Lindsay in 1867 (and his succession by Auldjo Jamieson as senior
partner) heralded a new era in fortunes. Under Auldjo Jamieson's
direction the practice was reorganized into cash, correspondence,
general, factory and copying departments and its clientele reputedly
'extended by leaps and bounds' (*Accountants' Magazine*, 1900: 511).
Table 2 reveals that average annual fee income increased by 64 per
cent between 1859-67 and 1868-78.

Findlay Blair Anderson (1848-1927) (*Accountants' Magazine*,
1927: 169-71), an ex-apprentice of L, J & H, became a partner in 1873.
Six years later, and as a result of the appointment of Auldjo Jamieson
and Haldane as two of the liquidators of the City of Glasgow Bank,
two other former apprentices and assistants - Thomas Whitson
(1835-1895) (Stewart, 1986: 162) and Francis More (1838-1905)
(*Accountants' Magazine*, 1905: 520-2; *Scots Law Times*, 1905: 74-5) -
were admitted to partnership. Table 1 and Figure 1 reveal that profits

peaked in the 1879 to 1890 period following the City of Glasgow Bank appointment and Table 2 shows that average annual fee income in 1879-91 was 79 per cent higher than in 1868-78. The increasing workload of the practice during the zenithal 1880s is also indicated by the fact that the number of clerks employed by L, J & H rose from eight in 1857 to fifty-four in 1887. In 1889 Charles J. G. Paterson (1858-1937) (*Accountants' Magazine*, 1937: 500-3), another former apprentice, was admitted as a partner.

The period from 1891 to 1918 was one of comparative decline followed by stability for L, J & H, punctured temporarily by substantial fees from casual clients (as in 1898-1900). A review of *Stock Exchange Year Books* (Skinner) from 1890 to 1900 reveals that the practice fell from first to third place in the league table of corporate auditors in Lothian, having failed to gain clientele from among the increasing number of manufacturing and mercantile companies in the region. The problems of operating in a highly competitive market for professional services from the 1890s were compounded by a loss of some important clients following the deaths of Auldjo Jamieson, More and Haldane within six years at the turn of the century. In accordance with a provision in the partnership agreements that a son of the senior partner may be admitted to the practice, Herbert W. Haldane (1870-1957) (*Accountants' Magazine*, 1957: 686-7) became a partner in 1898 as did Francis More, junior (1877-1951) (*Accountants' Magazine*, 1951: 150) in 1905.[3]

Significance of L, J & H in the Scottish profession

Until the mid-1890s, L, J & H headed a group of eight CA practices which dominated the profession in Edinburgh during the second half of the nineteenth century.

At the time of the genesis of the Society of Accountants in Edinburgh (SAE) in 1853 (of which L, J & H partners were four of the founder members), Donald Lindsay was reputedly one of three leading practitioners in Scotland (Walker, 1991: 261). His practice earned more commission from bankruptcy trusteeships than any other Scottish accountancy firm (see Kedslie, 1990a: 43). In 1890, by which time corporate auditing had become a major source of professional income for L, J & H, *The Stock Exchange Year Book* (Skinner) reveals that the firm held more appointments (18 per cent) of Lothian-based companies than any other practice in the East of Scotland.

There is ample evidence of the high status of L, J & H in the local profession. The partners trained more SAE apprentices registered between 1853 and 1914 (7 per cent of the total) than any other single

Edinburgh firm (Society of Accountants in Edinburgh Register of Indentures). In only ten years between 1854 and 1914 was there no L, J & H partner on the council of the SAE, while Auldjo Jamieson (1882-8) and James Haldane (1895-8) were each its president. Both Auldjo Jamieson and Francis More were presidents of the Edinburgh CA Students' Society and the senior partners were called upon to lecture to the society from its inception in 1886 on subjects ranging from political economy (Auldjo Jamieson), company law reform (Haldane) and goodwill (More) (see Lee, 1984: 9-11). Auldjo Jamieson's distinction in the profession is indicated by his membership of the Royal Commission on mining royalties in 1890; the Board of Trade Departmental Committee on the amendment of the Companies Acts (the Davey Committee) in 1894-5 (see Edwards, 1989: 201-2); and by his being called as an expert witness before the Hypothec Commission (1865) and the Law Courts (Scotland) Commission (1868-70).

Acquiring a clientele

The progress of L, J & H rested not only on the professional repute of the senior partners but also on the development of a complex network of kinship, business and social connections. Of particular significance was its close ties with the Edinburgh legal profession founded primarily on familial connections (Walker, 1988: 193-6). A mutually beneficial relationship was cultivated between L, J & H and certain law practices where brothers of its senior partners were gainfully employed - *Lindsay,* Howe & Co, Writers to the Signet (WS); Tods, Murray & *Jamieson,* WS; W & F *Haldane,* WS. The position of George Auldjo Jamieson's brother, James, at the 'head of the largest legal business in Scotland' (*Scots Law Times,* 1907: 101-2) was especially propitious. Other beneficial linkages were developed with J. & F. Anderson, WS (the senior partner was Findlay B. Anderson's cousin), with Dundas & Wilson, WS (L, J & H's law agents) and with Chalmers & Fotheringham, Advocates in Aberdeen (in whose office Auldjo Jamieson had been trained).

Directorships held by partners, particularly in financial institutions, were also an important source of auditorships, investigative remits and trusteeships. In 1895 the partners of L, J & H occupied seats on the boards of seventeen companies (Skinner). Anecdotal evidence also suggests that political and religious affiliations were significant to the acquisition of certain clients. Auldjo Jamieson and Haldane were office-holding Scottish Episcopalians and

Conservatives (Auldjo Jamieson was candidate for West Edinburgh in the General Election of 1885 and was a city councillor 1889-1900; Haldane was a founder of the Scottish Conservative Club) and were auditors of allied institutions.

Sources of income

The sources of income of L, J & H, as summarized from surviving income and expenditure accounts for 1859-1891 and analysed by major periods of change in profits, are summarized in Table II.

The nature of each form of employment and its significance to the contemporary CA profession will be discussed in turn.

TABLE II *Lindsay, Jamieson & Haldane: analysis of income 1859-91*

	Average annual income				Total
	1859-67	1868-78	1879-9	1859-91	
	£	£	£	£	%
Sequestration	260	289	234	8,550	2
Trusts and executries	1,756	3,879	5,205	126,135	26
Factories and curatories	783	1,270	1,325	38,246	8
Landed proprietors and estate management	420	1,884	3,189	65,968	14
Judicial remits	981	511	183	16,830	3
Investigations	14	248	867	14,110	3
Liquidations	2	6	2,933	38,223	8
Reconstructions	0	116	593	8,985	2
Audits	2,027	2,353	5,756	118,981	25
Charges for clerks writings	941	1,410	1,642	37,795	8
Other	294	268	9	5,840	1
Total	7,478	12,234	21,946	479,663	100

Source: Abstracts of Income and Expenditure.

Sequestration

Income obtained by Scottish accountants from sequestration (formal bankruptcy proceedings under Scots law), during the nineteenth century, has received close attention from historians due to its alleged pivotal role in the parturition of the earliest organizations of professional accountants. Kedslie has suggested that the appointment of accountants as trustees on sequestrated estates was the only area of work which provided significant employment opportunities for the mid-nineteenth century accountancy practitioner in Scotland (1990a: 49). Consequently, when the State proposed the reform of bankruptcy law in 1853 and threatened their appointment as interim factors, Edinburgh and Glasgow accountants were induced to constitute organizations for the protection of their principal source of income (Kedslie, 1990a: 53). The importance of sequestration work to CAs in the post-organization period is emphasized by Kedslie in a comprehensive analysis of sequestration awards in 1856-1904, although this did reveal a gradual diminution in bankruptcy work over time (Kedslie, 1990a: 114-34).

The fact that only 2 per cent of the income earned by L, J & H between 1859 and 1891 derived from sequestrations, however, suggests that the importance of bankruptcy reform for the organizational development of the CA profession may have generated an over emphasis on its significance to the work load of the contemporary practice. This hypothesis receives support from an analysis of *The Alphabetical Compendium of Scotch Mercantile Sequestrations* for 1851-3 which shows that L, J & H earned more commission from bankruptcies than any other Edinburgh CA practice, with an average of £547 per annum. Yet, in the same period the firm earned average business profits of £2,265 per annum.

A few substantial and complex bankrupt estates could yield high fees. In 1839 Donald Lindsay was appointed trustee on the sequestrated estate of George, Marquis of Huntly (Grant, 1979: 48) and, by the death of the Marquis in 1853, had earned commission of £13,450 (*Alphabetical Compendium of Scotch Mercantile Sequestrations, 1853*). James Haldane, as sequestrator of Laing & Irvine, manufacturers, Hawick, earned £2,838 in 1875-7. Such remunerative appointments were, however, exceptional - most bankruptcy trusteeships generated comparatively low commission for only one to two years.

Clearly, a substantial proportion of L, J & H's income derived from sources other than bankruptcy. One of the most important and hitherto neglected of these sources was trusts.

Trusts

The nature of trust related work Table 2 shows that a substantial proportion of the income earned by L, J & H from 1859 to 1891 derived from appointments falling under the common law definition of trusteeships (Marshall, 1975: 436). The partners of L, J & H were selected to administer property on behalf of others not only as trustees under the supervision of the judiciary (as in sequestrations) but also as extrajudicial trustees appointed outwith the courts under private trust dispositions.

The importance of trusts as a source of income for CAs can be gauged from the regulations of the new professional organizations in Scotland and from descriptions of the composition of contemporary accounting practice. The charters of incorporation (1854-5) refer to the selection of accountants on large voluntary trusts. Trust management and the framing of trust accounts featured in the professional knowledge sections of examination syllabuses from 1855 (Walker, 1988: 315-16, 326-7, 339, 347). Eminent practitioners, such as James McClelland, President of the Institute of Accountants and Actuaries in Glasgow (IAAG), referred to the employment of colleagues in family and testamentary trusts (1869: 12; see also *Interim Account of a Going Concern*, 1967: 9, 16-17).

A CA could be enlisted to perform several services relating to the administration of private trusts. First, the CA was well suited to perform the duties of a trustee who was obliged to 'keep proper accounts' for inspection by those beneficially interested in the trust estate (Menzies, 1913: 592). The Report from the Select Committee on Trust Administration, 1895 (p. 163) confirmed: 'it is usual to select one of those persons (generally accountants and businessmen) who really understand these matters' as trustees. Second, CAs might be employed by trustees as a factor - an agent whose duty was to conduct the routine management of the trust and who was usually a 'competent man of business' (Menzies, 1913: 120). Third, the trustees or their law agent might enlist the services of an accountant specifically to maintain the books in cases 'where the trust accounts are of an intricate nature or difficult to arrange' (Menzies, 1913: 147).

Extrajudicial trusts and L, J & H The detailed income and expenditure statements of L, J & H for 1859-91 show that the partners held eighty-seven appointments in connection with extrajudicial trusts and that these generated 25 per cent of the total fee income of the practice. An analysis of the distribution of commission earned from extrajudicial trusts revealed that 69 per cent of income derived from eleven appointments. In order to comprehend the nature of trust-related work, the key eleven appointments and a representative sample of ten others were investigated by searching the original trust dispositions in the Register of Deeds and the Register of Sasines for Scotland. It was discovered that the most remunerative appointments received by L, J & H were in connection with trusts constituted for the principal purpose of paying the creditors of insolvent landed proprietors. The results are summarized in Table III.

TABLE III *Lindsay, Jamieson & Haldane: trusts which generated more than £3,000 commission 1859-91*

Trust name/truster	Total commission 1859-1891 £	Duration 1859-91 (years)	Estate debts £
Lord Belhaven	19,292	33	226,451 (in 1859)
Earl of Glasgow	14,282	6	nk
Glamis/Earl of Strathmore	11,752	17	c. 205,000 (in 1863)
Marquis of Huntly	6,989	4	185,100 (in 1879)
John T. Gordon of Nethermuir	6,626	7	226,797 (in 1869)
George Dundas of Dundas	4,790	32	c.169,000 (in 1861)
Earl of Buchan	4,388	16	nk
Duke of Hamilton	4,315	4	167,000 (in 1879)
Penicuik/Sir George D. Clerk	3,786	8	183,100 (in 1883)
Baron Ruthven	3,782	26	41,137 (in 1865)
Ardkinglas/George F.W. Callender	3,626	15	37,700 (in 1876)

The trust dispositions reveal that the senior partners of L, J & H were appointed as sole trustees or as a joint trustee with an Edinburgh lawyer. On the Belhaven, Dundas and Ruthven trusts, the constitution of a voluntary trust for 'behoof' (benefit) of creditors with one of the partners of L, J & H as a trustee was a condition of the landed proprietor receiving substantial secured loans from the North British Insurance Company (of which George Auldjo Jamieson was a director) (Register of Deeds, RDS/1079: 175; RD5/1135: 718; General Register of Sasines, RS3/3405: 19, respectively).

The establishment of extrajudicial trusts increased following the decline in agricultural prices during the 1870s and 1880s and the consequent reduction in rentals (Lenman, 1977: 196-9). Those estates which relied heavily on the extraction of minerals also suffered during the 'great depression' (Marwick, 1936: 33-4). The fortunes of the Penicuik estate, for instance, depended substantially on coal and were subjected to a decline in mineral revenues of one half during the 1880s (Penicuik Trust Estates Act, 1883: 15). In 1869 the gross income from minerals (80 per cent) and land (20 per cent) of the Belhaven estates was £31,311; by 1883, 'owing to the great depression in the iron trade' and the exhaustion of the richest coal seams on the estate, revenues declined to £18,905 (Belhaven Trust Estate Act, 1884: 11).

The trust dispositions relating to the sample of ten less remunerative L, J & H commissions revealed that three were also constituted for behoof of creditors, five were testamentary trusts for the administration of the estates of deceased persons, one was an antenuptial marriage contract trust and one was formed for the management of surplus funds arising from the sale of land to pay estate debts.

The significance of extrajudicial trusts to Scottish CAs The frequency of extrajudicial settlements was seldom computed and published, but contemporary commentators reveal that they were as common as the formal process of sequestration. This highlights the limitation of historical analysis which has focused principally on the latter (Kedslie, 1990a; 1990b).

Where the debtor was reputable and could obtain the accession of his creditors, extrajudicial trusts were 'the course usually adopted' in insolvency administration (Wallace, 1914: 366) because they offered comparative secrecy, flexibility and low costs. Private arrangements offered an attractive alternative to the highly publicized process of sequestration which involved proclamations in *The Edinburgh Gazette,* public registration and examination of the bankrupt before the court (Bell, 1870: 488; Goudy, 1903: 519). Consequently, witnesses before the Select Committee on Fraudulent Debtors in 1880 stated that trust deeds were much more popular than bankruptcy in Scotland (p. 50). In 1889 the Scottish Institute of Accountants presented data derived from the *Mercantile Weekly Test* which showed that, in 1887-8, 49 per cent of insolvencies in Scotland were wound up under private deeds and that Scottish CAs held 332 sequestration trusteeships and 285 extrajudicial trusteeships (Privy Council, 1890: 14). Richard Brown noted their increasing prevalence in 1905 (p. 322) and Wallace considered that in 1914 at least as many insolvent estates were wound up under private trust deeds as under formal sequestration (p. 368).

The appointment as trustee under voluntary arrangements for the satisfaction of creditors was also a source of employment of considerable significance to early generations of Scottish accountants. Grant discovered that from about 1790 accountants were increasingly appointed as sole trustees under voluntary trusts for behoof of the creditors of landed proprietors in North East Scotland (1979: 48). One such practitioner was Charles Selkrig 'who had one of the largest practices in Edinburgh from 1786 till his death in 1837' (Brown, 1905: 194). Selkrig's surviving account book for 1812-24 reveals that he earned commission of £6,600 from 1812-22 in relation to the trust estate of the Duke of Argyll and other ducal families (GD.237/274/1). Other eminent practitioners - James Brown (*Accountants' Magazine,* 1900: 87) and James McClelland (Parker, 1986: 16), respectively the first presidents of the SAE and IAAG - were also heavily involved in this form of trust work.

Executries

The duties of an executor included the realization of the defunct's estate, recovery and payment of debts, preparation of inventories, managing the requisite probate, legacy or succession duties, and distribution of the residue to the beneficiaries. These duties were naturally performed by professional accountants in complex cases (Bell, 1861: 358-63) and were covered by professional examination syllabuses, though infrequently alluded to by contemporaries (Brown, 1905: 204).

Executry work was of marginal significance to L, J & H. From 1859 to 1891 twenty-two executry appointments generated commission of £4,733. One series of appointments, the executries of the 4th, 5th and 6th Earls of Aberdeen, comprised £2,809 of the total income from this source.

Factories and curatories

The appointment of Scottish accountants as factors and curators by the courts to administer the estates of others was another trust-related source of potential business. Under the Scots law of guardianship, those who are unable to manage their own affairs or do not have the capacity to contract may have tutors or curators appointed to act on their behalf (Marshall, 1975: 229). A tutor may be appointed to protect and act for a pupil, a curator is responsible for providing assistance in the management of the estates of minors or those suffering from mental infirmity (Lorimer, 1873: 71-93). In instances where there was no natural guardian or where parents neglected to nominate a tutor or guardian or their nominee failed to act, the Court of Session (after 1730) or the Sheriff Courts (from 1880) was empowered to commission an administrator - a factor *loco tutoris* or curator *bonis* - in their place. Other circumstances in which a judicial factor might be appointed included: a factor *loco absentis*, where an estate owner was resident abroad; a factor appointed under the Bankruptcy Act, 1856, to wind up an insolvent estate where the debtor died intestate or his trustee had died; and a factor appointed on a trust estate where the trust had become unworkable due to the decease, absence or disagreement of the trustees (Dickson, 1892: 48-52).

L,J&H and judicial factories External sources reveal that judicial factories and curatories comprised a significant component of L, J & H's clientele. An early example was Donald Lindsay's appointment as judicial factor on the estate of Sir J. C. Anstruther whose Fife estates were left in minority in 1831 (*Session Cases*, 1833-4: 657-9). The 1856 annual report of the Accountant of the Court of Session, under whose supervision judicial factories were placed after 1849, shows that the partners of L, J & H held five appointments as curator *bonis* and four as factor *loco tutoris* from which they earned total commission of £717 (CS. 323/1). Foremost among early factorial appointments was Donald Lindsay's as curator *bonis* to Charles Mackenzie of Kilcoy from 1854 to 1887 for which he received commission in excess of £9,200.

From 1859 to 1891 L, J & H earned commission of £17,396 from forty-three factories and £20,850 from thirty-three curatories. The majority of factorial and curatorial appointments each generated average annual commission of £25 and subsisted for an average seven years. Others were more lucrative. From 1868 to 1891 George Auldjo Jamieson earned commission of £8,283 as curator *bonis* to the mentally infirm William Cunninghame Bontine of Ardoch and

Gartmore (Court of Session, Copies of Printed Petitions, CS. 347/32: 1) and from 1885 to 1891 he earned £3,060 as judicial factor arising out of the Orr Ewing case (*Session Cases*, 1883-4: 600-50, 682-7; Morgan, 1986: 356-8).

Scottish CAs and judicial factories The persistent inclusion of judicial factories in Scottish CAs' descriptions of their work-loads and in the examination papers of their institutes indicate the significance of this branch of work during the nineteenth century (Walker, 1988: 11).

The 1856 annual report of the Accountant of the Court of Session reveals that twenty-one members of the recently formed SAE and nineteen members of the IAAG held commissions as judicial factors and curators (CS. 323/1). By 1881 Thoms, in a seminal *Treatise on Judicial Factories*, noted that 'of recent years accountants have been the parties usually suggested to the court' (p. 43). In 1888 it is known that CAs held 22 per cent of all judicial factory appointments (Privy Council, 1890: 14; Walker, 1991: 263) and in 1895 Lord McLaren commented before the Select Committee on Trusts Administration that 'the factor is generally an accountant, and I think the work is very fairly distributed amongst the profession' (Minutes of Evidence: 137).

Their appointment as Accountants of the Court of Session is further evidence of CAs' perceived expertise in judicial factory work. The conduct of that office and the regulatory framework surrounding factories was frequently discussed by the councils of the SAE and IAAG. During the 1860s to 1880s the Lord Advocate received several reports and letters from the Scottish professional organizations on the subject of unregulated 'open factories' and the inadequate (£600 per year) remuneration of the Accountant of Court - deficiencies remedied in the Judicial Factors (Scotland) Act, 1889 (Lord Advocate's Department, AD. 56/133: correspondence from C. M. Barstow, 1874; G. Auldjo Jamieson, 1883; W. Moncreiff, 1887).

Landed proprietors and estate management

It has been shown that L, J & H received a substantial proportion of commission from the administration of landed estates under trusts and judicial factories. In addition, the practice earned 14 per cent of its fee income between 1859 and 1891 (Table II) from appointments as factors or commissioners to superintend and centrally administer large estates which were under the local management of resident sub-factors or cashiers. Duties might include preparing estate accounts, dealing with proprietors' tax affairs, arranging loans for estate improvements and (particularly during the mid to late 1880s) organizing property disposals (Auldjo Jamieson, 1888: 545-7).

By 1865 George Auldjo Jamieson could assert that L, J & H 'have the charge, more or less directly' of thirteen estates in Scotland with a total rental of £100,000 (Hypothec Commission, 1865, Minutes of Evidence: 157). The most lucrative and prestigious clients were the Earls of Aberdeen. In return for performing the duties of commissioners on the 62,422 acre estate in Aberdeenshire, which had an annual income of £44,122 in 1883 (Gibbs, 1910, vol. 1: 18), and for administering the financial affairs of the Gordon family, L, J & H earned commission of £10,302 in 1859-91.[4] Other major landowning clients included the management of the estates of the 11th Earl of Haddington from 1874 - the year in which he was elected as a Representative Peer (Gibbs, 1910, vol. 6: 238) - and the administration of the Scottish estates of the 21st Baron Clinton from 1869 whose principal seat was in Devon (Gibbs, 1910, vol. 3: 323).

Grant (1979: 217) and Mepham (1988: 288-9) have emphasized the significance of estate administration to the development of the Scottish accountancy profession. L, J & H's archive reveals that this branch of work was not only a late eighteenth and early nineteenth-century phenomenon. Mepham summarized four services to landed proprietors which provided an impetus to the nascent profession - financing improvements, appointments as trustees for creditors, the administration of forfeited estates following the Jacobite Rebellion of 1745 and their employment as auditors of estate accounts. During the nineteenth century other developments increased the involvement of accountants in estate-related work. First, Edinburgh lawyers and accountants, through their appointment as directors, managers and agents of financial institutions and as administrators of trusts, were important channels to sources of finance for landed proprietors (Campbell, 1990: 132). Second, the increasing indebtedness of many estates, their engrossment, improvement and scattered location increased the need for efficient estate accounting systems and competent central management (Grant, 1979: 205-7). Law agents, who had centrally administered many large estates, were increasingly considered to be unfit for this work due to their esoteric and impractical 'habits and education' (Brown, 1869: 13; Select Committee of the House of Lords on the Law of Hypothec in Scotland, 1868-9, Minutes of Evidence: 164). Third, the exploitation of mineral and metal resources and the need for sound advice during periods of falling rentals necessitated consultation with men of business acumen.

It is no surprise, therefore, to find that the employment of CAs by landed proprietors features heavily in descriptions of the work undertaken by several of those who founded and headed the profession in Scotland during the second half of the nineteenth century (Stewart, 1986: 41-165); and that estate accounting and management was tested in professional examinations and was the subject of lectures presented to the CA student societies.

Remits and investigations

Judicial remits and references Most commentators on the nature of the business conducted by early Scottish CAs have referred to the significance of 'remits from court' - a branch of practice given prominence in the petitions of the SAE and IAAG for incorporation. Although historians have noted the frequent references made by contemporary practitioners to judicial remits, they have failed to investigate the true nature of this work. Kedslie, for example, appears to assume that remits referred to any form of work which was awarded by the judiciary (1990a: 38-9). From the perspective of the practising accountant during the nineteenth century, judicial remits and references were quite distinct from other appointments which were administered by the courts, such as sequestration trusteeships and judicial factories.

An incidental judicial remit was a procedure whereby the judge or sheriff, on the motion of the litigants, could engage the skills of a person with specialist knowledge to investigate and report on a matter of fact or dispute (Wallace, 1909: 290-5). Bell (1861) elucidated several forms of judicial process in which accountants received remits and these also featured in the charter of incorporation of the SAE in 1854 as significant sources of engagement (Walker, 1988: 308). Accountants were commonly employed to prepare statements of accounts under actions of 'count and reckoning' in which a creditor attempted to compel a debtor to pay amounts due, the accountant ascertaining the amount payable (Bell, 1861: 231). Under the complex process of 'ranking and sale', in which the heritable property of an insolvent debtor was sold under the direction of the court and the proceeds distributed to creditors, accountants were remitted to produce a scheme of division showing the apportionment of the funds realized for the creditors (Bell, 1861: 682-9). Similarly, in the process of 'multiplepoinding', accountants were remitted to prepare states of claims and preferences in cases where more than one creditor laid claim to the same assets (Bell, 1861: 580-2). Accountants were also remitted to report in disputes over trust estates, contracts of partnership and family settlements (Law Courts (Scotland) Commission, Minutes of Evidence, 1868-9: 406).

The employment of early CAs in connection with judicial references was initially less common than their involvement with remits. A reference or arbitration - whereby a controversy between disputing parties is settled outwith the court by a referee chosen by the court (Wallace, 1909: 295-302) - was frequently made by the courts according to Bell (1861: 712; also Muir, 1892: 10). During the last two decades of the nineteenth century an expansion of work for CAs as arbiters and skilled witnesses also occurred in cases arising out of liquidations and municipal improvement (see *The Accountants' Magazine*, 1929: 291).

Further evidence concerning the lucrative nature of judicial remits is available for the late 1860s. Remits (or 'accountings') were the subject of much discussion before the Law Courts (Scotland) Commission. A succession of senior lawyers reported to the commissioners that the system of remits to accountants was a cause of considerable grievance. Concern was expressed over the delay in preparing reports which were tedious, diffuse, of excessive length and failed to provide conclusive recommendations. Ponderous reports generated high fees which were borne by the litigants. Witnesses to the commission suspected that delays and the presentation of corpulent reports were devices invented by accountants to boost their fees (see Minutes of Evidence, 1868-9: 561; 1870: 696-7). Concern over the conduct of judicial remits was such that legislative intervention proved necessary. The Court of Session Act, 1868, codified the powers of the reporting accountant and introduced measures to obviate delay and reduce the volume and expense of reports.

L, J & H earned fees of £16,830 from judicial remits and references from 1859 to 1891 (Table 2). Among the most remunerative appointments were £1,363 for reporting in relation to several cases arising from the protracted liquidation (1857-77) of the Western Bank (*Session Cases*, 1872-1: 96-120); £945 in 1879 in a financial dispute between the 7th Earl of Seafield and his brothers (Strathspey, 1983: 42) and £599 in 1876-7 in the case *Kerr's Trustees v. Wharncliffe*, in which it was contested that an absentee landowner owed money to the deceased factor of his Scottish estates (Court of Session, Unextracted Processes, CS. 244/1528).

Investigations Edwards has observed the expansion of work undertaken by English accountancy firms to investigate suspected fraud, the conversion of businesses to limited companies and to report on the working of government institutions (1989: 270-1). The same was true of larger CA practices in Scotland (Dodd, 1909: 47).

L, J & H earned fees of £14,109 from investigative remits from 1859 to 1891, and Table 2 shows that this branch of work expanded considerably during the 1870s and 1880s compensating for the diminution of fees from court remits subsequent to the Court of Session Act, 1868.

The non-judicial remits awarded to L, J & H largely comprised a miscellany of minor, casual appointments to investigate: the administration of trusts; changes in partnership structures; irregularities at bank branches, and; questions remitted by royal commissions and local authorities. The most remunerative investigations conducted by L, J & H were undertaken for large industrial concerns established under the Companies Act, 1862. These resulted in the preparation of accountants' reports: for prospectuses on the flotation of co-partner businesses (such as Merry & Cunningham, coal and iron producers, Lanarkshire in 1872-4 (Board of Trade, BT.2/444; Slaven, 1986a: 30-3; 1986b: 52-3)); on corporate financing (such as the Benhar Coal Company in 1879 (Board of Trade, BT.2/389)); on proposals to sell or amalgamate companies (such as the Bute Docks Company in 1886 (Napier, 1991: 165-7; Williams, 1985: 775)); and on the causes of inadequate financial performance (such as the California Copper Co. Ltd. in 1885 (*Scottish Banking and Insurance Magazine,* 1885: 114-15)).

Liquidations and reconstructions

Liquidations In 1905 Richard Brown asserted that the great majority of the 50,534 liquidations in Britain since 1862 had been administered by accountants (p. 325). From 1856 to 1895 3,081 companies were registered in Scotland and 1,300 were dissolved (Payne, 1980: 19-21).

L, J & H earned small amounts of commission from two liquidations during the period from 1859 to 1878. Between 1879 and 1891, however, commission from liquidations averaged £2,933 per annum, although these amounts were primarily attributable to commission arising from a single liquidation, that of the City of Glasgow Bank.

The circumstances surrounding the City of Glasgow bank disaster, its prominence as the 'blackest page in the history of Scottish banking' (Munro, 1928: 275), its revelation of the dire consequences of unlimited liability, its significance for the development of external auditing and the notorious trial of the directors – 'probably the most important which has taken place in Scotland' (Wallace, 1905: 1) - have been extensively recounted (Kerr, 1926: 254-70; Tyson, 1974;

Checkland, 1975: 469-81; French, 1985; Edwards, 1989: 144-8). L, J & H's work in relation to the City of Glasgow Bank debacle commenced on 30 September 1878 when George Auldjo Jamieson (as a director of the Royal Bank of Scotland) was engaged by the managers of the Scottish banks to investigate the financial state of the City of Glasgow Bank which had made an urgent request for a cash transfer of £500,000 (Wallace, 1905: 48). The following day Auldjo Jamieson conducted an investigation in Glasgow and recommended against assisting the ailing bank which closed its doors as a result (Wallace, 1905: 50). On 22 October the shareholders resolved to wind up the bank voluntarily and appointed Auldio Jamieson and Haldane as two of the four liquidators.

The liquidation was expeditiously completed by October 1882. The deficiency between the bank's liabilities of £12.4m and its assets of £7.2m was redressed by two calls on the 1,819 stockholders. Within 18 months £1.6m of secured debts had been paid by the liquidators and five dividends had distributed £9m to unsecured creditors. Auldjo Jamieson and Haldane were rewarded for their efforts by receiving total liquidator's commission of £30,070.[5] L, J & H were subsequently appointed liquidators on a succession of smaller dissolutions such as: the Girvan & Portpatrick Railway Company in 1883 (commission £700), Dunblane Hydropathic Co. Ltd in 1884 (£100), Lanark Oil Co. Ltd. in 1886 (£185) and the Florida Mortgage and Investment Co. Ltd in 1888 (£550).

Reconstructions The services of George Auldjo Jamieson were increasingly enlisted in reconstruction and corporate recovery business. No commission was generated from such work from 1859 to 1867, an average of £116 per annum was earned from reconstructions from 1868 to 1878 and £593 per annum. from 1879 to 1891 (Table 2). Auldjo Jamieson's pivotal role in the resuscitation of the Arizona Copper Company from 1883 (Schmitz, 1990: 410; Jackson, 1968: 163-85; Board of Trade, BT.2/1116, BT.2/1304) and the California Redwood Company in 1885-6 (Jackson, 1968: 222-9; Court of Session, Unextracted Processes, CS.240/C2/4) largely explains the increase in income derived from corporate recovery work in the latter period.

Auditing

The assumption of auditing as the principal source of fee income of accountancy practices by the time of the re-introduction of the statutory corporate audit requirement in 1900 has been well documented (Jones, 1981: 51-6; Lee, 1988: xxi; Edwards, 1989: 263-9). An analysis of the changing profile of over 600 audit clients of L, J & H reveals that before 1879 a substantial audit clientele of landed proprietors, trustees, life assurance societies and learned institutions existed in the non-corporate sector: a client base in the later nineteenth century which has remained largely undetected by students of the Scottish accountancy profession and has resulted in misleading assertions concerning the significance of auditing at the time of the organization of the profession in Scotland (Kedslie, 1990a: 7).

Table 2 shows that over the 1859-91 period, L, J & H derived its second greatest source of income from audit fees. Table IV details the various components.

TABLE IV *Lindsay, Jamieson & Haldane: composition of audit fee income 1859-91*

| | Average annual income | | | Total 1859-91 | |
	1859-67 £	1868-78 £	1879-91 £	£	%
Landed proprietors/estates	578	985	1,632	37,257	31
Trusts, executries, factories	884	774	1,200	32,071	27
Insurance and banks	486	345	1,277	24,767	21
Companies	29	160	1,326	19,271	16
Unincorporated businesses	1	12	166	2,304	2
Educational, scientific and professional institutions	40	74	97	2,437	2
Local authorities	9	1	45	679	1
Churches and political parties	0	2	13	195	0
Total	2,027	2,353	5,756	118,981	100

Source: Abstracts of Income and Expenditure.

Estate auditing Grant (1979: 215, 251) and Mepham (1988: 288) have shown that the audit of estate accounts was significant to the development of the accountancy profession in Scotland during the late eighteenth and early nineteenth centuries. The increasing tendency of estate commissioners and law agents to act as suppliers of funds to indebted landed proprietors resulted in their inability to fulfil their traditional stewardship role as auditors of estate factor's accounts and their consequent replacement by a group of eminent (primarily Edinburgh) accountants.

Table 4 reveals that the audit fees received by L, J & H from landed proprietors increased consistently from 1859 to 1891. The complexity and variety of the economic activities conducted by larger landowners and the need for efficient estate administration during periods of depressed rentals increased the employment of estate factors (Napier, 1991: 164) which in turn induced the separation of the ownership and management of the estate and the consequent need for audit.

L, J & H's most lucrative estate audit appointment (generating fees of £6,673 between 1867-91) related to the interests of the 3rd Marquess of Bute, whose income of £151,135 in 1883 derived primarily from coal-rich properties in Glamorgan and Durham and from Cardiff Docks (Gibbs, 1910, vol. 6: 713). The audit of the colliery and Troon Harbour accounts of the Duke of Portland (the 9th largest landowner peer in the UK in 1883) (Gibbs, 1910, vol. 10: 598) generated fees of £2,288 from 1861 to 1891.

Trust, judicial factory and executry auditing The second largest amount of audit income also arose from extra-statutory appointments. The practice earned £32,071 (Table 4), principally from the audit of trustees' charge and discharge accounts and, to a lesser extent, from the audit of executors books and of factories and curatories which fell outwith the Pupils Protection Act, 1849.

The audit of trusts, as with landed estate work, was not unique to L, J & H during the second half of the nineteenth century. The obligation of the trustee to administer the trust property for the beneficiaries created the need for an audit. Alternatively, the appointment of factors or cashiers by the trustees to manage the trust estate induced the preparation of factory accounts and their audit by the trustees or an independent auditor (Menzies, 1913: 134-5). It also became common practice for the truster to provide for an audit of the periodical accounts and/or on the completion of the trust as a condition of the discharge of the trustees. By 1895 the audit of trust accounts was considered to be 'a practice very much on the increase' (Select Committee on Trusts Administration, Minutes of Evidence: 140, 143). Contemporary law texts recommended that the audit be conducted by 'an accountant of character and experience' (Menzies, 1913: 583), and by the early 1890s such work was identified as one of four major branches of the Scottish CA's audit practice (Drummond, 1891: 197).

One half of the trust dispositions examined in the study contained a provision for an audit. The deeds reveal that before the late 1870s the frequency of the audit and the name of the auditor were unspecified, the audit to be conducted when the trustees 'shall think fit' or 'judge it expedient' by an accountant named by the Lord Advocate or the Dean of the Faculty of Advocates. From the late 1870s (possibly in response to the City of Glasgow Bank disaster of 1878), the deeds of the larger trusts provided for annual audits to be conducted by a named CA.

Given the intermittent nature of the trust audit before the late 1870s, it is not surprising that only ten of the 256 audit appointments gained by L, J & H from 1859 to 1891 generated fee income in excess of £500. The high level of income from trust audits represents the sheer volume of such clients.

The audit of executry accounts (of which L, J & H held forty-nine appointments) on the termination of the distribution of the defunct's estate seldom earned fees for more than one year. Similarly, the audit of the accounts of judicial factories, which fell outwith the aegis of the Accountant of the Court of Session (thirty-three appointments), was a source of non-recurring fees - the audit being conducted at the termination of the factory or when the factor required interim approval of his accounts (Law Courts (Scotland) Commission, Minutes of Evidence, 1868-9: 617).

Financial institutions and companies Table 4 shows that a substantial increase in the audit fees earned by L, J & H occurred from the late 1870s and that this was attributable not only to the increasing prevalence of estate and trust audits but, more importantly, to the demand for audits from insurers, banks and other companies.

In 1837 Donald Lindsay was appointed as auditor of the Scottish Widows' Fund and Life Assurance Society (Maxwell, 1914) - the source of £14,625 fees from 1859 to 1891. To this prestigious auditorship was added that of the North British Mercantile Insurance Company in 1883 with a £750 annual fee. L, J & H also gained major new banking clients such as the Union Bank of Scotland (Tamaki, 1983: 124-7) and the Town and County Bank (Keith, 1936: 140) following the introduction of the statutory bank audit under the Companies Act, 1879 (Tyson, 1974).

In addition to the acquisition of new insurance and bank audits during the 1870s and 1880s, L, J & H gained a large number of corporate clients which reflected the numeric expansion and industrial profile of company formations in Scotland during that period (Payne, 1980: 56-68). The most remunerative corporate audits were concerns founded for the extraction and distribution of minerals by landed proprietors with whom L, J & H had an established connection. The audit of the Bute Docks Company in Cardiff generated average annual fees of £557 between 1888 and 1891; the Low Moor Iron Co. near Bradford likewise £219 between 1886 and 1891. The audit of four Scottish shale oil companies also generated fees of over £180 per annum during the 1880s.

Reflecting the investment trust movement in the East of Scotland during the 1870s (Burton and Corner, 1968: 43), L, J & H acquired the audit of the Scottish American Investment Company from its inception in 1873 (Weir, 1973). Auldjo Jamieson's involvement in companies formed in Scotland for overseas investment was reflected in the acquisition of several land and mining company audits during the 1880s. Of equal significance to the high fees gained from corporate audit clients was the relative stability imposed on the audit income of the CA practice by the annual reporting cycle of these institutions which contrasted with the less recurrent nature of income from the trust audit.

The foregoing analysis of the development of the audit clientele of L, J & H reveals that it may be too simplistic to assume that the expansion of the audit work of professional accountancy practices during the nineteenth century was purely a response to the statutory regulation of the railways, limited companies, banks and local government (Kedslie, 1990a: 135-71). An emphasis on legislative landmarks detracts from the considerable amount of auditing conducted by CAs in the traditional economy (landed estates) and in less glamorous spheres (trusts and judicial factories).

Conclusions

This paper has provided evidence to show that the nature of the practice conducted by Scottish CAs during the formative period of professionalization has been oversimplified by previous commentators. Based on the findings of this study, the imposition of an abstract thesis of the early significance of bankruptcy and its eventual replacement by corporate auditing (Stewart, 1986: 13-15; Kedslie, 1990a: 134) presents a superficial picture of the clientele of the Victorian CA firm. There are several explanations for the perpetuation of such generalized misrepresentations of the composition of accounting practice during the nineteenth century. First, the accounting historian's (and contemporary commentator's) tendency to concentrate on discontinuities - allying the developing work-load of professional accountants with the progress of major economic and legislative events in the maturing urban-industrial state and sidelining the evolution of older forms of work more closely associated with pre-industrial society. Second, the adoption of a tunnel approach to historical investigation - concentrating on the genesis of accounting practices of consequence today rather than arriving at a chronological destination and assuming a lateral view of the work-load of contemporaries. The results of such research, which fail to take the past on its own terms, serve only to misdirect future historical investigations. Third, the above problems are exacerbated by a lack of available primary evidence which increases reliance on secondary sources and perpetuates the misconceptions.

The evidence presented for L, J & H reveals the multifarious nature of the work conducted by a major professional firm in the East of Scotland during the mid to late nineteenth century. The dominant features of the practice were a concern with insolvency, in general, rather than the narrow definition of bankruptcy; the significance of trust, judicial factory, remit and landed estate work which confirm the much vaunted connection between the Scottish accountants and the legal profession; the early prominence of auditing and the expansion of both corporate and non-corporate external auditing following one of the greatest financial scandals of the age - the City of Glasgow Bank failure of 1878.

The central feature of the practice of L, J & H was that, although its partners increasingly provided services to the mercantile and manufacturing communities from the 1880s, its essential client base was the landed classes. That should not prove surprising because, although the political power of the Scottish landed interest was seriously diminished by the mid-nineteenth century, the same was not so of its socio-economic domination which was perpetuated until the First World War due to the continued importance of agriculture, the local and gradual progress of industrialization and the participation of landowners in the acquisition of the new industrial wealth (Campbell, 1990: 123). As George Auldjo Jamieson stated, agriculture was 'the most important interest in the country, as regards both its magnitude and its influence on the wellbeing of the community' (1885: 7).

The maintenance of the landed interest was ably assisted by lawyers and early generations of Scottish accountants who proved admirable as estate administrators (under factories, curatories, as auditors of estate accounts; and as financial advisers on sources of funds and the exploitation of estate resources). In return, the social status of the accountants was enhanced by association with landed society and the landowners' primary servants, the lawyers - and thereby conferred professional respectability on those who successfully organized the accountancy profession in 1853.

The findings reported in this paper are based on an analysis of the surviving records of a single, albeit major, Edinburgh-based firm. Similar contextual research, utilizing sources both internal and external to the firm, is desirable for other practices of different sizes, locations and generations. Without a deeper insight into the work mix of contemporary firms, the full critical history of the development of the accountancy profession in Scotland will prove elusive.

Notes

The author is indebted to Mr J. Martin Haldane, of Chiene & Tait, Chartered Accountants, Edinburgh for making the records of Lindsay, Jamieson & Haldane available for historical research, and to Tom Lee, Irvine Lapsley and the anonymous reviewers for their most helpful comments on previous drafts of this paper.

1. The archival material comprises: two-volume set of notes on the firm and its partners prepared by Herbert W. Haldane, CA, partner 1898-1957 (President of the Society of Accountants in Edinburgh, 1934-7); profit summaries 1845-91; detailed abstracts of income and expenditure 1859-91; expense accounts 1892-1905; clerks salaries summaries 1857-89; partnership agreements; documents relating to office buildings; and various client correspondence. Papers relating to L, J & H's involvement with the City of Glasgow Bank liquidation have been deposited in the National Library of Scotland (ICAS: F113-31). A series of client papers, mainly consisting of estate plans, are maintained in the Scottish Record Office (Haldane Brown: GD.255). George A. Jamieson's account book as trustee of the Ardkinglas Trust is deposited in the Antiquarian Collection of the Institute of Chartered Accountants of Scotland, Edinburgh.

2. Stewart (1986: 97) states that Lindsay established his own practice in 1823. The source of that assertion was Haldane's (1897: 496) discovery that Lindsay's name first appeared in the list of accountants produced in *Oliver & Boyd's Edinburgh Almanac* in 1823.

3. Beyond the period of this study the principal events in the history of L, J & H were as follows. In 1919 the fortunes of the practice were partly revived by the assumption of a 'new blood' partner, Alexander Morrison (1872-1955) (*Accountants' Magazine*, 1955: 436-7); the opening of an office in London in 1921; and by an expansion in post-war taxation and estate work (Haldane, 1955: 11-13). In 1967 L, J & H merged with another major late-nineteenth-century Scottish practice, Richard Brown & Co. (founded in 1885) as Haldane, Brown & Co (*Accountants' Magazine*, 1967: 139). Shortly thereafter Haldane, Brown & Co became the Edinburgh practice of Arthur Young, McClelland Moores & Co (Stewart, 1986: 176).

4. The Aberdeen appointment was gained following the resignation of George Hamilton Gordon, the 4th Earl (1784-1860) as Prime Minister in February 1855. During his premiership Aberdeen had been almost entirely absent from his family seat at Haddo House (Gordon, 1893: 301). Having been relieved of office the Earl directed his attention to estate matters and on discovering various debts and maladministration (Iremonger, 1978: 309), he requested Donald Lindsay to take charge of his financial affairs and to advise on family settlements (Haldane, 1954: 63).

5. Due to the existence of submissions to the Court of Session in May 1880 by Auldjo Jamieson and Haldane arising from a dispute between themselves and the Remuneration Committee of the City of Glasgow Bank (*Session Cases*, 1879-80: 1196-216), evidence is available concerning the profound impact of the liquidation on L, J & H. Auldjo Jamieson reported that the liquidation was originally conceived as a threat to 'the stability of our business': it had occupied almost all his time, half of that of Haldane and two-thirds of Francis More's (City of Glasgow Bank, 1880, Statements by Jamieson and Haldane, ICAS F.131/21). Although some important work was lost as a result of the appointment, an increase in the number of clerks (who processed 22,799 letters in relation to the liquidation October 1878-March 1880) and 'great personal exertions' had averted the risk to the practice.

Bibliography

Account Book of Charles Selkrig, Tods, Murray & Jamieson records, (GD. 237/274), Scottish Record Office, Edinburgh.

The Accountants' Magazine (1897-1970), Edinburgh.

The Alphabetical Compendium of Scotch Mercantile Sequestrations (1851-1853), London: Longman, Brown, Green & Longmans.

Annual Report of the Accountant of the Court of Session (CS. 323), Scottish Record Office, Edinburgh.

Auldjo Jamieson, G. (1885) *The Present Agricultural and Financial Depression: Some of its Causes, Influences, and Effects*, Edinburgh: Blackwood.

Auldjo Jamieson, G. (1888) 'Recent illustrations of the theory of rent, and their effect on the value of land', in *Report of the Fifty-Seventh Meeting of the British Association for the Advancement of Science held at Manchester in August and September 1887*, London: John Murray.

Baxter, W. T. (1991) Review of M. J. M. Kedslie 'Firm foundations', *Accounting and Business Research*, Autumn: 383-4.

Belhaven Trust Estate Act, 1884 *Local and Private Acts*, 47 & 48 Vict, c. 2.

Bell, G. J. (1870) *Commentaries on the Law of Scotland and on the Principles of Mercantile Jurisprudence*, 7th ed., Edinburgh: T. & T. Clark.

Bell, W. (1861) *A Dictionary and Digest of the Law of Scotland*, Edinburgh: Bell & Bradfute.

Board of Trade. Registrar of Companies for Scotland, Dissolved Company files, (BT.2), Scottish Record Office, Edinburgh.

Brown, R. (ed.) (1905) *A History of Accounting and Accountants*, Edinburgh: T. C.

& E. C. Jack.

Brown, R. E. (1869) *The Book of the Landed Estate*, Edinburgh: Blackwood.

Burton H. and D. C. Corner (1968) *Investment and Unit Trusts in Britain and America*, London: Elek Books.

Campbell, R. H (1990) 'Continuity and challenge: the perpetuation of the landed interest', in T. M. Devine (ed.) *Conflict and Stability in Scottish Society 1700-1850*, Edinburgh: John Donald.

Chandley, W. and P. Boys (1991) 'Hidden assets and secret reserves', *Accountancy*, June: 106.

Checkland, S. G. (1975) *Scottish Banking: A History 1695-1973*, Glasgow: Collins City of Glasgow Bank (1880) Remuneration to Liquidators, ICAS Collection, (ICAS F. 131), National Library of Scotland, Edinburgh.

Cornwell, S. V. P. (1991) *Curtis Jenkins Cornwell & Co: A Study in Professional Origins 1816-1966*, New York: Garland.

Court of Session. Copies of Printed Petitions for Appointment of Judicial Factors (CS. 347), Scottish Record Office, Edinburgh.

Court of Session. Unextracted Processes, Scottish Record Office, Edinburgh.

Dickson, T. G. (1892) 'Factorships', in *Transactions of the Chartered Accountants Students' Society of Edinburgh*, Edinburgh: Macniven & Wallace.

Dodd, A. F. (1909) 'The preparation of accountants' certificates for purposes of joint stock company flotations' in *Glasgow Chartered Accountants Students' Society Transactions for the Year 1909-10*, London: Gee.

Drummond, A. (1891) 'On the mode of conducting an audit', in T. A. Lee (ed.) (1988) *The Evolution of Audit Thought and Practice*, New York: Garland, pp.197-210.

Edinburgh & Leith Post Office Directory (1818-1970), Edinburgh: Morrison & Gibb.

Edwards, J. R. (1989) *A History of Financial Accounting*, London: Routledge.

French, E. A. (1985) *Unlimited Liability: the Case of the City of Glasgow Bank*, London: The Chartered Association of Certified Accountants.

General Register of Sasines, Reversions &c., (RS), Scottish Record Office, Edinburgh.

Gibbs, Hon. V. (1910) *The Complete Peerage of England, Scotland, Ireland, Great Britain and the United Kingdom*, London: St Catherine Press.

Gordon, Hon. Sir A. (1893) *The Earl of Aberdeen*, London: Sampson Low, Marston.

Goudy, H. (1903) *A Treatise on the Law of Bankruptcy in Scotland*, Edinburgh: T. & T. Clark.

Grant, I. D. (1979) 'Landlords and land management in North Eastern Scotland 1750-1850', unpublished PhD thesis, Edinburgh University.

Haldane, H. W. (1954) 'Lindsay, Jamieson & Haldane: some notes on the firm and the partners thereof from 1 January 1845 to 31 December 1891', unpublished typescript, Mr J. M. Haldane, Chiene & Tait, CA, Edinburgh.

Haldane, H. W. (1955) 'Lindsay, Jamieson & Haldane, 1892-1921; some further notes on the firm', unpublished typescript, Mr J. M. Haldane, Chiene & Tait, CA, Edinburgh.

Haldane, J. (1897) 'Eminent accountants of the past. Donald Lindsay', *The Accountants' Magazine:* 495-9.

Henderson, J. A. (ed.) (1912) *History of the Society of Advocates in Aberdeen,* Aberdeen: New Spalding Club.

Hypothec Commission (1865) Report of Her Majesty's Commissioners appointed to consider the law relating to landlords' right of hypothec in Scotland, *British Parliamentary Papers,* vol. 17.

Interim Account of a Going Concern: Some Essays on the History of the Firm of Mann Judd Gordon & Company (1967), Glasgow: privately.

Iremonger, L. (1978) *Lord Aberdeen: A Biography of the Fourth Earl of Aberdeen KC, K T, Prime Minister 1852-1855,* London: Collins.

Jackson, W. T. (1968) *The Enterprising Scot: Investors in the American West after 1873,* Edinburgh: Edinburgh University Press.

Jones, E. (1981) *Accountancy and the British Economy 1840-1980. The Evolution of Ernst & Whinney,* London: Batsford.

Kedslie, M. J. M. (1990a) *Firm Foundations: The Development of Professional Accounting in Scotland, 1850-1900,* Hull: Hull University Press.

Kedslie, M. J. M. (1990b) 'Mutual self-interest - a unifying force; the dominance of societal closure over social background in the early professional accounting bodies', *The Accounting Historians Journal,* December: 1-19.

Keith, A. (1936) *The North of Scotland Bank Limited,* Aberdeen: Aberdeen Journals Ltd.

Kerr, A. W. (1926) *History of Banking in Scotland,* London: A. & C. Black.

Law Courts (Scotland) Commission (1868-70) Reports of Commissioners to inquire into Courts of Law in Scotland, *British Parliamentary Papers:* 1868-9, vol. 25; 1870, vol. 18.

Lee, T. A. (ed.) (1984) *Transactions of the CA Students' Societies of Edinburgh and Glasgow,* New York: Garland.

Lee, T. A. (ed.) (1988) *The Evolution of Audit Thought and Practice,* New York: Garland.

Lenman, B. P. (1977) *An Economic History of Modern Scotland, 1660-1970,* London: Batsford.

Lord Advocate's Department papers, (AD), Scottish Record Office, Edinburgh.

Lorimer, J. (1873) *A Hand-Book of the Law of Scotland,* Edinburgh: T. & T. Clark.

McClelland, J. (1869) *The Origin and Present Organization of the Profession of Chartered Accountants in Scotland,* Glasgow.

Marshall, E. A. (1975) *General Principles of Scots Law,* Edinburgh: Wm Green.

Marwick, W. H. (1936) *Economic Development in Victorian Scotland,* London: Allen & Unwin.

Maxwell, Sir H. (1914) *Annals of the Scottish Widows Fund Life Assurance Society 1815-1914,* Edinburgh: R. & R. Clark.

Menzies, A. J. P. (1913) *The Law of Scotland affecting Trustees,* Edinburgh: Wm Green.

Mepham, M. J. (1988) *Accounting in Eighteenth Century Scotland,* New York: Garland.

Morgan, N. J. (1986) 'John Orr Ewing', in A. Slaven and S. Checkland (eds) *Dictionary of Scottish Business Biography,* vol. 1, Aberdeen: Aberdeen University Press, pp. 256-8.

Muir, J. (1892) 'A chat about accounting', in *Transactions of the Chartered Accountants Students' Society of Edinburgh,* Edinburgh: Macniven & Wallace.

Munro, N. (1928) *The History of the Royal Bank of Scotland 1727-1927,* Edinburgh: privately.

Napier, C. J. (1989) 'Research directions in accounting history', *British Accounting Review,* September: 237-54.

Napier, C. J. (1991) 'Aristocratic accounting: the Bute Estate in Glamorgan 1814-1880', *Accounting and Business Research,* spring: 163-74.

Parker, R. H. (1981) 'The study of accounting history', in M. Bromwich, and A. Hopwood, (eds) *Essays in British Accounting Research,* London: Pitman, pp. 279-93.

Parker, R. H. (1986) *The Development of the Accountancy Profession in Britain to the Early Twentieth Century,* Academy of Accounting Historians: Monograph Five.

Payne, P. L. (1980) *The Early Scottish Limited Companies 1856-1895,* Edinburgh: Scottish Academic Press.

Penicuik Trust Estates Act, 1883 *Local and Private Acts,* 46 Vict, c. 1.

Privy Council (1890) Scottish Institute Petition, In the Matter of the Petition of the Scottish Institute for Incorporation by Royal Charter, Scottish Dept., Edinburgh Central Library.

Register of Deeds and Probative Writs in the Books of Council and Session, (RD), Scottish Record Office, Edinburgh.

Report from the Select Committee of the House of Lords on the Law of Hypothec in Scotland (1868-9) *British Parliamentary Papers,* vol. 9.

Report from the Select Committee on the Fraudulent Debtors (Scotland) Bill; with the Proceedings, Evidence, Appendix and Index (1880), *British Parliamentary Papers,* vol. 9.

Report from Select Committee on Trusts Administration with Proceedings, Evidence, Appendix, and Index (1895) *British Parliamentary Papers,* vol. 13.

Schmitz, C. (1990) 'George Auldjo Jamieson', in A. Slaven, and S. Checkland (eds) *Dictionary of Scottish Business Biography,* vol. 2, Aberdeen: Aberdeen University Press, pp. 409-12.

Scots Law Times (1900-1907), Edinburgh.

The Scotsman (1888-1907), Edinburgh.

Scottish Banking and Insurance Magazine (1885).

Session Cases. Cases Decided in the Court of Session, Court of Justiciary and House of Lords (1833-1914) Edinburgh: T. & T. Clark.

Skinner, T. (ed.) (1880-1907) *The Directory of Directors,* London: Thomas Skinner.

Skinner, T. (ed.) (1885-1910) *The Stock Exchange Year Book,* London: Thomas Skinner.

Slaven, A. (1986a) 'John Charles Cunningham', in A. Slaven and S. Checkland (eds) *Dictionary of Scottish Business Biography,* vol. 1, Aberdeen: Aberdeen University Press, pp. 30-3.

Slaven, A. (1986b) 'James Merry', in A. Slaven and S. Checkland (eds) *Dictionary of Scottish Business Biography,* vol. 1, Aberdeen: Aberdeen University Press, pp. 52-5.

Society of Accountants in Edinburgh (1853-1904), Sederunt Books, Institute of Chartered Accountants of Scotland, Edinburgh.

Society of Accountants in Edinburgh (1855-1914), Register of Indentures. Institute of Chartered Accountants of Scotland, Edinburgh.

Stewart, J. C. (1986) *Pioneers of a Profession: Chartered Accountants to 1879,* New York: Garland.

Strathspey, Lord (1983) *A History of Clan Grant,* Chichester: Phillimore.

Tamaki, N. (1983) *The Life Cycle of the Union Bank of Scotland 1830-1954,* Aberdeen: Aberdeen University Press.

Thoms, G. H. (1881) *Treatise on Judicial Factors, Curators Bonis and Managers of Burghs,* Edinburgh: Bell & Bradfute.

Tyson, R. E. (1974) 'The failure of the City of Glasgow Bank and the rise of independent auditing', *The Accountants' Magazine,* April: 126-31.

Walker, S. P. (1988) *The Society of Accountants in Edinburgh 1854-1914: A Study of Recruitment to a New Profession,* New York: Garland.

Walker, S. P. (1991) 'The defence of professional monopoly: Scottish chartered accountants and "satellites in the accountancy firmament" 1854-1914', *Accounting, Organizations and Society,* 16(3): 257-83.

Wallace, W. (ed.) (1905) *Trial of the City of Glasgow Bank Directors,* Edinburgh: William Hodge.

Wallace, W. (1909) *The Practise of the Sheriff Court of Scotland,* Edinburgh: Wm Green.

Wallace, W. (1914) *The Law of Bankruptcy in Scotland with Forms,* Edinburgh: Wm Green.

Weir, R. B. (1973) *History of the Scottish American Investment Company,* Edinburgh: privately.

Williams, L. J. (1985) 'William Thomas Lewis', in D. J. Jeremy (ed.) *Dictionary of Business Biography,* vol. 3, London: Butterworth, pp. 773-7.

CHAPTER 12

The Influence of Scottish Accountants in the United States: The Early Case of the Society of Accountants in Edinburgh

Thomas A Lee

Introduction

In 1854, Queen Victoria granted a royal charter of incorporation to 61 members of The Society of Accountants in Edinburgh (SAE) (Lee, 1996). Under this banner of professional legitimacy, the SAE membership prospered and, by 1914, totalled 580 chartered accountants. However, not all SAE members admitted between 1854 and 1914 remained in Edinburgh. Research of the early history of the SAE reveals more than 23% of its admittants in this period moved overseas to develop their careers (Walker, 1988, p.44). Indeed, only 49% of the 726 SAE members admitted between 1854 and 1914 remained in Edinburgh after admission.

Fifty-nine SAE members emigrated to the United States (U.S.) between 1883 and 1926.[1] They comprise approximately 10% of the 600 admissions to the SAE membership between 1881 (the year of admission of the first SAE emigrant to the U.S.) and 1914 (the beginning of the First World War, and the year of admission of the last U.S. emigrant in this study). They were therefore a significant proportion of a growing chartered accountancy profession in Edinburgh in the late 1800s and early 1900s. Forty-six of the emigrants remained in the U.S. throughout their working lives, 8 returned to the U.K., and the remaining 5 moved on to other parts of the world to develop their careers.

The purpose of this paper is to report on the first phase of a long-term research program to identify the impact of U.K. accountants

Reproduced from *The Accounting Historians Journal*, Volume 24, Number 1, June 1997, pp 117-41, with kind permission from the Editor.

on the development of professional accountancy in other parts of the world. In this first study, the research focus is on the early SAE influence in the U.S. It is therefore an extended case study of the effect of emigration on the development of professional accountancy. As accounting histories such as Kedslie (1990a), Lee (1995), and Shackleton and Milner (1995) demonstrate, there were significant differences in the membership and organizational features of the early U.K. chartered accountancy bodies (i.e., with respect to members' backgrounds, training and examining standards, and clients). It is therefore important to examine each community on an individual basis prior to generalizing from the separate results.

In this study, the SAE is the body of professional accountants examined. Only accountants who were SAE members at the time of their emigration are included in the data base. The main empirical analysis therefore ignores SAE members who resigned prior to emigration, SAE apprentices who never became members, and Edinburgh accountants unconnected with the SAE. Future research will observe other U.K. bodies (e.g., The Institute of Accountants and Actuaries in Glasgow [IAAG], and The Institute of Chartered Accountants in England and Wales), as well as developments in countries other than the U.S. (e.g., Australia and Canada).

Within a general context of emigration to the U.S. in the late 1800s and early 1900s, and with respect to a theoretical perspective on emigration, the current study describes 59 identifiable SAE emigrants, and reports on what they achieved as professional accountants in the U.S. More specifically, the study attempts to identify the degree of influence these accountants had on the foundation and development of the U.S. accountancy profession (with particular reference to its institutionalization processes and practice formations).

Data sources used in the project are indicated in the bibliography with an asterisk. In this respect, it should be noted that available sources of information about the SAE emigrants were limited, and the detailed content of what was available was relatively restricted. Early membership records of professional accountancy bodies such as the SAE tend to describe mainly address changes.

Emigration to the U.S. and emigration theory

U.K. Emigration

The SAE emigrants in this study are examined in the context of a general pattern of emigration from Scotland to the U.S. in the late

1800s and early 1900s. Emigration from Scotland was part of a wider European migration which gathered momentum in the late 1700s, and began to diminish in the last two decades of the nineteenth century (Brander, 1982, pp.55, 73). More than 33 million emigrants from around the world arrived in the U.S. between the early 1800s and the early 1900s (Baines, 1991, pp.8-9; and Nugent, 1992, p.30). Over a comparable period, it is estimated that nearly 17 million individuals left the U.K. for other parts of the world (Nugent, 1992, p.30; see also Baines, 1991, pp.8-9). How many U.K. emigrants travelled to the U.S. is not precisely known, and those estimates which have been made tend to vary. Nugent (1992, p.45), for example, suggests that, for the period 1871 and 1900, between 60% and 70% of emigrants from England, Scotland and Wales arrived in the U.S. This datum drops to 37% for the period 1901 to 1914. Musgrove (1963, p.19) reports 60% of U.K. emigrants leaving for the U.S. in the 1890s.

Scottish Emigration

How many Scots emigrated to the U.S. is equally problematic. Prentis (1983, p.27) calculates that between 9% and 10% of U.K. emigrants from the 1850s to the 1890s were of Scottish origin. Baines (1991, p.10), on the other hand, estimates that the annual average Scottish emigration rate (per 100 of population) ranged from approximately one-half percent (for the decades from 1851 to 1880) to approximately one percent (for the decades 1901 to 1930). Nugent (1992, p.46) translates these rates into absolute terms, and claims that approximately 635,000 Scots entered the U.S. between 1871 and 1910. Aspinwall (1985, p. 113) estimates the figure at 800,000 for the period 1820 to 1950. Brander (1982, p. 104), on the other hand, puts forward a figure of 500,000 for the period 1861 to 1901. Berthoff (1953, p.5) states a datum of 567,000 for a century of Scottish emigration to the U.S. (i.e., from 1820 to 1920). In contrast, Anderson and Morse (1990, p.15) disclose two million Scots emigrants world-wide between 1830 and 1914, with an estimated one-half arriving in the U.S. between 1853 and 1914.

Despite these variations in emigration data estimates, it is clear that, within the period of emigration in this study (i.e., 1883 to 1926), many hundreds of thousands of individuals left Scotland for the U.S. The U.S. population census statistics bear this out. For example, according to Brander (1982, p.89), in 1790, the recorded U.S. population of Scottish birth was 189,000. Nugent (1992, p.151) reports it grew to 261,000 by 1910. This suggests a large number of Scots emigrants either died, returned to Scotland, or disappeared. For example, Nugent (1992, p.35) reports that 53% of U.K. emigrants to the U.S. between 1908 and 1914 returned to the U.K. Whatever the level of overall Scottish emigration to the U.S., however, it is certainly unsurprising to find (as in the current study) that it included a number of Edinburgh chartered accountants.

Emigration theory

There are two basic theoretical approaches to emigration (Woods, 1982, p. 131). The first approach relates to descriptions of emigrants and their emigration (including economic, political, and social reasons why they emigrated). The second approach deals with the economic, political, and social effects of emigration. The current study of SAE emigrants incorporates recognition of both theoretical bases in its analyses. For example, much of the paper's empirical content deals with descriptions of the SAE emigrants, and their emigration locations and employment. Also included are descriptions of how their careers progressed. What is lacking because of insufficient data are specific reasons for the SAE emigration. It is therefore useful to initially describe what emigration researchers typically state as the major reasons for emigration generally and emigration of skills particularly.

Emigration takes place for a number of economic, political, and social reasons. These can be generally categorized as "push" factors (e.g., economic decline, unemployment, and oppression), and "pull" factors (e.g., employment, better wages, education, and improved social status) (De Jong and Fawcett, 1981, p.20; and Lewis, 1982, p.100). Typically, emigration occurs because of differentials between the departing and host countries which allow emigrants to maximize on economic opportunity and social aspiration (Lee, 1969, pp. 285-7; De Jong and Fawcett, 1981, p.17; Lucas, 1981, pp.85-6; and Clark, 1986, p.80). The greater the differentials with respect to emigration factors, the greater the level of emigration (Lee, 1969, pp.289-92).

A common feature of emigration appears to be the frustration of the emigrant with conditions in the country of departure (Aspinwall, 1982, p.201; and Brander, 1982, p.73). It is therefore presumed in this study that the SAE emigrants were sufficiently frustrated with their economic and/or social conditions in Edinburgh to emigrate to the U.S. The latter supposition appears reasonable within the specific context of researched reasons for Scottish emigration in the second half of the nineteenth century. The major stimulus for such emigration was economic, particularly with respect to the importing of necessary skills from Scotland to the U.S. As Devine (1992, pp.2-3) reports, Scottish emigration during this period was a paradox because Scottish economic resources were sufficient to sustain a larger population. The emigrants left mainly industrial locations, and a large proportion were skilled and found similar employment in the U.S. (Aspinwall, 1985, p. 114). For example, Berthoff (1953, p.21) finds more than 40% of Scots emigrants between 1873 and 1918 had disclosed skills when they emigrated. Musgrove (1963, p.22) identifies a comparable effect. He reports that the proportion of skilled U.K. emigrants to the U.S. increased from 15% to 45% between 1900 and 1913.

The reason for the early transfer of skills between Scotland and the U.S. was the Scottish influence on industries such as textiles, railroads, cattle, coal, and engineering (Aspinwall, 1985, pp.95, 100, 115-16). However, with the later consolidation of large U.S. businesses, labor problems, and an erosion in value of imported Scottish skills and status, emigration from Scotland to the U.S. became less attractive (Aspinwall, 1985, p.82). For example, Scottish expertise was no longer needed in U.S. iron and steel industries by the 1870s, nor in coal mining by the 1880s (Brander, 1982, p.102; and Aspinwall, 1985, p. 120).

By 1914, the main emigration from the U.K. to the U.S. was what Musgrove (1963, p.28) describes as elite. Indeed, he concludes that middle class, white collar individuals were over-represented within the U.S. emigration population (Musgrove, 1963, p. 17). Of interest to the current study is Musgrove's more detailed finding that, as the emigrating proportion of individuals in the established professions slowed down in the late 1800s and early 1900s, the comparable proportion in the new professions increased (Musgrove, 1963, p.23). This would have included chartered accountants such as the SAE members. Professional qualifications were expected to give emigrants a significant start in the host country (Erickson, 1972, p.394), and the 1890 U.S. Census discloses 3.1% of Scots male emigrants were professionals (Berthoff, 1953, p.121). The equivalent datum for females is 3.6%. Within this general context, the SAE emigration in the late 1800s and early 1900s is not unexpected. Economic and social status differentials between Scotland and the U.S. were presumably sufficiently great to cause a significant proportion of SAE members to be frustrated enough to emigrate.

The literature of emigration contains general pointers of relevance to the location of the SAE emigration. Lee (1969, p.292) concludes that emigration is typically along defined routes. This can be evidenced more specifically in relation to Scots emigrating to the U.S. during the last half of the nineteenth century. For example, in the early part of the period 1861 and 1901, Scots emigrants located mainly in New York, Pennsylvania, and Massachusetts. Later emigrants were typically found in Illinois, Michigan, and Ohio (Brander, 1982, p.104). The major cities hosting these emigrants during the same periods were New York, Chicago, Philadelphia, and Detroit. The 1920 U.S. Census confirms these data (Aspinwall, 1985, p.123). Thus, in the current study, it is unsurprising to find a considerable proportion of SAE emigrants located in the above states and cities.

Professional accountancy in the late nineteenth century

The first SAE members known to have emigrated to the U.S. were W. H. K. Skinner (to Kansas in 1883) and T. R. Fleming (to Colorado in 1885). No information is available as to why they emigrated. According to SAE records, both men resided in the U.S. for three years. Skinner was the son of a lawyer and last recorded as an SAE member in Kansas in 1886. Fleming, the son of a banker, moved from the U.S. to South Africa in 1888, and remained there until at least 1924. Fleming's locations suggest he may have been concerned with mining operations.

The main SAE emigration started in the mid 1890s. Twenty SAE members arrived in the U.S. between 1883 and 1904. A further 39 entered between 1905 and 1926. Twenty-nine of the 59 emigrants were admitted as SAE members prior to 1905. The remaining 30 became chartered accountants between 1905 and 1914. Thirty-eight of the 59 emigrants were educated at four leading Edinburgh private schools (in order, George Watson's College, George Heriot's School, the Edinburgh Academy, and Daniel Stewart's College). The largest group (17) was educated at George Watson's College.

Walker (1988, pp. 40-51; see also Brown, 1905, p.332) characterizes the late 1800s and early 1900s in Edinburgh as a period of oversupply in professional accountancy, and this is supported by data in this study. All 59 emigrants were admitted to the SAE by 1914, and 47 had entered the U.S. by that year. Table I provides a complete analysis of the time period between admittance as an SAE member and arriving in the U.S., and the length of stay. It discloses that 42 (71%) of the emigrants entered the U.S. within 5 years of becoming SAE members, and 36 (61%) stayed for 21 years or more. Thus, for most of these individuals, emigration to the U.S. was a decision taken at an early stage in their professional accountancy careers, and resulted in these careers being located for the most part in the U.S.

TABLE I: *SAE membership, U.S. emigration and U.S. residency*

Period (years)	To Emigration	Of Residency
0 - 5	42	9
6 - 20	14	14
21+	3	36
Total	**59**	**59**

The significance of Table I is that it suggests the large majority of the SAE emigrants had time to materially influence the development of professional accountancy in the U.S. They were leaving a situation in which a local oversupply of professional accountants existed. In addition, they were members of an institutional body which was arguably well ahead of similar bodies in the setting of professional accounting standards. Each of the 59 emigrants completed a professional training involving a five-year apprenticeship with an SAE member, compulsory attendance at University of Edinburgh law classes, and passing several written professional examinations.[2] Forty-one individuals were admitted to membership under a national uniform system of training and examination which was administered from Edinburgh. Thirty-eight had SAE-managed evening classes available to assist in their examination preparation.

The 59 emigrants were therefore well qualified to practice their profession in the U.S. They were typical of admittants to the SAE between 1854 and 1914. The occupational classifications of the fathers of the 59 men are proportionally similar to those of all SAE apprentices identified by Walker (1988, p. 174) between 1837 and 1911. For example, 22 were from independent or professional backgrounds, 12 from manufacturing, commerce and farming, and 25 from lower middle and working class backgrounds. The majority (38) were educated at respected private schools in Edinburgh. The emigrants therefore do not appear to be significantly different as a social group from the total professional population of which they were initially a part.

Why the SAE emigrants left the U.K. is unknown. Lack of employment and career opportunities may fit most cases. Adventure and opportunity may be relevant to others. Escape from an impending World War may be yet another (13 of the 59 accountants emigrated in the years 1913, 1914 and 1915). Whatever the reason, the emigrants joined an accountancy community at the beginning of its journey to maturity, and in need of an influx of expertise.[3] Indeed, Brown (1905, pp.278-9) characterizes the U.S. accountancy profession at the beginning of the twentieth century as behind U.K. standards and undertaking work not usually thought of as mainstream practice in the U.K. (e.g., auditing).[4]

Most of the SAE emigrants entered a world in which organized and institutionalized accountancy was at an early stage. The first organized body of accountants (the New York Institute of Accounts [NYIA]) was formed in 1882, followed soon after in 1886 by the American Association of Public Accountants (AAPA). The AAPA was formed in Philadelphia by 24 individuals who were mainly chartered accountants from the U.K. Of the initial 10 AAPA Council members, 8 were from New York, and one each from Boston and Philadelphia. No SAE members were involved in the formation of the AAPA. The SAE influence on institutionalization was to come later in the AAPA's history. Indeed, 12 of the 59 emigrants are known to have become AAPA members, including J. B. Niven who was its Vice-President in 1915.

TABLE II: *U.S. accountants in the late 1800s*

Date	New York	Chicago	Philadelphia	Total
1870	12	2	14	28
1880	31	3	15	49
1890	66	24	35	125
1899	183	71	74	328

New York had the largest community of accountants in the late 1800s, as revealed by figures researched by A. C. Littleton (Zeff, 1988, p. 15) (see Table II). By 1899, there were 328 accountants identified in 3 of the largest U.S. cities. By way of contrast, the SAE in 1900 had a membership of 351, and there were 720 chartered accountants in the 3 Scottish societies formed in Aberdeen, Edinburgh, and Glasgow.

Public accountancy firms gradually emerged in the U.S. during the last decade of the nineteenth century. They were mainly founded by U.K. accountants fulfilling audit and company formation contracts in the U.S. (e.g., in brewing, steel manufacturing, and railroads). Examples of such firms include Barrow, Wade, Guthrie & Co. in New York (formed in 1883), Price Waterhouse & Co. in New York (1890) and Chicago (1891), Broads, Patterson & Co. in Chicago (1894), Arthur Young & Co. in New York (1894), Deloitte, Plender, Griffiths & Co. in New York (1895), Marwick, Mitchell & Co. in New York (1897), and Touche, Niven & Co. in Chicago (1900) and New York (1901). At least 32 of the 59 SAE emigrants are known to have been associated with one or more of the above firms at some time in their U.S. careers.

The U.K. influence of chartered accountants in the organization of the AAPA was increasingly resented in the late 1800s by other accountants with non-U.K. backgrounds (Miranti, 1990, pp.29-47). The greatest competition to the AAPA came from the NYIA which had been formed by non-chartered accountants with the intention of emphasizing "scientific" accounting.[5] In events reminiscent of activities in Scotland between 1884 and 1914,[6] the new U.S. professionals gradually organized to self-regulate public accountants and accountancy standards. The process was engineered through individual state legislation which licensed appropriately qualified individuals, and used state societies of public accountants and boards of accountancy to manage the legislation (Miranti, 1990, pp.48-68).

The first legislative provision was introduced in New York in 1896, and the New York State Society of Certified Public Accountants was formed in 1897. No SAE members were involved in the New York State Society formation, although at least 25 of the 59 emigrants became members of state societies. Other state societies included those of Pennsylvania (1897), New Jersey (1898), Illinois (1903), Ohio (1903), and Missouri (1904).

Legislative events similar to those in New York took place, for example, in Pennsylvania (1899), Maryland (1900), California (1901), Illinois (1903), and Washington (1903). By 1904, there were 21 state boards of accountancy (Brown, 1905, p.276), and 14 state societies. However, uniformity of standards was rare. This was a situation which also affected the early history of Scottish chartered accountancy.[7] However, there was some standardization between states. Many of the earliest members of state societies were admitted under waiver clauses which allowed previous practical experience to substitute for the passing of examinations. These waivers were of advantage to several SAE members coming to the U.S. For example, J. B. Niven was examined by the New York State Society (1904) but admitted under waiver to Illinois (1903), Ohio (1908), and New Jersey (1912). Fourteen of the 59 SAE emigrants joined the New York State Society, and 9 chose the Illinois equivalent (in all probability under the Illinois waiver clause in most cases because of SAE membership and previous practice experience).

The overall situation with state legislation in the early 1900s was one of differences rather than similarities. For example, states such as California, New York, Pennsylvania, and Washington did not permit reciprocity for certified public accountants from other states. Indeed, New York State Society membership was dependent on, first, passing examinations administered by New York University and, second, being a U.S. citizen (or intending to be so). This latter provision appears to have been deliberately aimed at U.K. chartered accountancy emigrants (Miranti, 1990, pp.56-62). In fact, 4 leading English chartered accountants (including A. L. Dickinson of Price Waterhouse & Co.) were denied membership of the New York State Society because they did not meet these standards.[8] As a result, they joined the Illinois State Society which had more liberal waiver provisions. Miranti (1990, p.61) comments that, by 1903, nearly one-third of the 54 Illinois members were from Price Waterhouse & Co.

The need for uniformity among states eventually forced national public accountancy firms such as Price Waterhouse & Co. to take action to prevent federal legislation being introduced to bring uniform standards. In 1902, they helped form and fund the Federation of State Societies of Public Accountants in the United States (FSSPAUS) (Miranti, 1990, pp.62-8). The New York State Society initially joined FSSPAUS but left in 1903 because most FSSPAUS members were also AAPA members, thus emphasizing the continuing tension between chartered and other certified professional accountants in New York at that time. The AAPA was re-organized in 1916 as the Institute of Accountants in the United States of America (IAUSA), using the U.K. model of centralization, and with membership not based on state society affiliation (Miranti, 1990, pp. 115-16).[9] Indeed, 10 of the 35 initial IAUSA Council members had U.K. or Canadian origins (Miranti, 1990, p. 116). The IAUSA was renamed the American Institute of Accountants (AIA) in 1917. Thirteen of the 59 SAE emigrants were founding Fellows of the IAUSA in 1916. The AIA eventually merged in 1936 with the American Society of Certified Public Accountants (ASCPA) to form the present-day American Institute of Certified Public Accountants (AICPA). The ASCPA was founded in 1921 in response to the lack of state society affiliation in the AIA membership rules - yet another example of the rivalries and associated tensions between different professional accountancy communities in the U.S. in the early twentieth century. No SAE member can be evidenced as a founding member of the ASCPA.

The above brief commentary describes the institutional and organizational framework of professional accountancy encountered by the 59 SAE emigrants entering the U.S. from 1883 onwards. The next two sections explain more about where they entered the U.S., and how they influenced its professional accountancy history.

The new emigrants

The 59 SAE emigrants arrived in the U.S. predominantly from Edinburgh. Forty-six appear to have travelled from that location, with a further 5 from other parts of the U.K. (including London), and the remaining 8 from various parts of the world (including Canada). Thus, 13 of the group had already moved from Edinburgh prior to relocating in the U.S. Their initial residence was typically New York. Thirty-two started work there, with a further 8 doing so in Chicago. The remaining 19 accountants started their residency at 12 different U.S. locations. In other words, most of the emigrants focused on the two U.S. cities with the largest populations of accountants (particularly of chartered accountants).

The majority of the new emigrants remained in the U.S. throughout their working lives. Twenty stayed at their original point of entry, and a further 26 relocated at least once in the U.S. during their careers. Eight returned to the U.K., and 5 moved eventually to other parts of the world (including Canada) . The emigrant group worked in a total of 23 states, with a major focus on New York and Illinois (consistent with their initial residency). Forty of the 59 emigrants worked at some time in New York, 16 in Illinois, 7 in Missouri, and 6 in California.

Despite difficulties associated with a lack of reliable data sources, it is possible to describe the types of employment with which the 59 SAE emigrants were involved. Table 3 outlines the broad categories of occupation, and also provides information regarding professional affiliations.

Table III suggests that at least 37 (80%) of the SAE emigrants were involved at some time in U.S. public accountancy. This finding is unsurprising as every emigrant was trained and educated in Scotland as a chartered accountant. Thirty individuals remained in public accountancy, and 17 moved from the latter into occupations in industry, finance or government. Seven accountants were employed in either industry, education, finance or government without entering U.S. public accountancy.

TABLE III: *Occupations of the SAE emigrants*

Public accountancy only	30*
Public accountancy and industry	12*
Public accountancy and finance (or government)	5*
Industry, education, finance, or government	7
No information	5
Total	**59**
* Public Accountants	
State society members only	2
State society and AAPA or AIA members	23[1]
AAPA or AIA members only	1[1]
Unlicensed public accountants	21
Total	**47**

[1] 12 AAPA members; and 21 (13 founding) AIA members.[10]

The major focus of this emigrant group was therefore public accountancy. Twenty-five of the 47 individuals involved in the occupation were licensed as public accountants by state boards of accountancy (23 were also members of either the AAPA or AIA). One individual was a member of both the AAPA and AIA without becoming a state society member. Twenty-one of the 47 SAE members appear to have practiced as public accountants without membership of a U.S. professional accountancy body. All 47 SAE emigrants who practiced as public accountants in the U.S. remained as members of the SAE during their public accountancy tenure. This perhaps emphasizes the importance to them of chartered accountancy, and its acceptance in the U.S. Interestingly, however, for those SAE emigrants for which there is an official record, none are found to be described as chartered accountants.

Of the 25 emigrants known to have been members of state societies in the U.S., 15 had a single membership, 9 dual membership, and 2 triple or quadruple membership. Fourteen of these individuals were members of the New York State Society and 9 of the Illinois body. Nine other societies had a total of 17 SAE members. Thus, as with their arrival and employment locations, the state-licensed SAE emigrants primarily focused on public accountancy in New York and Chicago.

The 47 SAE emigrants employed at some time in public accountancy were affiliated with a number of firms. Twenty-eight were associated with one firm, 17 with two, and 2 with three. Eighteen individuals worked with Price Waterhouse & Co., 9 with Marwick, Mitchell & Co., 5 with Touche, Niven & Co., and 4 with Arthur Young & Co. (all firms with strong Scottish connections). Nineteen individuals were employed by 11 other firms. Thirteen accountants were self-employed or partners in small firms. Of the 42 emigrants with national firms, at least 13 are known to have become partners. The latter group represents 28% of the public accountant group.

Table 4 below provides a review of the employment tenure of the 59 SAE emigrants. Thirty of these individuals had a single type of employment, and 24 changed the nature of their employment at least once. The employment details of 5 accountants could not be identified. Because of multiple employment, the figures in Table IV exceed the total of 59.

TABLE IV: *SAE emigrant employment experience*

U.S. Employment Experience (years)	PA	IND	GOV	FIN	EDU	NI
0 - 5	7	2	2	2	0	0
6 - 10	7	7	1	0	1	0
11 - 15	5	2	0	0	0	0
16 - 20	5	1	0	0	0	0
20+	23	5	2	2	0	0
No information	0	0	0	0	0	5
Total	**47**	**17**	**5**	**4**	**1**	**5**

PA = public accountancy; IND = industry and commerce; GOV = government; FIN = finance; EDU = education; and NI = no information.

The above data show that, for public accountants, 28 had 16 or more years of experience. For those in industry, the majority of 9 had 10 or less years of experience. For those in finance or education, most of the SAE members had less than 10 years of experience. These results support earlier findings that, at least for the majority of SAE emigrants in public accountancy and several others in non-public accountancy occupations, U.S. employment experience was long-term and, in many cases, permanent until retirement. Thus, emigration for these individuals was a matter which determined the nature of their life-long employment. Because of this, it is not unreasonable to suggest it also affected the history of U.S. professional accountancy. This can be seen more clearly when individual experiences are examined in the next section.

The high achievers

Several of the SAE emigrants had successful careers. This is not to suggest that others did not. It merely indicates that available information identifies those listed in Table V as the most prominent according to the data available.

TABLE V SAE high professional achievers in the U.S.

Name		Highest known position
Bassin,	T. A.	Comptroller, Nickel Processing Corporation
Brown,	R. C.	Partner, Touche, Niven & Co.
Caesar,	W. J.	Founding partner, Jones, Caesar & Co; partner, Price Waterhouse & Co.
Carruthers,	C. P.	Partner, Price Waterhouse & Co.
Charles,	W.	Partner, Price Waterhouse & Co.
Cuthbert,	H. T.	President, Arizona State Society
Cuthbert,	R. L.	Partner, Arthur Young & Co. and Deloitte, Plender, Griffiths & Co.
Drever,	T.	President, American Steel Foundries
Fraser,	E.	President, Missouri State Society
Grey,	D. L.	Partner, Price Waterhouse & Co.
Lowson,	F.	Vice-President, American Institute of Accountants
Mackenzie,	D. D. F.	Partner, Arthur Young & Co.
Mackenzie,	T. A.	Partner, Barrow, Wade, Guthrie & Co.
MacEwan	M.C.	Comptroller, Clark & Co.
Niven,	J. B.	Founding partner, Touche, Niven & Co.; and President, American Institute of Accountants.
Salmond,	C. W.	President, Pittsburg School of Accountancy
Sangster,	A.	Director of Accounts, New York State
Scobie,	J. C.	Senior partner, Price Waterhouse & Co.

Ten of the SAE emigrants listed in Table V became partners in national public accountancy firms (2 as founders). One other SAE member listed with addresses in New York and Chicago (G. A. Touche) had a considerable impact on the U.S. accountancy profession because of the firm he helped to found (Touche, Niven & Co.). However, most of his fame was established in London. He never became a member of any U.S. national or state accountancy body, and left the detailed management of his U.S. operations to his partner, J. B. Niven. Touche, the son of a bank agent, was originally apprenticed in Edinburgh to Niven's father, A. T. Niven, a founding member of the SAE in 1854.

Of the 10 partners in Table V, 5 were affiliated to Price Waterhouse & Co., thus emphasizing the important part that Scottish chartered accountants had in the formation and development of that firm in the U.S. The son of a Church of Scotland minister, W. J. Caesar was a founding partner in the firm of Jones, Caesar & Co. which acted as agent for Price Waterhouse & Co. in Chicago and New York from 1895 to 1900, and was involved in audits of breweries, railroads, and manufacturers such as the American Steel and Wire Company. Employees of Price Waterhouse & Co. visited the U.S. from 1873, and Jones, Caesar & Co. acted as individual agents for the firm between 1891 and 1895. The firm of Jones, Caesar & Co. eventually merged with Price Waterhouse & Co. in 1900 when Caesar left for Paris. He apparently was a difficult man who alienated clients, yet left a successful practice for Price Waterhouse & Co. (Jones died in 1898). Caesar was a member and trustee of the New York State Society, and a member of the Illinois Society. He was not a member of either the AAPA or AIA, and therefore apparently uncommitted to the U.K. centralist model of institutionalization adopted in the U.S. By contrast, J. C. Scobie, the son of a carpenter, and who emigrated in 1903 to work for Price Waterhouse & Co., was a member of the state societies of New York, Pennsylvania and Illinois, as well as the AAPA and AIA. He died in 1944 as senior partner of Price Waterhouse & Co. in New York. Scobie wrote a manual of audit procedures which became the basis for AIA publications on that subject. But he was best known for his careful and time-consuming recovery of the reputation of his firm following the 1939 Securities and Exchange Commission report on its client, McKesson & Robbins.

Of the other high achievers, 3 (H. T. Cuthbert, E. Fraser, and J. B. Niven) were heavily involved in the institutionalization process. Cuthbert was the son of a Clydeside ship-owner, and spent several years from 1906 in Chicago, then moved to Phoenix, Arizona where he formed a public accountancy firm of which he was senior partner. He joined the Arizona State Society in 1912, and was its President from 1919 to 1922. Fraser was the son of a schoolmaster, and also initially arrived in Chicago in 1903, stayed a short time (joining the Illinois State Society under the waiver clause), then moved to New York in 1905, working for the Audit Company of New York and Price Waterhouse & Co. In 1907, he worked in Chicago with Arthur Young & Co. Then he moved in 1909 to Kansas City, Missouri to found his own public accountancy firm, from which he retired in 1945. He was Treasurer of the Missouri State Society between 1919 and 1937, and its President between 1937 and 1942. He was chairman of the AIA Special Committee on Procedure in 1925, and was for several years a member of the Missouri State Board of Accountancy.

Niven is arguably the highest achiever of the SAE emigrant group. He was admitted to the SAE in 1893 and emigrated to Chicago in 1899.[11] He worked as a staff member with Price Waterhouse & Co. until he formed Touche, Niven & Co. with G. A. Touche. The firm rapidly became a national organization, and Niven was a member by examination in New York (1901), and by waiver in 3 other state societies (Illinois, 1903; Ohio, 1908; and New Jersey, 1912). He was admitted to the AAPA in 1904, and became a Vice-President in 1915 (when he was also Vice-President of the New York State Society). Niven was a member of the AAPA's Committee on the Journal (1913-14 and 1915-16). He became President of the New Jersey State Society in 1915, and occupied that position until 1921 (also being on the New Jersey State Board of Accountancy for many years). By this time, he was heavily involved in the affairs of the AIA. He was a member of its Council from 1917 to 1926 (*ex officio*, 1926-49); Executive Committee, 1918-22, 1924-5 (as chairman), and 1925-7; Committee on Federal Regulation, 1917-19; Committee on Publications, 1916-35 (chairman, 1927-35); Board of Examiners, 1917-24 (chairman, 1919-29 and 1921-4); Vice-President, 1921-2; and President, 1924-5. In addition, he wrote the tax section of the *Journal of Accountancy* from 1913 to 1920. He represented the Scottish chartered accountancy bodies at the first World Congress of Accountants in St Louis in 1904. He is reported as taking a prominent part in accountancy education at New York University (the gateway to membership of the New York State Society). Thus, Niven not only built a successful public accountancy practice in the U.S. (which is now part of Deloitte & Touche), but was also heavily involved in the institutional process at state and federal levels. He dealt particularly with education and training matters, and was both a contributor and supporter of the professional literature. He appears to have been one of the first tax practitioners in public accountancy. His role in the development of U.S. professional accountancy has been largely ignored, and appears worthy of further research.

One other SAE emigrant deserves detailed mention, if only for the fact that, despite a relatively short U.S. career, R. L. Cuthbert generated obituaries in the *New York CPA,* the *Journal of Accountancy, Pace Student,* and *The Accountants' Magazine* following his death on July 6, 1915 at Flanders (aged 47 years). Cuthbert had the unfortunate distinction of being the only New York State Society member killed in the First World War. He was the son of a Greenock shipowner, brother of H. T. Cuthbert, educated in London, trained in Edinburgh, admitted to the SAE in 1891, worked with Deloitte, Plender, Griffiths & Co. in London until 1895, when he emigrated to the U.S. He was member #16 of the New York State Society in 1896, joined the AAPA in 1905, and was a founding AIA member in 1916. At first a sole practitioner in the U.S., he formed a partnership in 1898, went solo again in 1900, then became a Deloitte, Plender, Griffiths & Co. partner in New York between 1905 and 1911. In 1911, he assisted Arthur Young to found his firm and was his partner until 1914, when he volunteered to join the Second King Edwards Horse as a trooper (despite his U.S. citizenship from 1894). He was killed in action at Flanders.

Other SAE emigrants who require further research include T. Drever (the son of a draper) who, following SAE admittance in 1905, emigrated to the U.S. and was, successively, Comptroller, Treasurer, President, and Chairman of American Steel Foundries based in Chicago. He joined the Ohio State Society (1908) and the Illinois State Society (1912), and the AAPA (1912) and AIA (1916). He earned an honorary doctor of letters degree. W. Charles (the son of a sugar merchant) also earned such a degree. Having joined the SAE in 1911, he emigrated to Canada in 1913 to work for Price Waterhouse & Co. He was with the firm successively in Chicago, Milwaukee, and St Louis, being a partner from 1935 to 1947. D. L. Grey (the son of an Edinburgh lawyer) was also a Price Waterhouse & Co. partner (1914-37), joining the SAE in 1899, emigrating to New York in 1902, and moving to Pittsburg and St. Louis with the same firm. He was a member of the Missouri State Board of Accountancy for several years. F. Lowson (the son of a Dundee linen manufacturer; and SAE member, 1903) spent his career in the U.S. in a partnership in a local New York firm (1905-24). He then joined the U.S. Treasury in Washington, DC (1924-46). In 1923-4, he was chairman of the AIA's Committee on Federal Legislation, a member of its Committee on Form and Administration of Income Tax Law, and a Vice-President. Finally, M. C. MacEwan (the son of a Presbyterian minister), who died of

pneumonia in 1899 in Chicago, was a partner in an Edinburgh
accountancy firm who went to the U.S. in 1896 to be the financial
manager of a thread manufacturer later taken over by the Scottish firm
of J. & P. Coats. MacEwan was a distinguished Scottish rugby
internationalist who captained the national championship team of
1891.

Other Edinburgh emigrants

It would be remiss to ignore non-SAE accountants who emigrated
from Edinburgh to the U.S. in the late nineteenth and early twentieth
centuries.[12] They have been omitted from the formal analysis in this
paper because of problems of identifying their presence as a group
either in Edinburgh or in the U.S. subsequently. However, during
research for this paper, several non-SAE accountants were discovered
to have travelled from Edinburgh to the U.S. for employment purposes.
They provide a flavour of the overall emigration to the U.S. of
Edinburgh accountants.

For example, Webster (1954, appendix) lists three Edinburgh men
working in U.S. accountancy at the end of the nineteenth century. Each
was a member of the AAPA. E. M. Noble qualified as an SAE member
in 1871 but resigned in 1875 when he emigrated to the U.S. He was a
sole practitioner in Washington, DC for many years, and was
Commissioner to the Court of Claims. The son of an Ayrshire minister,
Noble joined the AAPA in 1888 and died in 1892.

D. Rollo is described by Webster as an Edinburgh chartered
accountant although he was never an SAE member. Born in Perth in
1852, Rollo worked in various accountancy firms in Edinburgh from
1871 to 1890. One of these firms was a partnership with an SAE
member, J. J. Stuart, and it was described as a firm of chartered
accountants. Rollo emigrated to New York from Manchester in 1892,
and worked *inter alia* with Barrow, Wade, Guthrie & Co. prior to a
sole practice which ended in 1907. From that year until his death in
1914, Rollo was a corporate treasurer in Philadelphia. He became an
AAPA member in 1893, a Trustee from 1896 to 1903, Vice-President
in 1898, and President in 1899. He also became member #27 of the
New York State Society in 1896.

Webster also provides a record of an Edinburgh emigrant who
achieved success in the U.S. without a connection to the SAE or,
indeed, to any other U.K. accountancy body. D. MacInnes emigrated to
New York in 1880 at the age of 18 years. For the previous 6 years, he
had been a ticket-seller with the North British Railway in Edinburgh

and, from 1880 to 1897, he was timekeeper and accountant for railroads in the New York area. From 1897 to 1935, MacInnes was Deputy Comptroller of New York City. He became a Fellow of the AAPA in 1902, and was member #189 of the New York State Society in 1901. He was a member of the New York State Board of Accountancy from 1907 to 1909, and taught in Theodore Koehler's New York School of Accounts in 1905.

Concluding thoughts

This paper is not intended as a definitive study of the influence of Scottish chartered accountants in the U.S. Its scope is limited by a number of factors. Only emigrating SAE members have been researched at this point. Members of the IAAG, for example, have not been researched. These would have included James Marwick, co-founder of Marwick, Mitchell, & Co. later Peat, Marwick, Mitchell & Co. (see Wise, 1982). The period of analysis ends with SAE admissions in 1914, and it is possible that later SAE members may have influenced the U.S. accountancy profession. Records are exceedingly limited and dispersed, and further research is needed.

In the meantime, it is reasonable to suggest that this study provides sufficient evidence of an important influence in the development of U.S. professional accountancy. First, most of the 59 SAE emigrants remained in the U.S. throughout their working lives. Second, these working lives were predominantly in accountancy and, more specifically, public accountancy. Third, for those emigrants for whom information is available, most reached a senior position in their organizations. Fourth, despite their chartered accountancy qualification which enabled them to practice as public accountants, the majority of those men in public accountancy joined local and, less frequently, national accountancy bodies. Joining such bodies enabled a small minority of the SAE emigrants to become involved in their development and administration (achieving three state society Presidencies, three national Vice-Presidencies, and one national Presidency) (ignoring the national Presidency of a non-SAE accountant from Edinburgh). In addition to public accountancy, there are signs that a small number of individuals attained high office in industry and government organizations. In total, these individuals represent approximately 10% of the total group of 59 SAE emigrants.

The results of this study are also consistent with a theoretical perspective of emigration to the U.S. approximately a century ago. The SAE emigrants were highly skilled, arguably to a higher level than that associated with U.S. accountants of the period. This differential effect permitted the SAE emigrants not only access to an emerging U.S. professional practice, but also the opportunity to benefit economically and socially. Several of the subjects of this study are stated in their obituaries to be pillars of their communities, and to have followed gentlemanly pursuits such as shooting and sailing. The emigrants also consistently followed well-defined emigration routes from Scotland to the U.S. and beyond. The predominance of New York and Chicago as employment and residential Addresses is evidence of this point. Once located in the U.S., it is unsurprising that the skills and knowledge of the SAE emigrants was used successfully in forming and developing professional firms and institutional bodies. The training they received in Edinburgh may not have been put to use extensively in that locality. however, it is clear that it was of considerable use following emigration to the U.S.

Given the problems commonly associated with emigration (e.g., loss of family, friends, and cultural identity), and the immaturity of the U.S. accountancy profession at the time of emigration, the early SAE emigration record appears to be one of considerable achievement. The lack of information in this study undoubtedly errs on the side of understatement in this respect. Thus, it is reasonable to conclude that the Scottish influence on the U.S. accountancy profession went much further and deeper than the popular expositions of pioneers such as Marwick and Mitchell (Wise, 1982).

Notes

I am most grateful to Dr S. P. Walker for assistance on this project; an anonymous reviewer and the Editor of *The Accounting Historians Journal* for helpful suggestions; and to the Scottish Committee on Accounting History of The Institute of Chartered Accountants of Scotland, and the Hugh Culverhouse Endowment of The University of Alabama for financial support.

1. One other SAE member (J. V. Fleming, admitted 1898) emigrated to the U.S. However, he did so in 1941 on retirement after over 40 years of practice in Edinburgh. He has been excluded from the data set as he appears not to have been an emigrant in the sense of the other 59 members.
2. For details of these arrangements, see Lee (1995). At least two of the SAE emigrants (R. L. Cuthbert in his finals in 1891; and M. C. McEwan at the intermediate stage in 1885) were prize winners in their professional examinations.
3. For detailed histories of the U.S. profession, see Edwards (1960), Carey (1969), Previts and Merino (1979), Zeff (1988), and Miranti (1990).

4. Brown was particularly concerned about the lack of court-related work in the practices of U.S. accountants. Such work was a major part of many SAE members in the late 1890s and early 1900s, and was a major influence in the founding of the SAE (see Kedslie, 1990a and 1990b; and Walker, 1988 and 1995).
5. The driving force behind the formation of the NYIA was C. W. Haskins who, with E. W. Sells, formed Haskins & Sells in 1895 (Miranti, 1990). No SAE emigrant in the current study is known to have worked for Haskins & Sells.
6. The early history of both the Scottish and English accountancy bodies was characterized by inter-body rivalry. In Scotland, this resulted in successful court actions to maintain the monopoly of chartered accountancy (see Walker, 1991), and numerous unsuccessful attempts at obtaining U.K. legislation to effect the same result (see Macdonald, 1985).
7. Apart from rivalries between chartered and non-chartered accountancy bodies in Scotland, there was a persistent rivalry and hostility over professional standards between the SAE and its Glasgow counter-part, the IAAG (see Shackleton and Milner, 1995; and Lee, 1995).
8. It is not known whether any SAE members were similarly excluded.
9. One SAE emigrant (J. B. Niven) was heavily involved in the AAPA and had explicit reservations concerning the new structure not involving state society affiliation (Miranti, 1990, p. 115). Niven had been a Vice-President of the AAPA and the New York State Society in 1915-16, and was President of the New Jersey State Society between 1915 and 1921. He was a member of 4 state societies. Thus, not all chartered accountants were wedded to the U.K. model. Niven became President of the AIA in 1924.
10. Eighty-two of 206 (40%) AAPA members between 1886 and 1905 were from the U.K. (Miranti, 1990, p.41).
11. It is interesting that Niven went initially to Chicago. As previously mentioned, Illinois had a more liberal attitude to the licensing of professional accountants than did New York.
12. Webster (1954) reveals that, of 214 Fellows and 52 Associates of the AAPA between 1886 and 1904, 86 came from either England, Wales, Scotland or Ireland. Indeed, 67 came from England alone. Of the 86 U.K. emigrants, 19 were chartered accountants.

Bibliography

Accountants' Index: A Bibliography of Accounting Literature to December 1920. 2 Vols. New York, N.Y.: Garland Publishing, 1988.*

Allen, D. G. & McDermott, K., *Accounting for Success: A History of Price Waterhouse in America.* Boston, MA: Harvard Business School Press, 1993.*

American Association of Public Accountants, *Year Books of Annual Meetings*. New York, N.Y.: various publishers, 1906-16.*

American Institute of Accountants, *Year Books of Annual Meetings*. New York, N.Y.: various publishers, 1917-40.*

American Institute of Accountants, *Fiftieth Anniversary Celebration 1937*. New York, N.Y.: American Institute of Accountants, 1938.*

Anderson, M. & Morse, D. L, "The People," in Fraser, W. H. & Morris, R. J. (eds.), *People and Society in Scotland II 1830-1914*. Edinburgh: John Donald Publishers, 1990: 8-45.

Anyon, J. T., *Recollections of the Early Days of American Accountancy 1883-1893*. Privately published, 1925.*

Arthur Andersen & Company: The First Sixty Years 1913-73. Chicago, Il: Arthur Andersen & Company, 1974.*

Arthur Young and the Business He Founded. New York, N.Y.: privately published, 1948.*

Aspinwall, B., "The Scots in the United States,"in Cage, R. A. (ed.), *The Scots Abroad: Labour, Capital, Enterprise, 1750-1914*. London: Croom Helm, (1985): 80-110.

Baines, D., *Emigration from Europe 1815-1930*. Basingstoke: Macmillan, 1991.

Berthoff, R. T., *British Immigrants in Industrial America 1790-1950*. Cambridge, Ma: Harvard University Press, 1953.

Brander, M., *The Emigrant Scots*. London: Constable, 1982.

Brown, R., *A History of Accounting and Accountants*. Edinburgh: T. C. & E. C. Jack, 1905.

Carey, J. L., *The Rise of the Accountancy Profession: From Technician to Professional 1896-1936*. New York, N.Y.: American Institute of Certified Public Accountants, 1969.

Clark, W. A. V., *Human Migration*. Beverly Hills, Ca: Sage Publications, 1986.

De Jong, G. F. & Fawcett, J. T. "Motivations for Migration: An Assessment and a Value-Expectancy Research Model," in De Jong, G. F, & Gardner, R. W. (eds.), *Migration Decision Making: Multidisciplinary Approaches to Microlevel Studies in Developed and Developing Countries*. New York, N.Y.: Pergamon Press, 1981: 13-58.

DeMond, C. W., *Price, Waterhouse & Company in America: A History of a Public Accounting Firm*. New York, N.Y.: privately published, 1951.*

Devine, T. M. "The Paradox of Scottish Emigration," in Devine, T. M. (ed.), *Scottish Emigration and Scottish Society*. Edinburgh, John Donald Publishers, 1992: 1-15.

Edwards, J. D., *History of Public Accountancy in the United States*. East Lansing, Mi: Michigan State University, 1960.

Erickson, C., *Invisible Immigrants: The Adaptation of English and Scottish Immigrants in Nineteenth Century America*. London: Weidenfeld and Nicolson, 1972.

Ernst and Ernst, *Ernst and Ernst: A History of the Firm*. Cleveland, Mi: privately published, 1960.*

Haskins and Sells: Our First Seventy-Five Years. New York, NY: privately published, 1970.

Horne, H. A., *The History and Administration of Our Society: Fiftieth Anniversary of the Founding of the New York State Society of Certified Public Accountants.* New York, N.Y.: New York State Society of Certified Public Accountants, 1947.*

Jones, E., *True and Fair: A History of Price Waterhouse.* London: Hamish Hamilton, 1995.*

Kedslie, M. J. M., *Firm Foundations: The Development of Professional Accounting in Scotland 1850-1900.* Hull: Hull University Press, 1990a.

Kedslie, M. J. M. "Mutual Self-Interest - A Unifying Force: The Dominance of Societal Closure Over Social Background in the Early Professional Accounting Bodies." *The Accounting Historians Journal* (December 1990b): 1-19.*

Lee, E. S. "A Theory of Migration," in Jackson, J. A. (ed.), *Migration.* Cambridge: Cambridge University Press, 1969: 282-97.

Lee, T. A. "Richard Brown: Chartered Accountant and Christian Gentleman," in Lee, T. A. (ed.), *Shaping the Accountancy Profession: The Story of Three Scottish Pioneers.* New York, N.Y.: Garland Publishing, 1995: 155-221.

Lee, T. A. "Identifying the Founding Fathers of Public Accountancy: The Formation of the Society of Accountants in Edinburgh," *Accounting, Business & Financial History* (December 1996): 315-35.

Lewis, G. L., *Human Migration: A Geographical Perspective.* London: Croom Helm, 1982.

Lucas, R.E.B. "International Migration: Economic Causes, Consequences and Evaluation," in Kritz, M. M., Keely, C. B. and Tomasi, S. M. (eds.), *Global Trends in Migration: Theory and Research on International Population Movements.* New York, N.Y.: Center for Migration Studies, 1981:84-109.

Lybrand, Ross Bros, & Montgomery, *Fiftieth Anniversary 1898-1948.* New York, N.Y.: privately published, 1948.*

Macdonald, K.M. "Social Closure and Occupational Registration," *Sociology* (November 1985): 541-56.

Miranti, P. J., *The Development of an American Profession 1886-1940.* Chapel Hill, NC: University of North Carolina Press, 1990.

Musgrove, F., *The Migratory Elite.* London: Heineman, 1963.

"New York State Society of Certified Public Accountants," *Thirty Year Book 1897-1927.* New York, N.Y.: New York State Society of Certified Public Accountants, 1927.*

"New York State Society of Certified Public Accountants," *Year Book.* New York, N.Y.: New York State Society of Certified Public Accountants, 1938.*

Nugent, W., *Crossings: The Great Transatlantic Migrations, 1870-1914.* Bloomington, IN, Indiana University Press, 1992.

Prentis, M. D., *The Scots in Australia: A Study of New South Wales, Victoria and Queensland, 1788-1900.* Sydney: Sydney University Press, 1983.

Previts, G. J. and Merino, B. D., *A History of Accounting in America: A Historical Interpretation of the Cultural Significance of Accounting.* New York, N.Y.: Ronald Press, 1979.

Richards, A. B., *Touche Ross & Co. 1899-1981.* London: privately published, 1981.*

Robinson, H. W., *A History of Accountants in Ireland.* Dublin: Institute of Chartered Accountants of Ireland, 1964.*

Shackleton, J. K. and Milner, M. "Alexander Sloan: A Glasgow Chartered Accountant," in Lee, T. A. (ed.), *Shaping the Accountancy Profession: The Story of Three Scottish Pioneers.* New York, N.Y.: Garland Publishing: 83-151.

"Society of Accountants in Edinburgh," *Membership Records.* Edinburgh: Institute of Chartered Accountants of Scotland, various dates.

The Accountants' Magazine, Obituaries. Edinburgh: Institute of Chartered Accountants of Scotland, various dates.

Walker, S. P., *The Society of Accountants in Edinburgh 1854-1914: A Study of Recruitment to a New Profession.* New York, N.Y.: Garland Publishing, 1988.

Walker, S. P., "The Defence of Professional Monopoly: Scottish Chartered Accountants and Satellites in the Accountancy Firmament 1854-1914," *Accounting, Organizations and Society* (Vol. 16(3), 1991): 257-83.

Walker, S. P., "The Genesis of Professional Organization in Scotland: A Contextual Analysis," *Accounting, Organizations and Society* (Vol.20(4), 1995): 285-310.

Webster, N. E., *The American Association of Public Accountants: Its First Twenty Years 1886-1906.* New York, N.Y.: American Institute of Public Accountants, 1954.*

Wise, T. A., *Peat Marwick Mitchell & Company: 85 Years.* New York, N.Y.: privately published, 1982.*

Woods, R., *Theoretical Population Geography.* London: Longman, 1982.

Zeff, S.A., *The U.S. Accounting Profession in the 1890s and Early 1900s.* New York, N.Y.: Garland Publishing, 1988. *

CHAPTER 13

The Criminal Upperworld and the Emergence of a Disciplinary Code in the Early Chartered Accountancy Profession

Stephen P Walker

> Although most Chartered Accountants naturally conform to those unwritten laws which must of necessity govern the conduct of any body of professional men associated together for their mutual good, yet cases sometimes arise that render it a matter for regret that there exists among accountants no admitted code of etiquette (*The Accountant*, 21.7.1894, pp. 637-8).

Introduction

Biographical studies have long been conducted by accounting historians due to their potential for revealing the "influence of key individuals on accounting concepts, practice, and institutions" (Previts et al., 1990, p. 142). Recently, students of accounting professionalism, conscious of the exhortations of post-revisionist sociologists to investigate the "massive historical variation" in occupational experiences (Collins, 1990, p.21), have focused on the meso-level analysis of specific professional groups and the micro-centred study of pivotal figures in the construction and implementation of institutional strategies. In particular, Lee has urged the investigation of how professionalisation "is operationalised by a relatively few key individuals in positions of power and responsibility" (1996, p. x). Such biographical studies inevitably concentrate on luminaries and the role of the vocational elite in the emergence and protection of organisational structures. This paper analyses the impact of a small minority of

Reproduced from *Accounting History*, Volume 1, Number 2, November 1996, pp 7-36 with kind permission from the Editor.

practitioners who comprised an internal menace to the association - members who resorted to crime and misconduct.

Key actors are made audible and visible to historians through oral tradition and by the institutional and documentary legacies which testify to their positive achievements. By contrast, the focus here is on those individuals whose notorious and pernicious activities tarnished collective claims to professional status and thus ensured that they were considered best hidden from history. Yet, as will be shown, miscreant professionals also impacted on institutional configurations because their destructive behaviour could elicit organisational responses for the fortification or restoration of vocational standing. Historical biographies of the disreputable accountant may also provide insights into the motives, values and perceptions of a wider occupational populace and also reveal how contemporary social phenomena coloured the behaviour of the individual (Briggs, 1954). Analyses of the felonious practitioner may be particularly illuminative of the vocational attitudes and ideologies which prevailed in the early accountancy profession. The complexion of public responses to 'scandals' in the profession also assist attempts to locate the occupation in the contemporary social structure.

As an investigation into villainous members of the nascent accountancy profession the paper also seeks to extend the historical study of criminal behaviour among those who occupied middle and upper class statuses in advanced capitalism (Jenkins, 1987; Robb, 1992). The analysis of such 'upperworld'[1] crime contrasts with the more prevalent studies of 'underworld' criminality among the labouring masses (for example, Chesney, 1970; Emsley, 1987; Gattrell *et al.*, 1987; Jones, 1982; Philips, 1977; Weiner, 1990). As Robb has shown, the increasing complexity of finance and corporate structures in the maturing industrial economy offered substantial opportunities for the perpetration of white-collar crime (1992, pp. 6-7). Despite its contemporary significance and deleterious consequences for large numbers of investors, depositors and employees, the criminal upperworld of the nineteenth century has, until recently, received scant attention (ibid.). Given the occupational proximity of accountants to the commercial, industrial and financial communities, and the likely permeation of its ideals and standards of conduct to the business domain (ibid., pp. 177-8), the historical interfaces between white-collar crime and the accountancy profession are especially deserving of greater attention.

Recent historical investigations of professional conduct, ethics and discipline, such as those of Parker on Australia (1987, 1994) and Preston *et al.* on the US (1995), bear directly on the study of professional misdeeds and immorality reported in this paper. Parker's "private interest model of professional accounting ethics" provides a useful conceptual frame in which to consider organisational responses to revelations concerning the malfeasance of practitioners (1994, pp. 510-16). The centrality of the insulation function of codes of conduct, the symbolic role of disciplinary processes and the importance of "offence visibility" provide useful tools to understanding the emergence of rules for the expulsion of criminal chartered accountants which are discussed here. The investigation by Preston *et al.* into the content of ethical codes during the twentieth century is pertinent in its revelations about how perceptions of what constitutes 'professional' conduct are dynamic and reflect changing cultural contexts (ibid., p. 509).

This paper examines the interfaces between contemporary culture and professional (mis)behaviour in a different time and locale. The study differs from other recent work in that it applies depth biographical analysis to offending professionals rather than focusing on the changing content of formalised statements of conduct or the derivation of a model of professional ethics based on the scrutiny of numerous disciplinary cases. By examining the origins and activities of the few members of the Society of Accountants in Edinburgh (SAE) who were deemed guilty of criminal misconduct from its formation in 1853 to the end of the nineteenth century, insights are gained into perceptions of vocational behaviour during the infancy of modern organised accountancy in the context of a small, localised, and highly status-conscious professional community. The nature and extent of organisational responses to each case of wrongdoing also illuminate the character of accounting institutions during the second half of the nineteenth century and contemporary perceptions of professional morality.

Impediments to professional misconduct in Victorian Britain

In order to fully comprehend the several facets of accounting professionalism which are revealed in the stories of criminal behaviour discussed later in the paper, an analysis of prevailing attitudes towards professional misconduct is necessary.

Misconduct and the professional ideal

The royal charter of incorporation which was granted to the SAE in 1854 contained no references to the institution of disciplinary powers or procedures. In 1855 the Society issued its "constitution and laws". The closest which this document came to referring to the chastisement of disreputable members was the empowerment of the Council to consider and advise "on all matters" affecting the interests of the Society (Walker, 1988, p. 313). In fact, the SAE did not formulate a disciplinary code until 1883-4 in the wake of events which are related in the second part of the paper.

Given that the principal organisational model emulated by the public accountants in Edinburgh was the local legal profession, the absence from the early SAE rule book of any codified provisions relating to misconduct, is perhaps, surprising. The long-established institutions which represented and governed the profession of law in Edinburgh had introduced formalised disciplinary procedures well before the 1850s. Judges were vested with the power to reprimand, suspend or depose members of the Faculty of Advocates (the Scottish equivalent of barristers) (*Index Juridicus*, 1852, p. 145). The original regulations of the Society of Solicitors to the Supreme Courts in 1784 provided for the punishment of members who were deemed guilty or accused of malversation, dishonesty or breach of trust (Barclay, 1984, p.295). By the mid-nineteenth century the Council of the Society of Solicitors to the Supreme Courts was charged with the responsibility of adjudicating those instances of conduct by members "which may be considered derogatory to the Profession" (*Bye-Laws and Regulations*, 1851, p.3). Similarly, the rules of the more senior Society of Writers to Her Majesty's Signet provided for the appointment of Commissioners from among the members whose task was to consider cases of misconduct. As guardians of the profession, the Commissioners were given authority to inflict punishments on "delinquent" solicitors "for the good of the calling" (*Acts and Regulations*, 1811, appendix; *Index Juridicus*, 1852, p.63).

It is possible that the nascent SAE desisted from following the lawyer examples because the codification of disciplinary processes might have suggested (to a public suspicious of prevailing standards of business morality) that members of the new professional organisation were capable of unbecoming behaviour. However, the absence of provisions relating to conduct and discipline must also be considered in the context of prevailing professional ideologies. The latter also provide an essential backcloth to understanding contemporary responses to cases of professional crime and misconduct.

Preston *et al.* have illustrated how attitudes towards vocational conduct in the American accountancy profession during the early twentieth century reflected contemporary cultural values. Protestantism, "character" and idealism ensured that the occupational association relied on the admission of men of moral integrity; their practice of altruism, adherence to a "social ethic" and loyalty to fellow professionals in order to discourage misconduct (1995, pp.514-22). Hence, "The accountant's calling was governed not merely by written rules and regulation, but also by a belief in divine law and continuous examination by himself and his brethren" (ibid., p.522). A similar attitude prevailed in Britain during the nineteenth century.

Although some of the 'new' professions in Victorian Britain sought to enhance occupational claims by instituting regulations pertaining to the conduct of members (Corfield, 1995, p.204), the contemporary professional ideal emphasised the adherence by the individual practitioner to the 'spirit' or conventions of professional 'etiquette' as opposed to the formulation of codified rules of conduct and discipline (Reader, 1966, pp. 158-63). Compliance with acceptable patterns of professional behaviour was a matter of mutuality and loyalty to the association (Duman, 1979, p. 118). The 'pressure of opinion' exerted by professional brethren was often preferred to, or considered more effective than, the deterrent effects of disciplinary committees (Carr-Saunders & Wilson, 1933, p.420; Robb, 1992, p.177). Nineteenth century concepts of professionalism stressed the probity, dignity, honour and gentlemanly instincts of the practitioner. His self-definition and personal enforcement of the standards of propriety, 'civic morality' and altruism commensurate with his status were considered to be the primary safeguards against unworthy conduct.

The contemporary aversion to the codification of standards of conduct and the emphasis on social and moral controls to regulate vocational behaviour received expression in the accountancy press during the later nineteenth century. The accountant's adherence to conventional morality was considered essential to the maintenance of his professional demeanour. Good conduct would "not be attained so much by regulation and bye-laws, as by the moral influence which members of a chartered body will gradually exercise amongst themselves" (*Accountant*, 5.6.1880, p.4). At a general meeting of the newly formed Institute of Accountants in London in April 1871 the President, William Quilter, revealed the centrality of high morals to the standing of the public accountant:

> . . . something beyond mere professional knowledge and
> capability must be brought into the field of professional
> action, if the accountant is to maintain and consolidate the
> important position which of late years he has come to
> occupy in relation to the legal and mercantile community.
> By that *something more*, I mean the qualities of unswerving
> rectitude - fearless independence - and single mindedness in
> the conduct of the business entrusted to him . . . the due
> execution of which would be impossible in the absence of
> the moral qualities I have indicated. Without them, a man
> may be a clever accountant, but he will do nothing either to
> elevate his own individual status, or that of the profession to
> which he belongs (MS28/404/1, pp.8-9).

The institution by British accountancy organisations of codified
disciplinary rules to deal with cases of blatant or criminal misconduct
was also deemed inappropriate during the nineteenth century because
"as a rule, conduct of this nature is either amenable to the law, which
acts as an effectual deterrent, or it is so morally reprehensible that a
man may be trusted to abstain from it simply from regard to his own
interests" (*Accountant*, 22.3.1879, p.3).

It was in the context described above that previous to the 1880s,
the rules of the SAE contained no provision for instigating the
expulsion of a member (Walker, 1988, pp. 305-17). The name of a CA
who persistently defaulted in the payment of subscriptions or failed to
comply with the regulations of the Society, was simply and quietly
erased from the roll of members. Those rare instances of complaint
about the conduct of a CA (usually concerning the distribution of
circulars to solicit business),[2] resulted in a discussion by the Council
and a letter from the Secretary informing the member that such
behaviour was in breach of the "usual professional etiquette" (Sederunt
Book, 2/1, p.271; also Kedslie, 1990, p.272). A similar approach was
adopted by the neighbouring Institute of Accountants and Actuaries in
Glasgow. The official history of The Institute of Chartered
Accountants of Scotland relates how:

> . . . the Council of the Glasgow Institute, because of one or two
> cases which had been brought before the *Professional Etiquette*
> Committee, found it necessary in their report for 1908 to call
> attention to a Minute of Council dated January 30, 1865, bearing
> upon the question of canvassing for business, and to impress on
> members the extreme desirability of maintaining a high standard
> of professional etiquette in all their business relations with one
> another and with the public (*A History of the Chartered
> Accountants of Scotland*, 1954, p.54, italics added).

Socio-cultural filtering. Closure devices as social and moral controls

Despite the absence of written rules relating to the misconduct and discipline of its members, the SAE was not devoid of mechanisms to prevent the tarnishing of its organisational status through the dishonourable behaviour of a CA. Admission regulations were configured not only to restrict entry to those individuals who were deemed unlikely to bring the occupation into disrepute but also to encourage the internalisation of accepted norms of professional conduct.

Preston *et al.* have shown that during the early twentieth century, the reliance by the American accountancy profession on the integrity of the individual professional ensured that the organisation "need not be fully responsible for the moral development of its membership, rather it need only admit and retain those persons exhibiting 'proper character' (1995, p.521). This was also the case in the accountancy profession in Victorian Britain, particularly the SAE. As claims to the credibility and probity of the practitioner rested on membership of the professional organisation, the emphasis was placed by the association on the imposition of admission stipulations which would prevent the intrusion of those considered capable of malfeasance. Conditions of entry, qualification procedures and certification ensured that only those deemed competent and reputable were allowed through to offer services to the public.

In England and Wales, for example, the newly constituted Institute of Chartered Accountants (ICAEW) stressed its implementation of examinations and four "fundamental rules" to prevent the admission of "non public accountants" who were considered least likely (due to the nature of their business engagements) to conduct themselves in a "professional" manner. In particular, the royal charter of 1880 empowered the ICAEW to "lay down such rules respecting admission to membership and exclusion therefrom as would prevent Public Accountants from mixing the pursuit of any other business with the discharge of the *higher duties* devolving on them as Public Accountants" (*Accountant*, 12.6.1880, p.5, italics added; Millerson, 1964, p.163; Parker, 1986, pp. 57-9). The status implications which could arise from the combined practice of 'professional' public accountancy and 'commercial' broking (the latter activity not being constrained by the conventions of professional morality) is ably illustrated in Shackleton and Milner's analysis of a

mixed accountancy practice in Glasgow during the late nineteenth
century (1996, pp. 116-25; *Accountant,* 23.4.1892, pp. 329-30).[3]

From the outset, membership of the SAE had been confined to the
community of competent and *respectable* accountants (*Index Juridicus,*
1853, pp. x-xii; Sederunt Book, 2/1, p. 5; Walker, 1995). At the end of
the nineteenth century, despite the advance of the examination, senior
office bearers continued to maintain that admission was restricted to
"gentlemen of professional standing" (Sederunt Book, 2/2, p.161) and
that the Society was exclusive "as regards culture and conduct" (quoted
in Walker, 1988, p. xi). In 1892 the President of the SAE asserted that:

> We are willing according to our rules to admit any person into
> our Society of *good character,* who complies with the course of
> training and the requirements and qualification of the Society.
> We do not exclude persons otherwise, who satisfy what we
> regard as essential to *the proper practice of the business* (ibid.,
> italics added).

The ability of a potential member to pay substantial apprenticeship
and entrance fees was also perceived as evidence of vocational
commitment, pecuniary independence and gentility (ibid., pp. 129-31,
190-3; Shackleton, 1995, p.32). In this respect, the SAE was highly
emulative of the local legal profession. During the 1850s admission to
the Society of Solicitors to the Supreme Court was dependent on the
candidate being "of good moral character" (*Bye-Laws and
Regulations,* 1851, p.3). Similarly, entrants to the Society of Writers to
Her Majesty's Signet were expected to be "of good fame and
reputation" (Acts and Regulations, 1811, p.8). As Duman has observed,
although the recruitment of professionals was increasingly founded on
meritocratic criteria in late Victorian Britain, the primary aim of
selecting only those of good character "seems to have remained
constant" (1979, p. 123).

Other conditions of admission to the SAE obstructed the entry of
the individual considered likely to bring the vocation into disrepute.
New members could only be admitted at annual meetings (where they
would be visible to established professionals) and, in the early years of
the Society's existence, only following formal nomination, seconding
and on the approval of 75% of those present. Membership was also
restricted to those who intended to practice their vocation within the
relatively close spatial confines of Edinburgh. In 1882, the year of the
formative case of misconduct discussed here, there were only 164
members of the SAE. Covert behaviour was difficult given the close
social and occupational networks in the local professional community
which encouraged mutualism and fraternity (Walker, 1993, p.133). The

apprenticeship system was particularly important in fostering close connections and loyalties between practitioners. It comprised a medium for occupational socialisation and the inculcation of a professional ethos. Self-recruitment (particularly in the larger CA firms) was also a deterrent to unacceptable behaviour (Walker, 1988, pp.240-5). The good conduct of a CA father, son, brother, uncle or nephew was a familial as well as a professional obligation as the status ramifications of disgrace in such cases were not confined to the individual.

Further, from 1860 until 1875 (when it was discovered that the Society had no power to act in the event of a contravention) (Minute Book, 311, p.42), the potential entrant to the SAE was obliged to sign a declaration that "his exclusive object in Business is to follow the profession of an Accountant as defined in the Society's Charter" (ibid., p.59). This condition of membership ensured that the CA was restricted to contemporary prescriptions of 'professional' practice and was informally constrained by the standards of conduct associated with that status. The SAE member was thereby distinguished from the non-credentialed and potentially unscrupulous 'accountant' who owed allegiance to no professional organisation.

The three organisations of chartered accountants in Scotland have been compared with the Inns of Court of English barristers (Carr-Saunders & Wilson, 1933, p.210). In relation to their respective modes of regulating professional conduct during the nineteenth century the analogy is not wholly inappropriate. Although the 'benchers' of the Inns could wield disciplinary powers, as with the wider legal profession these were seldom invoked or were largely ineffective (Abel, 1988, pp. 133, 248-9; Duman, 1983, p.37; Lewis, 1982, pp.41-2). More effectual was the informal discipline and social control nurtured by the *esprit de corps* of a group of learned professionals who resided in close proximity to one another (predominantly in London). This ensured that "every barrister was the watchful guardian of the honour and integrity of his learned brethren" (quoted in Duman, 1983, p.37).

The SAE's apparent emphasis on the prevention of, rather than reaction to, cases of misconduct through: admission procedures, spatial and jurisdictional restrictions on practice, professional socialisation, the visibility of individuals in a small occupational populace, reliance on the public practitioner's compliance with the law, and adherence to contemporary standards of etiquette and personal morality, proved extremely effective in minimising internal threats to the status of the professional populace. In 1900 the SAE boasted a membership of 351. Since its inauguration in 1853 the society had admitted over 450 individuals to its ranks. Of this number only two CAs were removed from membership for committing crime and professional misconduct.

These individuals led undistinguished careers as sole practitioners, were largely secluded from the gaze of their fellow chartered accountants and were therefore less restrained by the socio-cultural impediments to dishonourable conduct.[4] The relevant cases were those of Henry Callender, and, more importantly, Donald Smith Peddie. Both were signatories to the SAE's application for a royal charter in 1854. Hitherto the cessation of membership of Callender and Peddie has been either unaccounted for (Brown, 1905, pp.364, 376) or hidden behind speculative and innocuous explanations pertaining to subscription arrears or retirement (Stewart, 1986, pp.58, 139).

The public and private worlds of two Victorian chartered accountants

Domesticity was one of the most potent ideals in Victorian society (Davidoff & Hall, 1987, pp. 180-92). The private world of home was rigidly separated from the public province of work (Thompson, 1988, p. 197). This uncoupling of domains has ensured that identifying covert social relationships during the nineteenth century is often problematic due to their being "veiled behind the Victorian culture of privacy and reticence" (Harris, 1994, p.89). However, when accepted norms of behaviour were breached, resulting in the interposition of the legislature, the courts and the media, the circumstances attending violations of the law and contemporary moral standards were often subject to sensationalised disclosure. In this way, the details of a miscreant private life could periodically and legitimately enter the realm of the public. It is through such exposure that there exists evidence of the villainous activities of Henry Callender and Donald Smith Peddie.

Henry Callender, CA

The first case of the SAE Council removing one of its number from the list of members for reasons other than arrears of subscriptions occurred in 1873. The case arose purely as a result of unfavourable reports in the press. The wrong-doer was expeditiously dispatched without any investigation into the credence of the revelations contained in the printed media.

The offender, Henry Callender, was an original member of the SAE (Stewart, 1986, p.58). He was outwardly respectable and established as a public accountant. Callender was educated at Edinburgh University and his father had been an accountant in Edinburgh (Matriculation Registers, 1823-35). Callender commenced in public practice about 1838 at the age of 29 and was subsequently Manager of the Scottish Life Assurance and Guarantee Association and of the Professional Life Assurance Company (*Edinburgh and Leith Post Office Directory*). Callender became an associate member of the Institute of Actuaries, was a director of the Scottish Imperial Insurance Company and was also one time Treasurer of the City of Edinburgh.

Callender's downfall concerned a municipal-related appointment. On 11 January 1873 *The Scotsman* reported that a meeting of The Water of Leith Sewerage Commissioners had been convened to consider "the state in which the books have been left by the late treasurer, Mr Henry Callender, who some time ago disappeared from Edinburgh" (11.1.1873, p.4). Defalcations were estimated at £2,600 and it was envisaged that further investigation would unearth more substantial frauds on the Commission. The press report concluded that the matter had "been placed in the hands of the Procurator-Fiscal" and that Callender appeared to have absconded to the United States (ibid.).

The publicised revelation of alleged criminality by one of its members induced a swift response by the Council of the SAE. Two days after the press report a meeting of the Council was convened where it was resolved that: "as appeared from public newspapers, Mr. Callender had left the country for America under heavy charges, they instructed the Secretary to delete his name from the List of Members of the Society when the same is printed" (Sederunt Book, 2/1, p.200). As there was no specific constitutional procedure for dealing with such matters, this executive decision was not brought before the membership of the SAE and no alteration to the bye-laws of the Society resulted from the case.

Compared to the Callender episode, the only other recorded instance of criminal misconduct by a member of the SAE during the nineteenth century generated a deluge of adverse publicity. As a result it elicited a greater and more enduring response from the professional organisation.

Donald Smith Peddie, CA

Outwardly, Donald Smith Peddie was an archetypal original member of the SAE. He possessed several attributes which stamped him as an estimable professional accountant of reputable origin. Peddie was a grandson of a Lord Provost of Edinburgh and was the second son of the Reverend Dr James Peddie (Brown, 1905, p.376; Stewart, 1986, p. 139). In addition to being a Moderator of the Synod of the United Presbyterian Church and an active participant in "the benevolent and religious societies of Edinburgh" (Kay, 1877, Vol. A, p.351), the Reverend Peddie was a prolific author and noted philanthropist (*Dictionary of National Biography*, Vol.XV, pp.648-9). As a result of his "unblemished and useful life" he "enjoyed the esteem and reverence of all classes and all denominations of his fellow citizens" (Kay, 1877, Vol.4, p.353).

Donald Smith Peddie's elder brother, James, was a Writer to the Signet (the most eminent branch of the solicitor profession in Scotland) (*The Society of Writers to His Majesty's Signet*, 1936, p.286). James Peddie's son, John Dick Peddie, was a classical architect of considerable repute and the Liberal MP for Kilmarnock at the time when his uncle's misdemeanours came to fight (Stenton & Lees, 1978, Vol.2, p.282). Peddie's younger brother, Reverend Dr William Peddie, succeeded his father as Minister of the Associate Burgher Congregation in Edinburgh (Small, 1904, pp.431-3). Donald Smith Peddie's credentials as an educated professional gentleman were enhanced by his having studied literature and law for six years at Edinburgh University (Matriculation Registers, 1821-8).

Peddie commenced practice as an accountant in 1831 at the age of 23 (*Edinburgh and Leith Post Office Directories*). Following a short period in the office of his lawyer brother, he spent the remainder of his relatively undistinguished career as a sole practitioner. Peddie was also the accountant and agent for the Edinburgh office of the Yorkshire Fire and Life Insurance Company (*Oliver and Boyd's*, Insurance Advertisements) and received several appointments under judicial factories and trusts (CS). From 1833 he assisted his ageing father in the treasuryship of the Friendly Society of Dissenting Ministers in Scotland. This organisation was established in 1797 to provide for the widows and orphans of (mainly United Presbyterian) clergymen (Jeffrey, 1919) and its Treasurer earned an annual salary of £45 (CH3/516/8). Peddie augmented his limited practice income by rentals from a residential property in Edinburgh and also secured returns on an investment as a partner in a colliery company in Fife (CS318/30/239, Inventory). He was also the trustee of mineral workings near

Dunfermline which he let to a coalmaster (*Scotsman*, 2.12.1882, p.6). Despite the variety of his interests, Peddie's pecuniary status was seldom stable. The cash books of the SAE reveal that during the late 1850s Peddie was in arrears with his subscriptions. In January 1864, the Commercial Bank of Scotland demanded that his cash credit of £1,500 be paid up due to its foundation on unsatisfactory security (Commercial Bank Minute Book, Vol.7, pp. 220, 261, 267).

Having been invited to join the newly formed Institute of Accountants in Edinburgh in January 1853 (Sederunt Book, 2/1. p.5), Peddie actively participated in the affairs of his professional organisation. He regularly attended annual meetings and from 1872 to 1876 sat as a member of the Council (ibid., p.196). Ironically, he was present at the meeting which removed Henry Callender from the list of members in 1873. It was only in the twilight of his career that Donald Smith Peddie was to gain notoriety. In order to comprehend the manner of his downfall and the SAE's reaction to it, it is essential to understand Peddie's relationship with a Mr and Mrs William Cornelius and the lurid disclosures which it precipitated.

An uncommon business relationship

William Cornelius was born in Hanover, Germany in 1830 (Census Returns, 1871, 685/2/46). He trained as an artist at the Royal Academy in Munich and sometime thereafter removed to London and became a British subject. In 1863 he married Elizabeth Brown, a professional musician. Six years later Cornelius moved to Edinburgh and started a small business as a decorative artist to the local nobility and gentry (CS243/1255, Condescendence; *Edinburgh and Leith Post Office Directory*, 1870-1). Cornelius's association with Peddie commenced when he rented a tenement flat from Peddie who was acting factor of the property which was owned by the Friendly Society of Dissenting Ministers (CS243/1255, Condescendence; CH3/516/10, p. 15). It was possibly due to his being in arrears for 18 months rent that Peddie employed Cornelius to undertake some house painting. Cornelius's business venture proved unsuccessful and in August 1870 he was bankrupted with realisable assets of £100 and liabilities of £370 (CS318/15/73).

Following his discharge as a bankrupt in November 1870, Cornelius, with the assistance of Peddie, commenced a new house painting business from a more central location in Edinburgh (CS247/4875, Condescendence). As Cornelius had no capital it was verbally agreed that Peddie would, for a time, "supply all moneys requisite for carrying on the extended business", direct the firm and also meet the expenses of the Cornelius household (ibid.). For his part, Cornelius would remit all the income from the venture to Peddie. Under this arrangement Peddie claimed to have advanced £10,000 to Cornelius between 1871 and 1878 (CS243/1255/4, Proof).

In addition to his painting business Cornelius became increasingly involved in property speculation. He raised funds from Peddie and the Scottish Investment Company to acquire 28 tenement flats in Edinburgh. He also bought a residential property on the outskirts of the city and embarked on the construction of two suburban villas (CS243/1255/4, Proof). The completion of the latter required several injections of new capital. Between 1878 and 1881 Peddie supplied Cornelius with a total of £9,500 on the premise that "I felt myself bound to carry on to a certain extent, for the sake of recouping myself" even though he claimed to have lost hope of recovering the whole of his investment (ibid.). From August 1877 advances totalling £1,800 were also secured from J. & W.C. Murray, Writers to the Signet. This law firm granted loans to Cornelius on the basis of his appearance as "a prosperous and well-to-do man" (ibid.).

Additional short term credit was extended to Cornelius by J. & W.C. Murray in order to provide working capital for his increasingly unprofitable painting business and to alleviate his mounting personal debts. In December 1879 Cornelius's problems were compounded by his losing a legal dispute with a firm of joiners (ibid.). By that time both he and Peddie had exhausted their meagre incomes and became involved in a "continual solicitation" of J. and W.C. Murray for more credit (ibid.). In the early 1880s Peddie "was in a perfectly impecunious state" and begged daily for money to meet his personal liabilities (ibid.).

As Peddie became increasingly unable to sink further funds into Cornelius's projects, the hitherto close personal and business relations between the two men fractured. In a series of letters written to Peddie in 1881, Cornelius accused his associate of breaching their business arrangement, of refusing to pay creditors and of attempting to cause his bankruptcy (CS243/1255/3, 10.1.1881). In 1881 Cornelius complained that his decade-long acquaintance with Peddie had brought nothing but debt. He wrote:

> . . . as often before I even had not a shilling to take home to keep house with, the consequence is, debts are incurred, & I am continuously worried by numerous Tradesmen, for payment. I asked you sometime ago, to be so good and give me your acceptance for a paultry sum of two hundred pounds, to meet this drain on me, but even that you have not done as yet, it is impossible for things to go on

much longer this way, something has to be done, and shall be done. I can not wear the fool's cap any longer (ibid., 22.4.1881; 21.1.1881).

From the autumn of 1881 Cornelius had greater cause to feel embittered. In November of that year J. & W.C. Murray issued a summons against Cornelius and Peddie for the recovery of £4,621 in advances and unpaid legal fees. Because most of the loans had been granted without guarantee or written agreement, the issue arose as to whether Cornelius (the principal) or Peddie (his agent), was responsible for making the repayments (CS243/1255/4, Proof). Despite a tacit admission of responsibility by Peddie, on 7th July 1882, the court determined that Cornelius was primarily liable for the amount sued for (*Scotsman*, 8.7.1882, p.5).

In May 1882 Peddie also raised a separate action in which he sought the recovery of £19,487 from Cornelius. This amount represented advances made from 1870 to 1881 (CS247/4875, Summons and Condescendence). Peddie claimed that unbeknown to himself, Cornelius had applied the funds to property speculation and that this was in breach of their mutual agreement to finance the extended house decorating business. In July 1882, being unable to comply with the pecuniary consequences of the court's decision in J. & W.C. Murray v. Cornelius and Peddie, and with judicial progression of the litigation instigated by Peddie imminent, Cornelius adopted an alternative strategy to improve his financial status and seek retribution from his former business associate.

Sexual immorality and the price of professional respectability

On the day of the judgement in J. & W.C. Murray v. Cornelius and Peddie, Elizabeth Cornelius left her husband's abode. One week later, Cornelius issued a summons against his wife and Peddie in an action for divorce. He alleged that Peddie and Elizabeth had committed adultery and sought £10,000 damages from the CA in compensation for the ruination of his "peace and domestic happiness" (CS243/1255, Condescendence). Cornelius alleged that from 1871 to 1878 Peddie (who was unmarried and then in his mid-sixties) had sexual intercourse with his wife in Peddie's office, the Cornelius residence and various other locations (ibid.). Cornelius claimed that in December 1878 he had discovered intimate correspondence written by Peddie to Elizabeth. In response, Cornelius composed the following letter to his wife's lover:

My long felt suspicions are then now at last realised into Truth, the enclosed is a Copy of one of your corruptious letters written by you to my wife, I might have sent you a Copy of an other one, but they are all so filthy, so much so that I do not like to soil my hands with them. These are the deeds committed by D.S. Peddie, Esq., my particular friend, [who] has gone every Sunday to Church, I say read this letter you fearful monster, you came as a Wolf in Lam Clothing to my house, why could you not leave me alone. Satan look at your destruction, what have you made of my poor Wife: a hur, a hur corrupted with your filthiness, poor soul. God have mercy on her and forgive her. do now what you like, you have done your utmost. if the Law of this Country would permit me I should know how to deal with you, give me satisfaction and do not turn a coward in the bargain. I am entitled to revenge, and will have it. . . I shall have some of this letter printed in large type and post them up on walls, yes even on the pulpit of your Church [sic] (C5243/1255/3).

On receiving this letter, Peddie sent his lawyer to Cornelius in order to protest that no impropriety had taken place. Cornelius claimed to have been placated until 1881 when he resurrected claims that Peddie had caused him "the greatest injury possible" (CS243/1255, Condescendence) by seducing his wife and once more threatened retribution by revealing Peddie in his "true colours before the publick" (CS243/1255/3, 10.1.1881). In January 1881 he wrote to Peddie: "I can assure you, you never made a greater mistake in your life if you think you have fairly saddled me with your prostitute" (ibid.). As their business relationship became increasingly acrimonious, Cornelius demanded that Peddie forward £601 to cover business and household expenses inclusive of £150 for "twelve months keep of your fancy woman" (ibid., 18.8.1881).

In their written response to the summons for divorce, Peddie and Elizabeth Cornelius offered an alternative description of events. Mrs Cornelius denied adultery and contested that her husband had deliberately attempted to prostitute her and desired that she develop a sexual relationship with Peddie in order to extort money. Elizabeth Cornelius claimed that on the basis of threats of public allegations of adultery, Cornelius had extracted £20,000 from Peddie and the current claim for damages comprised another attempt to fleece her co-defender (CS243/1255, Condescendence). Peddie concurred that Cornelius had "tried every means in his power" to encourage illicit liaisons between himself and Elizabeth Cornelius for the purpose of blackmail (ibid.). By contrast, Cornelius argued that his demands for money from Peddie were related to their unwritten business arrangement.

The Cornelius divorce case opened at the Court of Session (the highest civil court in Scotland) in early November 1882

(CS243/1255/1). As with the other litigation in which Peddie was embroiled in 1882, the proceedings were reported in the Scottish press. The prevailing anti-sensualism of Victorian Britain (Mason, 1995) and the increasing publicity which attended divorce cases in the wake of matrimonial legislation in 1857, gave an added piquancy to the revelations of marital infidelity which emerged from law-suits involving those, like Peddie, who were outwardly respectable (Hammerton, 1992, pp. 102-18). On 15 November the judge determined that William Cornelius was entitled to explain his case in open court. Witnesses would be called and havers taken in order to establish or otherwise the allegations of consent and connivance (*Scotsman*, 16.11.1882, p.3).

The prospect of detailed investigation into his private and business affairs and their public disclosure induced Peddie to flee. He left Edinburgh about 17 November 1882 and the next day wrote to his clerk from London that "he was obliged to go from home for a few days" (*Times*, 1.12.1882, p.7). It was subsequently reported that Peddie had absconded to Spain (ibid., 7.12.1882, p.7). On 22 December 1882 Peddie's property was sequestrated. The trustee revealed realisable assets of £4,656 - insufficient to satisfy his 36 creditors whose claims totalled almost £75,000 (CS318/30/239, Inventory). In January 1883 Cornelius too, was bankrupted (CS319/2754). On 31 January 1883 *The Times* reported that Peddie "was buried in Philadelphia two months ago in Potter's field, under the name of John North" (p.9).

Peddie's rapid departure from Edinburgh was immediately perceived by the press as evidence of his guilt. As *The Scottish Banking and Insurance Magazine* related:

> The story was received at first with incredulity, at least as far as the criminal defalcations were concerned. But the fama received its best proof in that its subject took guilt to himself by flight (December 1882, p.266).

The rumours of adultery and extortion induced Peddie's clients and creditors to scrutinise their accounting records. In particular, the suspicions of the Reverend William Peddie, nominal treasurer of the Friendly Society of Dissenting Ministers, were excited. A committee to examine the books of the Society, which had been kept by his brother Donald, was inaugurated (CH3/516/1, 22.11.1882).

Forgery and the misappropriation of funds

By the end of November 1882 the first revelations concerning Peddie's criminality were reported in the Edinburgh press. On 30 November *The Scotsman* noted that it had been discovered that bills for £8,500 (later revised to £8,050), discounted by the Commercial Bank of Scotland and drawn by Peddie in the name of a coalmaster in Fife, were forgeries (p.4). On the same day the manager of the Commercial Bank informed his board:

> . . . that in consequence of the discovery that certain bills which had been discounted to Donald Smith Peddie, C.A., Edinburgh bore signatures which were alleged to be forgeries he had intrusted the Bank's Law Agents to make a criminal charge against Peddie and that a Warrant had accordingly been granted for his apprehension. The Board approved of this step and agreed to defray according to customary outlay by the Police for telegrams & handbills with a view to his arrest (Minute Book, Vol. 11, p.21).

The warrant was duly issued on 1 December 1882 and on 2 December it was revealed that the total of forged bills on the Commercial Bank uttered by Peddie might amount to £11,000.[5] It was also suspected that Peddie had uttered forged bills of £2,000 on two other Scottish bank's and had composed deeds relating to heritable property which "are forgeries from beginning to end, even to the registration clause" (*Glasgow Herald,* 4.12.1882, p.6). Five days later the Chief Constable of Edinburgh issued a notice (see below) offering a reward for information leading to Peddie's arrest.

EDINBURGH CITY POLICE

£100 REWARD

This Photograph was taken several years ago

Specimen of Account's Handwriting

WANTED in Edinburgh, charged with having, on or about the 10th June last, Forged and uttered Bills or Promissory Notes for large amounts,

DONALD SMITH PEDDIE,

whose Likeness is here given,

an Accountant, 74 years of Age, about 5 ft. 8 in. high, slender or medium make, sallow complexion, prominent nose, protruding under lip, peculiar teeth (set like a saw), steel-grey hair, bald on top of head, small side whisker when he absconded about a fortnight ago, neck twisted to one side, leans forward and to one side, one shoulder higher than the other, slightly bandy-legged, slouching gait, furtive look, and reserved manner. Scotch accent.

Dressed respectably in dark clothes and black cloth topcoat (pockets behind) with velvet collar, or light grey cloth topcoat. Sometimes wears dress hat, and at other times a flat-topped round felt hat.

It is believed that the accused has gone abroad.

The above Reward will be paid for such information as will lead to the apprehension of the accused.

Police-officers are requested to make all possible search and inquiry for the accused at Hotels, Railway Stations, Out-going Vessels, and other likely places; and, if found, arrest, and communicate with the Procurator-Fiscal, City Chambers, Edinburgh; or the Subscriber,

W. HENDERSON,
Chief Constable

Chief Constable's Office,
Edinburgh, 7th December 1882.

Source: Reproduced with kind permission of The Royal Bank of
Scotland plc.

The defalcations committed by Peddie which caused most public outrage concerned his misappropriation of the funds of the Friendly Society of Dissenting Ministers. Having conducted a search of the records in Donald Smith Peddie's office, the committee appointed to investigate the Treasurer's Accounts reported on 6 December 1882 that only £5,000 of the £29,000 investments which were disclosed in the last annual report were secured (CH3/516/1, 6.1.1882; *Edinburgh Evening News*, 7.12.1882, p.2). At a subsequent meeting of the (140) members of the Society, it was resolved to institute a further examination of Peddie's involvement and to advise on whether legal liability for the frauds rested with the directors, the auditors, the actuaries and/or the treasurer (CH3/516/1, 20.12.1882).

The results of these deliberations were revealed in a comprehensive report which was issued to the members of the Society on 25 January 1883 and printed in the local press (CH3/516/10; *Scotsman*, 25.1.1883, p.5). It was shown that the total investments of the Society amounted to £30,940. Of this, £21,840 worth of securities were classified as "bad" due to their being either entirely fictitious (unsupported by deeds) or based on forged documents (CH3/516/10, pp.5-6). A further £4,100 of assets were considered "doubtful" because it appeared that the investments had been realised but the proceeds were never entered in the Treasurer's Accounts maintained by Peddie. The report identified familial collusion, apathetic directors and perfunctory auditing as factors which facilitated the defalcations of the CA. Among his many criminal devices for extracting monies from the Society (particularly during the 1870s) Peddie had assigned bonds to lunatics for whom he had been appointed curator by the courts and credited the funds to his own account (CH3/516/10, p. 16).

The report also showed that the Reverend Dr James Peddie was Treasurer of the Society from its inception in 1797 until his death in 1845 (ibid., pp.2-4). After 1833 he enlisted the assistance of his son Donald and as early as the 1840s funds were misappropriated by the treasurers. In 1844, anxious that frauds were not made public, the ageing Reverend Peddie recommended to the Committee of Management of the Friendly Society that Donald should formally succeed him as treasurer. It was decided, however, that Donald, who was not a member of the Society, was ineligible for the position (ibid.). In 1846 Reverend William Peddie was elected treasurer but due to his ignorance of the affairs of the Society, its management was left almost entirely to his accountant brother.

The report into the frauds also revealed that after 1846 the directors had shown increasingly less interest in the investments of the Society and concerned themselves only with scrutinising day-to-day receipts and payments. The annual audit of the accounts of the Society, which consistently revealed a large surplus of funds, had been conducted by two directors (clergymen) in a superficial manner:

> . . . the payments to widows and petty disbursements were carefully checked, and so were the various items of income . . . but the investments themselves (the capital sums) were never . . . properly checked with the deeds (ibid., p.4).[6]

The Reverend Dr William Peddie also regretted that:

> . . . it has not been the custom for a long period of time to call for a sight of the bonds and compare and examine them, otherwise the frauds would have been detected. The auditors, like myself, had confidence in my brother (*Scotsman*, 4.12.1882, p.5).

The response of the professional organisation

The public allegations of illicit behaviour by Donald Peddie came to the attention of the office bearers of the SAE via the printed media. In order to understand the reasons why the Council subsequently devised rules for the expulsion of CAs, it is necessary to comprehend the nature of the adverse disclosures which attended the Peddie frauds.

The need for professional insulation: the depth of public outrage

The circumstances surrounding Peddie's defalcations and their consequences were extensively reported in the press. *The Times* explained why:

> The extent to which crime is facilitated and encouraged by lax methods of conducting business receives frequent illustration; but it has seldom been exhibited more strikingly than in connection with the frauds lately discovered to have been perpetrated on the "Dissenting Ministers' Friendly Society" of Scotland. The story is a very painful one, because of the respectable position of many who are affected by it. It is also one of the most shameful ever laid before the public, because the persons defrauded are the widows and orphans of Dissenting clergymen, many of whom are wholly

dependent on the annuities of the society for their livelihood (30.1.1883, p.8).

The fact that Peddie, an overtly respectable professional of mature years who was born into a family of theologians, could commit adultery and perpetrate a fraud on a semi-religious institution to the potential ruination of those deemed most deserving of societal protection, shocked contemporaries:

> A VERY cruel blow has been given to an honoured name by the extraordinary course of fraud, immorality, and forgery pursued by Mr Donald Smith Peddie, C.A . . . [who] revealed himself to be a whited sepulchre, the dishonourer of a good name, the devourer of widows' houses, the reckless debauchee, the smooth-faced swindler and forger. The personal part of the horrid story that now fills all men's mouths receives perhaps a keener point from the knowledge that the hoary sinner is in his seventy-fifth year, and has been pursuing a life which would shame a man in "the May of youth and bloom of lustihood," and is positively appalling in a man of advanced years (*Scottish Banking and Insurance Magazine*, December 1882, p.266).

The press reported that Peddie had been renowned for his high social status, piety, and participation "in every religious movement for the benefit of the people" (*Scotsman*, 26.1.1883, p.4). He had maintained a facade of being "spotless in business" and had "the general reputation of a trustworthy man" (ibid.). The contrast between his public benevolence and private villainy to the detriment of 72 widows and a family of orphans induced *The Scotsman* to comment that "No more painful story of its kind has been told for many a day" (ibid.). The Reverend Dr William Peddie acknowledged that his brother's misdemeanours had not only caused considerable shock to "the public mind of the country", but also dishonoured God and hurt religion (ibid., 21.12.1882, p.5).

The abhorrence at the Peddie frauds engendered an outpouring of sympathetic philanthropy. Even before the Friendly Society announced that it intended to remedy the deficiency in its funds by appealing to the public, senior Scottish politicians such as the Earl of Rosebery, and several leading citizens wrote to the press to volunteer contributions for the relief of the innocent widows and orphans (ibid.; CH3/516/1, 25.1.1883). By the end of 1883 the Relief Committee of the Friendly Society had collected £13,249 (CH3/516/2, p.45).

So far as the Society of Accountants in Edinburgh was concerned, the criminal and debauched behaviour of one of its senior number not only suggested that its informal controls on professional conduct were insufficient but also that the perceived public altruism of the chartered accountant was a sham. It appeared to confirm the accusations which were made against the profession in an irreverent article published one year earlier in *The Financial Record, Economist, and Railway Review.* In "Trickeries of the Professions" the CA was portrayed as a conceited and mercenary character who, under a veneer of selflessness, was driven by an insatiable desire to overstep his rivals, advance his own interests, and grasp all for himself" (December 1881, p.281). The article asserted that the active participation of CAs in the church should not be construed as a symbol of devoutness and moral rectitude. Rather, it was an attempt to secure a clientele by nurturing congregational connections and to extend "influence and gain a recognised character for steadiness" (ibid.). It was also argued that displays of overt public-spiritedness by the CA, such as offering subscriptions to good causes, were similarly motivated by the need to create a favourable impression with potential patrons and thereby "contribute to his own profit" (ibid.). Peddie's dishonourable behaviour, despite his aura of professional respectability, philanthropy and association with religious institutions, served as a practical illustration of the apparent dichotomy between the public and private faces of the chartered accountant.

The SAE, whose members had acquired "inbuilt attitudes of social superiority and dominance" (Shackleton & Milner, 1996, p.98; Walker, 1988, pp. 12-21) over other public accountants was bound to act in order to ensure that the reputation of practitioners was not seriously tainted by the destructive conduct of one of its members.[7]

The formulation of a disciplinary code

Shortly after the Peddie defalcations broke in the press, the Council of the SAE were called to an urgent meeting to discuss "special business" (Letter Book, 74/1, p.414). On 5 December 1882 the President and Council convened to discuss the measures which might be taken in response to "the very painful rumours, which, within the last few days had gained so much notoriety regarding Mr D.S. Peddie" (Sederunt Book, 2/1, p. 12). The President considered that:

> . . . the uncontradicted narratives in the newspapers are alone sufficient justification for any action the Council may see fit to take: and I anticipate there will be unanimity in our resolution that his name shall not again appear in the List of Members of the Society (ibid., p.313).

However, as the annual list was not prepared and issued until early in the new year, it was not formally decided to remove Peddie's name from the roll until a meeting of the Council was held on 3 January 1883 (ibid., p.316).

At the latter meeting it was also resolved that the President, Secretary and law agent of the SAE should formulate a new bye-law giving the Council the "power to expel from the Society, any member who is found guilty of Breach of Trust, fraud or misdemeanour of a similar kind" (ibid.). This remit was to be acted upon immediately in order that a draft regulation could be presented at the annual meeting of the Society in February. Under the constitution of the SAE the bye-law would have to be submitted to an annual meeting and ratified at the succeeding AGM. Accordingly, the bye-law was adopted by the Society in February 1883 and confirmed unanimously one year later (Minute Book, 312, pp.236-7, 263-4).

The content of the bye-law was heavily influenced by the specifies of Peddie's misconduct. It was also wide ranging and uncompromising in its effort to prevent the profession from being tarnished by the behaviour of an individual miscreant. Public accusations of crime or "any wrong doing" were to be sufficient grounds for the President and Council to institute an enquiry which might result in a recommendation for the expulsion of a member:

> It shall be lawful for the Society, in the event of any member being convicted of Falsehood, Fraud and Wilful imposition, or Embezzlement, or Forgery or uttering any forged document, knowing it to be forged, or of any other crime or misdemeanour to expel such member from the Society: and in the event of any member of the Society being publicly accused of any such crime or misdemeanours as aforesaid, or of any wrong doing sufficient to disqualify him from being a member of the Society, or in the event of any written information to that effect being given to the President or Secretary of the Society, it shall be the duty of the President and Council to make intimation in writing to such member that they will proceed on some day not less than ten from the date of such information, to consider the conduct of such member, and if after such enquiry as they shall deem sufficient, and after considering any explanations which such member may tender, they shall come to be of opinion that the member accused is guilty of such crime or misdemeanour or wrong doing, they shall report the conduct of such member to the first Annual General Meeting of the Society or to any Special General Meeting to be called for that purpose in terms of the Society's Byelaws, and on a motion being and carried, such member shall be expelled from the Society, in the same manner as if *he had been*

convicted of any such crime or misdemeanour (ibid., 312, pp.263-4, italics added).

Although there is little evidence to suggest that it was used as a model by the SAE, the bye-law bore some similarities to the rules for expulsion which had recently been codified in the constitution of the ICAEW. The charter of 1880 enumerated six grounds for the initiation of proceedings leading to the possible removal or suspension of a member. These were: a breach of the fundamental rules of the Institute; criminal conviction; behaviour deemed "disreputable to a Public Accountant"; bankruptcy; engagements deemed incompatible with the practice of public accountancy; and, failure to pay subscriptions. However, ejection from the English Institute was only possible following a 75% vote by the Council of the Institute and on the accused having been heard (*Accountant*, 12.6.1880, p.7).

It is evident from the rules for expulsion which were devised by the SAE and the ICAEW during the 1880s that both organisations were largely concerned with protecting their members from the adverse status consequences of publicised cases of misconduct. A similar emphasis on professional insulation was revealed by the Scottish accountancy profession during the 1890s. As part of their attempt to secure the registration of chartered accountants, the Scottish chartered institutes formulated an Accountants (Scotland) Bill in 1896. The draft legislation proposed that a General Council would have the power to refuse to license an accountant who had been convicted "of a crime or a fraud, or to have been guilty of any act or default discreditable to a professional accountant" (Sederunt Book, 2/2, p.240).

Conclusions

The absence from the SAE's early constitution and laws of codified rules pertaining to matters of conduct and discipline, coupled with the perfunctory nature of much contemporary auditing and the professional's ability to maintain an aura of respectability, provided the vocational and cultural environment in which individuals like Donald Smith Peddie could, for many years, covertly lead a dual existence. When the public facade ruptured and the private life was exposed a single practitioner could potentially inflict considerable damage on the reputation of the occupation.

The need to protect the profession from the adversities wreaked upon it by the activities of the malefactor ensured that characters such as Peddie, though a minute fraction of the occupational population, could have as significant and enduring an impact on the institutions of professionalism as their more illustrious peers famed for constructive contributions to the organisation. The grounds for expulsion specified in the bye-law formulated in the wake of the Peddie frauds were to be retained by the SAE as late as the merging of the three local CA societies as The Institute of Chartered Accountants of Scotland in 1951 (*Charter of Incorporation*, 1944, p.28; McDougall, 1980, p.75). The findings of this paper suggest, therefore, that the institutional development of a profession is not only exhibited in the lives of "Its great personalities" (Peloubet quoted in Previts *et al.*, 1990, p. 137) but also in the shrouded existence of its more notorious members.

Preston *et al.'s* findings concerning the emphasis on unwritten rules governing early professional behaviour (referred to here as "etiquette") and the reliance on the 'character' of the entrant are supported by this study for an earlier time and place. However, unlike the early organisations of accountants in England, the US and Australia, the devising of ethical codes and disciplinary rules was not employed by the SAE at its formation in the mid-nineteenth century as part of an attempt "to confer legitimacy upon the professional body" (Preston *et al.*, 1995, p.510). When a formal statement on disciplinary matters was later devised by the SAE it was a defensive mechanism necessitated by the publicised activities of a member whose criminal behaviour conflicted with the contemporary perception of the professional ideal. In this sense, Parker's assertion that the propagation of codes is primarily motivated by the "protection of the accounting profession's self-interest" (1994, p.507) is supported.

The current study has confirmed the particular relevance within Parker's "private interest model" of the professional insulation and status preservation functions of organisational pronouncements. The revelations concerning the defalcations and immorality of Peddie required an institutional response in order to avert a threat to the hard won collective status gains amassed by Edinburgh CAs since 1853. It was also important that the SAE reveal that it had the capacity for instituting structures to enable the punishment of the dishonourable practitioner and thereby establish a potential deterrent.

The case presented here also confirms Parker's contention that the exercise of discipline by the professional organisation is largely emblematic. In the wake of press comment relating to the activities of one chartered accountant, the SAE devised a regulation for the expulsion of members which stood as a symbol to the public that the association would not tolerate unbecoming and discreditable behaviour. The importance of "offence visibility" is also evidenced in the findings of this study. In this instance, the conspicuousness of the offence was not a determinant of the punishment meted out to the individual miscreant. Rather, it determined the formulation of the behavioural standard by which misconduct would be subsequently judged. The Callender and Peddie episodes also reveal that organisational responses were positively correlated to the volume of adverse publicity which resulted from the activities of dishonourable practitioners. Callender's misdemeanours elicited little press coverage and engendered a correspondingly limited reaction by the SAE. Peddie's crimes, by contrast, though substantially unproven at the time, were sensationalised. Hence, the organisation not only expunged Peddie's name from the roll, but also acted expeditiously to institute regulations to uphold public confidence in the profession. The grounds for expulsion devised by the SAE in 1883 reveal the organisation's revulsion against any criminal behaviour or alleged act of wrongdoing which permeated the 'public' domain and had the potential to discredit the vocation. As Parker has concluded, in matters of ethics and discipline the need to protect the private interest of the profession "is ever present" (1994, p.523).

Notes

The author is grateful to The Institute of Chartered Accountants of Scotland and The Royal Bank of Scotland plc for access to archival material. Particular thanks are due to Andrew McLean of the Royal Bank Archives Section for assistance in locating relevant material. Many helpful comments were received during a presentation at the University of Essex in May 1996 and from Kerry Jacobs and Sue Llewellyn of Edinburgh University. The anonymous referees also offered suggestions which substantially improved the paper.

1. The derivation of the terms 'criminal upperworld' and 'white-collar crime' are explained in Robb (1992, pp. 6, 193).
2. Advertising and 'touting' were major issues of etiquette during the late nineteenth century, especially in the English accountancy profession (see *The Accountant*; Howitt, 1984, pp.27-8). Canvassing was associated with trade and the egoistic quest for 'profit'. It therefore conflicted with the ideal of the fee-earning, financially disinterested and service orientated professional (Carr-Saunders & Wilson, 1933, pp.432-41; Duman, 1979, pp.124-7; Reader, 1966, p.159; Walker, 1988, pp.58-9).
3. The Rules and Bye-laws of the Institute of Accountants and Actuaries in Glasgow also contained a provision which ensured that CAs who were engaged in "the business of a Manufacturer, Merchant, or Law Agent" would forfeit their membership of the Institute (Privy Council, 1890, p. 120).

4. According to Millerson, misconduct is most likely where a sole practitioner is involved in direct client relations, provides a fiduciary service and offers advice in complex matters (1964, p. 157).
5. In November 1883 the actual total of forged bills discounted by Peddie at the head office of the Commercial Bank of Scotland was calculated as £10,678 (the profits of the Bank during the financial year 1882-3 were £151,105) (Commercial Bank Minute Book, Vol. 11, p. 136). It was also revealed that the forged bills "had been in the circle for several years" (ibid.).
6. In their report on the accounts to 31 March 1882 the auditors stated that they had "found the Books correctly kept, vouched and summed up". The capital account was also examined "and found correct" (CH3/516/1, 9.5.1882).
7. Deprecatory articles in *The Financial Record, Economist, and Railway Review* in 1881 were not the only adverse publicity which confronted the SAE in the period immediately preceding the Peddie affair. In May 1882 the case of Lees v. Todd was decided in the Court of Session. Here, a shareholder raised an action against the directors of the Caledonian Heritable Security Company for issuing false and fraudulent balance sheets. Although the defenders were successful, the case illuminated the perfunctory nature of the audit practices conducted by a CA. Both the manager and the auditor of the company were SAE members and one of the judges referred to their "failure to perform their duty to the company" (*Session Cases*, 1882, p.852).

Bibliography

Manuscript Sources
Edinburgh Central Library:
Privy Council, (1890), In the Matter of the Petition of the Scottish Institute for Incorporation by Royal Charter.
Edinburgh University Library, Edinburgh:
Matriculation Registers of the University of Edinburgh.
General Register Office, New Register House, Edinburgh:
Census Returns for Scotland, 1841-81.
Guildhall Library, London:
Institute of Accountants in London, Minutes of General Meetings (MS28/404/1).
Institute of Chartered Accountants of Scotland, Edinburgh:
Cash Book, Society of Accountants in Edinburgh (94/1).
Letter Book, Society of Accountants in Edinburgh (74/1).
Minute Book of General Meetings, Society of Accountants in Edinburgh (3/1-3).
Sederunt Books, Society of Accountants in Edinburgh (2/1-3).
Royal Bank of Scotland Archives, Edinburgh:
Commercial Bank of Scotland, Minute Books.

Scottish Records Office, Edinburgh:
Cornelius v. Cornelius and Peddie, 1882 (CS243/1255/1-3).
Court of Session Processes, Index of Pursuers (CS).
Friendly Society of Dissenting Ministers in Scotland (CH3/516).
J. & W.C. Murray v. Peddie and Cornlius, 1881-2 (CS243/1255/4).
Peddie v. Cornelius, 1882 (CS247/4875).
Sequestration of D.S. Peddie, 1882 (CS318/30/239).
Sequestration of W. Cornelius, 1870 (CS318/15/73).
Sequestration of W. Cornelius, 1883 (CS319/27/54).

Books and Periodicals
Abel, R.L., (1988), *The Legal Profession in England and Wales,* Oxford: Basil Blackwell.
The Accountant.
Acts and Regulations of The Society of Clerks to His Majesty's Signet, (1811), Edinburgh: A. Balfour.
Barclay, J.B., (1984), *The SSC Story,* Edinburgh: Edina Press.
Briggs, A., (1954), *Victorian People,* London: Odhams Press.
Brown, R. (ed.), (1905), *A History of Accounting and Accountants,* Edinburgh: T.C. & E.C. Jack.
Bye-Laws and Regulations of the Society of Solicitors in the Supreme Courts of Scotland, (1851), Edinburgh: n.p.
Carr-Saunders, A.M. and Wilson, P.A., (1933), *The Professions,* Oxford: Clarendon Press.
Charter of Incorporation Rules and Regulations and Bye-Laws of The Society of Accountants in Edinburgh, (1944), Edinburgh: T. & A. Constable.
Chesney, K., (1970), *The Victorian Underworld,* London: Maurice Temple Smith.
Collins, R., (1990), "Changing Conceptions in the Sociology of the Professions", in R. Torstendahl and M. Burrage, *The Formation of Professions. Knowledge, State and Strategy,* London: Sage, pp. 11-23.
Corfield, P.J., (1995), *Power and the Professions in Britain 1700-1850,* London: Routledge.
Davidoff, L. and Hall, C., (1987), *Family Fortunes. Men and Women of the English Middle Class 1780-1850,* London: Routledge.
Dictionary of National Biography, (1917), Oxford: Oxford University Press.
Duman, D., (1979), "The Creation and Diffusion of a Professional Ideology in Nineteenth Century England", *The Sociological Review,* Vol.27, No. 1, pp.1 13-38.
Duman, D., (1983), *The English and Colonial Bars in the Nineteenth Century,* London: Croom Helm.
The Edinburgh Evening News.
Edinburgh and Leith Post Office Directory, (annual), Edinburgh: Morrison & Gibb.
Emsley, C., (1987), *Crime and Society in England 1750-1900,* London: Longman.
The Financial Record, Economist, and Railway Review.

Gattrell, V.A.C, Lenman, B. and Parker, G. (eds.), (1980), *Crime and the Law: the Social History of Crime in Western Europe Since 1500*, London: Europa Publications.
The Glasgow Herald.
Hammerton, A.J., (1992), *Cruelty and Companionship. Conflict in Nineteenth-Century Married Life*, London: Routledge.
Harris, J., (1994), *Private Lives, Public Spirit: Britain 1870-1914*, Harmondsworth: Penguin.
A History of The Chartered Accountants of Scotland From the Earliest Times to 1954 (1954), Edinburgh: ICAS.
Howitt, Sir H., (1984), *The History of The Institute of Chartered Accountants in England and Wales 1870-1965*, New York: Garland.
Index Juridicus. The Scottish Law List and Legal Directory, (annual), Edinburgh.
Jenkins, P., (1987), "Into the Upperworld? Law, Crime and Punishment in English Society", *Social History*, Vol. 12, No. 1, pp.93-102.
Jeffrey, Rev. L., (1919), "United Presbyterian Ministers' Friendly Society. Historical Sketch", unpublished typescript, Scottish Record Office, Edinburgh (CH3/517/61).
Jones, D., (1982), *Crime, Protest, Community and Police in Nineteenth-Century Britain*, London: Routledge and Kegan Paul.
Kay, L., (1877), *A Series of Original Portraits and Caricature Etchings*, Edinburgh: A. & C. Black.
Kedslie, M.J.M., (1990), *Firm Foundations: The Development of Professional Accounting in Scotland, 1850-1900*, Hull: Hull University Press.
Lee, T.A. (ed.), (1996), *Shaping the Accountancy Profession. The Story of Three Scottish Pioneers*, New York: Garland.
Lewis, J.R., (1982), *The Victorian Bar*, London: Robert Hale.
Mason, M., (1995), *The Making of Victorian Sexuality*, Oxford: Oxford University Press.
McDougall, E.H.V., (1980), *Fifth Quarter-Century. Some Chapters in the History of the Chartered Accountants of Scotland*, Edinburgh: Accountants' Publishing Co. Ltd.
Millerson, G., (1964), *The Qualifying Associations. A Study in Professionalization*, London: Routledge & Kegan Paul.
Oliver and Boyd's New Edinburgh Almanack and National Repository, (annual), Edinburgh: Oliver and Boyd.
Parker, L.D., (1987), "An Historical Analysis of Ethical Pronouncements and Debate in the Australian Accounting Profession", *Abacus*, Vol.23, No.2, pp. 122-140.
Parker, L.D., (1994), "Professional Accounting Body Ethics: in Search of the Private Interest", *Accounting, Organizations and Society*, Vol. 19, No.6, pp.507-25.
Parker, R.II., (1986), *The Development of the Accountancy Profession in Britain to the Early Twentieth Century*, Academy of Accounting Historians: Monograph Five.
Philips, D., (1977), *Crime and Authority in Victorian England*, London: Croom Helm.

Preston, A.M., Cooper, D.J., Scarbrough, D.P. and Chilton, R.C., (1995), "Changes in the Code of Ethics of the U.S. Accounting Profession, 1917 and 1988: the Continual Quest for Legitimation", *Accounting, Organizations and Society,* Vol.20, No.6, pp.507-46.

Previts, G.J, Parker, L.D. and Coffman, E.N., (1990), "An Accounting Historiography: Subject Matter and Methodology", *Abacus,* Vol.26, No.2, pp. 136-58.

Reader, W.J., (1966), *Professional Men. The Rise of the Professional Classes in Nineteenth-Century England,* London: Weidenfield and Nicolson.

Robb, G., (1992), *White Collar Crime in Modern England. Financial Fraud and Business Morality 1845-1929,* Cambridge: Cambridge University Press.

The Scotsman.

The Scottish Banking and Insurance Magazine.

Session Cases. Cases Decided in the Court of Session, Court of Justiciary and House of Lords, 1881-82, (1882), Edinburgh: T. & T. Clark.

Shackleton, K., (1995), "Scottish Chartered Accountants: Internal and External Political Relationships, 1853-1916", *Accounting, Auditing and Accountability Journal,* Vol. 8, No.2, pp. 18-46.

Shackleton, K. and Milner, M., (1996), "Alexander Sloan: A Glasgow Chartered Accountant", in T.A. Lee (ed.), *Shaping the Accountancy Profession. The Story of Three Scottish Pioneers,* New York: Garland, pp.81-151.

Small, R., (1904), *History of the Congregations of the United Presbyterian Church from 1733 to 1900,* Edinburgh: David M. Small.

The Society of Writers to His Majesty's Signet, (1936), Edinburgh: T. & A. Constable.

Stenton, M. and Lees, S., (1978), *Who's Who of British Members of Parliament, 1886-1918,* Sussex: Harvester Press.

Stewart, J.C., (1986), *Pioneers of a Profession: Chartered Accountants to 1879,* New York: Garland.

Thompson, F.M.L., (1988), *The Rise of Respectable Society. A Social History of Victorian Britain, 1830-1900.* London: Fontana.

The Times.

Walker, S.P., (1988), *The Society of Accountants in Edinburgh 1854-1914: A Study of Recruitment to a New Profession,* New York: Garland.

Walker, S.P., (1991), "The Defence of Professional Monopoly: Scottish Chartered Accountants and 'Satellites in the Accountancy Firmament' 1854-1914", *Accounting, Organizations and Society,* Vol. 16, No.3, pp.257-83.

Walker, S.P., (1993), "Anatomy of a Scottish CA Practice: Lindsay, Jamieson & Haldane 1818-1918", *Accounting, Business and Financial History,* Vol.3, No.2, pp. 127-54.

Walker, S.P., (1995), "The Genesis of Professional Organization in Scotland: a Contextual Analysis", *Accounting, Organizations and Society,* Vol.20, No.4, pp.285-310.

Weiner, M.J. (1990), *Reconstructing the Criminal: Culture, Law and Policy in England 1830-1914,* Cambridge: Cambridge University Press.

CHAPTER 14

Gender Segregation in Scottish Chartered Accountancy: The Deployment of Male Concerns About the Admission of Women, 1900-1925

Ken Shackleton

> Women have not so far exhibited any overpowering desire to become Chartered Accountants. Happily for the nation, most girls look forward to marriage as their ultimate destiny, and therefore regard any occupation they may have taken up as more or less as a stop-gap
>
> (Editorial, *The Accountants' Magazine*,[1] December 1919).

Introduction

This paper traces the masculine discourses which surfaced in the Scottish chartered accountancy profession during the first two decades of the twentieth century on the subject of the admission of women. From their formation during the mid-nineteenth century, admission to the training systems and memberships of the organisations of accountants in Edinburgh, Glasgow and Aberdeen had been exclusively male. The question of the admission of women to the profession first impinged on the consciousness of Scottish chartered accountants through a muted institutional reaction to the women's suffrage movement and the consequences of the Great War.

Reproduced form *Accounting, Business & Financial History,* Volume 9, Number 1, March 1999, pp 135-56, with kind permission of Routledge.

By 1919, however, a more direct consequence of the suffrage movement, the Sex Discrimination (Removal) Act, altered the scene.

The paper examines the divergent views expressed by the local professional organisations in Scotland on the issue of the admission of women. The gender segregated character of the solutions formulated by the male professional elite and the way in which these solutions were conditioned by the achievement of the larger goal of the registration of the profession are also explored. It is also suggested that, although the Sex Discrimination (Removal) Act removed one institutional impediment to the entry of women to Scottish chartered accountancy, its immediate impact was minimal in the face of more enduring social and cultural barriers within practising firms.

Histories of gender segregation in the accountancy profession

A substantial number of papers have emerged during the last twenty years which have examined the participation rates of women in public accounting during the twentieth century in a variety of countries. This literature reflects a broader concern with gender segregation which has focused on 'the inequalities experienced by women in an apparently consistent fashion throughout the world' (Glasner, 1987: 295; Moore, 1992). Most of the empirical work which has been reported to date has concentrated on the entry of women to membership of the accountancy profession and the obstacles which have blocked career progression since the 1970s (French and Meredith, 1994; Glasner, 1987). It was about this time that the participation rates of women in public accounting increased significantly and this was accompanied by changes towards sexual desegregation in managerial and professional occupations including accountancy (Beller, 1985; Jolly *et al.*, 1990).

A number of studies in this growing literature have offered historical insights on the admission of women to the accountancy profession and the barriers to career progression. Silverstone and Williams' survey of women members of the Institute of Chartered Accountants in England and Wales (ICAEW) at 1977 included an exploration of the slow growth in the number of women entrants to the English Institute and the persistence of 'considerable male prejudice within the profession' (1979: 107). Ciancanelli *et al.* (1990) provided a quantitative assessment of women's participation rates in the UK profession for the period 1977-88 which was founded on data drawn from the records of the ICAEW and the Chartered Institute of Public Finance and Accountancy. The authors expressed doubt about whether initiatives to enhance access to the profession would result in gender equality given the absence of changes in organisational and societal practices.

Lehman (1992), in a wide-ranging paper covering eighty years, explored the entry of women to the accounting profession in the UK and the USA. Lehman considered the possible mechanisms which obstruct the entry of women to the accounting profession and the secondary obstacles which restrict their advancement within it. The paper concluded that the barriers were founded on economic, political and ideological factors. McKeen and Richardson (1991) conducted an oral history investigation of the Canadian accounting profession from the late nineteenth century to the mid-1980s. These authors contended that the entry of women into accounting associations 'appears to have been closely related to the ebbs and flows of the suffragette movement in Canada' and that the admission of women mirrored the social attitudes of the day (1991: 11-12). McKeen and Richardson also highlighted how traditional patriarchal attitudes continued to restrict the entry of women. This was despite the belief by women that they had an expanding sense of their own right to participate in professional and commercial employment.

Foremost among studies on the history of female recruitment to the profession in Britain is the work of Kirkham and Loft. On the basis of their investigation of gender and the construction of the professional accountant from 1870 to 1930 Kirkham and Loft concluded that 'By the eve of the First World War, the 'professional accountant' had established a distinctly masculine identity. The clerk, however, was an ambiguous construct; its gender was being contested but was increasingly coming to be seen as feminine' (1993: 551).

Studies of Gender Segregation in Scottish Accountancy

Kirkham and Loft's influential study is primarily concerned with England and Wales. The authors speculated that the role of gender in constructing the professional accountant might be different in Scotland because:

Scottish   law,   education,   business   institutions   and   social
stratification, whilst having commonalities with their English
and   Welsh   counterparts,   nevertheless   have   developed
differently (Macdonald, 1985). Thus any understanding of the
relationship between the development of the accountancy
profession and gender in Scotland requires separate study
(1993: 517).

Indeed, the distinctive contextual factors identified by Kirkham and
Loft provide the backdrop for the emergence of the accountancy
profession north of the border which was several years in advance of
similar institutional developments in England (Willmott, 1986;
Walker 1995).

The only major empirical investigation of the admission of
women to public accounting in Scotland was conducted recently by
Paisey and Paisey (1995, 1996). This involved analysing post-1973
data relating to the Institute of Chartered Accountants of Scotland
(ICAS). The conclusions drawn indicated that there was increasing
discrimination   against   women   as   their   careers   progressed.
Furthermore, Paisey and Paisey claimed that the segregation 'which
existed at the beginning of the twentieth century persists at the end of
the century . . . albeit in different forms' (1996: 81). A review of the
activities of the ICAS Lady Members' Group, which existed between
1960 and 1995, was also published recently by the Scottish Committee
on Accounting History (ICAS, 1998).

The first official history of ICAS noted the contribution of women
to the accountancy profession during the Great War in the context of
'the increasing volume of work and shortage of male staff' (1954: 63).
However, the author of this history did not explore the issue of the
entry of women in depth, merely observing that 'the passing of the Sex
Discrimination (Removal) Act 1919 took the decision out of the hands
of the Societies' (ibid.). In his biographical study of the secretary and
president of the Society of Accountants in Edinburgh (SAE), Richard
Brown, Lee (1996) noted that the question of the admission of female
apprentices was considered by the Society during the 1910s and he
also provided a résumé of the SAE's stance on this issue. However the
divergent views within the Scottish profession on this subject were not
explored. Lee largely confined his remarks to an assertion about
Brown's willingness to accept 'a changing world' (218-9).

The current study seeks to trace in greater depth, and as far as the
sources permit, male responses to the question of the admission of
women to Scottish chartered accountancy during the first decades of

the twentieth century. The following sections trace the origins of the exclusively male profession from its organisation in 1853 to the passing of the Sex Discrimination (Removal) Act in 1919 and examines the immediate impact of this legislation.

An exclusively male profession, 1853-1900

Kirkham and Loft argue that in the mid-nineteenth century 'occupations and professions . . . were gendered, and for the most part they were gendered masculine' (1993: 519). The Scottish accountancy profession was no exeption. From the formation of the Society of Accountants in Edinburgh, the Institute of Accountants and Actuaries in Glasgow (IAAG) in 1853, and the Society of Accountants in Aberdeen (SAA) in 1866, recruitment and admission to the societies of Scottish chartered accountants were exclusively male. This gender-segregated labour market accorded with other professional occupations which emphasised Victorian values of *gentlemanly* respectability (Gourvish, 1988). At the first meeting of the SAE in 1853, it was minuted that: 'it had been resolved to use every effort to form a Society of *those gentlemen* who were recognised by the profession generally, as carrying on the business exclusively of accountancy in Edinburgh' (ICAS: 2/1, 1853, emphasis added).

Similarly in their requisition to fifteen senior colleagues, the Glasgow accountants who sought the formation of an organisation of practitioners in the West of Scotland in the same year, stated that:

> It has long been felt by *gentlemen* practising as Professional Accountants in Glasgow, that the formation of a Society or Institute of Accountants is in every way desirable by means of which they may be enabled to advance those objects in which they have a common professional interest (ICAS: 130/1, 1853, emphasis added).

Walker (1988), in the most comprehensive survey of all recruits (that is, not only those who were admitted as members) to the SAE, shows that issues concerning recruitment to the new profession were conducted in the context of patriarchal notions of generational advancement and social normalcy. Chartered accountancy offered an additional career option for the second *sons* of fathers in the legal profession and also constituted a path for the upward mobility of the eldest *sons* of those occupying lower social statuses (ibid.: 265).

Although the IAAG presented itself as operating a more egalitarian recruitment policy than the SAE, particularly on the issue of apprenticeship fees, its Council periodically demonstrated its adherence to the notion of an exclusively male organisation. It was recorded in the minute books in 1910 that: 'The feeling of the meeting was distinctly opposed to the proposal for the imposition of such an Apprentice Fee as would deter any large proportion of *lads* from which Glasgow Apprentices were principally drawn from entering into an Indenture with a Member' (ICAS, 130/5, p. 117, emphasis added).[2]

Although the rules of the chartered organisations did not explicitly debar female recruits to the profession, the legal, social and economic constructs of Victorian Scotland were so embedded as to prevent the issue from surfacing. The records of the three Scottish societies from 1853 to 1900 do not contain reference to a single enquiry about admission to apprenticeship from a woman.

The suffrage movement, registration and Scottish chartered accountancy, 1900-1914

Womens' quest for economic and social recognition and enfranchizement became an increasingly dramatic feature of the British political scene during the late nineteenth and early twentieth centuries. Up to the advent of the Great War the suffrage movement in Scotland had embarked on a number of overtly militant activities (see *The Glasgow Herald*, April-May 1913). The impact of first-wave feminism on the Scottish chartered societies arose in 1900, when it touched the issue of the registration of the profession. It was reported in *The Accountants' Magazine* in 1900 that the Scottish Womens' Liberal Federation had made representations to oppose the Scottish Accountants' Bill when this was presented to the House of Commons in 1899. The grounds for the opposition of the Federation had been that there was no provision for the registration of female as well as male accountants. The Federation's submission had stated that calls for the entry of women to professional accounting organisations had been made to a number of bodies but that these had all been rejected with the exception of the admission of a woman CPA in New York. It was concluded that 'we are not aware of any similar instance in Scotland' (*The Accountants' Magazine*, 1900: 191). This occurrence elicited no discussion of the issue by the councils of the Edinburgh, Glasgow and Aberdeen societies.

Other evidence that the question of the entry of women to the profession was surfacing in Scotland during the first decade of the twentieth century – to be met with patriarchal and stereotypical responses – is to be found in Brown's *History of Accounting and Accountants* (1905: 331). In this much quoted work, one contributor, Patrick, observed that: 'hundreds of women find employment as typists - and to a less extent as clerks in accountants' offices and their patience and manual dexterity seem to fit them admirably for routine and mechanical work'.

Patrick concluded that 'With all respect for the undoubted genius of women, it may be questioned if their faculties are at all specially adapted for accountants' work at large'. Nevertheless, he postulated that 'at the end of another fifty years lady trustees, receivers and auditors may be as common as lady doctors are now' (ibid.). This view was supported by a review of *The English Woman's Year Book and Directory* in *The Accountants' Magazine* which had noted the increasing participation of women in all walks of life: 'but we turn with some anxiety to accountancy. Here little has yet been attempted, but there is evidence that daring eyes have been raised towards this profession as well as to the few other remaining preserves of man' (1905: 40).

The pronouncements of Scottish chartered accountants during the early years of the twentieth century suggest that public accountancy was gendered male and was expected to be resistant to the 'invasion' of women. The latter prospect was perceived as being both remote and unwelcome. However, other forces were encroaching on the position of the Scottish chartered societies which resulted in the question of the admission of women being revisited.

During the nineteenth century 'the precursor organisations of the chartered profession were constituted primarily on a local basis in the major legal, commercial and manufacturing centres' (Walker and Shackleton, 1995: 469). The closure devices established by the chartered bodies encouraged the formation of second-tier bodies. The Royal Charters were found not to afford the chartered societies the complete monopoly which they coveted. The most effective means of securing market control was statutory registration. Consequently, a succession of registration Bills were presented by various accountancy societies from 1891 to 1911 (Macdonald, 1985; Kedslie, 1990; Kirkham and Loft, 1992). All such attempts at registration failed, primarily 'due to the inability of the accounting bodies to agree on any one measure and the ease with which contentious legislation for the profession, devoid of government support, could be successfully opposed' (Walker and Shackleton, 1995: 469).

The significance of registration bills to the quest for the admission of women to public accountancy centred on the fact that the pursuit of legislation exposed the constitutional arrangements of the accountancy bodies to a wider public and therefore opened up their affairs to greater scrutiny. The introduction of a registration bill offered any complainants an ideal opportunity to apply political pressure on matters which were not foremost in the minds of the promoters of the legislation.

The ICAEW was to encounter such difficulties when it embarked on a significant measure: the Registration of Accountants Bill which was presented to Parliament in 1909. The secretary of the ICAEW (Colville) wrote to his Scottish counterparts on 8 April 1909: 'I am directed to inform you that since sending you the draft we have been informed by the Board of Trade that it would be necessary to amend the (Registration) Bill so as to provide for the admission of women' (ICAS, 130/1: 45-6). The ICAEW complied with the advice of the Board of Trade. At the 1909 annual meeting of the Institute its President, Peat, vigorously defended the clause pertaining to the admission of women. The clause was accepted despite some opposition. The Society of Incorporated Accountants and Auditors (SIAA), who were joint sponsors of the Bill, also voted for the admission of women under the registration bill.

The Scottish chartered societies opposed the principles of the Registration of Accountants Bill, not on the grounds of the admission of women, but because it only provided for the registration of the profession in England and Wales. It is clear from the contemporary discussion printed in *The Accountants' Magazine* during 1909 that the Scottish chartered societies were more concerned with the threat posed by junior and 'irresponsible' organisations of accountants and the geographical limitation of practising rights than harbouring any concern about the admission of women. These concerns resurfaced in 1910. On this occasion the ICAEW and SIAA forestalled the opposition of the Scottish chartered accountants to a registration bill by ensuring that its scope was UK-wide. The resultant Professional Accountants' Bill was presented in March 1911. Clause 21 provided for the admission of women, subject to the normal conditions of entry relating to articles and examinations. The Bill was read a second time in the House of Lords but was subsequently blocked and foundered in the House of Commons.

The proposed raising of the constitutional barriers to the admission of women to the profession under registration bills in 1909-11 does not appear to have excited much debate among the chartered societies. This question was effectively subsumed by the far more important matter of instituting statutory protection for the existing practising membership. Controversy over the entry of women was also diffused by the need to adhere to the guidance offered by the Board of Trade on the issue. The Board's patronage was important to the success of any registration bill.

Given that it was raised in the context of the achievement of the greater object of registration, the question of the admission of women to the accountancy profession during the period to 1914 was secondary and relatively uncontroversial. Within a few years, however, the issue was disentangled from attempts to secure a statutory monopoly. Instead it was to become associated with an economic threat to the male membership of the Scottish chartered accountant profession. The First World War was to radically alter the scene.

The impact of the Great War

It was not until the Great War that there is a record of any formal or informal discussions within the councils of the Scottish chartered societies on the admission of women.

The First World War had a major impact on British society and the feminist movement (Marwick, 1977, 1991). Women involved in the suffrage movement abandoned the militant aspects of their campaign. The Edinburgh National Society for Women's Suffrage, for example, devoted its attention to the care of the wives and families of service personnel (*The Glasgow Herald*, April-May 1913). The equivalent organisation in Glasgow and the west of Scotland undertook fund raising for the war effort.

Before the outbreak of war in August 1914 many CA apprentices and younger members had been associated with regiments on a voluntary basis. Almost immediately on the declaration of war many of these left their professional offices to serve in the armed forces. *The Accountants' Magazine* of November and December 1914 published the names of 122 Scottish CAs, 235 apprentices and 281 assistants who had enlisted. The difficulties caused by the loss of accounting labour occasioned by large scale volunteering may be gauged from data compiled by the Glasgow Institute in order to make a case to the

Reserved Occupations Committee of the Board of Trade. The IAAG recorded that at 31 July 1914 there had been 131 firms comprising 145 partners and 892 male assistants. By November 1915, 28 per cent of partners were engaged in military or government service as were 59 per cent of assistants (ICAS 130/5, IAAG Council Minute Book 5: 550-1). In March 1915 the number of volunteers from Scottish CA practices was 712 and it was being openly acknowledged that the tutorial classes for apprentices were operating with 'much diminished numbers' (*The Accountants Magazine*, 1915: 148).

The shortage of male labour in Scottish accounting firms was increasingly met by the employment of female clerks. As in other industries and professions it was women who constituted a 'stagnant reserve army of labour' during wartime (Tinker and Neimark, 1987). By 1916 *The Accountants' Magazine* was to comment that 'There is no difficulty at present in getting good female clerks, who, with a little training, can do the work perfectly well' (1916: 186). Thus, during a period of crisis when men were volunteering for the armed services, accounting practices engaged women to perform tasks which had previously been considered to be the exclusive province of male apprentices and assistants. In order to preserve the interests of CAs and CA firms, the chartered societies in Scotland pursued policies which encouraged and nurtured the employment of women.

During October 1915 the council of the IAAG introduced a new recruiting scheme in an effort to allow firms to 'retain sufficient staff to continue "satisfactorily"' (ICAS, 130/5: 544). In December 1915 it also approved a recommendation that women be admitted to the tutorial classes which were to commence during the following Spring (ibid.: 565). A subsequent report of the IAAG on the experience of admitting women to these classes explained that:

> In all, about fifty young women enrolled themselves, and it was found necessary to divide the class into two portions. Mr. Hourston gives a very satisfactory account of the women students, and reports that they showed great interest in the work, and on the whole proved themselves thoroughly capable of mastering the elementary subjects embraced in his Prospectus. It was only to be expected that very few women would enrol themselves for the ordinary Tutorial classes preparatory to the examinations, but in the one or two instances in which young women attended these classes, the tutors report very favourably on their progress. Until some definite arrangement is made for complete education and qualification of women in the accountancy profession, it seems

unlikely that many women will avail themselves of the more advanced classes (*The Accountants Magazine*, 1916: 295-6).

The Edinburgh Society followed the example set by its counterpart in Glasgow and introduced classes for sixty-five women in October 1916. These initiatives were connected to a major reconsideration of the role of women in accounting offices and the question of admitting women to apprenticeships and membership.

Professional and legal obstacles to the admission of women

In 1992 Kirkham criticised Lehman on the grounds that '*her*story in accounting is recounted through the male discourse of professional accountancy which is contextualised within wider economic and political factors' (1992: 288). The same criticism may be legitimately levelled at the empirical reportage which is contained in the following section of this paper. However, the current study did utilise the primary source documents of the three Scottish chartered societies, the major benefit of which is that it permits triangulation insights to the considerable variety of opinions and explanations within a masculine discourse on the issue of the admission of women to the profession (Jick, 1979). These sources reveal that from 1915 there was considerable tension both within each of the Scottish societies and also conflicting views between them on the question of the admission of women. This was despite the fact that publicly, the Edinburgh, Glasgow and Aberdeen societies attempted to present a united position.

The first formal and traceable attempt in Scotland by a woman to obtain a CA apprenticeship occurred in Glasgow in September 1915. The Council of the IAAG minuted the receipt of a formal indenture between Bannatyne & Guthrie and Isobel Clyne Guthrie (the daughter of the senior partner, David Guthrie). David Guthrie was to play an instrumental role in the policy considerations of the IAAG on the admission of women. At the same council meeting it was decided to 'hold over Miss Guthrie's indenture meantime' and to formally ascertain the powers of the IAAG regarding the admission of women (ICAS, 130/5: 535-6).

Isobel Guthrie's application had actually been preceded by two enquiries in July 1915. On 19 July, the SAE reported the receipt of a letter from George Lisle, CA asking if 'the council would permit the registration of an Indenture to a female apprentice' (ICAS, 2/3: 234-5). Similarly, in a letter dated 22 July from John Mann & Co., the council of the IAAG was requested to examine whether the powers of the Royal Charter enabled the institute to admit women. The IAAG decided on 20 September to act jointly with the SAE and SAA on this question (ibid.).

The council of the Edinburgh Society determined to seek the opinion of its law agent (solicitor) on the matter. This was related thus: 'both the Charter and the Rules preclude the registration of an Indenture entered into between a member of the Society and a female Apprentice and he referred to decisions of the Court supporting this view' (ICAS 2/3: 237). The opinion was copied to the council of the IAAG in October 1915. The IAAG's own law agent reported in November. It was argued that the Charter of the Glasgow Institute, which referred to 'persons' was ambiguous, and that this required that its meaning be assigned 'in accordance with inveterate usage. Therefore we have no hesitation in saying that in our opinion women as a matter of right are not entitled to membership of the Institute under its existing Regulations' (ICAS, 130/5: 555-62; see also McKeen and Richardson, 1991). On a related question the law agent argued that the proper course of action for the IAAG to follow if it wished to alter its regulations so as to admit women would be to apply to the Crown for a Supplementary Charter giving it that power (ICAS, op. cit.).

The opinion of the law agent of the Glasgow Institute was transmitted to the SAE with the observation that in the circumstances the IAAG would not proceed unilaterally with the matter. It should be noted that at this time the local CA societies were considering proposals to create a Joint Committee of Councils of the Scottish Chartered Accountants (Shackleton, 1995: 36-39). The three Scottish societies were, therefore, anxious to move together on substantive issues.

A separate Society for Lady Accountants

When the issue of women apprentices was raised at a Joint Committee of Councils on 8 February 1916 it was agreed that 'it might be expedient to encourage the formation of a separate Society for Lady Accountants' and that enquiries should be made 'with the view of ascertaining what success such a movement would be likely to meet with' (ICAS, 130/6: 13-14). The Joint Committee expressed a readiness to consider any scheme which might be proposed and John S. Gowans[3] of the SAE and David Guthrie[4] of the IAAG were invited to formulate proposals (ibid.: 31; *The Accountants' Magazine*, 1916: 464).

Gowans and Guthrie presented a preliminary report recommending the formation of a separate *Society for Lady Accountants* to the Joint Committee in October and this report was sent to the members of the councils of the three chartered societies. In December 1916 the council of the IAAG agreed to the proposal in general but considered that 'the ultimate and logical outcome of such a scheme was . . . the admission of women to the present societies and not the formation of a separate Women's Society' (ICAS, 130/6: 67-8). The decision of the council of the Glasgow Institute (which was not unanimous) represents the first formal acceptance of the principle of female apprentices and, in consequence, their admission to the profession in Scotland.

The council of the SAE considered the subject of the formation of a 'Society for Women Accountants' at a meeting on 22 January 1917. The President was authorised to report to the next meeting of the Joint Committee of Councils in February 1917 that 'considerable difference of opinion existed in regard to this matter and that no definite decision could in the meantime be arrived at' (ICAS, 2/3: 278). The council of the Aberdeen Society was similarly 'of the opinion that the proposal was premature, as in their view there was at present, no necessity and no demand for the formation of a Society for Women' (ICAS, 130/6: 90-1).

At the Joint Committee of Councils meeting on 13 February 1917, Richard Brown, the President of the SAE, amplified the opinion of his council by asserting that a majority of its members were 'of the opinion that if this question was raised by the Councils it would be the occasion of serious difficulty and controversy and that the matter was best left alone' (ibid.). The implication was that further discussion within the Edinburgh Society would prove inconclusive, perhaps even acrimonious, and therefore pointless. Given the composition of the Joint Committee of Councils and the political realities which confronted it, the issue of women apprentices was also consigned to the backburner. At the Annual General Meeting of the IAAG on 29 January 1918, it was reported that over the past year the issue of admitting women had been considered by the Joint Committee but that views among the three Societies were difficult to reconcile. Consequently, 'it was inexpedient to take any action in the meantime' (*The Accountants' Magazine*, 1918: 128).

A further complication in the minds of the leaders of the Scottish accountancy profession was the position of apprentices currently serving in the armed forces. Undoubtedly, consideration of the admission of women would be affected by the attempt to create acceptable structures for the vocational rehabilitation of returning ex-servicemen when the war was over (Shackleton, 1995: 43). In 1917 *The Accountants' Magazine* published an editorial which concluded that 'These men are needed in the profession, and they may rest assured that they will receive every assistance and encouragement to take their places in it' (1917: 243-4). At no time in the discussion on how to treat returning members and apprentices was there any serious consideration given to the position of the women who had served in accountants' offices in their place. There seemed to be an unstated assumption that women would accept that the world was returning to its immediate pre-war state and that any aspirations which women might have to become chartered accountants were not sustainable. It does not appear to have occurred to the Scottish chartered accountants that women who had played a significant role in accountants' offices during the war years might not meekly accept their former status (Kirkham and Loft, 1993: 542). This would also be consistent with the argument that womens' position as a reserve labour force in times of war would be confirmed by their rejection on the return to peace (Tinker and Neimark, 1987).

A second scheme of gender segregation

At the beginning of 1918 it became apparent to commentators north of the border that the issue of the admission of women to the accountancy profession had assumed a new momentum. In January *The Accountants' Magazine* (1918: 7) noted that the Institute of Bankers had decided to permit women to sit its examinations although the question of their admission was to be deferred until after the War. The journal noted that this development might be regarded as a sign of the times. Confirmation that the movement towards the admission of women was being considered in other parts of the accounting world was provided by the publication of a report on the acceptance of the principle by the Australasian Corporation of Public Accountants (ibid.: 80), and a note that the Council of the Society of Incorporated Accountants and Auditors (SIAA) had called an extraordinary general meeting to consider the advisability of admitting women (ibid.: 86). The SIAA claimed that the extension of the parliamentary franchise to women under the Representation of the People Act of 1918 rendered inappropriate the deferment of this issue until after the War. The SIAA subsequently gained the approval of its membership and of the Board of Trade together with the sanction of the High Court for the admission of women to its ranks on the same terms as men (*The Accountants' Magazine*, 1919: 322).

In the summer of 1918 there began a process of reconsideration, reversion and prevarication as the three Scottish chartered societies gave further thought to the admission of women. The council of the IAAG considered the matter on 16 September when the President recalled that it was almost eighteen months since the Joint Committee of Councils had been unable to reach agreement on earlier proposals. It was decided to raise again the issue of admitting women at the Joint Committee called for the next day (ICAS, 130/6: 274). At this meeting the President of the IAAG claimed that: 'the matter was becoming somewhat urgent as women were being invited to join outside bodies of accountants' (ibid.: 86). Not for the first time in its existence the IAAG was moved, not only by arguments about equity, but also by concerns regarding its professional monopoly in Glasgow.

Consideration was deferred by the Joint Committee of Councils until its next meeting in November 1918, by which time the Edinburgh Society had also concurred that the matter should be reconsidered. However, this apparent willingness to readdress the issue at the Joint Committee was given reluctantly. The council of the SAE was seriously split on the issue and took the unusual step of taking a vote and declaring the outcome. This revealed that two of its members were prepared to admit women '*if that could be arranged*', two members voted for delay '*until after the War*', and six members voted for women to be admitted to '*a separate Society under supervision*' (ICAS, 2/3: 334-6, emphasis added).

When the issue was discussed again by the Joint Committee of Councils on 13 November 1918, the outcome was a reprise of the approach taken in 1915-16 whereby the societies undertook to obtain legal opinion on the admission of women under their Royal Charters and to commission, concurrently, a further report on training arrangements. The formulation of legal opinion took five months and it was concluded in April 1919 that the three Royal Charters did not entitle the societies to admit women (ICAS, 130/6: 354-5). At this

stage a new proposal was made which appeared to the majority of the
Joint Committee to offer an acceptable compromise: 'the Committee
were of the opinion that the best course in the meantime would be to
adopt some scheme under which women, after undergoing the same
training and passing the same standards of examination as men, but
on paying lower fees, *might become associates but not members* of the
Society' (ibid., emphasis added).

This invention of a segregated and lower status for women
accountants in Scotland was enshrined in draft rules. However,
lawyers suggested that the three societies were not competent to
entertain this idea under their Royal Charters. While the SAE and
SAA awaited the delivery of a legal opinion, the President of the
IAAG instructed the Secretary of his Institute to approach the Privy
Council for guidance on the subject of securing a supplementary
charter which would enable the admission of women. The reply from
the Privy Council of 17 May 1919 stated that 'the Lords of the Council
. . . would be prepared to entertain a proposal to that end' (ICAS,
130/6: 380-4).

This communication was reported to a meeting of the Joint
Committee of Councils on 9 June 1919. A copy of the Womens
Emancipation Bill was also tabled (ibid.). A Joint Committee meeting
on 30 June heard that further informal discussions with the Privy
Council had revealed that 'a large number of similar applications were
being received' from other organisations. The Joint Committee was
also informed that the Lord Advocate had suggested that 'there was no
prospect of the Womens Emancipation Bill becoming law during the
present Session of Parliament although legislation on similar lines
would probably be introduced later' (ICAS, 130/6: 393-4). In the light
of these views: 'it was unanimously resolved to recommend the
Councils of the three Societies to take the necessary steps to obtain the
consent of their members to make application for Supplemental
Charters providing for the admission of women to the membership of
the Societies' (ibid.).

The council of the IAAG responded expeditiously and
recommended to its members at a quarterly meeting in July 1919 that
a special general meeting be called to approve the application being
submitted to the Privy Council. The Edinburgh Society responded in a
more cautious manner due to complications relating to its Endowment
and Annuity Fund. This had been established by private Act of
Parliament in 1887 and was funded from the admission fees of new
members. The SAE's lawyers were of the opinion that if the Society
wished to exclude women from the Fund then an amending Act of

Parliament would be required. In the meantime J. Watt, the law agent for the Faculty of Actuaries, which was also based in Edinburgh, had informed the SAE that, following a petition from the Faculty, an amendment to the Sex Discrimination (Removal) Bill, which was then before Parliament, had been secured[5] (Davidson, 1956: 104). This 'would have the effect of allowing all Societies incorporated by Royal Charter to admit women without the trouble and expense of obtaining Supplemental Charters' (ICAS, 2/3: 364-9). The SAE decided to delay taking any further action 'until it was seen how the Bill was disposed of'. This position was also adopted by the Aberdeen Society.

Scottish chartered accountants and the Sex Discrimination (Removal) Act, 1919

On introducing the Sex Discrimination (Removal) Bill at its Second Reading in the House of Lords on 22 July 1919, the Rt. Hon. Lord Birkenhead (the Lord Chancellor) related that 'the Bill intended to fulfil the pledges given by various members of the Government during the general election, to remove such obstacles as prevent the appointment of women to public offices and the fulfilment by them of public functions' (*House of Lords Debates*, 5s, 891).

During the Committee Stage of the Bill an amendment was introduced. In its original form Clause 1 had provided that:

> A person shall not be disqualified by sex from the exercise of any public function, or from being appointed to any civil or judicial office or post, or from entering or assuming any civil profession or vocation, and a person shall not be exempted by sex from the liability to serve as a juror (*House of Lords Debates*, 5s, 123).

Lord Birkenhead introduced the following amendment after 'vocation': 'or for the admission to any incorporated society (whether incorporated by Royal Charter or otherwise)'. He explained that:

> this amendment is put down to meet a point which has been taken by certain persons interested in this question in Edinburgh. It was pointed out, and I think justly, that the words of the Bill would not ensure the admission of women to certain incorporated professional societies, such as the Faculty of Actuaries and the Society of Accountants in Edinburgh. On behalf of the former society this

amendment was asked for. The Scottish Office was consulted and
agree. The words will, of course, also allow the admission of women
to similar English societies (ibid.).

The amendment was approved without discussion. The Sex
Discrimination (Removal) Bill was given a Third Reading in the
House of Lords on 5 August 1919 and sent to the House of Commons.
The Commons devoted most of its consideration to the position of
women in the civil service and peeresses in the House of Lords. At the
time when the Solicitor-General expressed in Parliament the hope that
the Bill would remove occupational barriers to women, an event
occurred north of the border which suggested that his expectation was
not met with unanimous support.

At a special general meeting of the IAAG on 15 October 1919,
the President reported that the passage of the Sex Discrimination
(Removal) Bill was uncertain and that the membership should
consider a resolution on the admission of women. The latter had
already been recommended by the Joint Committee of Councils and
the council of the IAAG. Of the thirty-seven attendees at special
general meeting (from a total membership of 823) eleven voted
against the resolution. Given that major constitutional changes
required a 75 per cent vote the motion was declared as lost. The
constitution of the Glasgow Institute also provided for the calling of a
poll of the membership and this was invoked by the Council of the
IAAG. The result of the poll was reported at the quarterly meeting of
the Institute in October 1919 and represented something of an
embarrassment. On a 58 per cent turnout, 481 votes were recorded of
which 300 were in favour and 181 against the admission of women. A
majority of 62.4 per cent was insufficient to secure the motion. *The
Accountants' Magazine* speculated that:

> the opposition . . . came mainly from the younger members. The
> majority of these have been serving in the army for years, and some
> of them no doubt feel that the difficulties in the way of resuming
> their civil vocation are already serious enough without the addition
> of competition by a flood of women accountants (1919: 513-16).

The President of the IAAG remarked that:

> he need hardly say that the Council regretted what had happened.
> The matter had been under their consideration for a very
> considerable time, and they had recommended the Institute to adopt

the resolution after careful and mature consideration and only after the approval of the Joint Committee . . . had been obtained. There was no doubt that there was a demand by a limited number of women for an accountant qualification, and the Council feared that if the Institute did not open its doors, such women would be driven into outside Societies or into the formation of a Society of their own, a result which would be very regrettable. In the opinion of the Council, if women were to be qualified in any way, it was extremely desirable that their education and qualification should be in the offices of members of the Institute and under the ordinary Regulations, and it was fairly obvious that such requirements could not be made upon women unless the inducement of full membership of the institute was held out to them (ICAS, 130/6: 429-30).

Events were subsequently overtaken by the progress of the Sex Discrimination (Removal) Bill. The Bill cleared the House of Commons in October 1919 and at a meeting on 13 November the Joint Committee of Councils decided that further action by the Scottish Societies on the admission of women was unnecessary (ICAS, 130/6: 455). The Bill received the Royal Assent on 23 December 1919. *The Accountants' Magazine* noted that in Edinburgh and Aberdeen: "it seems probable that there is a substantial minority to whom the change will not be welcome" (1919: 514-15).

The impact of the Sex Discrimination (Removal) Act to 1929

The implementation of the policy of the Scottish chartered societies to admit women was enacted first by the council of the IAAG when, on 14 January 1920, it accepted the indenture of Miss Isobel Clyne Guthrie. This indenture was first presented to the council in 1915 and it was conceded that it should be backdated. The effect of this was to enable Isobel Guthrie to undertake a three year apprenticeship. She passed her final examination in 1922 and was admitted to the IAAG in 1923.[6]

Although the enactment of the Sex Disqualification (Removal) Act eliminated the constitutional barrier to the admission of women it had little immediate effect on the recruitment of women to the profession in Scotland and beyond. The inter-war period witnessed a revival of the domestic ideology which prescribed that women should remain at home and the marriage bar effectively closed professional occupations to legions of women. It should also be remembered that it was individual accounting firms which granted indentures and these were able to invite, accept or reject applications for apprenticeships on whatever grounds they wished and to do so outside the public gaze.

During the first decade after the introduction of the Sex Disqualification (Removal) Act, in the context of high levels of post-war recruitment to the profession, a total of forty women were admitted to CA apprenticeships in Scotland. This represented a mere 1.4 per cent of the total indentures recorded during this period. Further detail is provided in Table I.

Although indentures of women were proportionally more common in Edinburgh than in Glasgow during the 1920s, the data in Table 1 does not disclose that over one half (53 per cent) of the SAE apprenticeships were contracted in only three firms whereas the twenty-three indentures recorded by the IAAG were spread amongst eighteen different firms. This finding suggests that either there was less hostility in principle among Glasgow practices to the recruitment of women, or that Glasgow firms were prepared to operate 'tokenism' in their recruitment practices.

The findings of the study suggests that in Edinburgh a very small number of firms were strongly committed to the indenture of women apprentices whereas the vast majority of practices in the Scottish capital were indifferent or hostile to the notion. This point is reinforced when it is considered that two of the first female apprentices recorded in the books of the SAE were under the tutelage of John U.C. King, of Brown, Peat & Tilley in London. During the initial discussions on the admission of women to the accountancy profession, office bearers of the Aberdeen Society had indicated that there was no demand. The data reported in Table I reveals that no women were indentured to members of the SAA from 1920-1929.[7]

TABLE I *Male and Female Apprentices Contracted in the Scottish Chartered Accountancy Profession 1920-29*

Year	SAE Total apprentices	No. of women	IAAG Total apprentices	No. of women
1920	96	3	225	2
1921	78	3	190	0
1922	101	0	227	2
1923	96	1	211	3
1924	94	3	265	2
1925	50	0	154	2
1926	61	1	170	2
1927	63	0	156	3
1928	59	1	148	2
1929	50	3	176	7
Total	748	15	1922	25
(%)	(26.5)	(2.0)	(68.0)	(1.3)

Year	SAA Total apprentices	No. of women	Total Total apprentices	% women
1920	14	0	335	1.5
1921	16	0	284	1.1
1922	22	0	350	0.6
1923	16	0	323	1.2
1924	18	0	377	1.3
1925	7	0	211	0.9
1926	24	0	255	1.2
1927	10	0	229	1.3
1928	12	0	219	1.4
1929	16	0	242	4.1
Total	155	0	2825	40
(%)	(5.5)	(0.0)	(100)	(1.4)

Of the forty women who entered CA apprenticeships in the 1920-29 period, twenty-five qualified for admission, although two women did not apply for membership. Given the obligation to pay membership fees, which were particularly high in Edinburgh, application for membership would likely have been regarded as an uneconomic decision if the apprentice intended to marry shortly after qualification. The failure rate of women in CA examinations during the 1920s (at 37 per cent) was similar to that for male apprentices.

Summary

When confronted with the issue of the admission of women to public accounting, Scottish chartered accountants deployed a number of blocking strategies intended to shield the profession from threats to the gendered construction of public accounting. If the profession had been successful in securing its primary objective of a statutory monopoly, the admission of women would have been conceded as an acceptable trade-off with government. However, when the issue was considered in isolation, on its own merits, the intrinsically patriarchal attitudes of the members of the Scottish profession were reasserted.

The initial blocking strategy took the form of denial. It was claimed that there was no demand either within the profession or from women themselves to enter the vocation.   This argument was promulgated by one of the chartered societies even when the evidence demonstrated that it had become an untenable standpoint. A second strategy deployed by the Scottish chartered societies rested on legal and constitutional arguments. It was asserted that any variation in the rules of admission would require the alteration of the terms of the Royal Charters, and would also be subject to endorsement by the (male) members. Legal opinion was consistently of the view that the respective Royal Charters precluded the admission of women.   This stance became less secure when it emerged that the Privy Council would provide sympathetic consideration to any application for a Supplementary Charter which would allow women to be admitted to membership. Of the three Scottish societies only the IAAG determined to test formally members' views. Although there was support for the entry of women the required majority was not secured.

As it became obvious that influential opinion in the profession and wider society ran counter to the traditional views of the majority of its members, the Scottish chartered societies conceded the entrance of women but devised an admissions policy which was founded on gender segregation. Initially, it was proposed that the creation of a separate Society for Women Accountants, supervised and controlled by the chartered societies, would absorb exogenous pressures for constitutional change. When it became apparent that this would not be acceptable, an alternative compromise was reached, whereby women would be admitted to the existing societies but as lower-status members than men.

The evidence shows that without legislative reform, the Scottish chartered societies would have compromised on gender-segregated organisational structure. With the enactment of the Sex Discrimination (Removal) Act, 1919 the fractious institutional debate among the Edinburgh, Glasgow and Aberdeen societies on the admission of women was, however, rendered redundant. Following the Act, all formal legal and constitutional barriers to female admission were removed and the Scottish societies accepted indentures from female applicants. These early applicants had family connections to CA firms. In Edinburgh in particular, there existed a small number of practices which appear to have been committed to the admission of female apprentices. However, the evidence presented above suggests the continuing importance of the social and cultural attitudes in professional offices which had prevented women from entering the profession before 1919.

Conclusions

The extent to which women have been excluded, marginalised, exploited and alienated in society is a core issue in the feminist literature. Crompton (1987: 108) has observed that the exclusion of women from professions is so deeply ingrained that it is almost regarded as a natural state of affairs. The findings of the current paper suggests the tenacity of the ideologies and structures which encouraged the exclusion and segregation of women in the accountancy profession. Although legislative changes broke one set of organisational barriers, the reforms were not greatly effective at the level of accountancy firms. The foregoing review of the discussions on the question of the admission of women to the three Scottish societies during the early years of the twentieth century reveals that male concerns and responses were mixed and intertwined with other priorities such as the registration of the profession.

The paper also confirms the impact of contemporary developments, such as the feminist movement and the First World War, on raising the question of the admission of women to the profession. These wider social forces presented challenges to the prevailing systems of organisational power and control in particular occupational groups professions (Hopwood, 1987). McKeen and Richardson (1991) observed that the issue of the entry of women coincided with the ebbs and flows of the suffrage movement. The accountancy profession in Scotland was significantly affected by the social and economic impact of the Great War. As Kirkham and Loft have stated, in a wider context, 'War changed accountancy' (1993: 535).

It is also notable that the three Scottish societies considered the issue of the admission of women to public accounting in a less than homogenous manner. Although the research clearly shows that in their public commentaries Scottish CAs held uniformly sexual stereotyped views about women (Spencer and Podmore, 1987), their more private utterances suggested greater diversity according to such factors as geographical location, organisational affiliation and age. Unanimity among chartered accountants on the issue of the admission of women was, therefore, difficult to achieve. The solutions which emerged from their negotiations were schemes for gender segregation such as the formation of a separate Society for Lady Accountants, supervised by the established and dominant organisations of male accountants.

Economic priorities also became intertwined with the question of the admission of women. The Scottish chartered accountants appeared indifferent to the issue at first when it emerged in connection with registration. Their primary object was to secure monopolistic advantage. Similarly, after the War, the attitudes of Scottish chartered societies to the admission of women were influenced by economic concerns. In the only recorded vote on the issue, younger members of the IAAG perceived the admission of women as an economic threat and rejected constitutional reforms.

In the final analysis the passage of the Sex Discrimination (Removal) Act in 1919 removed the major constitutional barrier to the admission of women. Thereafter the accession of women to membership of the Scottish chartered societies was dependant on firms recruiting female apprentices. During the ten years after the Act a very small number of women entered into indentures, such that 'tokenism' appears to have been in evidence. Women entered the profession in only small numbers perhaps, as Zimmer noted, '*because* of their differences from other members (and) . . . to serve as "proof" that the group does not discriminate' (1988: 65). Most of the women who were admitted to apprenticeship were from privileged backgrounds and many had family connections to the firm in which they trained. In its fundamental structures and attitudes, Scottish chartered accountancy continued to be gendered male after 1919.

Notes

The author is grateful for financial support provided by the Faculty of Law and Financial Studies, University of Glasgow, which facilitated this research. The author acknowledges the permission of Peter Johnston, Secretary and Chief Executive of the Institute of Chartered Accountants of Scotland (ICAS) for permission to consult and quote from the archives of ICAS and its predecessor organisations. Staff at a Wards Research Seminar at the University of Glasgow (May 1998), my colleagues Mike Adams, George Harte (University of Glasgow), Stephen Walker (University of Edinburgh) and the anonymous reviewers made a number of helpful comments and suggestions on earlier versions of this paper, for which I am grateful.

1. *The Accountants' Magazine*, which was first published in 1897, carried on its mast head the inscription *A Journal for Business Men*.
2. A revealing insight into the position of middle class women is provided through the Sloan family in Glasgow. One of the most prominent Glasgow accountants of his day, Alexander Sloan (1843-1927) was the secretary and later president of the IAAG. He had a family comprising six sons and seven daughters. The eldest son D. Norman was apprenticed in his father's accountancy practice. All of the daughters received an expensive education but only Agnes became a professional (one of the first female doctors of medicine) (Shackleton and Milner, 1996: 90-1). Nowhere in the Sloan family papers is there a suggestion that Sloan's daughters should pursue a career in accountancy.
3. John Stuart Gowans was admitted to the SAE in 1883 and was a partner in the firm A. & J. Robertson, Edinburgh. From 1916 he offered his services (free of charge) as a lecturer on a course for women assistants in accountants' offices.
4. David Guthrie was admitted to the IAAG in 1890 and was a partner in the firm Bannatyne & Guthrie, Glasgow.
5. In the official history of the Faculty of Actuaries in Scotland, published in 1956, Davidson juxtaposed the unconventional habits of the President who 'built a yacht in his own dining room removing a window to accommodate it' with a paragraph on the question of the admission of women to the Faculty. The major part of the discussion considers the fact that only three women had become fellows of the Faculty, which was explained as follows: 'It may be that in actuarial life, at least, the severely statistical and practical approach to our problems leaves little room for those flashes of intuition with which the fair sex are generally

supposed to cope with life's little difficulties. In any case, the gruelling course of study for the actuarial degree, concurrent as it is with a busy official life, requires a degree of physical endurance and of singleness of purpose, which, without the least disrespect, may be considered as unlikely to appeal to the average young woman' (Davidson, 1956: 104).

6. Isobel Guthrie married Thomas Lockhead, a chartered accountant who had qualified in the same firm of Bannatyne & Guthrie. Thomas Lockhead was asked to go to London by John (later Lord) Reith of the BBC. Isobel Lockhead never practised.

7. During the period from 1920 to 1950 only three women were indentured to members of the SAA.

Bibliography

The Accountants' Magazine.

Beller, A.H. (1985) 'Changes in the sex composition of US occupations, 1960-1981', *Journal of Human Resources*, Vol. 20: 235-50.

Brown, R. (ed.) (1905) *A History of Accounting and Accountants*, Edinburgh: T.C. and E.C. Jack.

Ciancanelli, P. (1992) 'M[other]ing View on: "The Construction of Gender: Some Insights from Feminist Psychology"', *Accounting, Auditing and Accountability Journal*, 5(3): 133-6.

Ciancanelli, P., Gallhofer, C., Humphrey, C. and Kirkham, L. (1990) 'Gender and Accountancy: Some Evidence from the UK', *Critical Perspectives on Accounting*, 1(2): 117-44.

Crompton, R. (1987) 'Gender and Accountancy: A Response to Tinker and Neimark', *Accounting, Organizations and Society*, 12(1): 103-10.

Davidson, A.R. (1956) *The History of the Faculty of Actuaries in Scotland 1856-1956*, Edinburgh: The Faculty of Actuaries.

French, S. and Meredith, V. (1994) 'Women in Public Accounting: Growth and Advancement', *Critical Perspectives on Accounting*, 5(3): 227-42.

Glasgow Herald (various).

Glasner, A.H. (1987) 'Gender, Class and the Workplace', *Sociology*, 21(2): 295-304.

Gourvish, T. (1988) 'The Rise of the Professions' in Gourvish, T.R., & O'Day, A. (eds) *Later Victorian Britain, 1867-1900*, (New York: St. Martins Press), pp. 13-35.

Hopwood, A. (1987) 'Accounting and Gender: An Introduction', *Accounting, Organizations and Society,* 12(1): 65-9.

House of Lords, *Journals of the House of Lords,* Vol. CLI.

Institute of Chartered Accountants of Scotland (1954) *A History of the Institute of Chartered Accountants of Scotland from the Earliest Times to 1954,* Edinburgh: ICAS.

Institute of Chartered Accountants of Scotland (1998) *Forward with Confidence,* Edinburgh: Scottish Committee on Accounting History, ICAS.

Society of Accountants in Edinburgh,

2/1 Council minutes 1853-66

2/3 Council minutes 1903-21

Institute of Accountants and Actuaries in Glasgow,

130/1   Council minutes 1853-77.

130/5   Council minutes 1908-16.

130/6   Council minutes 1916-20.

Jick, T.D. (1979) 'Mixing qualitative and quantitative methods: triangulation in action', *Administrative Science Quarterly,* 24, December: 602-11.

Jolly, D.L., Grimm, J.W. and Wozniak, P.R. (1990) 'Patterns of Sex Desegregation in Managerial and Professional Speciality Fields, 1950-1980', *Work and Occupations,* 17(1): 30-54.

Kedslie, M.K.M. (1990) *Firm Foundations: The Development of Professional Accounting in Scotland, 1850-1900,* Hull: Hull University Press.

Kirkham, L.M. (1992) 'Integrating *Her*story and *His*tory in Accountancy', *Accounting, Organizations and Society,* 17(2): 287-97.

Kirkham, L.M. and Loft, A. (1992) 'Insiders and Outsiders: intra-occupational rivalry in accountancy, 1880-1930', Research paper presented at ABFH Conference, Cardiff Business School, September.

Kirkham, L. M. and Loft, A. (1993) 'Gender and the Construction of the Professional Accountant', *Accounting, Organizations and Society,* 18(6): 507-58.

Lee, T.A. (1996) 'Richard Brown, Chartered Accountant and Christian Gentleman' in Lee, T.A. (ed.) *Shaping the Accountancy Profession: The Story of Three Scottish Pioneers,* New York: Garland Publishing Inc, pp. 153-221

Lehman, C.R. (1992) '"Herstory" in Accounting: The First Eighty Years', *Accounting, Organizations and Society,* 17(3): 261-85.

Macdonald, K.M. (1985) 'Social Closure and Occupational Registration', *Sociology*, 19(4): 541-56.

McKeen, C.A. and Richardson, A.J. (1991) 'Gender and the Accountancy Profession: An Oral History of Women Pioneers in the Canadian Accounting Profession' unpublished paper, School of Business, Queen's University, Kingston, Ontario.

Marwick, A. (1977) *Women at War, 1914-1918*, London, Fontana.

Marwick, A. (1991) *The Deluge: British Society and the First World War*, Basingstoke, Macmillan.

Moore, D. (1992) 'Notes Towards Feminist Theories of Accounting: A View from Literary Studies', *Accounting, Auditing and Accountability Journal*, 5(3): 92-112.

Paisey, C. and Paisey, N.J. (1995) 'Career development of Female Chartered Accountants in Scotland: Marginalisation and Segregation', *The International Journal of Career Management*, 7(5): 19-25.

Paisey, C. and Paisey, N. J. (1996) 'Marginalisation and Segregation: the Case of the Female Scottish Chartered Accountant' in Masson, D.R., and Simonton, D. (eds), *Women and Higher Education: Past Present and Future*, Aberdeen: Aberdeen University Press, pp. 72-83.

Shackleton, K. (1995) 'Scottish Chartered Accountants: Internal and External Political Relationships, 1853-1916', *Accounting, Auditing and Accountability Journal*, 8(2): 18-46.

Shackleton, K. and Milner, M. (1996) 'Alexander Sloan: A Glasgow Chartered Accountant', in Lee, T.A., (ed.), *Shaping the Accountancy Profession: The Story of Three Scottish Pioneers*, New York: Garland Publishing, Inc, pp. 82-151.

Silverstone, R. and Williams, A. (1979) 'Recruitment, Training, Employment and Careers of Women Chartered Accountants in England and Wales', *Accounting and Business Research*, Spring: 105-21.

Spencer, A. and Podmore, D. (eds) (1987) *In a Man's World: Essays on Women in Male-Dominated Professions*, London: Tavistock Publications.

Tinker, T. and Neimark, M. (1987) 'The Role of Annual Reports in Gender and Class Contradictions at General Motors: 1917-1976, *Accounting, Organizations and Society*, 12(1): 71-88.

Walker, S.P. (1988) *The Society of Accountants in Edinburgh 1854-1914*, New York: Garland Publishing, Inc.

Walker, S.P. (1991) 'The Defence of Professional Monopoly: Scottish chartered accountants and "Satellites in the accountancy firmament 1854-1914"', *Accounting, Organizations and Society,* 16(3): 257-83.

Walker, S.P. and Shackleton, K. (1995) 'Corporatism and Structural Change in the British Accountancy Profession, 1930-1957', *Accounting, Organizations and Society,* 20(6): 467-503.

Willmott, H. (1986) 'Organizing the Profession: A Theoretical and Historical Examination of the Development of the Major Accountancy Bodies in the U.K.', *Accounting, Organizations and Society,* 11(6): 555-80.

Zimmer, L. (1988) 'Tokenism and Women in the Workplace: The Limits of Gender-Neutral Theory', *Social Problems,* 35(1): 64-77.

For Product Safety Concerns and Information please contact our EU representative GPSR@taylorandfrancis.com Taylor & Francis Verlag GmbH, Kaufingerstraße 24, 80331 München, Germany

Printed and bound by CPI Group (UK) Ltd, Croydon, CR0 4YY

08/05/2025

01864416-0001